Communist Intimacy

Communist Intimacy

Jasna Koteska

Washington, DC

Copyright © 2014 by Jasna Koteska

New Academia Publishing 2014
First published in Macedonian by Templum, Skopje, Republic of Macedonia, November 2008

Translated from Macedonian by Vera Trandafilovska and Rodna Ruškovska. Copyediting, Jeff Bickert and Maury Saslaff

All rights reserved. No part of this book may be reproduced or transmitted in any form or by any means, electronic or mechanical, including photocopying, recording, or by any information storage and retrieval system.

Printed in the United States of America

Library of Congress Control Number: 2014930485
ISBN 978-0-9899169-7-4 paperback (alk. paper)

New Academia Publishing
PO Box 27420, Washington, DC 20038-7420
info@newacademia.com - www.newacademia.com

Contents

Numbers to Compare	vii
I. Intimist	**1**
1. On the Emotions That Remained on a Bus	3
2. Intimist	9
3. Communist Crimes and Political Anesthesia	55
4. Poetry Between the Small-Town Mentality and the Secret Services	101
5. Lenin's Laughter	151
II. Phenomenology of Communist Intimacy	**163**
1. Paranoia	165
2. Intimacy	183
3. Waiting Room	203
4. Prosthesis	219
5. Body	251
6. Why is it Good to be Good	265
Children to Compare	283
Bibliography	287
Notes	297

Numbers to Compare

Numbers to Compare
Jovan Koteski

To my children Vasil and Jasna

While in prison
my prison number was 6412

In Homer's "Iliad"
verse 6412 reads:
"Now for your father
you will pay for the grave mistake."

Sometimes things
in time and space
rhyme even in spite of our will.
Be it.

(From the collection "Live Fire" 1990)

For many years, I read my father's lines as a mistake. My father's file was kept under number 5622, which meant that there was no way that number 6412 could be correct. When I first published the analysis of his file "Jovan Koteski, file 5622" in a journal, the number of the file was left in the title, probably as my unconscious attempt to avoid the *Homeric* call, the dialogue of Judgment, which these lines implied.

What was "a release" for me simultaneously meant that by contrast, my father would have to accept the only answer I could give. It was only when I was writing this book that it suddenly became clear to me that the number my father was talking about did not refer to the file but to the prison. That was the moment when for the first time, I accepted the last line of the poem as the only possible one.

I.

Intimist

1

On the Emotions that Remained on a Bus

I have never wanted to write this book, although no topic has ever been more important to me. Nevertheless, we do not choose topics, topics choose us. My father was a poet. Later on, I was told that such a profession does not exist. My father was my love, my joy and my pride. Even so, there is no street from my childhood I do not hate. Now I live on the other side of the city and each visit to my childhood district depresses me. I didn't cross a single street in my childhood, holding my father's hand, without him making me look back at least three times. If he didn't make me, I would make him. We were a parent and child–and allies. Still, this is not a biography about my father. Out of all the people on the planet we know our parents the least, that is the Hegelian dialectic, and it would be vulturous to claim the opposite. Even if I wanted to write a book about my father, I couldn't. This is a book about how communism and a small-town mentality hurt me, and not how they hurt my father. Be that as it may, at least my father found freedom in his death–from everybody, including his children. My father wanted to be remembered for and by his poems. They are his biography.

These few lines are mine. My father was arrested the same morning I first went to the high school with the ominous name "Josip Broz Tito." I submitted the necessary documents together with my friends from school, as we all had the best grades. Unlike the others, I had a lot of awards and diplomas, but unlike the others, my name was not on the list. Actually, it was, though below the line. At 6 o'clock in the morning on September 2, 1985, while my father was seeing me off to my first school class, and less than an hour before he was arrested, he was consoling me–certainly a mistake had been made, as it was impossible I had been left out, and they would certainly accept me. And he was right. I was crossed out from the list below the line with a pen and added above the line. I went back home running to tell my father the happy news, but my father was no longer at home. I was the 35th student in a class limited to 30. At that time I didn't know I was an extra student, just like four others, and I never did find out what sins our renegade group of five shared. In the years that followed, I won many competitions for my high school, and forgot that they had forgotten to accept me once. And I never thought my name was added to the list by the UDBA[1] people. Today, as it turns out, everything I know I owe to them. Thus, it is logical to dedicate this book to them.

Although they removed most of the documents from my father's police file in a most orderly manner, the UDBA people nonetheless subsequently decided to hand me one previously never received letter–my father's suicide letter from prison, which was written on December 12, 1985: "Dear Jasna, I know that this farewell letter will hurt you very much, but I don't want to live anymore. One day, when you grow up, when you think about it, maybe it will become clear to you why I acted like I did. I could endure everything, joy and poverty, but not injustice…" (that's enough, the rest is for me). They left this letter because they are cautious, and because they know some things will never stop hurting.

At Josip Broz Tito High School we had practicum at the metal factory, which was situated near the city's hippodrome, and it was there that we were introduced to the working process of socialism. While the others were assembling to watch the horses, I stayed with the working class. At that time, the prisoners from the Idrizovo prison were grooming the horses, and I was afraid that if I saw my father with the horses I wouldn't know what I was allowed to do. Once, in the school library, the librarian whispered to me that my father was a great man. In the letter to my father that month, I wrote that the librarian sent regards to him, and said that he was a great man. My father asked me not to mention any names in my letters anymore, that we mustn't hurt people. As a result, my letters became even colder, if that was possible.

People lie when they say they have memories of their traumas. When you suffer a trauma you build a parallel world. While we were being jolted along in a crowded bus on the way to the Idrizovo prison, I always imagined the same scene: walking my dog, which I didn't have, in the city park. It was always the same scene, and always the same dog. In the canteen in front of Idrizovo, we waited for hours and looked towards the main gate. The visitors were either very loud or very quiet; there was no misunderstanding among us. We were taken into a big hall called "the dining room," and although dining rooms are cosy, there was nothing at all personable here. We always sat at "our" table on the left side of the buffet, which offered the same five things sold in the canteen, and it was always the same table, and always the same five things. My father would come out first, which was no small thing considering the hefty prisoners who pushed from behind. Once he was seated at "our" table, he neither talked much, nor loudly. To our left, the police officer, who in the spirit of Lenin was called a militioner at the time, paced up and down. Afterwards, we took the same bus home. I put my face to the window glass, looking with open eyes at my dog in the park. I must admit, the city park remains disgusting to me to this day.

I started studying my father's file, and was driven by one overwhelmingly urgent, personal need. I was neither hungry to find out who my father's spies were, nor why they spied; I wasn't led by the need to understand the great history; I didn't want to dismantle the logic of Yugoslav communism, and even less the small-town version of Macedonian communism. This came later, when the emotions were released from everything that eventually made any difference, or could still make a difference. I had to leave them at a bus stop so I could continue. At that time, you know, there weren't many bus stops where our buses stopped…

I wanted to come to peace with my family's past. I felt some kind of past loss, some intangible sadness. Imagine for a moment a person living with the burden of a sadness that cannot be publicly grieved for. I seized the meaning of this when I was reading Judith Butler's, *Antigone's Claim* (2000). The last paragraph of the first chapter reads: "Antigone refuses to obey any law that refuses public recognition of her loss, and in this way prefigures the situation that those with publicly ungrievable losses–from AIDS, for instance–know all too well. What sort of living death have these people been condemned to?"² Knowing that the total official number of personal communist files in Macedonia is 14,572 (unofficial sources claim more than 50,000 files), I started counting the children and the relatives of the pursued and persecuted under communism, asking myself: Where are these people today? What are they doing now? What are they doing with their sadness?

I started talking with my friends and colleagues about my father's file. It turned out that they all knew my father was in prison, that my family was excommunicated. Even so, they never asked, and I never told them. It was as if we had made a secret pact to console each other in silence, as if we had no idea where to go with our stories from the communist time; it was a kind of cultural amnesia, a consensus–talk about everything, but *that*. Of course, from time to time, I talked about my father's imprisonment to a boyfriend or a close friend. "You know, my father was in prison once, under communism." After the fall of communism, their reactions were always either complete silence or uneasiness. Not because they didn't have any empathy, but because there was no recognizable ritual they could invoke, no pre-defined method with which they could reply. Where would they place my sadness? What name would they give it?

Once, on the day of the anniversary of my father's death in 2002, at the commemoration at the cemetery in my father's birth village of Prisovjani, my best friend asked me: "We all cried, why didn't you?" I answered: "If I start crying in public now, I will never be able to stop."

Once, much later, I read a book by Viktor Erofeyev called *The Good Stalin* (2004). Erofeyev was a child of the nomenclature, the golden youth under Kremlin protection. His grandmother once called his mother to tell her that the child vomited because he had eaten too much caviar. Here, no one ever wrote such a book; the sons of Dedinje, Pantovčak and Vodno³ played rock-and-roll, made "black wave" films (they were allowed), and from India they brought Buddhism and started living the "avant-garde." That sado-masochistic relationship between art and ideology finally ended when the majority of these sons later went *too right* to remember their childhood. In *The Good Stalin,* it is described how young Erofeyev's literary outbursts prevented the Old Erofeyev, who was at the top of his Soviet career, from becoming Andrei Gromyko's Deputy Minister of the Interior. Erofeyev concludes: "Who am I to condemn the fame of the 20th century? If there had been one less bullet, just one less crematorium oven, I wouldn't have been in this world as well."[4] And it turns out precisely that *they*, damn it, had always had a more interesting story than "ours." We emerge from the scum of life, from the displaced. "They" were born as heroes, from the blood of those who had fallen at the altar of their lives.

When I publicly spoke about my father's file in December 2005, I started receiving anonymous and partially anonymous threats to the safety of my family (see the chapter entitled "Hard Wing"). And nobody is an idiot. I can live without my father's past, but I cannot live without my son's future. It turned out that communist-related topics are still traumatic, and they are not as naïve as they would seem to be, and I stopped trying to understand whether the police group with whom my father was arrested was part of the UDBA's internal sub-structures. That cannot be found out anyway, except by "interrogating" the same structures. Besides, my father's communist tragedy is far bigger than *just* the hard UDBA story from the 1970s, and far more tragic than *just* his imprisonment in the 1980s, as his total communist Golgotha lasted more than 40 years.

It's only in these last few years that the idea for phenomenological insight into communism comes to me. What kind of human engineering was needed to establish that ideology? What did it mean? What did the combination of communism and the small-town mentality mean in the Macedonian version of the story? How was the sacrificing of such proportions possible, and why did communism require that? And finally, what did that "Intimist" mean? What did being an intimist in communism mean, an intimist in our small-town world? This book is one of the possible answers to these questions, and it is an answer to the question of how I understood the period, and of how I see the Macedonian rabble of communism and the small town today.

2

Intimist

Biographies–Wishes

They bring neither the treasures from the peaks, nor those from the wombs of the hills. But, there is a vivid memory which, like the caressing hand, mildly passes over all things worthy of remembering. One cannot inscribe himself in that memory with a clumsy hand and rough tools…
—Kafka

Biographies–Biographies are wishes, most frequently wishes to keep, to retain the Platonic memory of the person who is the subject of the biography. Even in the driest of biographies, there is a hidden but megalomanic ambition (recognized at least in that unique trivial detail), the ambition to grasp that something from that side in which the person who is the subject of the biography sang, loved, thought, danced, created and lived the ambition to meet him in that singing, thinking, creating, living…

And yet, not all biographical meetings are the same, since there are at least two types of wishes connected with the wish to memorize one's life. The first type of wish is comprised of meetings with the aim of greeting, led by the need for an impossible touch with the one who is no more–those are meetings such as greetings, meetings in search of a mutually blended scent. And there is the other type: the wish for a hard repetition of certainty, meetings such as a terrible need for re-memorization, for reproduction of the primal sight, for the first picture of the person who is the subject of the biography, a need to capture and freeze his cause and his movement; the wish to reach that invisible detail through which everything from his life will open, will spread, everything that can be (and because it can, will be) served up to the hyenas from the city, the wish to capture everything "to the sediment" of a single human life, so that firmly established sediment will become a condition for distortion, for punishment and annihilation.

Of course, both types of biographical meetings are records; they are records consisting of words, words that penetrate the innocent paper, destroy its smooth surface, its constant readiness to accept the record. Because of that penetration, the hand which writes the record is important, the hand that attends the paper's penetration. Therefore, the wish that moves the search for the lost past is important, for the memory of a life, for the remembrance. As we said, the biography consists of words, which are here to remind us. But how can words remind us at all?

As a scene of history, a biography, and particularly a literary biography as a memory of literary history, will always have to be a record that is gentle, a record that caresses, a record that hasn't set off towards the wish to cement, to kill and to destroy. A biography cannot be established by reproduction–each acceptance (which together with mystery makes a human life) is possible only in a symbolic way, in absentia, only when a biography itself stops at the doorstep of an entrance into somebody else's life, and at the doorstep it will decide to stop itself...

Biographies-Lexicons

It is early for the last word, I say,
I am talking almost from the end–first,
I wasn't at the scene you are accusing me of,
I myself was a scene in blood!
—Yevtushenko

So, there are at least two types of biographies. And, certainly, there is the third kind, the most frequent kind of biography–that which more or less consists of facts. The facts about Jovan Koteski, compiled from different lexicons–here is what they read:

Jovan Koteski (1932-2001) was a poet who belonged to the third generation of Macedonian writers, who begin in the 1950s. He was born in the village of Prisovjani in the Struga region as the fourth of five children of Petkana and Vasil Koteski. He spent his childhood working as a shepherd-servant, looking after other people's cattle, and in 1946 he enrolled in the Ohrid High School and lived in a boarding school. In 1948, his father, who worked as an emigrant-confectioner in Bratislava, Slovakia, was imprisoned by the Slovak Informbiro and sentenced to a nine-year imprisonment, the reason being that the Slovak secret services found a picture of Josip Broz Tito in my grandfather's apartment in Bratislava, the same Marshal, in whose name–and in the name of greater irony–my father stood many trials later for. Jovan Koteski met his father only twice in his life: once when he was seven and the second time when he was 26. Of the second reunion, in 1958, Jovan Koteski later wrote: "When he came back, he called one of my aunts, and she brought him to my hovel, which I rented when I was a student. At dusk, when I came back from the faculty, I see a guest in my room. And there it is–the hug of a barren, miserable life."[1]

Jovan Koteski was detained for the first time in 1948, when he was 16 years old, probably because that was the year his father was imprisoned in Slovakia, and it is known that the Yugoslav secret services collaborated with the secret services of the other communist countries. Koteski became suspicious to the Yugoslav Interior Service because of the communist logic that says–your father is suspicious, therefore you are suspicious too. In 1950, Jovan Koteski was detained again, and this time he was convicted and sentenced to three years in prison for a verbal diatribe against Marshal Tito, but he was released several days later. He was detained for a third time in 1952 while working in a youth brigade in the Mavrovo mountains in Macedonia, the fourth time in 1954, etc., whereas his police file under the code name "Intimist" was not officially opened until 1961.

In 1954, he moved to Skopje, the capital of Macedonia, and enrolled in the university to study literature, a study which he never finishes. He worked as a journalist at Radio Skopje for three decades, and in 1958 he published two collection of poems: *Land and Passion* and *A Smile before Dawn*, followed by *Evil Times* (1963),

Heaviness (1965), *Peplosija* (1966), *Shadows* (1972), *Green Gates* (1975), *Heraklea* (1978), *Sea-boards* (1981), *Wakes and Dreams* (1982), *A Chandelier* (1983), *Fruits* and *A Title Deed* (1985), *Live Fire* (1990), *Grindstone of the Sun* (1990), *Shivers* (1991), *A Mouse with Binoculars* (poetry for children, 1991), *A Plough Handle/Morning Star* (1992), *Evil Times* (1992), *A Cradle* (1994), *Loneliness* (1994), *Festivity* (bibliographical edition–manuscript, 1995), *A Searcher* (narrative poem, 1995), *Bars* (1996), *Dowry* (1997), *Landslide* (1998), *Destruction* (1999) and *Molehill* (2000).

On September 2, 1985, he was arrested and sentenced to a five-year prison term, being convicted for actions against the Yugoslav Federation and for creating an independent Macedonian state, which actually comes about seven years later. He belonged to the last group of political prisoners-intellectuals in the Former Yugoslav Federation. Jovan Koteski again stood trial, which was closed to the public, with one of my father's prosecutors asking for a 20-year sentence.

His release from prison was not initiated by the Macedonian writers, but by the American poet Allen Ginsberg, then a member of the PEN Freedom-to-Write Committee, and later its vice-president.

In 1986, Ginsberg attended the Struga Poetry Evenings in Macedonia as a laureate of the Golden Wreath poetry award. After the intervention of the Yugoslav PEN Center (based in Zagreb, Croatia) in July 1987, Koteski was set free after almost two years in prison. The person most responsible for his being freed is the Croatian writer Predrag Matvejević, who at the time was vice-president of the World PEN Center and president of the Croatian PEN Club, and who organized a petition with world famous writers for my father's release. During the 1990s, Matvejević himself fell out of favor under Franjo Tuđman's nationalistic regime in Croatia and fled the country. With letters to the District Court in Skopje and to the Federal Court of Yugoslavia in Belgrade, Matvejević succeeded in obtaining a reinvestigation of the procedure against Koteski and his early release from prison in July 1987. Koteski was employed as a librarian in a small library near his home, where he worked until his retirement. He traveled to Croatia and met Matvejević, and in 1995, he received an award for a narrative poem in an anonymous contest.

Koteski spent the last decade of his life in relative isolation at his home in Skopje, suffering from paranoia. In November 2000, seven months before his death, he managed to see selective parts of his file, which took up more than 300 pages and told how he was the subject of surveillance for more than 40 years of his life.[2] The last document from my father's file was from 1988, but most of the researchers think that the surveillance continued until 1990. If (rightfully or not) we believe that the surveillance of my father stopped in 1990, then the surveillance lasted for 42 years, while if (with interruptions) it continued up until his death, then my father was the subject of police surveillance for 53 years. He died on July 12, 2001 in Skopje, and was surrounded by his closest family.

Biographies of "One One"

Oblivium is that which effaces–effaces what?
The signifier as such.
—Lacan

Then, there are those biographies that are not that, biographies consisting of instinctive memories, those in which you have been constituted as "one one" (Lacan's first signifier that, for instance, I got to love *one* animal). And then there is "one two," when I place myself where the amount is, not on the level of "one," but on the level of "one two." Where the thing which is a record that penetrates the innocence of the paper starts to operate…

In the place where "one one" is, the place of I, his child, there are some isolated instances of memories, secretions and introjections which are (already) lame for all the reasons and for all the work behind the reconstructions. In that place I can see how I look at myself, but I cannot *see* anymore. That is the space which talks from a point that cannot remember anymore. That is a place of loss, where an exchange of phantasmas with reality occurs, something irreducible, something that may function as that Lacanian initial repressed signifier. Thus, from the place of "one one," here are some memories.

My father, the man entered under the name of Jovan Koteski in the Lexicons read Lorca's poem *Two Sailors on the Beach* to his daughter. And he interpreted the poem to her, explaining that those are not two but one and the same sailor, but one in him continued to travel by ship over the seas of the world, and the other in him stayed in an Asian port with the woman he would love all his life.

Another memory, another isolated: My father bought a painting. There is a vase with three flowers in it, Picasso style. Three hands are holding the vase. "The painting is nothing special, I can draw a better one" I say, and I am a child. My father smiles, asks me to get a piece of paper and try. I go to my room and I draw the same picture from memory. I show him the paper, my father says that I have drawn the same picture. "But better." "Yes (smile), but the thing is not to draw the same picture, but to draw *your* picture, just like the painter drew his"…

Third memory: My father rings the doorbell that Friday. It's the second year nobody rings our doorbell. The ringing–it is a movement of threat… in prison from this side of prison… That Friday, I open the door and I see my father arriving unannounced from prison, expressly released that morning, in a prison uniform, he didn't have time to change, all he thought about at that moment, that morning, was to get home as quickly as possible. I don't realize that in the meantime, in the place of my great love, a great dull hatred is born. My first impulse is to close the door in his face. So that each of us will continue living in prison, each in their own prison. I don't realize that if he had known how to love me a little less, if only I had better understood what was happening to us, I wouldn't have hated him as much as I did from the moment he disappeared. Each love seems self-sufficient, love in the time of bloody systems as well. You are not prepared for loss. I know I wasn't…

Fourth memory: My father in the house that lies in decay amidst poverty and hunger. My father comes home from work in 1994, and as always, asks if anybody called him. Nobody?

Fifth memory: My brother graduates that March, and now he is an atomic physicist. My father, drunk, holding my brother's graduation papers, goes out to find money, my brother has to go back to Belgrade, Serbia; he will be working at the Vinča Institute of Nuclear Sciences near Belgrade, they have an extinguished nuclear reactor. My father comes back and throws 400 German marks on the table. He is swaying. "I was sitting in the company of young people, businessmen, Jasna. One from my generation was sitting there… he told me, oh Jovan, don't make a fool of yourself, come sit with me, don't sit at a table with children… And then he saw, when the kid started to count… 100, 200, 300, 400… I stopped him. That's enough, I said, I will give it back to you, and he replied: Uncle Jovan, if you give it back to me, I'll beat you up. And I will give it back to him and that's why I say to him, beat me up, I'll count it out to you as you did now." He is swaying with the blue notebook "Graduation paper, candidate: Vasil Koteski, Faculty of Physics, Belgrade, 1994;" he sits on a pile of books, the pile falls, but my father still clutches the notebook "Graduation paper"…

Sixth memory: The process of a long reconciliation. A man I accidentally met at a conference calls me to work on a project, and since we don't have any money I'll work on anything. For months, he has been trying to persuade me to go to Budapest where he is a professor. He enrolls me at the university where he works, invites me to stay with his family, opens the door of his library to me, gives me Foucault and the Russian dissidents, and I read everything that has nothing to do with my studies. I avoid going back to Macedonia, even during the holidays, the country is as disgusting to me as it was when I ran away from it. Several days before the end of my studies, my professor shows me his grandfather's thick dossier. In fact, my professor is a grandson of one of the leading communist snitches in Hungary, which is his way of payback. After me, a girl moves into the house, escaping from Slobodan Milošević's Belgrade. She is also broke, she also reads the books our professor gives her… He helped us find a vocabulary to explain to ourselves the things that were happening to us in our historic times… The last morning on the train from Budapest to Skopje, for the first time in many years, I feel immeasurable happiness to be going back, after an entire decade, to my father again. Yes, my professor was the child of a former communist snitch.

My father, the day before he died: "This home is not a home. And we tried. Look, your mother put a picture here, and a flower here, and these shelves. Wonderful. But this is not a home. You will understand me, won't you? Everybody has to go home. I have to go home now…"

Biographies of "Friends"

> You would play upon me; you would seem to know my stops; you would pluck out the heart of my mystery; you would sound me from my lowest note to the top of my compass. And there is much music, excellent voice, in this little organ, yet cannot you make it speak. 'Sblood, do you think I am easier to be played on than a pipe? Call me what instrument you will, though you can fret me, you cannot play upon me.
> —Shakespeare

And then, of course, there are the hard biographies. They are usually written by those who smile at you while clutching a knife behind their back such as your friends, the Macedonian poets and writers.

When my father showed me the dossier for the first time in November 2000, it was only several months before he would die. That's how much time we had, time for reconciliation. Some among us, the children of political prisoners, didn't have even that much luck. The first thing he showed me was the section entitled: "Cooperation with Internal Affairs: none!" And then he read 300 (from who knows how many) pages, which he was allowed to see and keep from his file, with just a few names, half the pages crossed out with a felt-tip pen, so as to find out what he had known all his life: That he had been the subject of an investigation for at least 42 out of his 69 years. And then we realized that the paranoia was not paranoia, that the fear was not an irrational luxury, but a higher state of acknowledgement. And then you read, and it hurts, but at least you see that you are not crazy.

When my father got out of prison, it often happened that in the street his best friends, our literary doyens, our reading lists, would turn their heads away from him. The same happened to all of my family. We understand, it was difficult for them, they didn't know how to greet us and not bring harm to themselves. We understand them, but let's make it perfectly clear–they will never be understood by the poet and the child in my father, because for that child those mechanisms cannot be understood. And in the name of that child who didn't understand them, in the name of my father who is gone, I have but one simple message from the mouth of Croatian rapper Edo Maajka: "Fuck you."

When my father initially left me, the first basic question about the file for me wasn't–who, how or why?–but a completely different, infrastructural question. What did that machinery actually look like? Who typed this page? What was the typist's name? Who made this typing mistake? Who tapped my brother's telephone conversation while he was arranging his athletic training? Was that information worth it? What was the name of the telephonist? Did that actual informant, writer, our reading list, feel that he was doing something useful when he passed on that "information?" What did "the informant" look like? What did he have for breakfast that morning? What line did he use when he saw his kids off to school? Did he make his children happy and good people with the salary he received from his underground work? Because if he did, that is at least some kind of galactic, ethereal consolation, though if he didn't, that does not console me either.

Likewise, later, when you're waiting for a bus, suddenly a personal question comes to your mind. That bus happened to me one morning. When it became clear to me that the tapping device was put in our home around the time I said my first hello to my first infatuation. It was a secret between all of my close friends, but not to the state structure. If I had been able to choose, I wouldn't have wanted it to be like that. If my brother could have chosen, he wouldn't have wanted it to be like that either. But, you see, we had no choice.

Those are fundamental issues, and they are very important. You cannot tap the conversations of one nation without any consequences and then expect that nation to be normal. You cannot then tell them one morning: We should enter Europe, don't cross the street when the light is red. They, with their tractors, had flattened all of the intimate coordinates of our human lives, always crossing on **red**, they had run all the traffic lights of human intimacy; then they ask us to stop on green and be loyal to their conventions. That cannot be. To be fair, both sides need to be fair.

In my father's file, there is a document that says a tapping device was put in our home, but there isn't a document that says it was ever taken out. You will say, nobody is crazy enough to spend time listening to my retired mother's conversations, but you see–we don't know. Because that is the logic of the system. It has to keep you entangled in paranoia. It will not tell you when the tapping started, and it will not tell you when it stopped. It will not intentionally tell you when it stopped, so that you don't relax. That is the small-God logic: Nobody asks you whether you want to come into this world, nobody asks you whether you want to leave. To leave their panoptic view? They decide. That is the position of omnipotence.

And precisely because entire generations of children of former political prisoners remain silent, as I do, that's why that omnipotence is possible, although nobody has or ever will possess the legitimacy to give it to them. One of the basic jobs of ex-communist states is to create mechanisms that will make that page of their past visible, the suffering of entire generations and descendants of the victims in the political calculations. I apologize, but if it is possible today to see space in every third newspaper dedicated to people's complaining about how much their liposuction hurt, they will have to allow it to be said that this hurt too. My father was a political prisoner when Laibach and NSK[3] had already taken place in Slovenia, and when everything was falling apart. When nothing was left, some among us decided to equip themselves in order to tear apart those with heretical thoughts.

It occurred to me to mention the Idrizovo prison to people who I had known for years, and they would tell me that their father, stepfather, etc. were political prisoners. The first thing that came to my mind was the question: Damn it, how many are we? Really, how many are we? The basic question remains: If you have whole generations "tried for communism," the question is: How do states that emerged from Yugoslavia incorporate the experiences of the expelled today, how do they channel their energies? I speak on behalf of all the children of the political prisoners. And what connects us is the question: Do you know what these people were convicted of? They were convicted of living in a culture which asks from them submission to a type of cultural amnesia, as if there exists a generally accepted consensus to agree never to talk about the loss. The problem is not in rehabilitation. You will receive a document which says that everything is now all right, but that document is not worth the paper it is printed on. You will find employment in the institutions of the system, though nothing will be easier for you. You will seem integrated. Everything will be all right. But you know. Your fathers (and mothers) are branded. Entire segments of their lives are marked with a black felt-tip pen, as with the corresponding segments in their files, and likewise with your lives and the lives of their descendants. You, the descendants, don't know what to do with the black felt-tip pen. If the gods intended for your father to suffer, you cannot live on welfare, despite whatever coordinates you set for yourself. There is no such thing as a logic of health, order and reason. There isn't. And because there isn't, our general question is: Where are those people, how functional are they in and for their societies, and what about their publicly unacknowledged pain? If the post-communist states want healthy nations, they must submit to an extensive psychoanalysis, so as to better understand their mechanisms and know what happened to them and where they stand now. Unfortunately, we are too lazy to do even that. In the name of all of this, I invite the children of the former political prisoners to open the files they keep at home. I know they stay away from those drawers because it hurts them, but if they open them, once, maybe it will start hurting less.

The Violence of Macedonian Culture
(About the Macedonian Writers' Parade)

> Once more I am a wanderer, a pilgrim, through the world.
> But what else are you?
> —Goethe

"The biography of the friends," the one that your colleagues, the Macedonian writers and poets, wrote about you in the long decades between 1960-1990 without you knowing. What did those expert, creative quills manage to write in the "biography" genre on the topic, "one wanderer through the world," over all these decades?

My father's file shows the principles on which the control strategy was built in the cultural sphere in the years between 1960 and 1990. If you left your home, then you were observed. The streets were circled by managers, municipality representatives, policemen, collaborators, informants, DBK[4] servants and your friends, though you couldn't distinguish who was who. You were tied to your place, your place had a name, and in my father's case that name was "Intimist." You were an intimist, and as such, you were extremely suspicious. There was no reason to be an "intimist" in 1961, when all the others were sociologists.

A terrible parade of living and dead poets, literates, accidental people–and policemen–paraded through my father's file. The world of my father's file was an obscene combination of Macedonian writers and policemen who frequently merged into the same person, which was a world where you were without stable coordinates for friendship. Most of the "friends," colleagues and writers, were there to tighten the ring around their target. Everybody and everything was an ear.

It is clear from my father's file that the type of control that was exercised on him was based on a system of continuous reports, lists and records. An informant submitted a report to a manager, and the manager submitted that document to three other authorities: the information book, the UDBA Department and the file for a legal connection. In January 1988, a person X called my father at home to wish him "A Happy New Year." The content of this wish was then forwarded to THREE other authorities.

The records connect the center (the heads of the UDBA) to the periphery (my father's "friends"). Power was distributed in an exclusive way in the proper hierarchical order, from the lowest authority to the final pimp, who records every distress, which recording led to tragicomic situations. In the informant's document, dated April 1961, my father complained to his "friend" over lunch that he was not satisfied with the system; though "with good intentions," X reminded my father that for him personally it was good and that he had nothing to complain about. And then all of a sudden there was a "switch." I'm quoting from the file: "Jovan suddenly left the restaurant to talk to a person passing by." In translation, this means that my father went out to greet another friend, which was a very good cause for alarm within the hierarchical organization. As part of the routine operatives' notes, it was necessary to investigate who he greeted, and to set that person as a new target of observation. This organization demanded the real name of everybody you greeted, as well as wanting to know the real reason for your permanent criticism of the system, your surplus of meaning, your poetic sensibility and your "illness."

I would like to recapture for you the monstrous dimensions of this control, which were systematically exercised on my father for at least four decades. Imagine for a moment that you are my father, the Macedonian poet Jovan Koteski, in April 1961. On the 18th of that month you met your friend (his name is crossed out with a black felt-tip pen) to have lunch at the hotel "Macedonia." While talking, you complained that Macedonian villages were poor and that there was a strong Serbian influence in Macedonia. Your "friend" is actually an informant and he immediately passed what you said on to the authorities. In June 1964, you visited a friend. You were among a group of Macedonian poets who talked about some Slovenian magazines, and your writer–host was an informant. In that same month, you're strolling "along the promenade" (as it was written in the file) with three well-known Macedonian writers, and one of them was an informant. Together with three other Macedonian writers you visited a fourth in that same month and complained to the writers (quoting from the file) that: "Washington, in a program on Yugoslavia in Serbo-Croatian gives more detailed information than our press does." The Macedonian writer who was your host was also an informant. In October 1964, you, along with some other people, were in somebody's office (it is crossed out in whose office), which turns out to be "the office of a collaborator." Once again in that same month, you met five colleagues, writers, at the "Tourist" Hotel. You talked about "Khrushchev's resignation," you said that a "pro-Chinese policy" was being led by the state, and one of your friends was an informant. Lastly, a plane crashed in that same month on Avala (a mountain near the Serbian capital, Belgrade), and you were at a colleague's place, a poet, you were one of five Macedonian poets there. You were suspicious that a plane could crash on Avala just like that, and your host was an informant.

If you lived my father's life between 1960 and 1990, informants were always close to you. The government consisted of many bodies, but they didn't sit at the table next to you, they didn't peek from behind a pot, they didn't pretend that they were reading a newspaper in the lobby. This was not a movie, this was your life, and the informants were your closest friends and colleagues, the Macedonian writers. Like all people in this world, you talked to your friends about things that were important to you, things that hurt you, things that made you happy or things that disturbed you. You were a Macedonian poet and everything was important to you in relation to Macedonian culture and the institutions leading it, including the Macedonian language and the Macedonian villages. Because you wrote about them in your poetry, the ideology was important to you, because like every poet on this planet you also think you had a right to have an opinion about it. But while you talked to your friends, you didn't know that you were actually talking to a hybrid, a two-headed creature who had the face of a poet and another face–that of a police officer without a uniform. Your best "friends" were always next to you; In some documents you were at their place, in others you were at a restaurant, in a club, at a hotel, a reading, a meeting, in their business car, in a bar, in an office, whether it was yours, his or hers. All of the above listed places were actual locations from my father's file.

When you look at this diffusion of the government and its most perfidious penetration of your intimate world with the help of your friends, you cannot but ask yourself, where is the limit? Some of my mother's friends, our poets' spouses, are also unmasked as informants in the file. Where does the list end? What surprise awaits you behind the black felt-tip pens that hide the other identities?

Sadism

> The duty of the inn-keeper…(is)
> to shelter traveling families respectfully:
> to shave the man, to pluck the woman, to pick the child clean…
> This man and this woman were ruse and rage wedded–a hideous and terrible team.
> —Victor Hugo

When I first read the file I stood mute before the fact that the Macedonian writer of our more recent cultural history was so regularly and eagerly moving the machinery. The first question you are going to ask yourself is: What was the mental matrix of the Macedonian poets in a role of hosts of a stolen story or in the role of innkeepers that rob families, when they could perform such massive and collective violence? And the next is: What was their driving motive?

Personal benefit or gain, fear, basic ideological illiteracy, curiosity, spite, "philosophical" desire for insight, malice or the sadistic satisfaction of candidly observing someone? You see the sadism as being accentuated as one of the most important driving factors in this document. From one page of my father's file to another, you can cut through the sadism with a knife. You read and see the sadism of a culture and you remain mute, speechless. And you cannot speak a word of that for many years.

The sadism of the Macedonian writers in those many years was such that they wanted, at any price, voluntarily and in the name of any absolute absence of elementary empathy, to bow to the government. And the government for them was one concrete space bordered by the local cultural head and the UDBA services. The leading figure of Macedonian culture between 1960 and 1990 was embodied in the president of the Writer's Association of Macedonia, in the leading literary critic with an authoritarian attitude, in the boss of your cultural institution, in the one who was responsible for the cultural cashbox and in the faculty professor from whom you expected a good review. Finally, he was present in each local thug who, not having anything better to do, decides to become a writer, because in the years we are talking about, this was a highly competitive profession strategically financed by the state, with the aim of creating an "economic base" of–and for its literature. I'll give you an example: In one document from February 1988 (half a year since my father got out of prison), someone calls in the afternoon and introduces himself. That person (I'm now literally quoting from the file):

Asks to talk to Jovan Koteski. When he is told he is not at home, he leaves a telephone number and asks for Jovan to call him back when he comes home. Later, Jovan called the same number–stressing that somebody called him. He received an answer that nobody called him. Thinking that he dialed the wrong number, Jovan called once again.–The X's apartment? Jovan Koteski speaking. X: Yes? J: Somebody called me from there?! X: Nobody called you and it is better for you not to play games anymore. Jovan: OK! He hangs up, very anxious and disturbed. (document ends).

The Macedonian writer in the role of police officer was trembling not only from the perverse desire to torment someone, but also from the perverse desire, for just once in his police career, to tread on the food that will satisfy the never-ending metonymic appetite of his uncrowned boss of the Macedonian writing establishment and the UDBA services. But, in his primitivism, this man didn't know something that every animal knows–once it is fed it leaves the carcass because it doesn't need it anymore. He didn't know that the boss wasn't an animal, but a man who had an appetite that no amount of food in this world could satisfy. There is no food that can stop the hunger of the uncrowned master of the Macedonian cultural establishment between 1960-1990. He would swallow anything, not one, not two, he would swallow all of the good poems and all of the good poets of his time, so that he could rise above their corpses as the best and greatest author. The more he swallowed, the hungrier he was. From the file, it is clear that there was no end for a matrix that wanted to swallow the entire essence of everything you have ever said.

In my father's file, most of the people were crossed out with a black felt-tip pen. The only names left were those who were supposed to be burned. If it's any consolation to the writers who were present in the file with a name and a surname, there were even "worse" than them. Those that the UDBA wanted to protect. There were also those who were crossed out, or protected in another way, but you can recognize who they were anyway. Fifteen people worked on creating my father's file, the second listed under the name of Trajan Petrovski. Was he the president of the Writer's Association of Macedonia until 2007? You see, I don't know even this. But, if it is the same man, then the perversity continues. The same name, Trajan Petrovski, appears in my father's file in 1987, this time as a benefactor. According to the documents, after my father's release from prison, and when he was unable to get an appointment with anybody (from his colleagues to the Director of Radio Skopje where he had worked before), Trajan Petrovski offers to help him and has him employed at the library near my father's home, where my father worked until his retirement. There are documents from the sessions of the Writer's Association of Macedonia in the file, where the president at that time (who is also crossed out with a felt-tip pen), Macedonian poet Gane Todorovski, behaves as if the imprisonment of a member of his association is not his concern, and he leans on the UDBA services. In a document from January 1987, President of the Yugoslav PEN Center and Vice President of the International PEN Center, Croatian writer Predrag Matvejević, asks the District Court in Skopje for my father's release from prison. In the request is the following sentence: "We asked, and we are asking for an explanation (about the imprisonment–my comment) everywhere, from the Macedonian writers (who did not publicly make statements about this), from the literary organizations (which didn't defend him) and from the court (which tried him without public attendance)…" Even the Yugoslav PEN Center (a part of the Yugoslav infrastructure, the disintegration of which was the cause of my father's trial in 1985) is confused by the indolent attitude of the home Writer's Association."[5] But its president, the Macedonian poet Gane Todorovski, is not confused. He enjoys his position of the inviolable master of Macedonian culture, before whom all writers tremble. My father's example proves the reason why. In a text from 1998, Macedonian poet Eftim Kletnikov writes:

Once, when Jovan Koteski was still imprisoned, I met [Predrag] Matvejević at the Book Fair in Belgrade. I felt obligated to thank him personally for what he was doing for Koteski. He literally told me: "You know, Eftim, I knelt down before one of our well-known intellectuals, who held a powerful position [in Macedonia], begging him to intercede for Koteski because I knew that he could save him in one fell swoop if he wanted to. And you know what he told me? Leave him there. He deserved it!" I got goose bumps.[6]

This is very important. If this is the mental cultural matrix of our not so distant past, then we people working in the field of culture should ask ourselves what the position of our culture today is and what can we expect from it? Entire generations of high school students grew up with this literature. You read it to your children before they went to sleep, and I read it to my son before he went to sleep. But, you see, I am terrified when I open a book by anyone born before 1950, because I fear the possibility that they have written another type of poetry with the same hands. I lived in a neighborhood of decades-long terror.

The records that my father's file are based on have one binary function and branding: useful–harmful, insane–sane, dangerous–

humble, normal–abnormal. This is a key to the enforced labeling, the differentiation of each member of that community insofar as who is the man that you have met, where should he be, how should he be characterized and how to recognize him. There are a number of notes on the margins of the file by operative persons and inspectors, which give advice on how to continue future observation. Part of the advice deals with who would be best in continuing to implement a permanent and individual observation of my father. For example, in the first document of my father's file from 1961, there is the following note: "There is a condition and confidence to place X with this person (my father–my comment) because we think that Jovan confides in him."

The writer's sadism transpired in a close union with the police one, and later, with the prison one. In communism, political prisoners were treated worse than those who had committed the "usual" crimes such as murder, rape, etc. In the operative's note of my father's file, dated December 12, 1985, it is stated that his cell "roommate," the sadist Vasil Atanasovski-Šumski, is actually the police "operative link" who works as a prison extortionist. Šumski tortures my father in all ways possible, and my father tries to commit suicide. A note of the same date reads: "Our operative link, Vasil Atanasovski, indicates that the 'Intimist' is depressed, and has written suicide notes."[7] The irony of Vasil Atanasovski-Šumski's police sadism is actually something else. According to the operative's note from Idrizovo prison, after Šumski tortured my father and my father attempted to commit suicide, Šumski denounced my father to the Services, which then "extorted" from my father: "(A) promise that he will not contemplate such things any more" (from the operative's note to the chief inspector of SDB–III Department). Even death is not free or voluntary; if you look for an exit from the sadistic circle of prison torture, even that exit has to be approved by *The Services*.

Hard Wing

> The cadet's noses should be obtuse and bent, that is ordered by the rules, that think of everything and truly all our organs for odour are humbly and modestly bent. As if cut

with a sharp knife. Our eyes should always see in emptiness, and they have this in the Rulebook. Actually, we are not supposed to have eyes, because the eyes are impudent and curious, and the impudence and curiosity are doomed by all the healthy moral viewpoints. Our ears are very unusual. They can barely hear anything because of the everlasting intensive hearing.
—Robert Walser

But, the "easy" type of surveillance performed on my father (officially from 1961, and unofficially from 1948) continued until the late 1960s. The main actors in that "easy" surveillance were his friends, the writers–policemen.

Come the late 1960s the surveillance on my father suddenly stiffens. Now, the *writer–policemen* are no longer sufficient, and an unknown agency begins sending *policemen–writers*. They are not his friends, but their job is to become his friend and they succeed in doing that over four long years. All the documents from this period are censored in the file, but we can reconstruct it from the statements by my father (and the other players) during the investigation process. Around 1968, an unknown person knocks on my father's door. He is a policeman in a uniform, and he is in the active service of the police station in the district where my father lives at the time, in a small house that was given to him after the Skopje earthquake of 1963. The policeman is a neighbor and his duty is to make contact through literature. He introduces himself and asks my father to read his literary materials and to write him a recommendation for the publication of a book project of his. My father has already had a vague feeling that he has been under observation for almost two decades, and he is terrified by the uniform he sees in front of him and agrees.

A few months later, while my father is walking towards the bus stop, he meets the same policeman, now accompanied by another man unknown to my father, who is also a uniformed policeman. The first policeman introduces my father to the other as follows: "His good friend, a great Macedonian and a sufferer just like him. I thought that they, being police officers, were provoking and investigating me…" my father writes in his statement. Months pass, and the entire procedure lasts a total of four years. On one occasion, my father goes to a butcher. The same two policemen meet him, redirect him to another butcher close to one of their houses, and invite him to be their guest. After some time, an introduction to a third from the police follows. This meeting–in a supermarket–is also "accidental." Again that night, they invite him to be their guest.

I didn't understand what those people (policemen–my comment) wanted from me, but they were constantly telling me that the one who is not a good Macedonian will have his head fly off like a rooster's. I was overcome by fear and panic. The stated people never left me alone anymore… On several encounters, when they waited for me when I was going to the supermarket, they told me they would do their work and that I should stay still. Until the present day, I don't understand why all of that was done to me. (quoted from the police file)

From 1968 on, there was a turnabout in the type of surveillance performed. Now, there weren't just friends who informed, a multitude of bodies who "easily" informed with the aim of removing the mask of this suspicious man. Now, there was penetration of the law in the tiniest segments of life, and the so-called friendship was not being used, but was being constructed. After a while, the group of policemen inform my father that they have placed bombs in several strategic places in the city. My father, frenzied, moves to another part of the city. Meanwhile, he doesn't sell or lease his small house, but instead simply leaves it to his relatives and rents a new place. In this apartment, in 1972, one of the policemen comes and threatens him, saying that if he tells anybody about their activities they will kill his family. Moreover, in order to convince my father of the seriousness of their intentions: "When he (one of the policemen of the group–my comment) entered the apartment, in the kitchen, he took a hand grenade out of his pocket and holding the pin, started to unscrew it, telling me that he will throw the bomb in the apartment." My father, according to his statements to the investigative bodies, and according to Predrag Matvejević's letters to the Federal Court of Yugoslavia, holds me, at two years old, in his hands. "I was in the apartment with my little girl–a daughter (me) and he told me: You see this in my hand, it's a bomb. Your head will fly off and so will the kid's. We are the ones who throw bombs. Go on, say something." My father promises he will keep quiet and lives in fear from that day forward: "Then he asked me where we stand, and I told him that I will bury this inside me as a secret. After this, Slave (one of the policeman–my comment) left the apartment without any further delay." After a while, that group leaves my father alone and they lose all contact. "From that day on, I have been in deep desperation. I have never discovered their intentions, why they treated me like that."

I am not a criminologist, and I don't know how or why this second "hard wing," which keeps my father under permanent police surveillance, suddenly becomes "radical." But several questions must remain in the game. Is there such a thing as "radicalizing" police officers? In this system of hierarchy, those policemen are also part of the panoptic view, and their professional agenda consists of (as seen in each segment of the file) constant control and supra-control. They are aware of their permanent visibility because only in that way can automatic, ongoing functioning of the state be assured. As active policemen, they know that the effects of their surveillance are permanent and uninterrupted. Is this group part of an internal police sub-structure or not, or did they have some other, more hidden agenda?

Why hadn't they been discovered for 12 years in a world of such pervasive police and "police" control, and were only discovered much later, in 1984? Who protected them, and why? Why was the leader of this group, otherwise a UDBA inspector, assigned the task of looking for "the bombing group" in the long years that followed, which actually meant looking for himself? Why were they all of a sudden arrested 12 years later? Why did one of the members of the group die in prison? Why was the other killed by the Greek counter-intelligence services in Canada? And finally, why was my father arrested with them? All of the documents covering this extensive period are missing from the file. Because I cannot speculate, I must leave these questions open, hoping that they will be resolved by future generations of Macedonian historians.

In June 2008, a young historian came to see me at work. For three years, he had been studying the case of "the bombing group" with whom my father was arrested, and he reported new information that he had come across in the interim. It is true that one policeman from the bombing group died in prison from a beating. Another officer from the group managed to escape from prison, acquired an illegal passport, crossed the Yugoslav border and went to Canada, where he was murdered at a pedestrian crossing by the Greek secret services. Why by the Greek secret services? What is the truth about the aim of the operation of the group–those were questions he couldn't answer. I asked him whether he thought the group was operating on their own initiative or were part of a hidden UDBA agenda, and whether the Macedonian secret service created this group for their own purposes. Why was my father selected to be "the intellectual" of the group, and did it "help" that he had been observed for almost two decades? The visitor told me that he had talked with an unnamed inspector from SDB[8] who thought that the group was organized on a self-initiative basis, without the participation of the secret services–that was to be expected from an SDB employee. On the other hand, over the past three years I talked with several historians who thought that if a part of the group had been motivated by patriotic convictions it is possible that the other part had an "assigned" task by the UDBA, which included terrorism (two police officers in the group were experts in explosives). The historian told me that during the two years (2007-2008) he was actively asking about "the bombing group" (where the members of the group lived, where the families of the group members lived, and at the State Archive of the Republic of Macedonia where he was looking for their files and the inspectors who had handled the case), he received an anonymous threat, by phone, telling him to stop studying the file, because he had gone "too deep."

These kinds of threats were hardly news to me. In 2005, when I first spoke about my father's file publicly, I was receiving tens of anonymous calls for days, with threats that I was endangering the safety of my family. In January 2006, my mother was invited to a "dinner" by one of my father's past friends, a former employee of the Ministry of Foreign Affairs and part of the embassy circles here. My mother told me about the threat that I would lose my job, and was putting my family (including my small son) in danger as well. My husband took this second round of threats seriously and asked about the nature of the threats: Are the threats by a scared "neighbor," or by people at the secret services trying to send us a message? Most people told us that if a certain sub-structure wanted to warn you not to go digging up and exposing state secrets, the warning would sound "different." Ultimately, however, no one could be sure of the nature or the seriousness of the threats; and all of this simply meant that certain communism-related topics remain highly problematic, even traumatic for many, and that many are not as innocent as they might appear. I leave these issues to be resolved by the historians.

At any rate, in September 1985, my father was arrested, convicted and sentenced to a five-year imprisonment because of his "relationship" with this (police) group, in addition to being tried at a closed proceeding. The leading prosecutor in my father's case is Jovan Trpenovski, later the President of the Anti-corruption Committee in the independent, post-Yugoslav Republic of Macedonia. The other prosecutors are Gorgi Naumov (minister in the first expert government in the Independent Republic of Macedonia) and Mihailo Manevski (the current Minister of Justice in the Government of the Republic of Macedonia). (This last name was revealed by one of the historian–researchers studying the bombing group.) A little later my father's sentence is reduced to a four-year imprisonment. My father gets out of prison after less than two full years in July 1987.

Even so, the surveillance of my father does not end there, but instead is doubled. There are documents which indicate that intensive observation was required, as well as continuous control over all of his movements and statements. Two pages detail strategies for continuous observation, uncovering his interests, checking all people who come into contact with him, plans and activities to evaluate his interests, comments, investigations of those people who contact him, and "depending on what is needed, measure X (crossed over with a felt-tip pen) is to be implemented"–with all of this coming after all the measures, including the "continuation of the measure and monitoring of telephone conversations and numbers" already being in force. So, what were these additional measures? According to the documents from the file, under this monitoring procedure his colleagues, the writers, are back in the game, but this time doubled up with professionals from the UDBA. Once again, the whole machinery of writer–policemen as informants is activated.

Can you see the absurdity of the system? My father had been under maximum observation his entire life and served a prison sentence, but the surveillance only became harder and larger.

In February 2009, through a journalist and reporter from BBC Macedonia, Cvetin Chilimanov (presently one of the Counsellors to the President of the Republic of Macedonia), I was told about the mastermind behind "the bombing group" from 1972. He was Gjorgji Docev, and he was still alive. I had the chance to meet and talk with him, and Docev said that he had no idea who my father was back then. Nor did he know how my father and the police around him ended up in the story. In 2008, he published his memoirs and explained in them how he had made the bombs, where he placed them and why. It was done out of personal rage against the Yugoslav communist collectivization–for two decades he had been acutely dissatisfied with the system, and decided to resort to terrorist actions. Shortly after the rest of the group, he was arrested in 1972 and convicted. In 2009, he told me hadn't any as to idea how my father had been implicated in the story, nor why.

This serves to illustrate that my father's "communist story" is far larger than just "the bombing group," and far more tragic than his imprisonment alone. The surveillance on my father began when he was 16 years old, and it didn't stop until just two years before the disintegration of Yugoslavia. The excruciating role for which he was written into "the bombing group" is but one part in his communist Golgotha.

About Help

Kelly: What's this?
Alexander: It's a secret spy mask.
Kelly: Hey man, this is a sock!
—Fine and Friedkin, screenwriters of *I Spy* (2002)

One of the last documents in my father's file before his arrest is an operative's note dated July 3, 1985, according to which the well-known Macedonian poet Ante Popovski asks for a meeting at the RSVR[9] service of the Socialist Republic of Macedonia in order to retell the unusual conversation he had with my father the previous day.

I quote the note from my father's file in full:

On July 2, 1985, around 9 pm, Ante Popovski and Jovan Koteski met at the Club of Social and Political Organizations. Jovan asked Ante to take him home in his car because he had something to tell him on the way. He started with Živko, a former police officer who had now been arrested along with a group of terrorists for the bombings in Skopje. He said that about 20 years ago, Živko wrote a collection of poems and Jovan Koteski wrote a review for him. Ante expected that he would tell him something more, but here Jovan stopped. In answer to Ante's question–how all that related to him and why he was telling him this–Jovan mumbled something incomprehensible, from which Ante drew certain conclusions on the basis of which a process was set in motion in which others too would "burn." Ante pretended to pay no attention to his babbling and they parted. Ante told the source that he hadn't slept all night and the next day at 7:00 am went to the source to ask for advice or information about whether all of this was true and how it might be related to him. He then produced a text (the line is crossed out with a felt-tip pen–my comment), and said: Here is how the UDBA can package it. The text was written by a journalist who followed the trial of Ordev, Dinevski and Eftimov, written for the daily "Nova Makedonija."–A director of the daily, Ante kept the text. The text was written as presented by the source to retain its originality.

The text is followed by the operative notes by the inspector.

When we say that the hard UDBA wing starts with the surveillance and torture of my father in the late 1940s, and the "light surveillance" of my father by his colleague-poets ends in the late 1960s, this does not mean that the writers and my father's colleagues discontinued their informing activities, as we can well see from the above quoted note from 1985.

Imagine, for a moment, that you are Macedonian poet Ante Popovski. Your friend (my father) asks you (Ante Popovski) to meet and talk about something that scares him. He wants to talk to you about a group of police officers, who, 12 years ago, threatened him and his family with death, and proclaimed him the ideologist of their "movement." But they are not naïve people, and this is not a film; they are police experts in explosives, they brandished a bomb in front of him and his two–year old girl (this is me) and blackmailed my father into keeping quiet–and he kept quiet and lived with that terrible burden for an entire decade. With that burden he took his children to kindergarten; with that burden he walked his children to the city park and waved to them while they were riding on the merry-go-round; with that burden he got up and went to bed, every single day of those 12 years. Now, imagine that your friend Jovan Koteski suddenly heard the names of those same people on television, which tortured him for years, and that they have been arrested. For 12 long years, your friend, my father Jovan Koteski, couldn't confess his UDBA burden to the police because the communist police to whom he would have taken his problem to were the same police who had threatened him with death. Or, as is written in the operative's notes from my father's file dated November 28, 1985: "One thing has to be emphasized: Who could Jovan have told then, when they themselves wore uniforms? Actually, he should have told the same people." Therefore, when your friend, Jovan Koteski, suddenly finds out that the same police group was arrested, he finally wants to tell somebody–and not just anybody, he wants to tell you, his friend Ante Popovski. He wants to ask for advice because he thinks that you will be able to help him, because you are at the top of the writer's hierarchy, and are also a director at the most important communist daily. He starts talking to you, but you pretend that everything that he is saying is unimportant, and you make a face as if to say he is talking nonsense.

Of course it's 1985, of course Tito has been dead for five years and of course the intimate poetry has been written for a long time, and even *he, the Intimist*, is writing it, which you know very well. *They* still haven't left the scene, and you should be careful. Therefore, as your friend finally opens up to somebody to tell him about the nature of his problem, you at the same time start calculating what you might get and what you might lose from this unexpected confession by your "friend?" You try to ask more questions, as you cannot hide the curious note in your questions very well, and you question him as if he is still–or already guilty. You expect him to tell you something more, some juicier material. He is confused by your rejection, by your police-like curiosity and he withdraws. He starts talking in a confused manner, he understands that you are not the man who can help him in this tragi-comedy that was happening to–and enforced on him for decades; he wants to get out of your car, and goes. You shut the door of the car behind him and you go home, but you cannot sleep, you wait for daybreak, you wait to become active again, and to become applied and employed. Of course, you are already employed as a director, you are also a respected poet, but you have material which shouldn't be neglected, and it's unclear what advantages the material might bring you, or certainly, might also take from you. On the desk of the leading Macedonian newspaper, of which you are the director, you already have material–a journalist's piece on another case (which is crossed out in my father's file for the rest of us), and in it there are names of people who are not part of the case your "friend" talks about. In any case, you look at this unusual "confession" by your friend with "nervous exhilaration," you collect all the similar materials you have on your desk and the first thing you do at 7:00 am the next morning is to immediately ask for a meeting at the UDBA services. There you sit and comfortably retell all that you have noticed about your friend; he didn't really tell you anything of real significance, but that's why you feel that it's enough to recount his bewilderment, his fear, his "talking nonsense" and his confusion. You want everything to become transparent, but not in a way in which you and your friend will exchange *his* intimate trouble; you will try to think of what can be done to help him tell the story, and to hear his truth, but you will not alarm the Writers' Society of Macedonia of which you are both members.

You are not a hero, and in the end you are merely an ordinary man; such is the system, and you know that very well. Of course, that was 1972, and now it is 1985, but the system in Macedonia simply became suspended in time for an indefinite period. And you, you are not a hero. Therefore, you decide to go home and ignore all of that, you will probably pretend you haven't heard anything and maybe you will even use Jovan Koteski's confusion as gossip at a family dinner. So what? This is what neutral citizens do, that's good. You too will do that because the system is stronger than you, something you know all too well.

But no. You decide that you can do all of this in another way, *their* way, *the most transparent* way, and that is through the communist paradox–you will call *the secret services*, the ideological–police nomenclature, who will evaluate and think about this. You are at peace with yourself, and *after* an entire sleepless night you have fulfilled your civic and patriotic duty. You leave for a new work day toward new victories. Maybe you will even profit from all of this.

Nonetheless, we shouldn't be naïve. My father's file hides many names of his "friends," the Macedonian poets and writers who are crossed out with black felt-tip pens. If Ante Popovski's name was left, it was left to be burned. And it was left to be burned because Ante Popovski too offended the State, but for another reason entirely. As the director of "Vardar Film," the only Macedonian film production and distribution company under communism, he is accused of financial embezzlement and punished, though not imprisoned, because in communism there is no other serious mistake outside of the ideological. He is punished by having his director's position taken away and being given another one; at any rate, a certain embarrassment remained. Was Ante Popovski recruited as a spy from the literary sphere at the time he himself fell from grace, or did the director's position at the film company automatically mean that he needed to ideologically contribute with a little bit of solid communist snitching? I don't know, but for my father's case this is irrelevant.

What is relevant is that the communist world is so constricted that nobody can seek or receive help. If you cannot talk to the police, you will logically turn to your friends and colleagues for help. But what happens when your best friends are collaborating with those selfsame police?

How Much Can a Living Being Endure?

One eye sees, but the other feels.
—Paul Klee

My father had manifested a disturbing awareness of being observed all his life. In one transcribed telephone conversation from July 27, 1987, my father complains to X that: "Since I exist I have been constantly provoked, and a living being can endure that much… I will tell you, you will be disgusted…" But the more you talk, the more you come across deaf ears, and the more you complain, the more people wave you off. You have no way of proving your "mere" intimation feeling of being observed. Part of that obscene State structure is for you to become completely lonely, to be cornered in a way that your informants will remain your best "friends." Even with this vague feeling that he had been observed all his life, when my father opened his file he was astounded by the Kafkaesque scenario, by the rate of the ever-present look, by the long lasting surveillance and finally by the observer's sadism.

Loneliness is their goal, it is good (for you) to be alone. They will do everything so that you are left alone after everybody has deserted you. When my father is released from prison, the operative's note from September 10, 1987 reads: "We find that Jovan was deeply affected by the fact he had been deserted by his former friends. At the moment, he feels psychologically worse than he did in prison. Their financial situation is bad and they have a lot of debts." Several months later, in a note from February 2, 1988, the operatives conclude that the surveillance proved successful, as nobody has yet approached my father. "Jovan Koteski, as we have informed many times already, has contacts only with his brother Naum. Occasionally, he talks to his sister from Struga." According to the wiretapped conversation, when the first writer, Ilija Todorovski, calls my father on July 27, 1987, my father tells him: "If I had been Eichmann, somebody would have called by now. I've developed the complex of a scarecrow–nobody has called… You are the first who has and I won't forget that, thank you very much. I hope they are listening, let them know how I feel!" The inspector's note beside these lines is brutal, my father's complaint that he is lonely drives the inspector to this sadistic conclusion: "Jovan Koteski is consistent in his dishonesty and his lies. He gives the impression that he believes in it. Objectively, this condition is equally complex to him, as it was when he was in prison. His activities must be observed to the maximum extent…"

I was frequently asked how my father survived the relentless political pursuit, as only those who have lived through torture can know this. At times, the man who is subjected to torture for decades becomes only pain. The pain becomes an object without human attributes and content. I will describe an ordinary day in my father's life, from 1994, though all of the years before and after were the same. 1994 is seven years later, seven years after my father has already been freed, after Macedonia has gained its own statehood and after his heretical thoughts are no longer heretical but lucrative.

My father tried to sleep during the day. It was unbearable for him to be awake when there was light outside. For one who has survived torture, light is a particular problem. The one who is watched all his life, and himself cannot see, the one who is an object of information and never a subject in communication, shuns light because the visibility guarantees the functioning of the system. When he was awake, my father walked nervously from one room to another. He would go into a room and leave it immediately. He would stand in the hallway and listen to what my mother was doing in the kitchen; he would knock on my door to see whether something terrible had happened to me, he would find some excuse, for example "I'm reading Tsvetaeva," and without waiting for a response would quickly leave. For hours, from behind the curtain, he would worriedly watch the dustman who had decided to spend the last three hours of his working day sitting on the sidewalk under our window. What if he was not a dustman? Many dustmen in the file turned out to be "official persons from the UDBA." He will go to sleep. He sleeps with one eye open and jumps at every sound, and asks for explanations about what has happened; he wants to see, to be reassured. He lives as if at any moment the most important person will come and bring the most important decision that will manifest the prophecy of his life.

The man who endures 40 years of political persecution builds strategies for survival. When the doorbell rings, he thinks: Who is the next to be tortured? If somebody rings the doorbell, he stops to listen to the breathing of the one who rings the bell. He barely finds the courage to look through the peephole. Even when he knows the person who is ringing well, he watches him for a long time. Sometimes I try to open the door, but for him it's a matter of life and death to be the first to open the door, so nothing terrible will happen to me. And in the end: "Ah, it's you Vera, come in, yes, Jasna is at home."

The man who survived torture, after being subjected to surveillance all his life, becomes the one who cannot be reconstructed through identification with those closest to him. His world becomes a world which is not based on dialectics. That is an absence from the absence. It is pure presence. A man who survives torture develops an impossible paradox, a disconnection with the representation and too many representations. He has millions of pictures of the terrible possibilities of the system and pictures which do not conjure any memories. That man who survived four decades of torture is my father, the Macedonian poet Jovan Koteski.

Application Adopted!
>The repulsive courtesies began once again,
>one of them passed the knife over K. to the other, who then passed it back
>over K. to the first. K. now knew
>it would be his duty to take the knife,
>as it passed from hand to hand above him
>and thrust it into himself.
>—Kafka

My father took his file in November 2000. All the people who took their files that year in Macedonia knew that they had to sign a form, which literally reads as follows:

With regard to the protection of data and information about private and family life, I request that the entire content of the file remain secret until (100 years from my birth, and in my father's case it is entered–my comment) 2032, provided it is not destroyed but given to the Archive of Republic of Macedonia.

Once you sign the form you see the cynical ending that follows: At the bottom, it says that the application "is adopted."

You see that the horror of the police file is not just the fact that my father lived a life where the police assumed the faces of his closest friends. The horror lies in one supreme agency in which his world is even narrower than the narrow world of the ancient Greek heroes who address the sky with the cry, "I suffer injustice." The Greek man suffers a terrible punishment, without subjective guilt, but when he wants to discover the name of that agency by which he suffers, the sky and the earth turn so that he can *see*. When Oedipus wants to know what happened in his past, a witness stands ready to appear already in the next act.

My father waited 40 long years to *see*. And when he stopped petrified in front of the UBK[10] door, before the authority that had tormented him all his life, as before with the last chance for him to *see*, the UBK services made him submit an application in which he asks that his only hope never be fulfilled. On the form, my father has to ask that the thing under the name for which he suffered remain forever closed. He submitted an application wherein he asked for his file to be available to him in 2032, and in the meantime he should "voluntarily" grant them permission, should they so want, to burn his file. My father wanted to see that he was not crazy in his claims that he had been observed all his life, but everything that he essentially wanted to see was for what *good* all of that was. And he had to read that his application–never to see the resolution of his living tragedy–"was adopted!"

In rare moments of humor, my father called his file the "biography of friends." That is Don Quixote humor. First you smile, then you form a complex expression, gradually realizing that you are laughing at the face of pure sadness. That's the humor of somebody who has survived prison despite their innocence. When you receive a document saying that you are rehabilitated, that document is not worth the paper it is printed on. You can be the best poet of a State, as you were only born to write about her beauty, her golden voice, to write about the ground beneath her special feet. You could have written the most beautiful poem about the unfulfilled love of a generation, "Ana," but it will never become required reading or make the list, because for these dunces even Ana's hair is debatable. After you have survived the pogrom of your time, in which your colleagues wrote your biography without you ordering or authorizing it, all that is left for you is to live each day, a Kafkaesque reality of the UDBA daily routine, for the rest of your life. And to the infinity of your earthly loneliness repeat the verses: "Oh my friends, there is no friend!" Even so, my father left forgiving everybody.

The Phenomenology of the Informant

> (A man) cannot express what he is; he has to
> announce just that which he himself is not–that is, the lie.
> A certain rate of truth may only be found in a choir.
> —Kafka

It is clear from a rough analysis of my father's file that the system of control upon which the communist system was founded was based on one assumed subject–the holder of the assumed "truth"–who is the informant himself. The informant is the person who knows. The informant becomes the Great Other, the holder of the interpretation and the truth. He becomes the most omnipresent subject who is assumed to know–he becomes God, small, local, political, but God nevertheless.

On the other hand, the spied on one, the surveilled, is not a being who talks, although he is observed talking all the time, he is the subject of an experiment and has to be silenced. The experiment will subject him to a lot of disturbances, and cause every type of disorder, but because he is not a being who talks, as Lacan puts it in commenting on Pavlov's experiment, he is not asked to question the experimenters' desire, the informant' s wish to *know* everything down to the last minute detail.

Even from the first document of my father's file, we can read the important directives that sketch a profile of the informants who obscurely worked on modeling the ideological and cultural horizon of the Macedonian communist past. This is a five-page document, in which on April 18, 1961 the informant (crossed out) retold "in his own words" before the SVR service (and sent to: Information Book, DB-Ohrid Division and the legal connection file) about a conversation that he had had with my father at the Hotel Macedonia. That conversation contains several important and entirely unexpected switches, and as we will see below, the switches are key in establishing the logic of the victim because these switches represent an excess in the informant's system.

So, they met at the Hotel Macedonia, "to have lunch. Jovan came to the table." He bragged that he was now: "A journalist at a radio station, he told X the column he was writing, only X didn't remember." When my father bragged that he had now had a regular income, he unexpectedly "nervously" said that all personal wealth meant nothing because (quoting from the informant's report) he wants, "to withdraw completely to a most remote village in order not to see anything happening in the present society and around him." According to the unknown informant's statement, my father continues with the idea that something is not right, because, "where the Macedonians actually lived in the remote villages, nothing was written about them and nobody paid attention to those people." X contradicts my father, offering that "he as an individual cannot do anything by reacting."

When the point of his complaint is not understood, my father suddenly tells X that he "couldn't understand what he wanted to tell him, and wasn't surprised because X had limited intellectual capabilities." According to the file, X decides again to "bring my father to his senses." He repeats that, "Macedonia and the Macedonian people have gained their rights, and the issues of nationhood have been resolved." My father doesn't listen to this suggestion and continues to complain to his "friend" (according to his notes) that, "Lots of money flows in the capital Skopje, as if only Skopje should survive, they'll let the villages die." And when for the last time X decides "with good intentions" to remind my father that he is doing just fine, in this conversation that's falling on deaf ears a new switch transpires about which we talked before. "Jovan all of a sudden left the restaurant because someone was passing by (and) he went to talk to him."

The operative's note that analyses the informant's profile reads that "the person had no tendency to add things and exaggerates them, he reported realistically." Those two, the informant and his supervisor, are experts. That means they are seen as people who are capable of evaluating, even measuring something–something as unmeasurable as people's motives. The informant is hired to determine the motives of the suspicious poet's behavior, and the controller is hired to determine the motives and confidentiality of the informant.

From beginning to end, however, we have but one Cartesian procedure at work here, one that basically does not lead to *knowledge*, but only to certainty. The informant is not somebody who knows, he is somebody who is *known to the system*. There is nothing *on the other side* that guarantees the credibility of this informant insofar as he will accurately recount the conversation. There is nothing *on the other side* that guarantees that *this* superior is capable of estimating who might be trustworthy. And it is from these types of paradoxes that all of the tragicomic elements in the file emerge.

My father said that "he was writing books, and now he'd written a book about the Macedonian migrant workers, which was published in Zagreb, and he'd made big money from it." But you see, my father never wrote such a book, and because we don't know who the informant was, we can only speculate about the various possibilities. Here is one. My father grew up in boarding schools and dorms. He had nothing; all he had was a talent for poetry. Maybe the informant lived comfortably, maybe he spent his summers in Croatia, maybe he despised my father, maybe his poverty aroused sadistic impulses in him. My father succeeded in providing a certain existence for himself, and now he decided to invent a book in Croatia. As a poet, maybe he really did have a book in his head that he imagined publishing one day in Croatia. Each poet is a little bit of a Münchhausen. If he doesn't speak the objective truth, that doesn't mean that there isn't one. When Don Quixote sees a giant in a windmill, it doesn't mean the giant isn't out there somewhere.

But the result of the operative's note is such that the inspector asks for a more detailed investigation of my father's connections with Croatia. He "himself is suspicious of my father's connections with Zagreb and with Croatia in general." We see here how Zagreb becomes Croatia, how the (non-existent) published book becomes a *"connection,"* etc. What becomes clear from this short report of my father's file of 1961 is that the communist cultural sphere was covered with a system of control that essentially believed in *the certainty of the subject,* and in the certainty of something so complicated, complex and uncertain as the behavior of the subject.

The informant and the controller behave as if they have the capacity to understand one another. They have unlimited faith in their ability to break through, and to see through the other. What has this omnipotent competence granted the informants? Who has given it to them? It is given by the only one who can (that is in the position to do so)–the system of control. It is not important that the subject of surveillance is, as is any other subject, actually endlessly and infinitely complicated. It is important that the informants who drive the control machinery believe in the certainty of the subject. The subject–like any other–who is observed in his spontaneous behavior can be led by the wish to brag, to complain, by the need to present himself better than he really is, worse than he is and different than he is. Actually, that subject is always so complicated that there is nothing to guarantee that the explanation of one man's behavior will (ever) be objective. But this truth is not important for the invisible power structures. In other words, the informant is the subject who is assumed to know, Lacan's *sujet supposé savoir*. He is the holder of the transmission. He lacks criteria, but what he lacks, the informant nicely makes up for, and substitutes with ceremonies, and with simulations.

As Kafka said, "A certain amount of truth can only be found in a choir." The informant can operate only if there is a choir of informants. There is nothing on the other side which guarantees the authorization of the informant to perform the tasks assigned to him. But, trust is not required, it revolves around the certainty of the system, and the system guarantees the informant's desire to serve the system. From beginning to end, nothing here essentially leads to knowledge (for the spied on one, for my father, for Jovan Koteski) nothing will ever grasp the truth about him, but only his certainty before the system, and his certainty is called guilty–because we observe him! We would be stupid to waste time. We will do everything to justify the logic of our existence. He should end up in prison. We must prove his primordial guilt. Actually, we don't even have to prove it, it is enough that he is already registered as suspicious in our complex system of control and surveillance. Our ultimate proof is our surveillance. That is exactly why the surveillance must never stop–it should last at least as long as our system lasts. The surveillance, and the informant as its holder, are the crutches on which our system lumbers forth.

The Search for Pathological Excess (About Primordial Guilt)

> No, said the painter, I neither saw the figure, nor that armchair,
> all that is invented, but I was ordered to paint it.
> —Kafka

According to various sources, in the years from 1960-1990, in Macedonia, along with the regular police forces and counter-intelligence officers in the active service, the surveillance structures over the "suspicious" people were also fed by 12,000-40,000 informants who worked for the State Security Services. They also operated among Macedonians working in culture (were actually part of them). Not only were they the bearers of the system, but they were the bearers of the truth as well.

How were these spies recruited? In my father's file from October 1985, there is the following sentence, written by an operative and referring to the informant and his profile: "I talked to the source for the first time, I haven't met her before, and she came to me on the recommendation of my friends from the City Council." In July 1987, after my father's release from prison, there is an "Official note for the transfer of a file in operational processing," which reads that the "Intimist remains of interest to SDB, the processing should be linear, and attention should be paid to selective people from cultural fields, who will serve SDB's processing purposes."

So, what did these informants hope to discover, what was their final sanctuary, what truth did they expect to uncover? According to the centralized and uninterrupted recording on which the system was based, it is clear that their task was to record everything they (personally) found to be pathological. Any excess was pathological. When somebody received a salary and still complained about the social order, he was a pathological case. Each poet's relation to his excess had to pass through the state authorities.

When my father was arrested, there was a whole series of (tragi-) "comic" situations. Neither my immediate family nor my relatives could find my father for several days, who, the day when he was arrested, simply vanished from the face of the earth. When they finally find out that he was in pre-trial confinement, my relatives exchange endless speculation and assumptions over the next few days over the phone about the cause of my father's arrest. According to the wiretapped telephone conversations from my father's file, the UDBA services are alarmed about each one of them. Here are some of those excess assumptions (I have put all my relatives under X, which will allow me to protect them, as for decades they were visibly exposed):

September 3, 1985:

"X: Is it about the forest?
X: I don't know, they didn't tell me anything.

X: What is (relative) X's number?
X: I don't know his number.
X: And those from Lisiče? (a district in Skopje, where three of my cousins then lived; JK)
X: I don't know, I have never talked to them."
The inspector's note under this conversation is crossed out, but the words Lisiče and forest are underlined.

September 3, 1985:

X: "It must be about the forest."

September 3, 1985:

X (police officer–relative): "I'm sorry he never took my advice. I have warned him so many times not to talk in front of everybody. I have told him that our people go to restaurants to listen to such conversations, that's how they earn their living."

September 4, 1985:

X: "It must be related to the Struga Poetry Evenings. He definitely overdid it with the talking and drinking… (You should) explain to them nicely that the man was provoked and stressed because they had cut his trees, etc."

November 12, 1985:

X: "When we were left alone, he told me: Jovan has been a friend of our family since 1954. He is a lawyer from Kavadarci (a city in Macedonia–JK), deputy public prosecutor. If Jovan is convicted of anything, he is just a single lyre in the poetry–he neither did, nor can do anything!"
Inspector's note: "… (illegible) to eliminate these intrigues (illegible)…. What can (illegible) I do? Who is the deputy prosecutor?"

November 3, 1985:

X: "I only wanted to tell you, the doctor sent his regards… he said that X is very interested in him."
The inspector's note "reveals" the doctor's identity. "It seems he is a gynecologist in (illegible)…"

And so on. The State Security Services which, after my father's imprisonment, follow all the "quakes" in his family, have full hands of "new evidence" of his essential guilt before the System, and that evidence is as follows: the forest, the cut trees, the doctor–gynecologist (?), the deputy public prosecutor, what exactly my father talked about and said at the Struga Poetry Evenings, Skopje's Lisiče district as assumed pseudo-utopian bastion of resistance… All of these attributes, locations, states, names, lack of names, clear and unclear positions are in excess. And that excess is a problem.

When the system establishes a case of excess, it starts "disinfecting" it. That disinfection is effected by recordings and by alarm over the most trifling absurdities. These absurdities, i.e. this "excess" and these "pathologies" of the confused relatives, certainly led to yet more misinterpretations in the State Security Services–and the recruiting and employing of yet another army of informants.

In my father's file from June 26, 1987, when there is an initiative launched for my father's release by the Croatian PEN Center, there is a document according to the field operative's record, which says: "There is a tendency that Jovan Koteski will be seen as a repressed writer," and therefore the inspector "thinks that the date of his release should be postponed in order to avoid the possibility of his attending this year's Struga Poetry Evenings."

On July 27, 1987, there is a note in which my father's conversation with somebody is taped. It is my father's first conversation after getting out of prison, after his early release.

"X: How are you?
My father: Fine."

But you see, the essence of the whole mechanism is that nothing is fine there. Nothing is fine in a police state. When my father gets out of prison, there is a document called "PLAN of measures and activities for processing Intimist during 1987," and it is dated January 26, 1987. Several days after my father is released in July 1987, there is an operative note by the inspector: "Jovan Koteski's activity should be observed to the maximum and his connection with certain people as well, because he is now ready to connect with anybody."

The absurdity of the system lies in *the impossibility of exit*. My father was observed all his life, he had already served a prison sentence, even though he was innocent, he got out of prison, and according to the judicial process and standards he was free. But now, according to the information from the file, remarkably, he is less free than ever! Now begins the doubling and fortifying of the surveillance. No proof was offered for his guilt during the trial. But for the system, that is not necessary because it is clear. The ultimate reason for his imprisonment is precisely that he was imprisoned because he was observed, and because his conversations were tapped and recorded over many long decades. The thing is that for this machinery you are *primordially guilty*, and the machinery must continue to prove the essence of its existence.

Branding (the Body, the Spirit and the Work)

> Polonius: Do you know me, my lord?
> Hamlet: Excellent well; you are a fishmonger.
> —Shakespeare

I have often been asked the question: Why my father? And to that question there isn't a good answer, for that is a question of the type treated by ancient Greek tragedy. You are not a victim of deserving subjective guilt, but you have to suffer because the gods intended such a prophecy for you. But that is exactly the question of the essence: Why did they determine such a prophecy for you? Is it because you were hubristic and excessive in your characteristics and behavior, were you angry too much, were you confused, were you confused in a way that the State didn't like, or does the fact that you were a poet make you suspicious from the beginning and on into eternity?

Have you been branded? There is a document in the file from March 18, 1986, in which a writer is quoted (name deleted): "Even from his first appearance in the Macedonian literature (although a strong poet), he is physically unattractive and has often been neglected." And he adds: "What is positive in this 'Intimist' tragicomedy is that he is convicted... because if he hadn't been convicted by society, the writers themselves would have simply 'eaten him,' because it wasn't a simple thing to be the third poet in the country."

In another document, it is stated that: "Although he had immense talent, he was short and had no way of imposing himself in an environment where 'charismatic' leaders ruled." I want to pay attention to these details. Because part of the answer to the question regarding the essence of the modern political tragedy from the communist decades is that somebody suffers by virtue of being branded (as well).

The soldier of the system is recognized from a distance. He distinguishes himself by his pride, his body radiates bravery and strength. It doesn't matter that he doesn't know his trade (notice how in the guard there are always people who don't know how to handle the weapons, but who, as Foucault writes, distinguish themselves by their march, by holding their head just so, by their physique and their dignified appearance). The army of obedient bodies is an army shaped by the corporeal dough, which learned how to hold itself. In Macedonia, from 1960 on, it is a problem if you don't know how to hold your body.

Please explain who knows how to hold their body if they are interested in "the Russian issues" of essence, life, ideologies, freedom and rights? The body is an object and a target of the State. It is a body that is manipulated; if you don't know how to hold your body in such a way as to represent your socialist ideology, you are also suspicious.

The spirit is a problem too. For instance, my father was more relaxed than was recommended, he talked here and there; like Don Quixote, he rebelled over this and that. He didn't like the socialist ideology, thus he was not a suitable soldier of the system; he had excess, which the system wanted to eliminate.

And finally, and the most importantly–your work represents a problem. In my father's file, there is a document in which an "influential writer" (his name is crossed out) offers my father a bargain: freedom, if he stops creating, which we will agree is ridiculous by all standards of authorship. In that document, it is literally stated what this writer proposed: "Give up writing poems in the future and I will provide you freedom." This communist version of the Salieri approach serves as an important inspiration for part of this book. When my father goes to prison, two different versions of the Macedonian literary journal "Razgledi" are published; in the first, there are two poems by my father, while in the second they are removed and the entire run is reprinted. When my father was imprisoned, all of his collections were withdrawn from the bookstores and libraries. A part of the rebellion that Allen Ginsberg tried unsuccessfully to provoke among the Macedonian poets referred to the censorship of my father's work. An operative's note from October 15, 1987, submitted by "our operative" employed at the city library reads: "After Koteski's imprisonment, all of his works have been withdrawn and prohibited."

Opening the Archives

> Naturalists tell of a noble race of horses
> that instinctively open a vein with their teeth
> when overheated and exhausted by a long course, in order
> to breathe more freely.
> I am often tempted to open such a vein,
> to procure for myself everlasting liberty.
> —Goethe

In December 2005, extracts of this text were published in the Macedonian political magazine "Focus." This came about independently of the Council of Europe's initiative for the international condemnation of crimes of totalitarian communist regimes in January 2006, for which Macedonian representatives voted neutral. The publication, i.e. "the opening" of my father's file, came about as a result of coincidence.

The Macedonian writer Blaže Minevski contacted me a few months prior to ask permission to publish the information that two books were seized from my father and never returned to him. The publication of this information was certainly legitimate, but for years I have had material that was far more hardcore–the dossier itself (it later turned out that those books had been seized from another political prisoner). I have known Blaže Minevski from days past, as probably the only Macedonian writer who in 1991, in the Macedonian daily "Nova Makedonija," published the text "Art is Defended by Art," in which he posed the question: "How is it possible that at the time, one Allen Ginsberg was more interested in the destiny of the Macedonian poet Jovan Koteski than the (entire) Macedonian Writers' Society?" He also stated that in all those years there hadn't been (in Macedonia) a single book subject to the standard censorship process. "Does that mean that the Macedonian writer didn't know how to write a book which would be forbidden?"

The answers to the questions raised by Minevski 23 years ago seem understandable today from the perspective of the police files. My father's file (together with the remaining 14,572 official personal police files kept for those considered and treated as "interior enemies" by the communist government in Macedonia) provides insight into the terribly cemented mental matrix of the culture of the imprisoned mind. Together with random individuals, a vast parade of those working in culture–the number of direct snitches is estimated at 12,000 to 40,000–participated in that tiring work of the liquidation of thought in Macedonia.

Studies on political prisoners in Yugoslavia indicate that the character of dissidence was less ideological than it was national– but that doesn't mean that they were mutually exclusive. The debate over the values and delusions of the communist system currently taking place in Europe must also proceed via an analysis of the police files. By facing up to the communist past, we will see revealed a history which will not be so attractive, and we will see "Stalins in the Souls" in those who built our cultures. We will face the root of the permanent, subtle and perfidious censorship that lasted for decades and left far more terrifying consequences than any direct political censorship. Prohibition was performed via the mechanisms of threat, and not as direct conflict.

In a country where in principle everyone was free, no one dared to write anything really free. As if in the Macedonian (and ex-Yugoslav) version of communism, there wasn't even some nominal need to provoke the system. The system didn't have to take the thought seriously (which is essential in each "sound" system of censorship) because it had (already) seriously understood the potential strength of the thought, and watched it in every way, and wherever it could; it physically canceled it.[11]

In February 2006, (Macedonian writer) Blaže Minevski's research on the accessibility of police files for the period from 1944-1990 appeared in the Macedonian political magazine "Focus." In 2002, 14,572 official personal files of the State Security Services were handed over to be kept in the State Archives of the Republic of Macedonia. On July 5, 2000, the "Law on Handling the Files

Kept by the State Security Service" was adopted in Macedonia. According to Article 21 of that law, the law would remain in force for just one year. In other words, it entered "into force on the eighth day after its publication in the 'Official Gazette of the Republic of Macedonia,', and will be implemented from the day it enters into force." But this law was also incorporated into the "Rulebook on Using Files at the Archive" adopted on January 1, 2003. Additionally, the Rulebook had one new element which didn't yet exist in the already invalid law.

Namely, the person who wanted to see his file, along with a photocopy of his identity card, also had to submit a verified statement at the notary that, "under full material and criminal responsibility, the person who has insight into the file will not deliver personal data about other physical persons who appear in his personal file." This meant that "The Rulebook on Using Files at the Archives" was even more problematic than the already invalid law, because in the law there was no such article that required the signing of a statement at the notary. In Blaže Minevski's words, "The snitch has a reputation, and the victim has neither reputation nor can he consider publicly pointing out the person who destroyed his reputation or, perhaps, his life in general... Thus, if the victim publishes the name of his executioner, the state will help the executioner by rendering his old victim a victim again, and the executioner, an executioner."[12] Therefore, the following question remains: How could it be that until today in Macedonia, it is still impossible to look at documents which are 60 years old, without holding accountable before the law the one who looked at them and made them transparent to the public? Let's assume that the State Security Services have intelligence information, which for the well-being of all of us, is important to remain a state secret. Is it possible that all of the nearly 15,000 files are of such great gravity that (the integral) disclosure of those files would still, today, represent such a (political) problem?

In February 2006, I was at the State Archives of the Republic of Macedonia and I asked to see my father's integral file (i.e. without the crossed out parts), but refused to sign a statement at the notary. The employee working with these files told me that protection was needed for my own safety, and because of the fact that problems might arise, "Someone might want to kill somebody." I find this illogical, not only because the statement does nothing to protect the one who was the direct or indirect victim of the system, but again, the snitch is protected; more importantly, because the main argument for non-transparency is completely illogical. In the loneliness of the archive room, the victim can see the identity of his/her snitch, but must then return home with that knowledge, and without the possibility of–or the recourse of catharsis. And that is precisely the instance when "someone might want to kill somebody."

On January 22, 2008, the Macedonian Parliament voted unanimously–with 73 votes "for" and none "against"–to support the "Law on Determining Additional Conditions for Performing Public Function" proposed by the leader of the Liberal Party of Macedonia, which was seen as a first step towards the implementation of the lustration and demystification of the (Macedonian) communist past. This process of lustration was drafted to cover a period of 46 years, from 1944 to 1990, and to be further implemented over a period of five years. According to the scheme, all current and future officials should provide a statement declaring he/she was not a collaborator with the secret services, which applies to both those who gave the orders and those who used the information. The authenticity of the statement is checked by a committee selected by the Parliament with a two-thirds majority, consisting of the President, Vice-President and nine members. But the problem with this solution is that again, it included a mediative authority (this time the Committee, which mediates between the past and people), which means that even now the archives are not actually free. The law was also subject to criticism because it "made equal" the snitches and the high officials, which did not differentiate whatsoever with regard to their character or degree of accountability.

However, the main problem remains, as someone or something again mediates the past, this time it is the Committee, which is the only one that has unrestricted insight into the past. In some (other) communist countries, some new players entered the Archives after the fall of the regimes, and performed an inventory and description of everything they found there. In Macedonia, from 1990 until today (2013) the police archives are, at least in principle, closed to public view; that is, they remain accessible though with serious restrictions. The historians hide behind the information that the archives of the former Yugoslavia were burned in the bunkers of Bosnia, but all intelligence documents were regularly re-sent to at least three other authorities, which means that if the main archives were burned, the regional archives were not burned, and that there still remain material for examination and research.

Today, the upper floors of the building that once served as the headquarters of the Stasi–the Counter-Intelligence Service of East Germany in Berlin–have been converted into an historic archive service (while the lower floors are a museum). The Stasi files are accessible to anyone. Germany is not indifferent to what was happening in their past, but it would have been more indifferent if what had been happening had remained hidden. During the 1990s, there were numerous debates in Germany over what to do with the files. Today, it is simply assumed that they should be kept and studied, with the hope that "history will not repeat itself."

The price of transparency is not small, but paradoxically, it hurts much less than secrecy. The spirit of this book pleads for a complete opening of the archives of the counter-intelligence services of communist countries. Radical transparency is a condition for the ordinary, simple truth. Contrary to the skeptics' fears that the files will give rise to revanchism, spectacle and the like, it has been shown that *only* the citizens from the former East Germany who opened their archives entirely did not suffer any undue damage from said newfound insight into their own past. You can profit from the past only if no one or, at most, a very small group of people have access to it.

3

Communist Crimes and Political Anesthesia

"There isn't anything, is there?"

In September 2007, I visited the former headquarters of the Stasi service in Berlin. The massive building, once the former base of the East German secret police, is now a museum. In front of the massive gate, the tourists, mostly animated Americans, had located on their maps of Berlin the rest of the 10s of ex-Stasi buildings across the city. Now that we were at the zero point, in the epicenter itself at the headquarters, the group was optimistically planning their visits to all of the buildings in a single day.

By contrast, the woman checking tickets was tense. I asked where I could buy books, films, materials, anything? She redirected me to the archives on the upper stories, everything is there, everything is available, but she doesn't speak English, and this is not a tourist destination, "There isn't anything." She pushes me ahead of her, behind the desk (I enter more out of embarrassment than need); do I see anything that can be sold? I withdraw, I apologize repeatedly, I think vaguely that it can't be easy to sell tickets every day for the story of somebody's past hell, she is not here to inspire or inject meaning in the communist stories of the past for the visitors, damn it, she sells tickets as her job for a salary, she has a family to feed, she is not here to deal with our search for meaning, do I understand now?

I go up the stairs heavily. There are 30 offices on each floor, and a lot of stories. In each office there is but one thing, specifically one color–administrative gray. There is one armchair, one desk, one or two telephones and a filing cabinet for documents, and somewhere a map of East Germany. And that's literally everything. Every office is similar to the previous one, each the same as the next. There is no substance to–or in this building. Somebody performed his damnable assignment here for a modest salary. I go up to each of the upper stories with increasing heaviness, while in me some exacting and pedantic urge rises, some urgent need to enter every office. What if I find an explanation in the next one?

It was raining when I left the museum. I couldn't move from the spot, not from the shock of what I'd seen, but because I didn't see anything. Death hangs in the air on each of those out of date telephones, tens, hundreds and perhaps thousands of counter-revolutionaries were convicted in endless rows. But today it smells of Domestos, and thick red-braided ropes hang before each shabby armchair. In front of the gate, in the rain, a German approached me. "There isn't anything, is there?" "Nothing," I said staring at the ground. "It's strange," he continued, "I lost everybody I had because of that building. Since they've turned it into a museum, I come here every day. I cannot stop coming. There isn't anything, is there? That's why I come. Every day I have to look at that exact same *nothing*. Do you understand me?"

I used all of the shampoos in the hotel room. Everything can be cleaned, every abject substance, if somebody bleeds or vomits on your new shirt, if you shit on your own book; what cannot be washed away is the bureaucratic disengagement, the grayness of the furniture left behind *them*. Only *nothingness* cannot be washed. I watched Shrek 3 on the hotel television. At least here the monsters had a recognizable face–the scary looked scary, the good looked good. And that's how I fell asleep.

And then I woke up. And my questions were as follows: What is our awakening like today, what view is still possible on the communist experience? And then this: Why another retrospective on the theme of communism today, when it was successfully criticized even during the time it existed? Where does the necrophilic desire come from, to shoot the dead ideological corpse for the second time, when I, speaking as an analyst, claim there isn't a more tiresome topic than the communist, and that those books and that frozen epoch can be read only with immense effort.

My reasons are personal. I could console myself that my father was a victim of the gods, but that kind of romanticism is irresponsible. All people are victims of the gods, but some people are additionally victims of other people, of the systems perpetrated by other people. We are always being convinced that things are not personal, but that is not true. Each thing has its own personal name. The name of the ideology behind my father's tragedy was called communism. If you write about communism, does that automatically mean that you are fond of capitalism? To everybody for the past few years who commented on the topic of this book, saying "It is silly to attack communism, look how bad capitalism is," I have a question: "If one system turns out to be gray, does that mean the other will be less black?"

The three greatest ideologies of the 20th century–New Deal capitalism, fascism and communism–operated according to similar mechanisms. A review of communism like this one can only be useful to the critics of capitalism. These two systems are mirrored, what is found in one is mirrored in the optical distortion of the other, and vice versa. Look how the Tito-themed cafes, bars and restaurants in today's Macedonia ("Broz café," "At the Marshal's," etc.) as well as those tables and outlets selling artifacts exploiting socialist nostalgia (posters, remakes of Yugoslav radio hits, films and the entire image) are pure, free-market entrepreneurial projects, capitalist cash cows for the milking. It is only logical today to support the body of socialist nostalgia if you are a capitalist, which paradoxically means that if you write against communism, you are nostalgic! And is there some correct dosage in our approach towards our past? Nostalgia does not bring the frozen socialist past back into history, nostalgia places the memory of socialism in the "absent" time of today's capitalist world. Capitalism is a civilization with cancelled time, "the first world civilization without a world," as Badiou says; it has infrastructure, but instead of (the socialist) postponed time, it has the capitalist cancelled time–and these two forms of ideological time are related.

Four Comments on the Nature of the Analysis that Follows

1.

In this book, I use the term communism and not socialism, NOT because: 1. The term was key in the jargon of the winners of the Cold War (who never accepted the name socialists for their opponents); 2. The parties representing the real socialism called themselves communists. But because everything that existed in reality was communist ideology, which was consequently framing itself as a *phantasm of socialism as transition*, "in itself more than itself" (real communism in socialism, more than socialism), the communism we were waiting for didn't come because it was already here.

The three-year rule of the Khmer Rouge Government in Cambodia (1971-1974), during which two-thirds of the adult male population was killed ("As far as I know, the closest approach to the Socialist ideal in history"–Shafarevich[1]), shows that the wiping out of the phantasmal frame of the socialist transition led to total anarchy of everything that existed. In the last official census of *today's* Cambodia, *half* the entire male population is *under* 21 years old. The attempt to fully implement the ideology outlined in the "Communist Manifesto" (abolition of the state, private property, family, separation of children from their parents, etc.) would mean destroying everything, including the Manifesto itself. Socialism wasn't the "positive" substance, but the symptom, the blind spot, "the parasite" latched onto the body of communism, which paradoxically "protected" it from disappearance, in fact *guaranteed* it.

2.

I agree with Katherine Verdery that it's irrelevant to study one country as typical because, "*No* socialist country was 'typical,'" as it cannot be said that the Netherlands, New Zealand, Japan or America are typical, but are variants of the unique capitalist system.[2] What follows is an attempt to analyze the common points through which communism operated–not only as an ideology, but also as real socialism (as the difference between the promising platform and the unpleasant reality).

3.

This book is organized as an analysis of *exceptions* because I believe that the exception is more important than the rule: "The exception explains the general and itself ... If (the exception) cannot be explained, then the general also cannot be explained ... the general is not thought about with passion, but with a comfortable superficiality. The exception, on the other hand, thinks the general with intense passion,"[3] says Kierkegaard. Similarly, Althusser offers that there isn't anything in history but *exceptions*. "There is no ultimate rule that allows one to measure 'exceptions' against it–in real history, there are, in a way, nothing but exceptions."[4]

4.

The analysis of communism herein can also be applied outside its historical context. Some of the phenomena described can be recognized in different forms of political and popular living in different stages of all of the post-communist realities from 1989 onward. Of those current in the Macedonian present reality, the following (similarities) come to mind as regards: *exoticism and eclecticism* (the interest in the Hunza people, the region's Antique heritage as opposed to the inability to have a dialogue with its neighbors; see the chapter entitled "Exoticism"); the Government's call for *shock work* against the inbuilt acceleration of time, characteristic of capitalism (see the chapter entitled "Arrhythmia of Socialism"), *expanding the role of the secret police* (with the rebalancing of the 2008 budget, the Intelligence and Counter-Intelligence Administration of Macedonia was allocated far more funding compared to previous years; see the chapters dedicated to the secret services), etc. The ideological premises and approaches of communism can be replicated and applied in different forms of political rule–without direct–historic or logical–political heritage. This book *also* serves as a reminder of those dangers.

Malevich's Squares
(On the Bureaucratic Banality of Evil)

When we talk about the social logic of communism, what are we actually talking about? We certainly aren't talking about the formal logic, about the abstract relation between A and B. We talk about "communist grammar" (which in the Macedonian case was mixed with "small-town grammar"), we talk about a cluster of rules according to which some people are included in the system, and others are excluded. That "grammar" is a form without substance.

Communism, like New Deal capitalism and fascism, is based on administrative emptiness, and on *pure form*. There is nothing in communism that identifies the human life and its inherent value in and of itself. The cynics may say that human life is also an empty abstraction, a form without content. Yes, but that would mean that emotion and pain don't exist as well, which is not true. With a little bit of good will, only the opposite must be said. If something really exists, in the sense of trauma, stroke, of Lacan's Real ("I'm alive")– that is *the emotion*. Everything else is convention, empty bureaucracy, like the empty Stasi-offices in Berlin.

The Soviet communist Pyatakov, expelled from the Bolshevik lines, in exile in Paris wrote:

We are not like other people. We are a party who makes the impossible possible; transfixed with the thought of violence, we direct it to ourselves, and if the party demands it, if it is necessary or important for the party, we will be able by an act of will, to expel from our brains in 24 hours ideas we have held for years… Shooting someone in the forehead with a gun is a trifle in comparison to the fulfillment of the will I talk about.[5]

The will Pyatakov talks about is precisely the will of the empty administrative machinery of communism. Because it is empty, the will of the Party is chaotic, in the sense that each substance can take part in filling it. The party can oscillate between terribly left-wing and terribly right-wing options, but it does not announce them. The Party, with the greatest of ease, demands from its subjects that they give up everything today which they believed in yesterday, and that can only be explained with the total bureaucratic absence of *sense*. There is only the chaotic "work" of the writer–bureaucrat, of the UDBA snitch, of the radio employee, of the neighbor you had coffee with, etc. They are the "flesh" through which the bureaucratic machine operates, the pure form of the Party as the Great Other, which, like God, has no positive or negative value by which to be "accountable" before the people.

Kołakowski wrote that the former Yugoslavia was a country of "ideological chaos;" you could be opposed to the regime, but you could also end up in prison easier than in the most liberal Soviet countries, Hungary and Poland.[6] Moreover, at the peak of the dictatorship, Tito's regime could be tolerant, and in the freest of decades one could end up in prison (my father's case being proof of this). The bureaucratic apparatus in Yugoslavia was far more chaotic and far less thought through than is commonly believed. Much/all depended on the local small-town interpretations of the ideology. You could be free in Serbia in 1949, but arrested in Macedonia in 1985, while in Slovenia in 1985 the alternative art groups such as Laibach and NSK were doing projects exploiting pro-fascist symbology and iconography.

The best metaphor for senseless bureaucratic communism (of the pure form) was offered up by the best abstract painter of the very young Soviet Union. Two years before the October Revolution, Kazimir Malevich exhibited *Black Square* in Petrograd (former name from 1914–24 for St. Petersburg) in 1915. Just one year after the Revolution, Malevich replaced the black square with the final square solution, the minimalistic *White Square,* in 1918. Here is a painting where there is literally *nothing*! In 1919, Malevich left his final testament to the communist artists: "I have torn through the blue lampshade of color limitations and come out into the white. After me comrade aviators sail into the chasm–I have set up the semaphores of suprematism… Infinity is before you."[7] When ideology freed itself from substance, through the semaphores of supermatism, it could only sail directly into the pit, into the perpetual, infinite hole of the communist bureaucratic nonsense. It is hardly by chance that the detached ideological apparatus of communism recognized its favorite genre in science fiction.

The relationship between *science fiction and communism* is well documented. The Soviets translated Jules Verne and H. G. Wells, while thousands of authors could not work; Tarkovsky made his movies, and the fact that his unique, complex art succeeded in seeing the light of day owes much to the epoch's love of science fiction. Communists loved fantasizing. The Soviets described the ideal Marxist society on Mars (Alexander Bogdanov's *Engineer Manny,* 1913). In Yugoslavia, through the *Sirius* editions and the SF comics, science fiction was the most widely loved and read young people's literature, and was admired by numerous, prominent communists. Three years after the October Revolution in 1920, H. G. Wells, the author of *Time Machine,* travels to Russia to meet the leaders of the Revolution. At the Kremlin he interviews Lenin, who states: "If we succeed in making contact with the other planets, all our philosophical, social and moral ideas will have to be revised, and in this event these potentialities will become limitless and will put an end to violence as a necessary means to progress."[8] (There is a well-known Yugoslav pun, where after a lecture on Marxism, a student, confusing Marx with Mars, asks: "But, tell me, is there life on that Mars anyway?"[9])

Communism was an ideology with philosophical appeal because it promised people "the oceanic feeling" for everybody in a "clearer" way than did the other two great ideologies of the 20th century (capitalism and fascism). What Lenin outlines in his conversation with Wells is the collapse of all ideas, a cleaning of the whole substance in the name of the pure form. The problem, of course, is generic. As with cleaning myself in Berlin, what will remain after the cleaning of the substance is an empty form, the terrible pit of *nothingness,* to which, nonetheless, any substance can stick–any evil which, because of the bureaucratic banality, becomes what Hannah Arendt describes as "the banality of evil." Similarly with the Stasi museum: There is nothing there, but this is not a nothing of empty form–it is always the nothing as *bureaucratic, banal and totally evil.*

Wells also precisely documented this disparity. In the West in the 1920s, it was fashionable to like communism, but Wells noticed that while they were showing him the Kremlin, they didn't let him see the hungry streets of the city, the devastation in the Soviet "White Square," and he wrote: "Communism is like a magician who forgot to take the dove and the dwarf with himself, so he cannot take out anything from his hat."[10] The magic of Malevich's post-revolutionary "White Square" is the magic of the pure bureaucratic form, and Wells is terrified. Science fiction was a genre that emerged as a necessity to warn of the terror of the abstract universe, where the pure form conspired (one of the most important books acutely critical of the system belonged to the same genre: Yevgeny Zamyatin's *We,* 1921). Science fiction represented the same artistic resistance as Malevich's squares. But communism wasn't able to capture that parodic distance at all, and that absence of humor proved to be fatal for millions of people.

Kremlinology as a Symptom

The study of communism faces one obvious problematic phenomenon–an uncertainty of the facts studied. One obvious example is as follows: When Khrushchev succeeded Stalin, the era of quiet "de-Stalinization" began. Khrushchev talked about the "thousands" of Stalin's victims, when the wildest estimates spoke roughly of a "modest" 2.3 million dead who disappeared under Stalin's dictatorship between 1930 and 1953. When a more systematic view of his rule was later established, various researchers, including the writer Solzhenitsyn, talked about something between 8 and 12 million people killed. After opening the archives of the Soviet governments in 1989, the number reached as many as 20 million victims, and that number is still not final.[11]

Nancy Adler writes that when Robert Conquest's book "The Great Terror" appeared with the estimate of 20 million Stalin victims, some revisionists put it down to the anti-communist hysteria reminiscent of McCarthyism in the USA of the 1940s and 1950s. In the American communist chase, the Rosenbergs were executed and many Americans were excommunicated because of their sympathetic position on communism. Conquest replied to the accusations that the analogy between Soviet communism and McCarthyism would be appropriate provided that during those two years, the Americans had shot the majority of their civil servants, 3/4 of the members of Congress, hundreds of writers and thousands of military officers.[12] And only those from the ranks of the political nomenclature, and not from among the politically "irrelevant": peasants, workers, everybody who doubted, wrote a poem, told a joke, stole an apple (between 1930 and 1940, 20% of the inmates in Soviet gulags were political prisoners, with the average (forced) laborer a kolkhoznik, who'd stolen an apple and been proclaimed a counter-revolutionary.[13])

Like the Nazis, the communists also left too much paper behind for their most shameless crimes. But the obvious problem remains, how to get hold of those papers? And when you do get hold of them, how credible are they? With the exception of East Germany, the other former communist countries have applied different solutions to the issue of accessibility of the archives–and not always the best ones. The problems are especially acute in Russia. In 1989, the Soviet archives were opened to foreign and national researchers. Subsequently, the President's archives were proclaimed increasingly off limits until they were completely closed, and today's FSB archives are accessible only to the families of the repressed and to former employees.[14]

The science that studies the Soviet files is called Kremlinology, which was named after the headquarters of the Soviet Government. The Kremlinologists' general complaint, which resembles the complaint by the Macedonian historians, is that the files from communism are inaccessible, that they are fabricated, that they have to be read "between the lines," and that the research is primarily based on gossip (this one heard that that one was a spy, who is certain that he heard that in the camps...etc.). One should be careful on which photograph, which member of the Comintern was later photoshopped; to see whose portraits disappeared from the textbooks and when (Trotsky in Russia, Đilas in Yugoslavia, Čento in Macedonia); to look at the small details on the pictures, who sat next to Stalin's chair in 1931 and who in 1933, who was called to a conference with Tito on Brioni in 1941 and who in 1966, where did Đilas disappear after 1950, why did Kardelj disappear from the chairs in 1960s and is back again in 1973; who stands next to the Marshal on May 25 or who is on the slet at the Red Square, on the slets in China and North Korea and so on. In all of this, the obvious phenomenon is overlooked, that exactly the archival "impossibility" is the symptom itself, according to Žižek, of the mechanisms through which the socialist regime operated as a saturated universe of signs.

Neutral Citizens

Donald Rayfield says that when in 1996, the book *Hitler's Willing Executioners* by Daniel Goldhagen appeared, it caused a lot of controversy because the author claimed that: 1. The number of killed Jews was known to the majority of Germans; and 2. The refusal to participate in the genocide of the Jews was neither punished by death nor by any other injustice.[15] Opening the Stasi archives in Germany confirmed that as well–those who refused to collaborate with the communist secret services didn't suffer any personal damage. Moral choices were possible, especially for the intellectuals. The problem is that the intellectuals are most frequently the state's servants and pecuniarily dependent on it. They are the extended hand of the machineries of education, educated to support the professional and ethical codes of the abstract state machinery.

These insights show the *parameters* under which massive crimes can occur. Massive crimes are only possible with the silent cooperation of everyone with everybody, and it is provided through an ideological shield. Similarly to the fascist and capitalist ones, the bureaucratic communist machinery was based on the use of the "bare life" (Agamben) of the nameless bureaucratic screws. They are neither the informants, nor the victims. They are the so-called neutral citizens.

Communism was capable of producing big crimes because it was guarded by the idea that it was the best system in the world. Petty crimes are committed out of greed or habit, while the big ones out of faith and conviction. Only the great idealists commit big crimes without regret, as the ideals free them of a guilty conscience. If the intellectuals in the horrible regimes most often knew or guessed what was happening, than the question is the following: Why, for God's sake, wasn't there any serious resistance in the communist regimes, although they were principally supported only by fanatics, sadists and cynics? Tito's regime mostly experienced verbal resistance in the circle of the nuclear family–there, you could hate Tito, be ironic towards slet, be disgusted by the systematic injustice, talk about national issues, etc. but never out of your home.

When the prosecutors in Nuremberg asked the witnesses against Eichmann the following questions: "Why did you not protest? Why did you board the train? Fifteen thousand people were standing there and hundreds of guards facing you–why didn't you revolt, and charge and attack?"[16] Hannah Arendt rightfully says that the questions are cruel and stupid. The whole triumph of the sadistic structure of the SS was based on a type of torture in which the victim allows himself to be taken to the pit without protest, giving up any kind of human resistance; as a former prisoner of the

Nazi camp said: "The system which succeeds in destroying its victim before he mounts the scaffold... is incomparably the best for keeping a whole people in slavery."[17] It is best to create a system in which people will voluntarily walk as "puppets towards their own death." In communism, the regime destroyed the essential resistance in the same way Nazism did because the regime generally functioned without major shocks.

Studies about prison torture confirm this. Torture in the most general sense is not functional at all, you cannot receive any relevant information from the person you torture, torture survives as a myth with a reason. In an interview about his book, *Torture and Democracy* (2007), Darius Rejali says:

Torture is not useful for collecting information. People think torture worked for the Gestapo, for example. It didn't. What made the Gestapo so scarily efficient was its dependence on public cooperation. Informants betrayed the resistance repeatedly in Europe, and everyone knew this, but it was more convenient to say the Gestapo got the truth by beating it out of us.[18]

In a sense, these two insights "rehabilitate" the neutral citizens. Neutral citizens were aware, they weren't ignorant, but that knowledge couldn't have been of significant use for critical resistance. The regime was based on a systematic breaking of resistance.

Slavoj Žižek took out the following sentence from Marx's *Capital* (1867) as the most basic definition of the ideologies: "They do not know it, but they are doing it." But this sentence isn't precise enough. People weren't politically unaware of the principle of blindness, they always assumed that something was happening, but they chose not to react. I think that a more precise definition about the ideology is the dialogue from Beckett's *Waiting for Godot (1953)*. When Estragon nervously tells Vladimir: "I tell you I wasn't doing anything," Vladimir replies calmly: "Perhaps you weren't. But it's the way of doing it that counts." The leader of the ideology is Vladimir, while "the neutral citizen" is Estragon. The ideology first anesthetizes you not to do anything, and then it consoles you that you're doing nothing is completely all right. That merging of two ideological fists between which the "neutral citizen" is pressed, as well as his nervous reaction, is the ideological pillow to which the nervous "neutral citizen" is comfortably lulled.

Socialism as "Released Territory"

Immediately after the fall of the Berlin Wall, the Italian Marxist Massimo Fini wrote for the Yugoslav media:

I hope that the Eastern countries will not simply repeat capitalism, but that they will find a third solution. The Protestant logic on which capitalism is based is not like the East imagines it to be, but it implies paying the price. What price do you have to pay? It can be reduced to one answer–unhappiness. The wealthiest capitalist country in the world, the USA, is the biggest user of psychopharmaceutical products. Every second man is deeply unhappy... The East dreams the dreams of the others. The wealthy supermarkets in the West are a dream to the Westerners themselves.

Fini was not alone in this thesis. After 1945, there was massive rejection of capitalism throughout Europe; for the Western left-wing, communism remained a valid "experiment" they still looked at, expecting the ideological "solution" in the long decades after the Second World War.

What the Yugoslav readers at that time, exhausted by the experiences of socialism and incapable of a "new answer," couldn't see in Fini's melancholic lines, because of the logic of their jovial desire (*I* too want to see those supermarkets first, and buy *my* Coca Cola can), was Fini's wish itself, his *own* exhaustion from participation in the project called capitalism. And they didn't see Fini's comfortable left-wing lethargy–"the new answer" should be sought elsewhere, while I will continue my relatively prosperous life. "The third way" will be sought by the pitiful from "The third world." Probably the worst favor you could do for somebody is to tell him on his death bed that he spent his life in the wrong neighborhood. Certainly, that can also be interpreted as enlightenment. Fini's procedure, according to Lacan's concepts, could be put down to the so-called economy of the other's desire, which Lacan explains like this: "Desire is always desire of the Other." Fini hallucinates that communists live better than capitalists. "You don't need our overloaded supermarkets, they are a lie, I see something better on your side."

But the same logic of hallucinations was true for the communist citizens as well–I also want to hold *my* Coca Cola can. Yugoslav communism, which did not have a rigid prohibition of Western books and films compared to the people of the so-called Eastern

Block, paradoxically just increased the anxiousness of the citizens. The desire, we have known since Freud, sexualizes the object. Coca Cola cans appeared for the first time in Yugoslavia at the Olympics in Sarajevo in 1984, the can held by the world champion in karate, opens the most urgent request for sexualization. He is not just the world karate champion, but the world sex champion on the longest tracks. We should remember Lacan's love formula. "Love is persuading the other, he owns that which will complete you, that is, persuading yourself that you can continue not recognizing exactly that which you lack."[19]

There is always some lie in desiring. There are empty desires and crazy desires, and there are desires for the forbidden, but without exception they are all desires of the Other. The West liked communism because that was Lenin's desire. The East liked capitalism because that was Wilson's dream. We see consciousness as an expression of prestige, but consciousness is not prestigious–when people want something, they want what *the Other has*.

Žižek offers that this explains why Yugoslavia, along with Cuba and Nicaragua was, for Western left-wing intellectuals, a kind of realized ideological dream, a kind of "released territory"–"released" from Stalinist dictatorship, but also from inhumane capitalism.[20] That's Fini's paradox. I live in socialism and I desire capitalism and vice versa–this paradox is essentially incorporated in the ideological world. Yugoslavia was Arcadia for the Western left-wingers: There are no free elections, yet nor is there a consumption-driven society, people travel freely, they have access to Western books and films, they don't wait in front of embassies for visas and they have cheap electricity; but the question is, does the question exclude the fact of totalitarian governance? If you worked as a magazine publisher in the 1980s in Yugoslavia and you asked the authorities for advice on whether you could publish something, they would reply: "We are a self-management society, think with your own head!"[21] Which always meant–think with *our* head. The censorship may be hidden, but the political dictatorship over individual thought is nevertheless rigid; thus, self-censorship was the main driver that moved the system.

Yugoslavia didn't even have the liberalizing period like the Czechoslovakian historiographic renaissance in the period from

1964-1969, when the Czechoslovakians spoke openly about their gulags and purges.[22] Yugoslav historians couldn't publicly admit their gulags and political prisoners until the mid 1980s.[23] In 1979, the official historian Branko Petranović wrote that the magazines of the opposition must be suppressed because, "The country is still undergoing revolutionary processes and changes."[24] Tito was destroying the opposition in a Soviet style, and only Yugoslavia didn't have a "modest" transitional phase towards socialism, characteristic of the other countries of Eastern Europe between 1945 and 1947.

To the present day, "neutral" citizens are proud that Yugoslavia avoided the "Stalin's lap," but also the cruel capitalist acceleration, and that Tito introduced participative democracy, minority rights, etc., that Macedonian socialism brought us statehood (it is difficult to criticize something which constitutes you), that the people are nostalgic, if not after Tito's system than at least "after the youth," and that they have every right to their own memory and so on.

When Tito's regime is criticized today, it is always seen as either a globalization impulse or as right-wing nationalism. Even the biggest liberals in Macedonia proclaimed Resolution 1481 of the Council of Europe for "The need for international condemnation of crimes of totalitarian communist regimes" of 2006 as "controversial," calling it a nebulosis taken out of "the small brain of the Brussels bureaucrats." When, in March 2007, the Macedonian Parliament gave a green light for the first Lustration Law, the reaction of the public was divided. For the opponents of lustration, the communist spies just performed the dirty work in one system, which was unjust in itself. They said that the spies can be just as guilty as the so-called "neutral" citizens who knew that the spying practice existed, but still didn't do anything about it. Among the public calls against lustration in Macedonia, traces could be found of a certain nostalgia towards the UDB. That means that the opponents of lustration believed that the Macedonian KGB was just some kind of unimportant invasion into peoples' privacy, unlike present, omnipotent and yet abstract and anonymous insight into people's intima, characteristic of the capitalist panopticon.

And at first glance, it seems that it is not easy to make a good representation of Tito's Yugoslavia when it is known how bad Stalin was. The real value of living in Tito's Macedonia will become visible only after the opening of the dark pages of the counter-intelligence services, calmly and not on the principle of spectacle or a hunger for gossip. Tito and Stalin are alike because they destroyed the opposition with the same methods in order to introduce the governing of the unique Communist party. And that happened with a lot of political mistakes, individual horror and political victims. The current wave of nostalgia about communism can be used *not* to release people from their memories, but to "release" the memories themselves, to release the memories which until now were forbidden by the collective memory. The need to glorify the socialist past is maybe necessary, but is also useful, because we get more relevant knowledge about the past, with more (forbidden thus far) available information.

Personal memories are a valuable tool for an ethical future. People have a tendency to remember "that then" mainly as it looked *to them*. But each one of us has a different version of the past. For some, living in communism was an era of a happy childhood. For the others among us, it meant an experience of prisons, ex-communication and terror towards the members of their families. Around half a million Yugoslavs were observed by the communist secret services in Yugoslavia. In Macedonia, there are 14,572 official personal police files today (unofficial sources claim more than 50,000). Those are the people who do not share the bright picture about the past, as their memories differ from the happy families' stories.

What is missing in all the cases is an *ideological* confrontation with Tito's regime in a double sense–in terms of transitional justice, but also in an analysis of the specific *human engineering*, which was needed for that ideology to be established, but also the realsocialism, as a difference between socialist platform and unpleasant reality. This effort is important, not because the re-named communist parties won the elections in most of the countries in former Yugoslavia, as well as in Poland, Hungary and Bulgaria, but because communism is still a valid political option–in February 2008, in Cyprus, which is a member country of the European Union, the option of the real communism won, namely that legitimate elective victory shows that communism should be regarded not as past, as an acute presence, but also as possible future. In the last few years, some Macedonian blogs opened debates about the place and role of Tito, Stalin, Mao, and left-wing blogs with Marxist orientation were also opened, and in them many humanist, manifesto messages (solidarity, unification, freedom....), and what is more likable than that? In May and June of 2008, when the jubilee of the 1968 student demonstrations was celebrated, the motto, "Be realistic. Demand the impossible," became relevant again. Just a few people know that this wasn't the demonstrators' sentence, but most probably Jacques Lacan's. Several years before the revolution of 1968, the great French psychoanalyst worked the French students over in the paradoxes of the psychoanalysis from the bench, telling them that they can, that the world offers impossibilities, be realistic! He gave them his full support when they took the motto to the streets. But just a few people know that their teacher told them that same day in the afternoon: "What you, as revolutionaries, aspire to is a Master. You will get one."[25] At the peak of the celebration of the jubilee in June 2008, I heard Lacan's motto in one celebrity talk show on Macedonian television. Lacan's sentence became famous, the demonstrations fell through, but the people got a Master.

Anesthesia

Doctors confirm that not feeling pain is more dangerous for a patient than feeling pain. But the problem with the communist anesthesia is that it was so successful that it almost entirely incapacitated the patient. Look at the cultural decay today in the countries of the former real-socialism, where, with some honest exceptions, we find a complete "absence of philosophy," in the sense that culture should produce concepts and not cultural workers–pharmacists.

Why was the communist anesthesia so successful, more successful than even the Nazi's? Beyond the (previously discussed) notions of neutral citizens and real-socialism as a left-wing dream, there is this:

1. Killing "Others" as opposed to killing your "Own."

Rayfield says that however cruel it may sound, Nazism had a certain "logic" behind its barbarism. Supported by the Nazi businesses and the Army, the Nazis were directed towards destroying *the Other* (Jews, Slavs, homosexuals, communists…). The average German could put on pink glasses and live his life as under any other regime.[26] The communist regimes directed their cruelty towards their "own": their neighbors, their own army generals, the professional elite, even members of their own families (the schoolbook example is Stalin's relationship with his own son Yakov when, in 1928, Yakov tried unsuccessfully to kill himself, and Stalin laughed at him; and when Yakov was arrested in 1941 by the Germans, Stalin not only refused to negotiate his release, but when the Germans used Yakov's picture for a (propaganda) pamphlet, Stalin ordered the Spanish communists to infiltrate the agents' lines and kill Yakov. "Stalin's politics were entirely a result of his own paranoia, as Stalin turned on his own people. He waged a war against his closest allies."[27] There were only a few people close to Stalin whom he didn't wish to kill, and very few things in life that he (openly) appreciated. What happened to the innocent victims in the USSR is no different from the treatment of victims of totalitarian regimes everywhere, but the difference is that those other regimes rarely, or never, turn on "the closest ones."

2. "It's their fault."

In a system where it was unclear who was a friend and who was an enemy, and where the victims were recruited from the same ethnic, management, professional and family structures, the blurry notion prevailed that those 100 million victims of communism *somehow deserved* what happened to them. If they weren't Others, and yet were slated to be sacrificed, this was proof that certainly somewhere along the line they did wrong. The average citizen of communist regimes could well don the pink glasses, but this was no guarantee that he would be spared from the governing ideology. Those who survived didn't accept their survival as self-evident, but as a kind of teleology, some hidden sense, governed and guaranteed by a higher logic, as well as by the fact that they personally never did any wrong, anywhere.

3. Condensed against spread time/space of the crime.

Nazism is a totalitarian ideology and was, under Hitler's leadership, the practice of the Nazi (National-Socialist) Party, which refers

Communist Crimes and Political Anesthesia 73

to the politics of the Government of Germany between 1933-1945, the period known as the Third Reich. The systematic execution of the Jews transpired in a condensed time and space. Communism, however, spread across an entire third of the planet, and in each country displayed features characteristic of that country. In the Soviet variant, communism lasted for 75 years, in Eastern European countries for 55 years, and still exists elsewhere today.

In the Nazi camps death was the goal, while in the communist camps life was not worth a penny. It is a strategically different position (as Marcuse says, communism is a civilization, while fascism is barbarism), though statistically the distinction is not a significant one. In the communist gulags where people went "to work," the mortality rate varied between 0.6%-25% in the years from 1920 to 1930, and rose to 60% in the years from 1940-45, which means that during the Second World War the mortality rate in both types of camps was identical. Because of their program of extinction, the Nazi camps remained in our memory as the very topos of evil, scary cancers; the communist camps hid behind the illusion of retraining, and to the present day their "declarative" determination remains their best ideological shield.

4. Revision of everything I know?

Political amnesia results from an epistemological inability to revise everything you learned about the system under which you lived. One of the researchers of the Soviet archives, Grigory Pomerants, describes it thusly: "(I)magine being an adult and nearly all the truth you know about the world around you... has to be absorbed in a matter of a year or two or three."[28] After a while, people will get tired, they will not want to talk about the victims anymore, and the victims themselves will feel cheated and ill-treated.

5. Adaptation to repression.

The system(s) of the past created mechanisms for an adaptation to repression. Prisoners learned that life consisted of injustices, families had to adjust to the absence of their closest ones, even high officials had to learn that they could–to use János Kádár's favorite self-labeling of 1989–at any time, become "scapegoats" within the scheme of the same repressive apparatus.

When some former Macedonian party secretaries came out with the position in the 1990s that they had been repressed, they were met by the public with laughter and disbelief. But a classification of the victims of the communist regimes shows that the number of political victims from the ranks of the nomenclature reached 10%. The system was based on constant control, which besides being external and directed towards the people, was also internal and periodically applied to the officials themselves. If the system is adapted to the system of repression, then discoveries about the authorities and their official recognition carries with it the risk of destabilizing the system.[29]

Let's look at the terrible proliferation of "honesty" when a leader falls from power. Both Khrushchev and Gorbachev kept quiet when they were in a position to actively change the system from the highest possible station–after having lost their power they spoke up, claiming they themselves were "victims." After falling from power, Khrushchev publicly said that his son Leonid had been a victim of Stalin. During the Second World War, his son was interned at a Nazi camp and later released by the Soviet troops. As a consequence, like millions of Soviets in German captivity, he was proclaimed an enemy of war by Stalin's regime (he was guilty of having touched fascism, even as a victim–those touched by the "impure" were particularly suspicious to the paranoiac Stalin). Khrushchev sent appeals everywhere, even to Stalin, but Stalin remained mute.[30] (The first official denunciation of Stalinism is the well-known Khrushchev speech at the 12th Congress of the Communist Party of the Soviet Union in 1956. The speech was sent to the KGB and was debated for two days. Christopher Andrew writes: "None dared to ask the question which Mitrokhin[31] was convinced was on everybody's mind: Where was Khrushchev when all this crime was happening?"[32])

We know the same of Gorbachev: After he lost power, he felt safe enough to publicly declare that his family was also a victim of the repression, more specifically, the family members of his wife Raisa Maksimovna had been arrested as kulaks and sent to gulags.[33] Both of them knew that the destinies of their families were far from exceptional, and that the same destiny was shared by "thousands" of others, but from their place in the Government, they kept quiet.

6. Society without consequences.

Communism was a "society without consequences," actions were not followed by legal or public judgment, and the people learned that it is enough to be in an anesthetized relationship towards the regime in order to survive. If there is any *fundamental* difference between capitalism on the one side and communism and fascism on the other (with all the media impossibilities of capitalism), it lies in the fact that you can profit by having a different opinion in capitalism, and that it is a condition for the different opinion to become *possible*. If it is possible, your actions can find some test in the public arena–but they don't have to.

7. The victim must be worth it.

There are situations when suggestion is powerless: One such situation is when you cannot help the fact that the children of the communist victims regularly stand on the side of their parents' executors. This phenomenon is characteristic not only for Macedonia, this relationship towards a sacrificial past is well documented in the former Soviet Union. Most frequently, the descendants of the victims of communism, even the victims themselves, and even after long decades of torture and suffering, think that communism is the best possible system, and that their sacrifice is justified only when it is placed on the communist altar. In these cases, it seems we can talk about identifying the parent's claim (or your own) not in the acceptance that communism was a sacrificial ideology, but the other way around–the parental victim is logical only if it is "incorporated" into the socialist body.

The majority of public or hidden calls against lustration in Macedonia were led by the children of the victims of communism (more extended examples in our country were Mirjana Najčevska, the former President of the Helsinki Committee for Human Rights, and Vladimir Milčin, President of the "Open Society Institute Macedonia," mentioned here because of their important roles in Macedonian society). Although they, as descendants of persons persecuted under communism, and according to the terms of transitional justice, were themselves victims of the past system, they spoke out against the opening of the files. What we need to say here is that communism didn't create a monolith of heroic victims, victims who fell because of–or for *a* goal. As a matter of fact, it was completely the opposite: The dimensions of the ideological catastrophe of our recent past lies in the fact that the victims of communism were, most commonly, completely *pointless victims*.

The communist system regularly announced: "Is there anybody among you who will voluntarily submit themselves to our sacrificial ideology?" Because no such person was to be found, they chose themselves. To admit this is not a simple thing, whereas to ignore it is irresponsible. Nevertheless, our endless search for meaning does not end here.

8. "We don't have time for the past."

In Macedonia, there is the idea that we don't have time for the past, that we have more urgent issues. In 2006, when I came across an announcement on the Internet from a German-Hungarian organization dealing with an analysis of the communist heritage in their two countries, under the patronage of the European Union, I applied with an essay. I'm neither German nor Hungarian, but in Macedonia these topics were too far in the past, too retro. We are running ahead–who will look back now?

My paper–and by extension, myself–were accepted. The essay about my father turned out to be the most pained and painful of all; it stood out from the others by the extent of the surveillance over my father and by the combination of small-town intrigues and ideological confusion of the surveillance agent. With 42 years of police surveillance, my father placed "first" as the best illustration of the relationship of communism towards human intima.

Our "innocent" communism turned out to be scarier than "their" Eastern European experiences. Croatian historian Ivo Banac was right when, in his book *With Stalin Against Tito* (1990), he was the first in Yugoslavia to ask for acceptance of a simple fact–that the Yugoslav version of communism in the first years of its existence was more rigid than in the other countries of the Eastern Block;[34] and because of the ironic fact that Yugoslavia was seen as the softest communist dictatorship and the DDR as the hardest, giving rise to the paradox of the ideological chaos of the "freest" regime, this opened up even more perverse space for pointless ideological sacrifice.

9. Problematic capitalism.

Capitalism has succeeded today in organizing, in making civilization recognizable as we know it, but it was the same in the years of communism as well. And Verdery offers a brilliant insight into the communist subordination before the capitalist definition of civilization: "The irony is that had debtor regimes (from the communist countries–my comment) refused the definition imposed from without–had they united to default simultaneously on their Western loans (which in 1981 stood at over $90 billion)–they might well have brought down the world financial system and realized Khrushchev's threatening prophecy (i.e. his pronouncement "We will bury you! Your grandchildren will be Communists!"–my comment) overnight. That this did not happen shows how vital a thing was *capitalists' monopoly on the definition of social reality*" (my emphasis).[35]

If things were therefore back in the decades of communism, the ultimatum is now complete: Today's capitalism holds a monopoly over reality, and it is understandable that people don't like it.

Furthermore, transition is terribly problematic: In the Macedonian case, this doesn't only mean that people are lazy and fed up with Tito as subject–topic, but also that the capitalist reality is a cruel one. As a result, the liberal doesn't want to enter the closed epistemological circle, to be caught out as a supporter of the capitalist doctrine, though the point is exactly the opposite: If you corner people (here) and force them into taking a position, they usually come out against liberal democracy, opting instead for some kind of communal version of the past–which makes Yugoslavia still a traumatic topos, and silence seems to be the only exit; to maintain the official mask of "solidarity" with the transition (in the sense that there simply isn't another "valid" political choice), and to nurture some intimate sympathy towards "the past," whose open propagandizing would otherwise earn us the ignoble label of radical political "immaturity."

But the truth is entirely otherwise. Today, it is easy to hate capitalism, all the world hates it, and everybody will agree with you. Similarly, the worst way to approach communism is to pretend that you have the formula ("the third way") that the left-wing needs. Capitalism was widely and overwhelmingly rejected by the majority of European nations at the conclusion of the Second World War. And let's remember that the DDR was seen as the anti-fascist alternative of the Federal Republic of Germany, which was seen as some as the "historic heir" of the Third Reich.[36] The left is always ready to search for (and discover) a new answer–and they are right, as Žižek claims, when they claim that the three world orders of the 20th century–New Deal capitalism, communism and fascism–are based on the same uniformity, bureaucratic orientation and administration.[37] But the protest that Badiou, Guattari, Žižek and the left-wing raise that the impossibility of openly pleading for the fascist option is censored is madness. The symptom they rightly identify is precisely the opposite: In a sense, everything that is talked about politically is just a different form of social fascism.

Parents on Respirators (About the Communist Dream)

So, how can the former communist patient wake from the dream? And whose dream, actually, are we talking about?

The best story about the communist dream comes from Wolfgang Becker's film, *Good Bye Lenin* (2003), in which the hero's mother awakes from a coma, upon which her doctors warn her son that it will be a great shock for her to find out that while she was in a coma, East Germany ceased to exist. So, the son starts to recreate the DDR as it used to exist in his mother's apartment. From the mother's viewpoint, this is an excellent lesson that changes in the real political universum are always realized or expressed as a nightmare–while people are in a coma. From the child's viewpoint, this film touches upon the right diagnosis in connection with the historic changes–the burden of maintaining the parental homeostasis falls on the child. In her brilliant analysis of communism, *Dreamworld and Catastrophe* (2000), Susan Buck-Morss offers this from Benjamin: "We must wake up from the world of our parents." And adds: "But what can be demanded of a new generation, if its parents never dream at all?"[38]

The problem stated in Becker's film is that the parents who under communism dreamt extensively, and whose dreams are abruptly interrupted by political developments, fall into such a type of long-term dream-state, into such an extended coma, that they deliver the symptoms of the unconscious to the next generation, to their children, in the form of a question: Is there still a place in this world for me, the Yugoslav parent? In Lacan's second seminar from 1954-55, we find an excellent operational dream for the interpretation of mechanisms of generational change: Lacan's dreamer dreamt that he was swimming in a sea, which is some type of uterus, but also a sea composed exclusively of numbers that refer to his date of birth.[39] In his dream, the dreamer actually asks: Am I my parents' legitimate child? On the other hand, in Becker's *Good Bye Lenin*, it is the mother who is dreaming, and her unconscious asks: Am I still a legitimate "child" of the new epoch? The child is left to answer to what extent is his mother legitimate.

In almost all of the former communist countries, this type of child hesitation exists–should I perform artificial respiration on my parents, should I keep the parent–family universum from slipping into the unconscious of history, hang communist-era wallpaper and pretend communism didn't go anywhere (Becker's solution), or start, shockingly, questioning their world? Most of the sons and daughters adopted the solution from *Good Bye Lenin*, because *this* eventually represents some kind of generational empathy; but the problem, as it is correctly posed by Benjamin is, when should the awakening from their world take place? In most cases, these countries adopted the solutions of the wider Euro-integration process as the only alternative, but the former Yugoslav drama–"We had everything Europe had, only second-hand quality"–remains the same: We still have everything Europe has, but it is still second hand.

Communists dreamt extensively–that we know. They saw dreaming in the most prosthetic, most mechanical sense. Susan Buck-Morss offers the example that in 1929 in the Soviet Union, there was a proposal to build a dream community in the surroundings of Moscow, the so-called "Green City," intended to be a place for common rest, recuperation from work. Konstantin Melnikov proposed building a central hotel, the "Laboratory of Dreams" in the Green City, with the explanation that: "Man sleeps one-third of his lifetime… 20 years of lying down without consciousness, without guidance as one journeys into the sphere of mysterious worlds…"[40] And Melnikov proposed a hotel–laboratory where as a *nomenclature*, millions of followers would be led, in what he called a "sonata of the dream": "All beds here were to be built-in, like laboratory tables; to obviate the need for pillows, the floors sloped gently to the ends of the structure. The walls were broken with great sheets of glass, for sleep would be encouraged at all times of day and would, under some circumstances, require sunlight as well as darkness."[41] The experts will encourage the aural dream, and they will also orchestrate it: "The rustle of leaves, the cooing of nightingales, or the soft murmur of waves would instantly relax the most overwrought veteran of the metropolis. Should these fail, the mechanized beds would then begin gently to rock until consciousness was lost."[42] Melnikov sent the Green City building board the following message: "Cure through sleep and thereby alter the character … Anyone thinking otherwise is sick."[43]

Such ideas are not unknown to the New Age capitalists in similar versions, in the experiments of the so-called lucid dreams, in which the dreamer is trained to be conscious of the dream while dreaming. In revolutionary 1968, a book by the same name of *Lucid Dreaming*, appears by Celia Green, but the whole idea comes to us from the ancients (in practice, for instance, the Tibetan Buddhists use the technique in the performing of yoga exercises). The (mis)use of the dream has attracted all of the significant ideologies since time immemorial, and particularly the totalitarian ones. What intrigues in the dream, however, is this: Why does ideology need the dream?

In the most famous "dissident" debate before the foundation of Yugoslavia, "The Conflict in the Literary Left,"[44] which started in 1928 and lasted up to 1952, the dream is mentioned in one important text. The biggest supporter of Miroslav Krleža's[45] line about freeing literature from socialist realism is the Serbian writer Marko Ristić, the author of the essay, "Don Quixote's Dream and Truth." In the essay, Ristić pathetically says that on the path of truth and freedom everybody has to be subdued, but the poet must *not* bow his head, and must not forget the starry sky. In other words, everybody should believe, without question, but the poet should continue to doubt. Ristić connects the poetic dreaming to Don Quixote's ideology–and for a reason. In Cervantes's novel, the reserved believer is Sancho Panza. It is easy for Don Quixote to go forward–he would be a communist leader, but contrary to the popular interpretations, the real poet in the novel is precisely the down-to-earth Sancho Panza, who says: "My master is crazy, but I will follow him anyway." It is easy to follow if you are convinced that your leader is wise. But for your leader to be constantly wise, you must constantly be in a state of dreaming, in a type of impossible coma.

Once the leader is unmasked as crazy, everybody falls into a collective coma and the whole of post-socialism floats through an era of clinical coma. Hence, I think that, paradoxically, the first gesture of Macedonian parents' real awakening from the communist dream occurred with the first Yugo-nostalgic facilities, which provided vertiginous confirmation that we have lived through a change in the political world. When the president of the new political party, "Tito's Left Forces Union," stated in Macedonia in 2007 that he preferred "the pensioner as an electorate," this was a clear sign of health–they are pensioners and want to talk about the problems of pensions; yet at the same time, it was proof that Tito's forces are part of a dead, past time. Now we want to validate his decisions–are they still functional, what was good in the system? In other words, a clear distance from the communist tradition can only happen when people begin to see communism as a period "other" than my (their) own. That is the first clinical sign that communism finally died and the children are free to take down the communist wallpaper and wake up from the nightmare of the parent universe.

When in 2007, on the streets of Kiev, I started asking whether there was a Museum of Communism, people looked at me in disbelief, shaking their heads. One man told me: "We don't need a museum, everything you see around you is a walking museum." Paradoxically, there is freedom from communism only where it returns to life again, back to the world again from a state of death, as nostalgia–and not where it is still living an acute everyday life.

"Better 28 Years Old in a Camp than 93 Years Old in Freedom" (About Communist Nostalgia)

In 2007, on a panel about communist nostalgia in Budapest, a Hungarian Jew told me: "My mother is 93 years old and she still talks about how good her youth was. In 1942, she was 28 years old. When I asked her how it is possible for a Jew to be nostalgic about a period of the Third Reich, my mother replied: It is better to be a 28-year-old girl, even in Nazi Hungary, than a 93-year-old grandmother in today's Hungary."

This is probably one of the best expressions of nostalgia–when I long for the past, I long for (my) youth. Besides, the past is always manipulated so I can say: "I was happy," but now I am not. Things are not remembered in "memory blocks," memory is always re-membering as *omitting*–I always remember something other than what it was really like.

Psychoanalysis teaches us that a person can never desire the situation he/she is in. It is impossible, Lacan claims, for a person to say: I want this.[46] Desire is particularly impossible in the realm of ideologies. People's most basic experiences teach us that you cannot meet a person who, without reservation, without resistance and without minimum comic distance, will tell you: "I completely like the life in this system; God, how well this ideology suits me!"

Nostalgia for the past is always equated with some morality of the world. "In the old days, there was respect." For instance, this is how people often address the world and its generally downward decline into corruption. The past remains a kind of holder of "true" relationships, which became corrupted along the line.

But what do we do when the past is a proven dictatorship? János Kádár, the controversial Hungarian leader of the "happiest barrack in the Soviet Block," the murderer of the popular revisionist Imre Nagy (who after the unsuccessful revolution in 1956, seeks refuge from the Soviet tanks in the Yugoslav Embassy in Budapest, which delivers him to the Soviet troops, and in a secret process, is sentenced to death by hanging), who in 1989 in his last speech before his Party, said: "Only the beautiful things, I remember."[47] For him, there was both good and bad in the past, but he decides to remember just the good, and this is true not only for the nomenclature, which is personally responsible, but also for the so-called "neutral citizens." Even today, Hungarians are nostalgic for the Kádár era as an era of "goulash communism" and a moderate "soft dictatorship," as the Macedonians are nostalgic for the Tito era. Kádár reformulated dictator Rákosi's communist maxim: "Whoever is not with us is our enemy" into: "Whoever is not against us is with us."

This phrase, which is actually from the New Testament, Mark 9:40, had its followers in all of the communist countries–in Yugoslavia, Slovenian communist Edvard Kardelj had the license on the "softened" version of enmity. The point about nostalgia's position in the context of or relationship to the totalitarian past is this: Whatever they were, they were "mine."

Meeting Lacan's Real is always some form of disappointment; when people turn back towards the past, they seek the enjoyment they do not get in the Here and Now, they escape from the present, which appears as some kind of non-reality. Robert Pfaller analyzes the agonizing Real via the work of the Belgian painter Rene Magritte, and his painting, *The Treachery of Images* (1928). The painting depicts something which looks like a pipe, and under it, there is the text: "This is not a pipe." This painting is closest to an authentic depiction of the Real. The Real is when there is something like a kind of meeting with the Truth, and with the Here and Now; yet it seems as though something is always missing, as in *Magritte*'s comment: "This is not a pipe," which is correct. And meeting the Real is really "not that;" what is missing is–precisely Magritte's comment–"this is not it!" And it is this addition that makes the Real *bearable*.[48]

In 2007, on several occasions in Hungary and in Germany, I met Artyom Kosmarski (born 1982), editor of the magazine "Komunitas" in Moscow. Several years after the disintegration of the Soviet Union, Artyom decides as a teenager to start listening to retro-music, British pop from the seventies, like Genesis–all flutes and mellotrons, reminiscent of the muddy outskirts of the English suburbs, everything that has nothing to do with his time, his post-Soviet Russia. Artyom described it thusly: "My project was refined and very private. I did not long for Europe. Acquiring minute knowledge of English culture of the 1970s, *I made myself* a European." Eight years ago he started feeling a strange sense of nostalgia for the "epic and heroic Soviet times," "marked not only by gulags, but also by great feats, victories and enthusiasm,"[49] and then began intensively downloading Soviet songs as MP3s from the Internet. When I last met him in 2007, Artyom was listening to Irish and French 15th century troubadour music.

Artyom's experience is neither new nor unusual. The enormity of these paradoxical experiences is well known (my friend told me her father, under socialism, dreamt about capitalism, and now defends socialism with great conviction). Kierkegaard reminds us of the well-known psychological pairs: "The melancholic has the best-developed sense of humor, the most extravagant person is often the one most prone to the picturesque, the dissolute one often the most moral, the doubter often the most religious..."[50]

The question is, what triggers these paradoxes? I can, perhaps, identify myself with some ideological facets, with bits and pieces of those systems, but can I do so with entire systems? Do my desires always belong only to the Other? In the sense that the Bolshevik wants to be a Bourgeois (having access to Western supermarkets, which was allowed for the nomenclature) and vice-versa, when the wealthy bourgeois dreams of the Revolution (Engels's case)? We know the case from Dostoyevsky's *Crime and Punishment* (1866), when the Bible takes on an entirely new meaning only when it is read in the boudoir (Raskolnikov's case).

The ultimate answer is that the Order is ambivalent, and the man in it is ambivalent. This ambivalence drives people to complete contradictions, and this thesis must be brought to its biological paradox, and conclude without any overreacting that the final desire behind every human social program is complete *annihilation of the humane* and a fall into total animalism–that paradox of "man into prosaicness," which Kierkegaard formulated for the first time through this event: "In Leipzig, a committee has been formed which, out of sympathy for the sad end of old horses, has decided to eat them!"[51]

Communist Artifacts

Nevertheless, there is something else in communist nostalgia and that is the capitalist demand to commercialize past aesthetics. At a working meeting about communist nostalgia in Berlin in 2007, I bought a piece of the Berlin Wall in the East Germany museum. Printed on it was: "Certified by West, Limex Bau, Export–Import. It is hereby certified that this grey segment pursuant to contract no. 08-999/10000/0038 of March 27, 1990 is an original piece of the Berlin Wall that marked the border between West Berlin and East Germany from 1961 until 1989."

That was my first communist prey. Although my friends made fun of me, personally, it didn't bother me that somebody was making some money on nostalgia (that is a fake problem), nor whether the wall was really certified (realistically speaking, even the original wall would not have been any more real for me than this stone). Five months ago, I met the same working group from the communist camp "Zanka" on Lake Balaton in Hungary, and with this group went through different camps and prisons of communist Germany and Hungary.

During one of the meetings, somebody suggested choosing Miss and Mr. Nostalgia, but the suggestion became a cruel joke when, all of a sudden, it somehow became clear to everybody that behind it hid not just an ordinary game of stereotypes, but an essential style identification. Without any conscious intention, the Russians and the Belarusians looked so retro, as if they had only recently taken straight from a communist joke–well, damn it, the Russians have always turned out to be the best communists. And I recalled Erofeyev's statement: "The absence of style is a terrible Russian whip. I don't know who designed the American uniform for the Second World War, but it was a super uniform. In it, everybody looked like a winner.... And the Russian Army uniform is pure stylistic misunderstanding... If somebody wears glasses, they are inconceivably disgusting. And the state elite! They put on suits, but didn't change the socks–they go and show off with short, turquoise ones. All the corruption in our country is a derivative of those socks... Or the intellectuals: They discuss Joyce and Borges, and they are dressed and combed like the Soviet–Soviets... It is impossible to invent a style out of nothing."[52] And then, isn't it that such stylistically perfect recognition arouses a new sympathy for their "fallen" ideological–stylistic solutions (who still likes winners today)?

At one of the meetings, we all agreed to bring an object that would identify our personal communism. Szabina from Hungary brought a video game with Peanuts' Snoopy, a gift from a relative who emigrated to America. "I have never had such a toy"–Rèka, also from Hungary, said. "That's why I brought it, this is a nostalgic status object," replied Szabina. Somebody suggested dividing us up into two groups–those who had never played with status toys to take them, and the children of the "nomenclature" to play with ours. I didn't bring my father's police file and Florijan from Romania, who worked on the topic "Romanian socialist terraces," didn't bring a piece from a communist terrace. I didn't have any objects older than 2001 at home, apart from old family photographs, so I brought a small statue of Tito, which I dug out of my father-in-law's basement, who was a former Yugoslav People's Army employee. In the end, I brought the pocket Tito in vain, because everybody started playing with Snoopy, so we didn't get to my communist object. This stupid social game is nonetheless not insignificant. In the course of these quasi-experiments, I came to the question of my past objects: Did I have any past that I wanted to call up through "my" object? Did I still want to listen to the music from (our) communist times? Did I like (our) past topics and films?

Nostalgic objects attract, they acquire new lives, and sometimes they grow legs and leave. Somebody suggested writing a "Manifesto for Release from Objects" as an extreme left idea of resistance to consumption to the nostalgic communist objects for sale today. At the time, that seemed wrong to me; five months later, I bought my first private Berlin Wall.

What does it mean–to release souvenirs from capitalist abuse? Not in the sense that it is a supreme communist gesture, but does that mean that capitalism "revolutionizes" the material conditions in order to exploit the communist past? There is one simple nothing in the place of that stone, and it is not the Berlin Wall–not because it is a stone, but because philosophy should re-define problems (not necessarily resolve them). Like the objects that trigger socialist nostalgia, this stone from the Berlin Wall is a fake problem. If this "Berlin" stone was the real problem, than we wouldn't need philosophy.

About Collective Guilt (Karl Jaspers)

How, then, can the former communist patient be aroused from his political anesthesia? How can he/she be expropriated from the dream (and not from the nostalgia) of the past? This is possible with a certain insight into the questions of responsibility in politics.

The shortest definition of politics is a public statement of judgment. Politics exists for the public, but paradoxically, only the actors in the events count in politics, which is particularly important for the so-called neutral citizens. It is a (pre-)condition to believe that collective guilt *doesn't exist*. The International Criminal Court of the United Nations Security Council for War Crimes in the Former Yugoslavia ruled in March 2007 that the former Federal Republic of Yugoslavia (a state that existed from 1992 to 2003) was not responsible for the genocide in the wars in Bosnia and Herzegovina at the beginning of the 1990s. In other words, The Hague found that one state, and one nation in particular, cannot be responsible for the crimes that that state committed in their name. The Hague decision confirms that collective guilt does not exist, similarly as there is no document in international law which says that the whole of Germany is responsible for the crimes of the Nazis, though there are many internationally binding legal documents in which Germany was judged liable to compensate for (pay off) the Nazi-related guilt; that alongside the fact that generations of Germans grew up with a feeling of collective guilt after the Second World War. Collective guilt has never been officially proclaimed, and I think that is important. I personally think together with their closest assistants, that only a certain percentage of the governing structures in a single state nomenclature should be considered guilty. The others are not guilty. There is no collective guilt, there is guilt that concrete people bear, people with names and surnames. Therefore, the following question is important: What happens to the public as recipient of politics?

Nancy Adler examines the work of Karl Jaspers, who in 1947 distinguished among four types of responsibility for healing society once the sobering process begins. The first type of responsibility is criminal–when there is a clear breaking of the law; the second is political–every person is responsible for the way he/she is ruled; the third is moral–"an order is an order" is an unacceptable dictum because the crime you commit remains the crime you commit, even if ordered by another. For Jaspers, the fourth type of responsibility is metaphysical responsibility; one person should be solidary with another: This is basic planetary metaphysics, and this is the real transcendence that is almost impossibly difficult. Everybody is co-responsible for the mistakes and for the injustice, and for not preventing or stopping the crime.[53] This means that (in general) collective guilt does not exist, and that the whole of society shouldn't be considered guilty. It is morally absurd to condemn people. Jaspers says there isn't a common feature for everybody who belongs to one group, to one ideology; that's why all the people shouldn't be politically accountable. But what the people need without exception, according to Jaspers, is political cleansing. And the victims are not the only ones who need this cleansing. Social cleansing means an *awareness of the guilt*, solidarity and co-responsibility. It is not the feeling that I am personally guilty, but it is a recognition of the mistakes made in the past by the system in and by which I lived. Political systems form a base for terror, but the terror is perpetrated by individuals, which means that you are responsible for *seeing* that the rule was unjust.

Bad Tito?

Where should the ideological healing begin? In the next three chapters, I have summed up several censored phenomena from the ex-Yugoslavia, (well) known to historians, but which are nonetheless worth repeating. If there was censorship in Yugoslavia, it was only applied to these four topic areas: 1. One mustn't attack the cult of Tito; 2. One mustn't write about Bleiburg and related events; 3. One mustn't question the way in which the Yugoslav Revolution happened in the Second World War; and 4. One mustn't write about national topics. Even Goli Otok (an infamous secret prison and labor camp in the northern Adriatic) wasn't an entirely forbidden topic–at least not after 1985. All other topics were relatively open to criticism, but precisely because only these four generally censored topics existed, they constitute the symptom upon which Yugoslavia was built. Any serious criticism must begin with these points of prohibition.

In a scene from the documentary, *Tito: The Post-Mortem Autobiography* (2003), by Russian director Sergey Kostin, Tito's personal doctor, Predrag Lalević, says that when the Marshal visited Hamburg, the Mayor of Hamburg raised his glass in a toast to the Marshal and asked him: "We know that 50 years ago, you were a worker in Germany, and I wonder, what would have happened if you had stayed here?" Tito replied: "I would have been the biggest capitalist of all." At the meeting in Napoli, in August 1944, Tito tells Churchill that he doesn't want to introduce communism in Yugoslavia. That is no mere game on the part of Tito in his dealings with Britain and Stalin. There is much evidence pointing to Tito as the biggest Yugoslav capitalist. Maybe the most absurd of the anecdotes was told by his personal chef, Jozef Oseli: when the Marshal fell into a coma, he was served cosmonaut food.[54] Some 1,000–1,500 people saw to Tito and his welfare, including bodyguards, technical personnel, cooks, teams of doctors, masseuses, tasters checking the food he ate, war technicians checking the facilities where he stayed, etc.[55] In 1968, Tito visited the opening of the Željava underground military air base (near the city of Bihać in Bosnia) for the first and last time, which cost 4 billion dollars at the time. The base took 10 years to build, had an infrastructure to support 1,000 people living and working there, and was destroyed in the Yugoslav wars in 1992 by the same Army that had built it.[56]

There are a lot of portraits of Tito–but which is the most accurate? Is he the creator of the idea of "socialism with a human face," the only living person on the planet to cross Stalin and stay alive? Or is he the biggest capitalist in his great factory of "Yugoslavia"? People from the former Yugoslavia find it hard to accept the phantasm about the bad Tito, and today they still eat up documentaries about Tito and listen to endless anecdotes about him. They still love him, almost unchanged. In October 2006, upon the celebratory occasion of 60 years of the victory over fascism, Branko Crvenkovski, then President of the Republic of Macedonia, proposed erecting a statue of Josip Broz Tito.

However, exactly one year later in October 2007, the German weekly magazine "Bild" published a list of the 10 biggest murderers of the 20th century. The honor of last place went to Josip Broz Tito. The magazine estimates that during his 35-year-rule in Yugoslavia, he killed one million people. Undisputed first place went to Mao Zedong with 50 million victims, the second to Stalin with 40 million and the third to Hitler with 20 million, while Lenin comes in fifth with 6 million, etc. Certainly, the right-wing "Bild" exaggerates: Hitler's bloody count is reduced to 20 million on account of doubling Stalin's to 40 million. Tito's body count is probably doubled too, but what about those half-million victims?

According to various sources, Tito is responsible for the liquidation of 450,000 to 600,000 political opponents. And these numbers represent a "low" estimate, given not having insight into the Yugoslav archives. Part of the files of the secret services of Yugoslavia were destroyed in the bunkers in Bosnia, though my father's file shows that intelligence records were re-sent to several authorities. If the central archives were destroyed, it is possible that not all of the municipal archives were destroyed with the same consistency. Taking into consideration the Soviet experiences before and after the opening of the Soviet archives, when the numbers of communist victims turned out to be far higher than the most fantastic estimates (after opening the Soviet archives, the number of Stalin's estimated 2.3 million victims rose to more than 20 million), it can be easily said that *Bild's* estimates of Tito's crimes may not have been right-wing exaggerations after all.

In the documents of the American Central Intelligence Service (CIA), which were declassified in August 2006, one letter to Truman states: "Tito killed more than 400,000 people of the opposition."[57] This information refers only to the first two decades of Yugoslavia, from 1945 to 1964. John Cabot, a CIA agent, sees Yugoslavia in 1947 before the Informbiro clash with the Soviet Union like this: "(The regime) is as suspicious, arbitrary, brutal, intolerant of opposition, fanatical and tortuous as the Russians…"[58]

The first victims of Tito's scheme fell during the Second World War. During the long decades that followed, Yugoslav generations studying Tito's partisan movement claimed the movement was massive. The truth is, Tito's Party had a mere 6,600 members and around 17,800 SKOJ members in October 1940, and only became massive in late 1943. Alongside the battle against the fascists, Tito led extensive battles to liquidate his rival, Draža Mihailović. Mihailović was also fighting against the Nazis, but unlike Tito, worked on the principle of sabotage and smaller actions against the Germans in order to avoid unnecessary losses for the civil population, as the German revenge was known to be particularly cruel. Mihailović's movement was far larger than Tito's, and neither Britain nor the Soviet Union supported Tito until 1943. They supported Mihailović's politics, primarily because he wanted to reinstate the King who was in exile in London.[59] Tito had another strategy: he wasn't out to avoid human loss, he'd been the leader of the left-wing Yugoslav Communist Party since 1937. But before 1943, the partisans were not numerous. The majority of people in the former Yugoslavia waited to see which course would prevail, Tito's or Mihailović's, and acted accordingly.

When the allies occupied Italy, Tito's partisan movement became massive,[60] making the occupation of Italy the single most important date in the history of Tito's rule. "Western politicians were inclined to solely blame Moscow for Tito's actions, but the historical documents show a completely different picture," Banac writes.[61] In 1943, Britain and not the Soviet Union, was the first to persuade the King to stop negotiating with Mihailović and make an agreement with Tito. Stalin only accepts Churchill's request, and recognizes the Anti-Fascist Council for the People's Liberation of Yugoslavia.

Once Tito came to power, he left his ultra-left position, says Banac,[62] and became more like Stalin. In 1943, after gaining the support of both Britain and the Soviet Union, Tito turns The Anti-Fascist Council for the People's Liberation of Yugoslavia (AVNOJ) into the core of his government and confers on himself the rank of Marshal. The Stalinization starts immediately. In early 1944, he warns the Croatian partisan printing office not to create the impression that there is a communist revolution going on in Yugoslavia, which of course, is a double game. Later, in his speeches, Tito compares anti-fascism with the Yugoslav Revolution, though at that time it seems clever of him to play along with Britain. Yugoslavia was seen as different from the Soviet Union because of this dualistic position, and later as well with the civil liberalization of the 1970s and 80s. However, this did not mean that society was any less restrictive.

"With Stalin Against Tito"

Tito reveals the first traits of Stalin and Stalinization in Yugoslavia after the Second World War. Stalinism, firstly and fundamentally, means uniformity. The most important characteristics of Stalinism, writes Ben Fowkes,[63] are control of the single political party, oligarchic rule in practice (the politburo makes all the decisions), the absence of the rule of law and the predominant governance of the security bodies. All of that exists in Yugoslavia. According to Ivo Banac, Yugoslavia is the closest to the Soviet model of party dictatorship, far more so than any of the other East European countries.⁶⁴ Unlike the East European countries that established coalition governments, Yugoslavia proclaims exclusive governance of the National Front from the beginning, and opponents of the party promptly begin to disappear. Unlike Yugoslavia, Hungary (in November 1945) and Czechoslovakia (in May 1946) organized truly free Parliamentary elections.

When elections were held in Yugoslavia in 1945, they resembled the classic "one-horse race." Voting against the National Front was possible, but candidates were not allowed to run against it. At any rate, a certain courage was needed to put the ball in the other box intended for those who voted against. In Slovenia, 17% did so.⁶⁵ A total of 9.25% votes went into the "black box," while almost 11.5% of voters appeared not to vote. The first Constitution of Yugoslavia was drawn up according to Stalin's Constitution of 1936, and was adopted in January 1946. Tito was crueler towards the opposition (true or false) than the measures implemented and doled out in either Poland or Bulgaria. A lot of ustash and cetniks were shot in the summer of 1945, while the countries of the Eastern Block accepted into the party ranks most everyone who repented. August Kosutić was the Vice-President of the Croatian Peasant Party, and although he voluntarily joined the partisans in 1944, he was later arrested– "The first example of communist repression directed towards an anti-fascist politician in East Europe in the last phases of the war," writes Banac.⁶⁶

During the event known as the Bleiburg massacre, Tito's partisans killed from "several hundred" to "200,000" prisoners of war and civilians (the second number is supported by Slovenian historians and by the Serbian researchers of the secret archives, including Marko Lopušina⁶⁷) who refused to surrender to the Partisans at Bleiburg, but were hoping, instead, to surrender to the British occupying forces. Contrary to the codes of international war, the British delivered them directly to Tito's forces; once they were marched back to various regions of Croatia, Slovenia and Serbia, they were shot en masse. When the former Slovenian communist official Mitja Ribičič defended himself in the 1990s, saying that KOS (The Counter-Intelligence service of the Yugoslav People's Army) carried out the liquidations without Tito's knowledge, he was refuted by the Slovenian OZNA officers (OZNA was the Department for Protection of the People with State Security Directorate) insofar as the liquidations lasted until 1953, and that all of the decisions were made by Tito.[68] Some 450 mass graves of these victims were later discovered in Slovenia, and to date, the remains of some 1,000 Croatian soldiers (who were killed as Partisan prisoners in 1945) have been disinterred from the Tezno forest (near the Slovenian city of Maribor). And that number comes from only one of the anti-tank trenches where they were thrown after being killed. Each trench is 1.5 km long, and the number of victims only refers to that part dug out as a single trench. To date, 70 meters from one of the 450 trenches have been dug out. In 2004, the German newspaper "Frankfurter Allgemeine Zeitung" published a piece on Tito's OZNA secret services, in which it stated that Yugoslavia never returned the looted estates to their Jewish owners, and Tito never visited Jasenovac (the largest concentration camp from 1941-45) during his entire 35-year-rule. According to historical documents, immediately after the liberation in 1945, between 15,000 and 30,000 people suffered political prosecution in Belgrade alone.[69]

The Yugoslav Army and the secret services were formed according to the Soviet model, with Soviet instructors who actively participated in the establishment of the Yugoslav state. According to Banac's research, one-third of the first generation of the Yugoslav Military Academy studied in Suji, in the Western part of Russia in the period from 1945-47.[70] In 1946, the Serbian communist Aleksandar Ranković took over the secret police OZNA (Department for Protection of the People with State Security Directorate),[71] and the first high-ranking victim was Agrarian party leader Jovanović, who questioned the rule of the Communist Party of Yugoslavia and was opposed to collectivization. Tito tells Ranković: "He has to be arrested," to which Ranković says: "It will be difficult to find anything on him," and Tito replies: "Then accuse him of anything."[72] Milovan Đilas, the most famous Yugoslav dissident, started talking about "the new class," the communist elite which is being created; paradoxically, Đilas's case indicates that only those who seriously took the term "classless society" suffered, while all opposition media were suspended until the autumn of 1945. The Yugoslav communists were the first in Eastern Europe to start a series of trials against the people of the church. These people were tried according to the determinant–spying for the West–which was interpreted in the widest possible sense. Yugoslavia was the first to put its own opposition from the lines of the National Front on the prosecution bench. In October 1947, for example, the process against the leader of the Serbian left farmers, Dragoljub Jovanović, began, even though his party was a pre-war communist ally.

Yugoslavia, the first to do so in Eastern Europe, launches processes against its own members–the so-called Dachau process (April, August 1948 and July 1949). In terms of its dimensions, it is a smaller trial process compared to that of Moscow 1939 (in terms of the number of accused and victims), but crueler in terms of the methods used.[73] Some 27 mid-rank communist officials, who were taken to the concentration camp at Dachau during the war, were tried–but now they were tried as Gestapo collaborators, the same principle Stalin used against all of its Soviet soldiers who had been arrested by the Nazis during the war. The ones who touched the "dirty" Nazi (the paradox is even greater–as Nazi victims) had become dirty themselves. Of these almost 30 officials, 11 were shot.

In June 1945, Tito still tolerated a multi-party system: "We are not against parties, especially as some of them already proved useful in collaboration with the National Front... We tell everybody who doesn't want to be in the Front; whoever wants to have their own party, they can have one and form one." This text was legally published in Belgrade, but when opponent Milan Grol resigns in August 1945, he explains: "A single party program is established and it excludes any difference of opinion."[74] At the 3rd Congress of the National Front in April 1949, Tito declares: "A member of the National Front cannot be a member of a political organization with a program contrary to the Communist Party program."[75]

Yugoslav communists also imitated the Soviet economic model, and were the first in Eastern Europe to nationalize the estates of anyone who was thought to be a "collaborator with the enemy," and this too was given the widest of interpretations. The Yugoslav Five-Year Plan of April 1947 was the first five-year plan in Eastern Europe, and is an exact copy of the Soviet one. Until 1952, 27% of the national income was to be invested in each year of the five-year plan, the number of experts was to be doubled, a smaller portion of land was to be collectivized and farmers were not to hold more than 35 hectares of land in order to avoid establishing a peasant bourgeoisie.[76] "The Communist Party of Yugoslavia took a hard hand towards the farmers,"[77] writes Banac. Apart from Bulgaria, no country in Eastern Europe was closer to the doorstep of a complete collectivization of agriculture than Yugoslavia. The Yugoslav farm cooperatives were the first forms of village collectivization, and by the end of 1948, there were 1,318 farm cooperatives, the most in Eastern Europe. When Tito sends his two close collaborators, Edvard Kardelj and Ivan Šubašić, to Moscow after the war, Stalin, much to Kardelj's amazement, discloses the percentage agreement with Churchill.[78] This agreement, according to which Yugoslavia would enjoy greater freedom than the other communist countries in relation to the Soviet Union, would later prove fatal to the Yugoslav version of Tito's Stalinist rule in Yugoslavia. According to Banac, it had "negative consequences for political pluralism in Yugoslavia," which ceased to exist from that moment on. Up to that point, Churchill's demand of holding free elections in Yugoslavia, where via a referendum the people would decide on future of the monarchy, was still in play.[79]

Goli Otok (or, Why Didn't Yugoslavia Fall Under Stalinist Rule?)

Goli Otok (literal translation: Barren Island), Yugoslavia's island prison camp in the northern Adriatic, is not a myth, but paradoxically, Goli Otok threw a mythic shadow of blindness on Tito's other victims, and it remained remembered in history as Tito's greatest crime. But this is far from the truth. Tito, particularly in the early decades of his rule, governed using Stalinist methods, and this is the reason he was the only man on the planet to cross Stalin and stay alive.

Tito almost certainly didn't have the strength to deal with any potential Stalinist aggression against the country. In order to study the possibilities of using the Yugoslav-Soviet crisis to their (the West's) advantage, American counter-intelligence drew the following picture of Yugoslavia in 1950: "Yugoslav armed forces could not... under any circumstances withstand a serious Soviet attack."[80] Ben Fowkes writes:

Why did Eastern Europe fall under communist rule? A simple,

rough answer is that Stalin wanted that and he could do it at the end of the Second World War. If Stalin didn't intervene in Yugoslavia in the early stages of its constitution, and left it under the Communist Party of Yugoslavia leadership, it is because he didn't want to, and not because he didn't have the strength to occupy it.[81]

Yes, but the question is, why didn't he want to? And the answer lies not in the quotas set out in the Stalin–Churchill agreement, but largely in Tito's rule that was based on acquiring power according to Stalin's model. Stalin saw Tito's independence as unbearable. He tried to use the Cominform[82] and infiltrate his people into the secret police, but when he didn't succeed, there was a furious exchange of letters between Stalin and Tito in March 1948, after which 12,000 out of the 470,000 members of the communist party of Yugoslavia were arrested and sent to Goli Otok.[83] The internal politics of Yugoslavia in the first few years was no different from those of the surrounding communist states, except that it was far more tyrannical than anything Eastern Europe had seen before. According to existing records, 55,663 people were tried because of their connection with the Informbiro, of which 12 were participants in the October Revolution, 36 were Spanish soldiers, 23 were republic and federal ministers, two were presidents and two vice-presidents of republic governments, 39 were deputy ministers, 36 were federal MPs, over 21,000 were participants in the National Liberation Movement in the Second World War, 1,673 were partisans from 1941, 4,153 were KPJ officials, 1,722 were policemen and some 2,600 were military officers.[84]

According to Ben Fowkes, the purges in the period from 1949-1953 differed from country to country. If we generalize, it was best to be a Muscovite (if you were in the Soviet Union during the Second World War) than elsewhere; and the most dangerous was if you were in the resistance at home—or even worse if you took part in the Spanish Civil War.[85] After 1949, the purges in Eastern Europe became far more sweeping than those in Yugoslavia. In Hungary, for example, the country of "soft dictatorship" and "goulash communism," 350,000 people were expelled from the party, 150,000 were imprisoned and 2,000 were killed. But Yugoslavia's early Stalinization driven by Tito's cruelty is the sole reason for the absence of a more fundamental resistance later. Using reverse logic, we could say today what the apologists of Goli Otok still offer–"If it hadn't been for Goli Otok, the whole state would have been Goli Otok,"[86] when in fact the exact opposite is true–because of the pedagogic force exerted on Goli Otok, the entire state became one big Goli Otok later.

The gulags were a socialist practice, but according to Michel Foucault, the idea was French. At the Criminologists' Congress in Saint Petersburg in 1894, a French criminologist suggested for the first time that the Russians use its vast, wild and uninhabited Siberia as a warehouse for its prisoners, and analogously, Yugoslavia, found such uninhabited land in its Adriatic islands.[87] The first prisoners were brought to Goli Otok in July 1949, and we know about life on this island in its most active period until February 1951, mainly from prisoners' testimonies. The first two groups had to perform physical labor, while the psychological torture began with the third group, which was forced to navigate through the so-called "columns"–the scariest part of prison life after April 1950. The so-called "warm rabbit" was a procedure, whereby prisoners had to go through two columns of crazed prisoners armed with sticks, who had to beat the new arrivals in order to show they had been retrained. According to various calculations, columns stretched from 500 to 1,500 meters, and there was a doctor at the halfway point who performed check-ups on prisoners to determine whether they could survive the column to the end, and even former generals were not spared the columns. Besides the columns, there were also rooms dedicated to beatings. Sometimes prisoners were beaten in circles, sometimes they played "barking at a light bulb," whereby several victims were bound together while the others beat them. At any rate, according to Ivo Banac, the most difficult aspects of life at Goli Otok were two other practices: one saw prisoners tortured with Sisyphian work, which meant that they had to carry stones from the quarry to the top of the hill until they heard the command to bring them back. The worst aspect of Goli Otok lay in the fact that the prisoners were, in principle, managing the camp themselves. The prisoners met their bullies in the faces of former prisoners, but they never met the commander of the camp in person. The prison was managed by a prison hierarchy, which meant that the columns were organized by former prisoners who were, at the same time, beaten and forced to beat. The least sign of hesitation to participate in the "warm rabbit" was interpreted as permissiveness towards the Informbiro bandits (which lasted from 1948 to 1955), and a sign that one was not completely converted. "You are clean only if you are active (in beating others),"[88] Banac says. One of the conditions for release from Goli Otok was keeping silent about the island. According to the information by Ranković, by November 1952, 7,039 former Informbiro prisoners had been released from Goli Otok. Only 1.9% of them had been brought back to Goli Otok until that date, which means that they neither talked about the island camp nor about the Informbiro.

Today, Goli Otok constitutes the biggest criticism of the Yugoslav Federation, and there is a general impression that this topic has been open for discussion in Yugoslavia for some indefinite period of time–at least as far back as the 1960s. But the first public statement referencing Goli Otok goes back no further than 1980. Note Svetozar Vukmanović Tempo's[89] statement from his last book of memoirs, *Memoirs: Campaign or Polemics* (1985), in which he explains why he didn't mention Goli Otok in any of the books of his "Memoirs" until 1985: "Not in order to avoid talking about it, but for the simple reason that I didn't know there was a camp for communists on that island. Of course, I knew that we arrested such communists, but I thought they served their sentences in (conventional) prisons."[90] This statement, whether true or otherwise, only serves to illustrate the extent of censorship surrounding Goli Otok. If, as a high-ranking member of the party leadership, Tempo knew and kept silent–and even if he didn't know–this only underscores the fact that a very small cadre made the decisions in Yugoslavia, and that the secret services (always) had the last word.

Goli Otok was closed in 1987 after the Winter Olympics in Sarajevo, after an article in the Slovenian magazine "Mladina" appeared in which Dobroslav Paraga published the first testimonies in Yugoslavia about the terror on the island.

But these "pieces of history" are not included here to reveal or relate the final truth about Yugoslav socialism over its many decades. Nor do they serve to clarify the reason for my father's communist fate. But what the defendants of the Yugoslav (consequently the Macedonian) communism could never clearly see was that our socialism (as with the other totalitarian ideologies of the 20th century, even in their softest versions, if we see Yugoslavia as such) was built on bloody foundations. All of the both smaller and larger blocks of prohibitions and victims were a derivation of those very foundations. Therefore, we go from the wider historic picture to the specific Macedonian mixture of communism and the small town– what did it consist of?

4

Poetry Between the Small-Town Mentality and the Secret Services

When I analytically approached my father's file for the first time, I had only the secret services on my mind. They soon proved insufficient in explaining the dimension of his communist Golgotha. When I tried to read the file solely from a small-town point of view, something was still missing–this time what was missing was the "secretive" police factor. It turned out that the file could only be read as a combination of the secret services and our small town.

UDBA Code Names

When the secret services were opening the police files, how did they come up with the code names? My father was "Intimist" to the police, which is undoubtedly a beautiful name, but how did my father become Intimist?

The answer lies in the way the small town operates when it gives nicknames to people. If somebody in a small town has a distinguished talent for something, or a physical flaw of any kind, that talent or flaw becomes a nickname, a feature by which that man differs–and is differentiated–from the others. But the talent is not stressed: "To be respected and honored, but to be mocked and to be in a way constantly before the eyes of the small-town spirit, which remembers everything, omits nothing, and leaves nothing unnoticed" as the Serbian philosopher Radomir Konstantinović writes in his famous study of the "spirit" of the small-town *Filozofija palanke (Philosophy of Provincialism)* from 1969.[1]

In communism, there is a similar small-town *dramatization* of a person. Nobody is special, actual, a living person, but he/she is a specialty elevated to a nickname, to a code name of the secret service. This man is the Intimist, the other is the Cruel, the third is the Lover, the fourth is the Blacksmith, the fifth is Death, etc. People became a simulation, emptied of their "full" contents, cubes on the communist table, cliche roles in the comedy del arte, which are scattered across the big stage of life, where the battle between Good and Evil is played out.

This comparison might appear strange: While the small town implies tyranny of the *public*, insight of everybody into everything, the secret police implies only *secrecy*. But, the paradox of this tautology is that the public is already incorporated, and implicitly materialized in the UDBA's life. The public was the basic essence of the secret police and it could only operate when it censored that function, only when it "hid" the axis around which the UDBA's desire revolved and found equilibrium.

Another similar example lies in the question of why gays weren't allowed in the Yugoslav's Peoples Army. Not because gayness posed an active threat to the phallocentric military power, Žižek writes, but because the solders in the Army were exactly connected by the "gay code" of manhood, that manly–brotherly closeness which guarantees social cohesion in the army.[2] Censorship always misses its point, not because censorship impacts an enhanced marginal force status, but because censorship creates a schism in the power of the social group. Censorship reveals precisely why the system was built. In the case of the UDBA, the reason for the existence of a secret service was the public in all its best small-town ways. In order for the UDBA to function, it needed all of the public, all of the neighbors and colleagues you had coffee with. The service "remained" secret because it had the widest public platform.

The secret services were *diligent* in the same way that the small town was constantly employed as the "godfather's spirit which never gets tired," says Konstantinović on provincial mentality.[3] The secret police "incorporated" people in its theater; in a symbolic table of values, one code name became intertwined with another, and thus, the world of the secret police was an endlessly repetitive system. It was not a real system, but it was vital. The UDBA always found a reason to go back again to the lower spheres, among the people, because it loved everyday routine in its purest stupidity, in the most banal triviality. Consequently, the paradox: When people open their secret files, their most frequent comment is that their files are full of the biggest banalities, trivialities which the secret service archived most pedantically, when instead everybody expected to see "heroic," hidden details in them.

The secret police coded people in order to create a *live theater*, a simulation of life. People were not *these* actual people, but an abstraction of "pure" contents–the "Intimist," the "Cruel," the "Blacksmith," etc. The man was not an individual man, but part of the communist table, as the person *interpreted* his/her role without knowing it. The Romanian dissident Serbulescu wrote: "In the Socialist Block, people and objects exist *only* through their files. Our entire existence is in the hands of those who own the files, and is formed by the one who composes them. Real people are just a reflection of their files."[4] We can find a perfect example of this radical theatricalization of life in the first years of Soviet communism. When the third anniversary of the October Revolution was celebrated in Petrograd, the celebration, which was entitled *The Storming of the Winter Palace* (1920) and directed by Nikolai Evreinov, resembled mass theater. The performers included 10,000 participants from the Army and Navy, those same soldiers and sailors who actually participated in the 1917 Revolution, and behaved towards the Winter Palace as towards a "giant actor."[5] Some 100,000 people from the audience (1/4 of Saint Petersburg's population at that time) took part in this live theater, and the "acting" of the Revolution was performed in the same place that the Revolution had actually taken place three years before. Suzan Buck-Morss quotes the famous Russian formalist, Viktor Shklovsky, when she says: "Some kind of elemental process is taking place where the living fabric of life is being transformed into the theatrical."[6] The elementary process Shklovsky talks about is the transformation of the person into a symbol–not an abstract art symbol, but live human material. This means that the aestheticization of politics implies a formal distinction and separation of the person proper and the theatrical version of the person.

Similarly, this was the fate of the Slovenian communist revolutionary Jože Jurančić during the Second World War. After the capitulation of Italy in 1943, he led the rebellion of the Yugoslav prisoners in the concentration camp on the island of Rab in Croatia, where 2,000 starving prisoners disarmed 2,200 Italian soldiers. After the war, Jurančić was arrested by the communists and sent to Goli Otok, and while there in 1953, he mobilized with his Goli Otok inmates to build a monument for the celebration of the 10-year anniversary of the Rab rebellion; in other words, he mobilized to build a monument to himself.[7] The message is that this man was not an actual man. He was not Jože Jurančić, leader of the Rab rebellion. He was any communist, anybody else could just as well have been Jože. There is no individual act, every act is performed by the community. And this is precisely the reason why it was possible to develop such a cult of personality in communism–only in a culture without individuality does the leader acquire the position of a Person, he becomes a person for everybody else. The leader becomes a director: Totalitarian leaders act towards life as towards a big scene. Hitler was like a film director, he wanted to destroy decadent European civilization; Stalin wanted to make the world a "complete work of art," and so on.[8]

Why did communism want to turn live, human tissue into a theatrical one? The answer lies in the concept of "permanent Revolution" (developed by Marx and Engels between 1845 and 1850). When Marx predicted 15, maybe 50 years of civil war to the proletariat, Mao Zedong was prepared to go further and said that in the name of constant Revolution he was ready to accept the eradication of half of modern humanity in a nuclear war.[9] We will be in a state of permanent revolution only if/once life is turned into a massive theater. Ultimately, what is wanted from revolutionary emotion is the complete sadistic destruction of everything that exists. The frames from Eisenstein's film *October* (1927), in which the soldiers enter the wine cellars of the Winter Palace and break the expensive bottles of wine, were soon treated in Russia as historic, documented scenes of the Russian Revolution. Buck-Morss writes: "When later Soviet generations 'remembered' the October Revolution, it was Eisenstein's images they had in mind."[10] There is no difference between the excess of the euphoria of the theater/film and the one the Revolution wanted. Therefore, the most accurate definition of the revolutionary is Bakunin's: "The bandit is the first and only revolutionary in Russia."[11] Incidentally, Bakunin was not alone in equating the revolutionary with the bandit–see how Marx eulogizes the production capacity of the criminal to absurd excess in the 4th volume of "Capital":

The criminal produces not only crimes but also criminal law, and with this also the professor who gives lectures on criminal law... The criminal moreover produces the whole of the police and of criminal justice, constables, judges, hangmen, juries, etc. Torture alone has given rise to the most ingenious mechanical inventions, and employed many honorable craftsmen in the production of its instruments... He produces not only books on criminal law, but also art, belles-lettres, novels, and even tragedies... The criminal breaks the monotony and everyday security of bourgeois life. In this way, he keeps it from stagnation... Would locks ever have reached their present degree of excellence had there been no thieves? Would the making of banknotes have reached its present perfection had there been no forgers?[12]

The Revolution must be ecstatic about the principle of banditry, of crisis; everything should collapse and this should create immeasurable joy. In a letter to Marx, Engels wrote: "I feel the same as you do. When there was a crash of the stock exchange in New York, I couldn't find peace in Jersey, I felt excellent because of the general collapse. The crisis will help my organism like swimming in a sea. That's exactly how I feel."[13] Marx tells him: "Dear Engels! It is now that I received your letter, which uncovers all the pleasant perspectives of the economic crisis."[14] In another: "The American crash is superb and not yet over by a long shot. That means that, for the next three or four years, commerce will again be in a bad way. This is our chance *(Nous avons maintenant de la chance.).*"[15] Similarly, Mao Zedong's was joyful about crises: "Everything is falling apart, so everything is ok." Crises are good for the organism. Revolution should teach people to "dream radically," to demand the impossible (in the sense of the May 1968 motto: "Be realistic. Demand the impossible."), which senses or prophesies its final goal–a type of monumentality in which life becomes theater, and vice versa. In 1917, Lenin counted the days to prove that the Soviet Revolution would last longer than the Paris Commune, but if the revolution is similar to perfect theater, what happens the proverbial "morning after" when, as Žižek says, the revolutionary wakes up and starts to approach "the prosaic work of social reconstruction?"[16]

The realism of "the day after" is paralytic, and shows that the theater simply mustn't stop. When Tito visited Macedonia in 1978 for the 16th and last time, he was greeted by 400,000 Skopje citizens (almost the entire population of Skopje at that time), and the Marshal held a euphoric toast in the Parliament of the Socialist Republic of Macedonia: "Hundreds of thousands of citizens have been uninterruptedly standing on the streets for two days. What does that mean? It means we are on a good path."[17] In his book, *Tito for Macedonia, Macedonia for Tito* (2005), the Macedonian historian Petar Karajanov exultantly concludes: "This (euphoria–my comment) could not have been designed by any masterful protocol, nor by any order by the state or party bodies. It was a spontaneous expression of people's feelings."[18] And he's right. An event of such proportions could only be orchestrated by the complete dramatization of life in Macedonia. Theater has that *tension*, that surplus emotional excess that is desired by any revolution. When Tito gave his first interview for the Macedonian media in 1972, he explained how he felt when he visited Skopje, Kumanovo and Tetovo: "When a person passes by and looks at the joyous faces of the people, he has the impression as if these were the *days after liberation*... People were standing on the streets for three, four days when we passed by (my emphasis)."[19] It took Tito an entire 27 years after the Revolution to grant the Macedonian press an interview, but what is more interesting is that even so long *after* the Revolution, people delivered the revolutionary emotion to the leader as if "these were the days after liberation"–the masses were ready to play the revolutionary theater long after the actual revolution.

How is this possible? The answer is to be found in the secret services. When the Slovenian communist leader, Edvard Kardelj, criticized the Yugoslav masses in 1977, that continuous revolution didn't mean "pronouncing the word revolution with three R's,"[20] he explained how the continuous revolution should look like every day: "The Party *should always be there, where the masses are active*"[21] (Kardelj's emphasis). Kardelj's idea is possible only through the secret services, which constantly "dramatized" the massed, they divided it by roles and sub-roles, by groups of actors who constantly *acted* at being in the revolution. In those divisions, a lot of citizens got code names and files, and this concept found its final realization in Mao Zedong's thesis that a *cultural revolution* (whatever that means) is a condition for each revolution; the cultural (permanent) revolution now has to be a radical revolution, never sufficient in emotional scope and force, and it can be stabilized, effected, only through small-town methods. Tito said the same thing in the aforementioned interview for the Macedonian daily "Nova Makedonija" in 1972, when he saw the *military* euphoria on the faces of the Macedonians: "Every communist must be aware that he is *a soldier of the revolution...*, constantly bearing in mind that the people are looking at him (my emphasis)."[22]

The most popular children's game in Yugoslavia was "Take it Easy," a kind of projection of life in the barracks. If chess is a game of kings, an issue of control and power, "Take it Easy" was a kind of preparation for future soldiers, for the massive military psychosis and for directing revolutionary theater. Josip Broz Tito's favorite saying was as follows: "We live as if there will be peace for 100 years, but we prepare ourselves as if there will be war tomorrow" (Unlike the games reproducing the idea of the permanent revolution, there were also children's games in Yugoslavia, such as "The Brotherhood of the Tree Group," utopias about the ideal child community, which had everything it needed–a yard, a wooden house, a tree and a caring sister as a parallel universe, a capitalist sentimental projection about an *intimate* place for "us," contrary to the theatricalization of the revolution). Immanuel Wallerstein writes that although Marx predicted that the first communist revolutions would occur in the most technologically developed countries, the successful conquering of power happened only in the world's most pheripheral economies–Russia, Eastern Europe and China.[23] It's not by chance that communism only succeeded in semi-developed states, states with a small-town mentality and (semi)feudalism–and the very success of the communist revolution depended *precisely* on the secret services, which suited the small-town spirit perfectly.

According to Konstantinović, the small town has "an urge for the "story not heard so far," for the secret which is disclosed and revealed."[24] The small town constantly sheds light on peoples' secrets, the lives behind those secrets and on intimacy. The small town loves the story because of the story itself. It doesn't know why it tells and retells all of the gossip about its people. The gossip is told without any deeper aim, except to exhaust the need for experience–when I'm relating some gossip about somebody else, it is as if I am living it. At the same time, while I'm relating it, I neutralize the danger in the story. Hence, I conclude that life is not restless, not tragic. In the urge for gossip, the small town is anti-tragic, the gossip is told in order to say that there is no reason for anxiety. We stand firmly on the ground. And when we accept the temptations which life brings, we look at life with bright eyes. Communism was based on a similar philosophical optimism. Any kind of tragedy is driven away from our lives, the restlessness of the metaphysical is finally calmed; but a condition for rationality and sobriety (in communist jargon: dialectic materialism) is to establish a service that will know all of the secrets. The Secret Police (the middle name of all totalitarian regimes) were most successful where there existed a base of citizens who *provincially* supported the (rightness of) insight of everybody into everything.

Secret services operate secretly, but their network is comprehensive only in its dependency on public cooperation. Thus, the connection between the small town and the police state is established most naturally. The proof is Soviet Russia, which shouldn't confuse us with its magnitude–a small town is something inherent to *mentality, not territory*! The secret services of Soviet Russia directly saddled on to the previous practice of insight into (intercepting and reading) everyone's personal letters. Ever since Tsarist Russia, Donald Rayfield writes, personal letters of its citizens were read with astonishing determination. And in 1882, perlutrators (personal letter readers) individually read 28,000 private letters per year,[25] which was almost as much as the total number of letters sent (although according to the law this was illegal, as it was illegal later according to the Soviet Constitution). Based on this smalltown logic of insight into everything, Soviet Russia soon became a rare case of primordial belief in the banal–everything became important. Towards the end of 1923, 5,000,000 personal letters and 8,000,000 telegrams were read by the GPU each year; of these, each snitch (perlustrator) read 250 personal letters and 2,500 telegrams per day.[26] The system was developed in such a way that anyone who wrote mail had to be certain that they would be read by the services. As a result, Soviet Russia became a place of the most concrete embodiment of the small-town desire for omniscient insight into everything.

Lenin was the creator of the first Soviet secret service, the Cheka. The first unit of the Cheka was established at the peak of the Revolution in order to protect the revolutionary headquarters in Petrograd, but on December 20, 1917, the Cheka acquired a far larger executorship, and in February 1918, it was authorized to kill without interrogation and without trial. Inside two months, in September and October 1917, Lenin killed approximately 10,000 people, more than all the people killed over an entire century in Tsarist Russia. By June 1918, just eight months into the Revolution, every part of the Soviet Empire had its own Cheka service. Even the pro-Bolshevik lawyers were terrified by the fast growth of the secret services of the Soviet Revolution. Only two years after the Revolution, the Cheka amounted to over 20,000 armed men and women from different backgrounds, who, if they weren't recruited out of enthusiasm, participated out of panic–it was better to be Cheka than not. Rayfield writes that in Petrograd, the head of the Cheka was replaced every few weeks,[27] and nobody knew if he would still be alive tomorrow. One of the slogans of the early Soviet Union read, "Welcome to the Red Terror." Inside a very short time, the Cheka had over 300,000 paramilitary forces, which protected the Revolution. In 1918, Lenin and Trotsky opened the first concentration camps, and Trotsky loudly proclaimed Lenin's agenda: "Human life doesn't have a holy character," which paved the way for the "Nazification" of the communist universe.

The Yugoslav symbiosis of small town and communism ended with a similarly tragic outcome. Radomir Konstantinović's masterful study, *Philosophy of Provincialism* (1969), was not only a comprehensive analysis of the Yugoslav provincial mentality, but also a visionary book. The last two chapters of the book, entitled "Poetics of Serbian Nazism" and "Serbian Nazism and Language," proved that on the basis of his philosophical analysis, the Serbian philosopher Konstantinović foresaw what would happen with the disintegration of Yugoslavia in 1989–the small town (in combination with communism) ended in the bloody Nazification of Yugoslavia.

Humor

When I talked about my father's file on a television show, one of the guests told me during the commercial break that he too had a communist file, as my father had. But what did he do with the file? Nothing. When he read it, he decided to laugh because the file was not to be taken seriously.

Humor is the second common element between communism and the small town. Radomir Konstantinović writes that when a person gets a nickname in a small town, he should laugh at his nickname with the same intensity as those who created and conferred it, because if a person doesn't laugh, then he confirms that he is an object of the small town, and he must endlessly remain in the game.[28] Therefore, the only laugh in the small town is the *sarcastic laugh*, it can never appear as free laughter. And it's the same with communism. Here is one joke about the communist camps: One prisoner tells the other–"I got 10 years, what about you? I got 15. What did you get 15 for? For nothing. Listen–the first replies–if you want us to be friends, we have to be honest with each other. In order to get 15, you must have done something. Ten years is the sentence for nothing."[29]

The desperation that grows out of the cruelty of the communist system is overcome with sarcasm, as the person puts him/herself not only in the position of victim, but also in the position of being "included in the game," even in a kind of a nomenclature. You look at your file and it does not cause revolt, but laughter. Thus, you don't admit there is a difference between you and *them*, you save yourself with the cunningness of choice. You choose to be cunning, to "conclude" that the system isn't so terrifying after all. Nevertheless, the paradox is that the choice to be cunning and to laugh at the system isn't yours, that choice has already been made. The system is constructed in such a way that with laughter you only harmonize your place in the system, you accommodate better, you approve it all the better and you integrate better. A small town is a theater of nicknames, they are given to provoke mockery. In order to say there isn't essential tragedy in life, everything is a form of humor. Paradoxically, theater is played out in order to prevent the tragedy, as you must play yourself so that true emotion will never surface. If you play yourself, you are always alienated from the point of true pain, you become a mirage of yourself, and nothing hurts you. Like the small town, communism also transforms people into actors. When they play themselves, they are separated from their being so that nothing will hurt them. Communism loves rationality–reason is a tool against tragedy, and against metaphysical restlessness. Tragedy is for fools, as only the fools can be deceived. The communist chases existence, and then they try to outsmart each other. Hence, the person in communism becomes an artificial person, a person outside the tragedy. He/she doesn't have a face but a mask, and nothing can hurt the mask.

And at any rate, humor has a complex value. If you say: "I don't like communism," that rigid sentence drives away those who might still display some empathy. Humor makes it easier to persuade people to make a re-appropriation of their previous experiences. Could this be the reason why the best anti-Nazi films–Ernst Lubitsch's, Charlie Chaplin's and Roberto Benigni's–were (dark) comedies? Like Nazism, communism saw its most beloved portraits drawn in films; the first such was the warm *Goodbye Lenin* (2003), one of the first humorous East German films that didn't portray the sacrificial side of communism, and brought nostalgia back into pop-culture in a big way. Before *Goodbye Lenin*, there was Hausmann's naïve *Sonnenallee* (1999), a story about 17-year-old Misha, who listens to forbidden rock music, goes to parties and has troubles winning the affection of Mirijam, who is in a relationship with a boy from West Berlin.

Even so, there is something else here. The German weekly "Der Spiegel" claimed *Sonnenallee* presented an idyllic and false picture of life in the DDR, and Slavoj Žižek wrote similarly about Benigni's portrait of Nazism in *Life is Beautiful* (1997). In Benigni's film, father and son are prisoners in a Nazi death camp, and the father starts building an imaginary world in order to protect his child from the horrors of the reality. Benigni's message was that innocent humor can defeat radical evil. Žižek asks: What was good in Benigni's father? And answers, behind the polite mask, that the father hid the infinitely brutal order, not letting his child grow up. "The real horror for the child would be to have a psychotic father like Benigni,"[30] says Žižek. With his protective mask, the father doesn't protect children from the sadism of the world. He only dons the mask to hide his children from the excessive sadistic pleasure embedded in patriarchy. The representation of the 20th century father achieved its "political" goal–total paralysis of resistance, and herein lies one of the basic lessons of psychoanalysis. Benigni's father built a world of false consolation, an invented world, to hide the catastrophic sexual, political and family relationships in two of the most sacrificial ideologies of the 20th century–communism and Nazism. While everyday life is radicalized to terrible sadism, the worst variant is to adopt the mask of an illusory absence of trauma, and in turn place it on the children. The political lesson is then precisely the opposite. Parents must tell their children where the brutality of the system lies, they have a responsibility to help their children see where the political evil lies, and consequently where the potential for resistance is to be found.

The main argument of the black humor proposes that communism shouldn't be taken too seriously–don't accord it some monstrous strength, one which that system, in the end, didn't really have (as if the number of one hundred million victims weren't monstrous enough. And it wasn't–communism could always have done better). Thus, "Der Spiegel" was right, in that humor is most often used as a crutch for infantilism and playing "dumb" before the sadism of the world. We know from psychoanalysis that repeating a single topic–for instance, the communist–isn't a decision; when you go to return to a topic you do that more out of compulsion, on the principle of traumatic neurosis. When people open a topic with humor, they open it only to remove the place that was left censored. This may be partially true for humor itself. No matter how sarcastically communist citizens laughed at their system, it is a fact that communism always turned out to be bloodier than they could outlaugh it. Communism didn't like jokes. In Stalin's time, some 200,000 people were imprisoned for telling jokes,[31] and humor was kept as a weapon for *oneself*. In a letter to Kugelmann in 1867, Marx wrote: "The only policy we have to stand for now is the silence, until our enemies start speaking. When they start speaking…, then we should tell cheap jokes."[32] The policy of jokes against the enemies suggests that humor is never naïve. This is also true for the humor afterwards: After the fall of communism, the first true sympathies emerged in the form of funny portraits of communism. Communism becomes a desired good only because (at the moment) it is already dead. When a person today remembers communism with a shade of humor, he/she partially releases the place which was censored there, the place of the laughter itself, as he/she replaces the former sarcasm with capitalistic laughter, which is also not naïve. Capitalism installs robots who laugh at sitcoms in order to train the audience, and we naïvely see the laughter as a kind of "earthquake" in the order when the signifiers get mixed (as when a professor farts in class it is funny, because some release of the signifying chains occurs there); but the thing is that capitalism isn't naïve when it uses humor–as Marx too was not–the laughter is a powerful weapon, and where possible, laughter is regularly instrumentalized.

Poor, Clean and Sensitive

A small town fosters the ideal of cleanness and poverty, embodied in the maxim "poor, but clean." The secret services liked this conjunction, as the list of enemies included the rich and the "unclean." In 1918, Lenin makes the first list of two categories of citizens to be wiped off the face of the Earth: the bourgeois and the "irresponsible" (the second, quite ambiguous category literally covered everybody, mostly workers and peasants), and he delivers the list to the first secret services. When somebody suggests in February 1918 that Lenin rename the "Ministry of Justice" the "Ministry of Social Extermination," Lenin discards it as a good but not well formulated thesis–though the bottom line of Lenin's project was precisely the *sanitation* of the world (social extermination), and the clean form should be filled afterwards with "new" people. The secret services supported the small-town ideal of cleanness in another sense as well. The recruits of the first Soviet secret service, the Cheka, were sought from among those with "brave hearts, cool heads and clean hands."[33] Gerhard Gehlen expressed this best: "The work of the spy, that second oldest craft in the world, is so dirty that it can be performed only by the cleanest people."[34] The leader of the Cheka, Felix Dzierżyński, becomes an example for all future leaders. He worked day and night, and like Stalin, lived an ascetic life. He ate tea and bread, worked in an unheated office and covered himself with his coat; he cherished the ideal of poverty, asceticism and control, which the small town liked as well.

Konstantinović writes: "The small-town spirit is appalled by wealth, it will sometimes… mention a word about its poverty, it will even complain about it, but that complaint about its own poverty shouldn't be believed: It likes that poverty, and *it must like it* like uniformity is liked."[35] Small-town life implies routine, and Dzierżyński (like Stalin) didn't like shocks, the cult of cleanness referred to the objects of the material world, but also to the ideals; therefore, Dzierżyński pushed away even the slightest idea of transformation, in the sense that only uniformity is innocent. Finally, like Stalin, Dzierżyński left the dirty work of killing to others. Dzierżyński personally killed only a drunken sailor who swore at him; the rest of the work was done by the combination of the small town and the secret services. The secret services were required to work without any great emotional shocks; instead of emotions, sentimentality was preferred, the same sentimentality attributed to the small town "sympathy" of those closest to you. Today, it seems strange that the small-town sentimentality found its ideal continuation in the most cold-blooded murders of the secret services, although they shared similar tastes. The first man of the Soviet secret service, Dzierżyński, only read Polish romantic poetry and Marxist treatises. In his free time, even Marx only read romantic novels by Paul de Kock, widely popular in his time, which he justified by saying that he read them in order to know the taste of the workers. Dzierżyński liked the pallid Universe of melodramas and chansons, and Rayfield quotes Lockhart as follows: "There was nothing in (Dzierżyński's) character to indicate the inhuman monster he is commonly supposed to be. He told me that he suffered physical pain every time he signed a death sentence."[36] This type of behavior is common in the small town. When the small town torments its victims, it expresses an immediate surge of sympathy together with the victims. Not only that, in return the small town asks for an understanding of its sadism from the victim. But like empathy, the understanding is only an illusion–both are outside the realm of experience. The small town performs them because it is already previously abstracted from the emotional realm; the small town lives a life under masks, the man is transformed into a theatrical version of a man, and consequently sentimentality is a replacement for the essential empathy.

Poetry Between the Small-Town Mentality and the Secret Services 115

The small-town spirit of the secret services can turn against the leader of the services because the collective spirit is greater than each individual. The former factory director, later one of the most successful of Lenin's diplomats, Leonid Krasin, wrote about his leader: "Lenin has become quite insane, and if anyone has influence over him it is only Comrade Feliks Dzierżyński, an even greater fanatic and, in essence, a cunning piece of work who scares Lenin with counter-revolution and the idea that this will sweep us all away, him first. And Lenin, I am finally convinced, is very much a coward, trembling for his own skin. And Dzierżyński plays on that."[37] Although Lenin was initially against Dzierżyński's idea of destroying all of the counter-revolutionaries, after he was hit by a bullet on August 31, 1918 (it is first thought that the assassin was the anarchist Fanny Kaplan, but was later confirmed that it was Kannegiser), the Cheka's activities escalate and the next three years sees orgies of killings, and an explosion of criminal sadism spreads throughout Lenin's empire. The Cheka's murderers begin acting independently, and when Dzierżyński approves the killing of 500 people in Moscow, a Cheka operative, Gleb Bokii, kills 1,300 people by himself. In 1918, Lenin considers introducing the practice of hanging so that people will have the opportunity to contemplate the corpses.[38] Women also participated in these killings with the same intensity, and Rozalia Zemliachka, Béla Kun's lover, kills approximately 50,000 White Army officers with Lenin's approval. Zemliachka, who was educated in Kiev and at the Sorbonne, burned the officers alive in pairs, and managed to enjoy a quiet retirement.

According to Rayfield, what makes the beginnings of Lenin's secret services different from those of Hitler and Stalin is that the purges in the period from 1918-1922 were: (1) Class oriented and not racial, (2) The majority of survivors never had the opportunity to tell their experiences to the West, and (3) The papers of the secret services from this period were destroyed more systematically than they were later (as Stalin said "Winners are not put on military trial."[39]). The enormity of the crimes from the time of the first secret services is estimated today largely from census records of the time. In the period from 1914-1917, less than three million people were killed in the war, while between 1917 and 1920, the population in European Russia alone drops a whole six million (5% of the population); and there are also proportionate statistical disappearance rates in the populations of the Ukraine, Belarus and the Caucasus regions.

One of the best-known Lenin-related anecdotes says that when he was listening to the music of Beethoven he started to cry, but stopped himself abruptly and said that he couldn't allow himself surface sentiments because that made him appear to be weak. (Well known is the case of the German publicist Schlamm, who was rejected from the high communist structures in 1919 because of his pronouncement: "I am prepared to give everything for the party, except for two evenings a week, when I listen to Mozart."[40] In the Soviet version of communism, there are no hobbies and no music; the Party is a profession–and a hobby, and music.) Lenin's critics use this anecdote to prove and analyze his cold self-control and cruelty, but for Žižek it is proof of his humanity–he must keep his sensitivity under control in order to lead the political battle.[41] And he offers a reverse parallel between Leninism and Nazism: The highly ranked Nazi combines musical sensitivity with horrible cruelty without any problem whatsoever. After a "tiring day" of killings, Holocaust architect Heinrich enjoyed relaxing with Beethoven. Without any problem, he combined high culture and political barbarism because he abstracted himself emotionally, while Lenin had to suspend his love of music because he was still searching for an exit from the irreconcilable antagonism between art and the political battle. Nonetheless, both of these interpretations are incorrect. Lenin's suspending of (his) emotions isn't a matter of he, otherwise a cruel man, having to exercise self-control (the critics), nor because he, an otherwise sensitive man, had to be emotionally abstracted (Žižek). Stalin (like Hitler) was an extreme ascetic: With half the world under his rule, he lived in a simple room and slept on an uncomfortable bed; he had little interest in physical pleasures, he ate simple food, didn't appreciate luxurious tastes (and always checked whether his food was poisoned), and almost never drank or smoked–the well-known pipe a mere prop, a pose.[42]

Do these suspended emotions mean that Hitler was less of a sadist than Heinrich, and Stalin less of a sadist than Trotsky (the latter was an artistically disturbed soul, a sometime lover of Frida Kahlo's, proof of "humanity" in Trotsky the revolutionary)? Sadism emerged alongside the disciplining of the emotions (Lenin, Stalin, Hitler). On the other hand, in the Yugoslav and Asian communism, we find the cases of the shameless Kim Il-sung and Tito–extreme hedonists, with all of the decadence of a real leader. They didn't think they should act out the historic "modesty" together with the masses. (This included the rest of the upper Yugoslav command: It is well-known that Sarajevo's airport was closed for four hours because the Bosnian communist leader Dzemal Bijedić was learning to ride a bicycle.) In the past few years, Slovenian philosopher Slavoj Žižek has made great efforts to suggest the merits of Leninism (and generally of communism) to Western academia by publishing the critical papers of Lenin, Trotsky and Mao Zedong as an alternative to global capitalism. And Žižek differentiates communism and fascism as follows: 1. There is no fascism with a human face, there is only socialism with a human face. 2. The fascist leader accepts his audience's applause coldly, while the communist leader starts applauding together with the mass as a message that he, like the audience, is "material of history." 3. From Marcuse, Žižek takes the general idea that while socialism still represents civilization, fascism is beyond civilization–it is on the other side of civilization (we cannot contradict this point). But, while Žižek's analysis doesn't explain why Leninism is a good choice (according to various sources, Lenin alone is responsible for the death of five to seven million people), it does, however, propose that communism was an era of *suspended emotion*.

Communist leaders were elitists. According to Rayfield, the most common mistake of researchers on Stalin is their underestimating how educated he was. Stalin was a phenomenal, careful and dangerous reader.[43] He was familiar with 20,000 books in his personal library, and by the age of 30 had read piles of classics, including Western and Russian literature, philosophy and political theory. He read up to 500 pages on days when he was not active, left notes in the margins of the books he read, and although he complained of holes in his memory, he could remember phrases and arguments from books years later. A copy of Dostoevsky's *Brothers Karamazov* (1880) was among the books that were not looted from Stalin's library. Stalin underlined the sentence where Father Zossima considers active love: "Active love in comparison with dreamy love is a cruel and terrible thing."[44] For Stalin, loving the people actively was disgusting. Love, hate, trembling and fear are all reduced to the level of small-town sentimentality.

When he (the leader) is an ascetic (Stalin, Lenin, Hitler) and when he is a hedonist (Tito, Kim Il-sung), the small-town ideal of sensitivity "abstracts" the leader from empathy for (his/the) people. In a letter to Marx, even Engels writes: "The masses are terribly stupid."[45] The socialist thinkers were horrified by the masses, particularly the peasants. On the covers of his book, Mellier left the following note: "I got to know the delusions, abuse, vanity, stupidity and baseness of people. I hated them and despised them,"[46] and of the peasants he wrote: "It is fair to say there isn't anything more rotten, more primitive, nothing more worthy of contempt than the meek peasants."[47] Fourier said that: "(I)n their extreme primitivity, (they) are far more similar to animals than people."[48] The leader hates the masses and is "tired of sympathizing" with them. Although Lenin declaratively claimed that, "Clever idealism is closer to clever materialism than stupid materialism,"[49] in all of the versions of communist rule what governs, to the contrary, is the stupid materialistic mathematics, which is the double small-town face: The leader is "separated" from the banality of the world in *elitism*, but in his elitism he separates (and doubles) exactly this small-town sensitivity; sensitivity towards the people ends the moment a person faces the world, which simplified the aristocracy of the spirit. The aristocracy of cheap emotions is common to both the leader and small town alike.

The Hysteria and the Industry of Files

Freud tells us that culture asks too much from us, and he establishes a difference between the principle of pleasure and reality. In reality, there are but a few sources of pleasure, every inner urge for pleasure is regularly followed by denial and constraint. Therefore, perception regularly takes on the forms of hallucination–I have to *deceive myself* that there is still some pleasure in the world. This distorted perception is the best explanation for the hallucination following the October Revolution. In 1920, at the celebration of the three-year anniversary, and upon witnessing the collapse of the country, Trotsky appears before an audience and most earnestly announces: "If then, three years ago, we had the opportunity to look ahead, we wouldn't have believed our eyes."[50] The formula *eyes that don't believe* reveals the way in which the leaders dealt with reality (what we see) as opposed to pleasure (what we wanted to see). Trotsky, the anti-bureaucrat, art lover, supporter of psychoanalysis and friend of the surrealists, clearly shows that there is a hallucinant filter in place. Even if you had showed us then where we would have ended up, we still wouldn't have believed our eyes, Trotsky says. Neither then is there reason to believe that now.

The Soviet theater of the absurd consists of the fact that at the moment they see the horror following the Revolution, the reaction of the leaders is acutely opposed to the expected one. Instead of despair, they are caught up in euphoria. The catastrophe is proclaimed victory, *this* becomes the short cut to communism, *this* is already communism. Trotsky introduces an experimental discourse, which will later become Stalin's primary tool, when he says:

There won't be coercion in socialism... in socialism we will all be moved by the feeling of responsibility, by the work habit and by the attractiveness of work. That is undisputed. But this undisputed truth *has to be expanded a little*. Actually, in socialism the apparatus of coercion will not exist, that is, the state; because it will be completely merged in the community that produces and spends. Anyway, on the path to socialism there lies a period of the best possible strengthening of the state. Both you and I are now passing through that period... the cruelest form of state... (my emphasis).[51]

This assurance–worst is best–is what Lacan, in his seminar *The Ethics of Psychoanalysis* from 1959-60, called "the need to read reality as a fiction,"[52] to see theater in reality. Is my imagination materializing, does the revolution continue? It continues! The object is not good now, but we are going to "recuperate it" in our hallucinations. The tension cannot be resolved in a humane way, therefore, "we will introduce a force of inhumanity,"[53] as Lacan says; we are going to "recuperate" reality with a little bit of good hysteria.

But there is something else at work here. Contrary to the "common knowledge" that hysteria is emptying affects (he/she is in a crisis of tears, shouts, now he/she will be relieved), Freud explains in a letter to Fliess that hysteria is an utterly calculated and regulated action, "Everything is all right, this is what we wanted to achieve with the Revolution." Therefore, Lenin and Trotsky's hysteria is not mere simple hysteria–their hysteria is a calculated action. The neurosis of the leaders *after* the Revolution displays a symptom, the thing that Lacan called "the object that literally gives too much pleasure."[54] The more everything collapses, the more the leaders' pleasure grows. Witness the excess enjoyment present at the outset of Tito's Yugoslavia, when in 1948, the pursuit of Cominform people reaches its zenith, Tito sends several of his most trustworthy collaborators, including Đilas, Svetozar Vukmanović Tempo, Koča Popović, Todorović and Ivan Rukavina to Moscow, "each at their own task,"[55] which, according to Tempo's testimony, generally consisted of "idleness." Tempo writes:

We went to the Art Theater regularly. After returning from the theater, we frequently discussed the play we had seen... One evening, we saw the play *Dead Souls* by Nikolai Gogol. We talked about the characters... and without noticing we started pointing out related characteristics in ourselves: they called me Sobakevich, the man who addresses everybody in an insulting manner and who treads on the feet of the people he talks to; we renamed Đilas Nozdryov, who cannot open his mouth without telling a lie, the Blue one (Mijalko Todorović–my comment) became Manilov, always in the clouds...[56]

While the purges in Goli Otok (the Yugoslav island prison camp) progressed in Yugoslavia, the nomenclature is unusually happy, jovial, fulfilled, and not on the principle of bypassing the excess, hiding the excess personal non-virtues, but, to the contrary, by emphasizing them, "the way we are," good for nothing–with all our inconsistencies in the characters, we take pleasure from the system. The best cadre in Moscow insult, lie or hallucinate, and they legitimate this among themselves through theater; and yet, the world opens up more for the sadist "excessive pleasure" incorporated into the communist ideology.

Approximately half a million Yugoslavs were watched by the Yugoslav secret services.[57] The secret services *produced* files. As Andrei Şerbulescu says: "The first great socialist industry was that of the production of files... This new industry has an army of workers: the informants."[58] Each citizen existed for the services simply or only through his file. According to Kathrine Verdery, the producers of files were paid much better than the producers of commodities. And like employees in other branches, the police also exaggerated the results of their production, and it was often more important simply to enter information into the system than to determine whether it was really true.[59] While the producers of files were well paid, the small-town snitches didn't join the Yugoslav secret police by completing an application form; they worked on the basis of their word of honour, for little money, but out of great patriotism (at the Stasi, for instance, collaborators completed an application form). In Yugoslavia, the choice of spying was organized on the principle of a Serb watching a Serb, a Muslim watching a Muslim, a Macedonian observing a Macedonian and so on, and according to a Serbian researcher of the communist files, Marko Lopušina, this scheme was applied so that: "The illusion of objectivity was accomplished and the loyalty of the ethnic groups towards the Government was proved. The most reliable judges were those who collaborated with the political police, and the same was true for the witnesses as well."[60] According to Lopušina, once they submitted the required documents to the commander, the operatives could no longer follow the destiny of the watched target, so the operatives often knew only what they did.[61]

Three secret services operated in Yugoslavia, following the example of the Soviet model: KOS (Yugoslav People's Army Counter-Intelligence Service) was derived from OZNA (People Protection Department), the UDBA (State Security Administration, in 1966 re-named into SDB–State Security Service) and SID (Information and Documentation Service). There isn't a Yugoslav politician from the older generation known to have bypassed the Ministry of the Interior. As Lopušina says: "Being a police officer was an honor, but in the last years of Yugoslavia it was an embarrassment, therefore some of the politicians left that information out of their biography."[62] The first schools for counter-intelligence were opened in Split (Croatia), then in the Serbian capital, Belgrade, (The UDBA Higher Education School, in operation from 1952 to 1967), then in the Croatian capital, Zagreb (MUB), in the Serbian city of Zemun, and towards the end of 1970, a Faculty of Security was also opened in Skopje, Macedonia.

These institutions fulfilled only part of the needs of the secret service operatives, while other employees were recruited from the lists of scrutinized students from the Faculties of Law, Economy, Philosophy, Philology and Political Science; and their scholarships were three times higher than the standard public ones. KOS was a more mobile unit, and thus more dangerous. "KOS was a perfect political machine for killing people,"[63] Lopušina writes, and it was hence more powerful than the UDBA (which was more suitable for the small-town mentality and its passion for archiving the trivial everyday living). KOS could arrest UDBA people, or force them to pursue each other. The power of KOS lay in its mobility, with just under 80% of KOS people being operative in the field, and a mere 23% in bureaucracy and administration. The UDBA was pure bureaucracy and more often, therefore, the subject of employee purges. Half the KOS employees were Serbs, one-fifth Croats and 6.5% Macedonians.

The communist secret services are among the largest in the history of these underground political bodies. At its height, the agency of the East German secret police, the Stasi, employed 91,000 spies in a country of 16.4 million. It was the biggest German spy network, three times bigger than the Nazi Gestapo, and their spying took place on a territory just 1/4 that of Nazi Germany.[64] In the DDR, spies were recruited voluntarily (for money) or by force, and they usually had to sign a Declaration for Accession that was then archived. By 1989, 173,000 collaborators had signed such a declaration, and of them 91,000 worked as active spies. Spies met their superiors regularly and personally reported to them about their colleagues, friends and neighbors. The Stasi indexed more than 5.6 million people and was likely one of the biggest secret bureaucracies of all time. They had a file for every person who crossed the border of East Germany at any time, even for a holiday. In 1989, just after the fall of the Berlin Wall, the Stasi issued a directive to destroy the files. When the paper shredders of the agents, the so-called Papierwolfs (Paper Wolves), broke down, they began tearing papers by hand. Some 45 million tons of paper were torn inside a period of two months. Over the past 17 years, more than 1.7 million people submitted applications requesting to see what the Stasi knew about them, and after the release of the German film, *The Lives of Others* (2006), requests for files grew greater yet.

The secret services archived a range of absurdities. In the summer of 2007, one of the most bizarre activities of the secret services was released to the public. The secret Stasi agents broke into the homes of those under surveillance, located their dirty underwear, collected the odor from them with special tools and conserved the odor in jars! When I visited the Stasi Museum in 2007, some of these jars were still displayed on the shelves. The idea of keeping bodily odors is so astonishing that no one with an ounce of elementary mental health could imagine this bizarre collection scheme. But, the Stasi-services, similar to the psychopath from Süskind's novel *Perfume* (1985), succeeded over the long years of the communist regimes in convincing themselves that they could capture the *being* of each subject of surveillance, if only they could store his/her bodily odor in a jar. (I assume this was in order to be able to sniff him/her with dogs if he/she decided to run. No other "normal" explanation, with regard to the secret archiving of people's shit, comes to mind!) Today, the odorous Stasi jars are the final proof that communist paranoia had no limits. The secret communist services existed at the edges of every logic, and the communist police was and remains an ontological scandal!

Operating on the other side of the Berlin Wall was MAD (*Militärischer Abschirmdienst*, the West German Military Intelligence Organization). In 1984, it was discovered that among the more than half-million citizens that MAD had indexed, there were names of six-year-old children! The six-year-old Petar L. was reported as suspicious, together with his friends from his kindergarten; additionally, along with the pre-school and school-age children, some 12,000 men over the age of 80 were also watched.[65] The reason we know today of the many sordid and nebulous details of the work of the Stasi and MAD is the fact that only Germany has opened its archives to–and for scientific examination and study. Like their Yugoslav counterparts, the Soviet archives contain well-hidden secrets that have still not been made available.

Although espionage is an ages-old practice–traces of which can be found on 4,000-year-old clay plates from the Euphrates River– the first civil and military espionage efforts were only made official in the 17th century (England), and later in the 18th and 19th centuries (France and Prussia). Still, the counter-intelligence services only truly came to blossom in the 20th century in the two world wars (the biggest counter-intelligence centers appear in Paris, London, Casablanca, Istanbul, Cairo, Berlin and Rome), and most of them were founded and became fully operational during the Cold War, when so-called "total espionage" becomes relevant.

We don't know much about the Soviet secret services. In 1989, the Soviet archives were opened to foreign and national researchers, but a year later they were gradually closed–first the Presidential archives were made unavailable, then all of the archives were completely closed. Today's FSB archives are available only to the families of the repressed and former employees.[66] But something succeeded in coming to light nonetheless. In 1999, one of the most secret and best kept archives in the world was opened–the archive of the first KGB Headquarters (together with the most secret part of that archive, Directorate C, the list of KGB foreign spies). The owner of the archive was Vasili Mitrokhin, a major and senior KGB archivist. When the German magazine "Focus" stated in 1996 that a former KGB agent was in Britain and had names of "thousands of Russian spies," Tatyana Samolis, spokeswoman for the Russian SVR, announced that this was absolute nonsense; anybody could have the names of one, two or perhaps three spies, but not thousands![67] Before the fall of the Berlin Wall, Mitrokhin was an operative and traveled to the Olympics in China as an agent, but withdrew to archiving when he was appointed to supervise the movement of 300,000 documents from the old KGB headquarters to a new one in 1972, a position in which he served for 12 years.[68] During this entire time, he copied secret documents, with the oldest dating back to 1918. He was pedantic, and he wrote by hand with monastic stringency and ascetical rigor. On Wednesdays, his duty was to seal the KGB Directorate C. He took the copies home, and hid them under his bed; then moved them to his summer house and put them in cardboard milk boxes, and in this way packed over 25,000 pages. In 1992, after 20 years of copying, he took the cardboard boxes to Tallinn to the American Embassy in Estonia. The FBI rejected Mitrokhin's archive as a work of fantasy. But the British accepted it, and in a secret operation, MI-6 officers moved Mitrokhin's materials to London in six suitcases and consequently issued British passports to his family. Christopher Andrew, Chair of the History Department at the University of Cambridge, studied Mitrokhin's archive, and together they published it under the title, *Sword and Shield, Mitrokhin Archive* in 1999. In 2001, the American historians announced that all of that may have been true, but that no one simply could know–for sure. And they were right. The attraction or allure of the topic of secret services lies in the fact that one can never really be sure that what you read is true. Those documents were written by people trained in the practice of the most thorough deception and distrust, and were written for readers with the same distrust. The suspicion of the American historians is indeed understandable: You read it, but it may all have been a fairy tale. Who can guarantee that it's true?

Nevertheless, what is certain is that Yugoslavia was similar to the Soviet Union in terms of the very *massiveness* of the secret services. According to the best known researcher of the secret communist Yugoslav files, Marko Lopušina: "Such a large concentration of the secret police structures in the Government of Yugoslavia can only be explained by the fact that Yugoslavia was born in a war."[69] The country's new communist leaders were either part of the security bodies or army commanders. From 1944, Yugoslav specialists were trained in the KGB Academies in Moscow and Leningrad, and there are numerous photographs of the first incarnation of the Yugoslav secret services in Cheka uniforms, while party education in Moscow was tightly connected to that of the police. This includes and refers to Josip Broz Tito as well, who joined the counter-intelligence service in 1914 at the Austrian-Hungarian front, and later attended training by the Russian NKVD (Ministry of State Security). Well-known is an event from 1948 when Tito, who was angry at Stalin's attacks, was at a dinner with Ranković, Tempo and Krajakić, said: "Look how they attack us, and we gave them our best people–even I worked for the NKVD."[70] But in the some 900 books written about Tito in Yugoslavia, there is little information about his counter-intelligence work in Moscow. The Yugoslav secret services started operating during the Second World War, and in 1942 Tito adopted the first "Instruction for the Intelligence Service." Whenever a part of the territory of Yugoslavia was liberated and counter-intelligence zones were established, the networks were highly centralized, and Tito reigned at the top of the network. Due to the level of secrecy, the services easily got out of control, and in the 1970s cooperation between the headquarters in Belgrade and the services in the field were decidedly bad. The national and provincial leaders of the SDB forged confidential information for their own interests, and they broke the holy rule that all information must be submitted to headquarters directly, and without processing. Thus, the services became closed bodies that easily mutated into orgies of UDBA people who kept the destinies of hundreds of thousands of people in their hands.

It is well known that in 1988 Slobodan Milošević (who some years previous entered the main stage of Yugoslav politics) found a wiretapping device on the wall of his apartment. He asks the Head of the State Security Service, Dragan Mitrović, to see the coded names of the collaborators from his file. He receives the surprising answer that even if he wanted to, Mitrović could not tell him who the informants were because he didn't personally know their names, and that the heads of the departments didn't know them either. Much disturbed, Milošević calls the Minister of Police, Lalović, but he too doesn't know who tapped Milošević's apartment. Under pressure from Milošević, there are attempts in the secret service to reconstruct various events. They come to the conclusion that the tapping may have been ordered by Admiral Branko Mamula, who as Federal Secretary for National Security, didn't like Milošević as a Serbian nationalist.[71] This just goes to prove that several people (even the political "bosses") could intervene in the structure and workings of the police, as they were bigger than the party and all of the attendant political games. Even Milošević, who in the following years will become "the boss" of Serbia, couldn't get the information from the secret services. In the film *The Bourne Ultimatum* (2007) by Paul Greengrass, the plot is structured around the CIA heads fearing that it will be discovered that the CIA has become a de facto police state. The evidence confirming this is being kept in a secret place in a safe, and the film's main character is trying to get to these secret documents. The logical question is then why, at this moment, does one of the bosses not simply burn the content of the safe; why doesn't he eat, or simply destroy the documents? However, this fact does not mean that the film is naïve. On the contrary, we know that the Gestapo, the KGB and the UDBA kept comprehensive records archiving all of their actions, and that the secret police always had baggage that couldn't be destroyed or left behind. The secret police *had to* archive itself. And the question isn't why the secret police couldn't give up their archiving, but whether the secret service could become so radical as to transform itself into a parallel (police) state? The answer is twofold. If we believe that the secret police could be radicalized into a police government we are right (many people believe in conspiracy theories, and that the anonymous bosses of the secret services actually lead their respective states). And if we believe that this was just a film, then we are right again.

The trick of the secret services lies in this dual role: The idea that I am constantly an object of somebody's gaze is a fantasy, though at the same time, I have a phantasmic fear that according to the ideology I may not be visible at all (am I so unimportant?). It is precisely this ambiguity that is central in each ideology, and it explains the essential obsession of the secret services. In the German documentary, *No Lost Time* (2004), former Stasi prisoner Günter Herrig offers: "From today's point of view, I underestimated and overestimated the Stasi. They weren't as omnipresent as I thought, and from the file I see they were incautious, and that they didn't know many things. But it was also impossible to hide from them." The secret services exist so that a certain morality or ethic is respected; at the same time, nothing is respected. This is the radically contradictory position on which the success of the secret services is based. This *uncertainty* is one of the reasons why the spy retains the status of a mystery in the equation, even for the police structures. The essence of the existence of the secret services is their internal invisibility. Nobody knows anything about anybody. The more it doesn't know, the safer it is–not the system, not even the spy, nor the possible discloser, but precisely the ideology.

Intelligence and Secret Intelligence (About "Prison Schools")

There is one trivial detail in the biographies of the heads of the secret services which more closely explains the obsession of the *secret* intelligence with the intelligencia (poets, artists, scientists). The leader of the secret services always begins his biography–in prison! In the biographies of the biggest Federal and Republic executioners, as well as the leaders of the secret services in Yugoslavia–Josip Broz

Tito, Lazar Koliševski, Edvard Kardelj, Aleksandar Ranković, Stane Dolanc (similar to the Soviet Lenin, Stalin, Trotsky…), we find a euphoric *celebration* of their prison days as a period of "expanding their theoretical and political education." For example, after five years of "prison studies" in the Croatian and Slovenian prisons of Lepoglava and Maribor, Tito became "something like" an engineer, and in Tito's biography, *Tito Speaks* (1953), his most famous biographer, Vladimir Dedijer, describes the prison in Lepoglava in the most poetic terms. Why did their days in prison impress the leaders of the secret services? Because that's where they started their *real* education. If according to the well-known ancient doctrine–the body is a prison of the soul–then in communism, prison becomes freedom of the soul. Shortages of food and sex, physical and emotional punishment, solitary confinement, all of this serves to cleanse the spirit. Tito explained to his biographer Dedijer how the Lepoglava prison cells slowly became Party cells. "With a few books and means available…. we organized study courses and lectures."[72] In Dedijer's biography, Tito praises Yugoslav revolutionary Moša Pijade, who liked painting landscapes and who was a particular master of clouds ("they are his best paintings," Tito explains), but immediately adds: "In the headquarters, with me, he liked supervising the work on the machines."[73] All of this means that the Party cadre, though sometimes gazing at the sky with a touch of the bourgeois, find their earthly "duty" in the machines. Just as Tito learned from Pijade how to be an intellectual, Pijade learned from Tito how to be a worker, as Bosnian philosopher Ugo Vlaisavljević explains in his book *Lepoglava and University* (2003).[74] In prison, Moša Pijade translated Marx's *Capital* and learned from Tito how to operate the machines. Thus, as Vlaisavljević writes, Lepoglava becomes a perfect *proto-University* because it reveals to the communists the essence of education: It should be such a technology of knowledge, such a combination of science and technique in rigorous conditions of asceticism, that later factitiousness and poetics will no longer be allowed; no liberating, poetic "craziness," knowledge will become a combination of spirit and body, science and technology, some type of or variation of comprehensive education.

Therefore, it's not at all strange that the secret services had a "special" attitude towards intellectuals, especially those who "strayed" from the path. Communism created political prisoners, but it was also afraid of them. It created them, but it also kept watch on them. And it did so for a reason. When they get out of prison, they will be "new people;" prison will "make them people," better than those who never went through the prison school system. When Goli Otok (Yugoslav island prison camp) was opened, its existence was explained with notions of "school" and "transformation." And Foucault writes that no socialist country functioned without a more or less developed system of gulags. The gulag operated in such a way that it was seen in the collective fantasy as a kind of zoo, a lonely place outside civilization (Siberia, Goli Otok), populated with every type of "beast" who were there to become human, "to become people (again)." Petty criminals weren't sent to Goli Otok, but the intellectuals, even those with the greatest reputation in Yugoslavia, were. Knowledge had made them *beasts*, and prison should give them back their humanity.

In 1948, Yugoslavia inherited a network of relatively modern prisons that were used for petty criminals. Goli Otok was a place for the rehabilitation of non-people, a place of ultimate socialist education, something like a warehouse for the incorrectly intelligent. That made Goli Otok a type of "anthropology–technology" (Vlaisavljević): It was not a "natural place," but a "zero point" where the supreme technology for creation of correct intelligence started. And yet the opposite is true as well: the universities under communism (which were opened in Yugoslavia at the beginning of communism) became a type of anthropology–technology. The Philosophical Faculty was not philosophical–it was political. The Philological Faculty was not philological, it too was political, etc. This attitude towards education also shows the complex relationship between the secret services and the intelligence–the first produced the second, and vice versa. In my father's file, for instance, one of the snitches was a university professor, who, as it happened, was my professor when I was studying literature at the Philological Faculty in Skopje. In the operative's note from November 25, 1985, and at the UDBA's initiative, there was a meeting between the inspector and a collaborator, Prof. Nada Momirovska, which took place at the hotel "Kontinental" from 11:00 to 11:30 on the morning of November 22, 1985. The document says: "The aim of the conversation was that the collaborator would present findings relevant to the security and information about the comments at the Philological Faculty regarding the trial of Intimist." The document continues: "The findings are received orally, (and) the operatives' costs are 300.00 denars."

How is this relationship between the secret services and the intelligence explained? This relationship is best explained, again, through literature. In the world of literature, the detective genre was introduced by Edgar Allan Poe. In Poe's most famous detective story, *The Purloined Letter* (1844), written half a century before the global ascent of the secret services of the 20th century, Poe writes about a letter stolen by a politician. The police search him, ransack his house, check every book in his library, look in every drawer, tear open every duvet, collect every discarded butt in a bag; they search everywhere, but they cannot find the letter. Then, Dupin comes to the scene: He says the police are wrong, and that only a child hides something in a place where everybody will look. Dipen comes to the politician's house and finds the letter on the table. The letter the whole world has been looking for lies in plain sight of everyone. The ideal illustration of this same phenomenon is the case of Radovan Karadžić, the leader of the Bosnian Serbs, who was responsible for the genocide in Srebrenica from 1995 to 2008 while the entire world was looking for him, and who was living as a spiritual healer in Belgrade right out in front of everyone. They're not going to find you only if you are not hiding. Poe's short story, written half a century before the secret services grew to their later massive proportions, made for the first time the hidden essence of the secret services public–secret services don't look for something that cannot be seen, but for something that is in plain sight of everyone; they search for that which is most banal.

Edgar Allan Poe introduced the detective genre as *an intellectual genre*. "The crime is solved by one *abstract reasoner*, and not by the informant or the carelessness of the criminal,"[75] says the Argentinian writer Borges in his analysis of Poe's story. The one who solves the riddle is the intellectual who mocks the police. While the police literally plough through everything in a physically closed world, only the intelligent agent (secret intelligence) solves the drama. The information the snitch searches for is identical to this short story–it is a search for the obvious, for the banal. In Poe's first detective story, *The Murders in the Rue Morgue* (1841), the first parameters of the spy's behavior are set. Here too, the story is not adventurous, but intellectual–the crime is solved in an intellectual operation, and not in an action involving firearms; through a proper investigation of people, and not by pressuring them. Knowledge is the essence of the snitch, but the police officer loves the event he can reconstruct more than he does the real case. That makes the police officer a *writer*. Poe's story is told while the city sleeps, so that the spy can, as Borges writes: "…feel the crowd and the solitude at the same time, which stimulate the thinking."[76] In Poe's short story, the detective (the man of the services) is a "foreigner," and although he is part of the small town, he must be a distant outsider at the same time; he feeds himself with small town secrets, but lives differently from it.[77] By introducing the topical issue of the police officer in literature, Poe broke a longstanding illusion. The people's watcher is not a foreigner, as he is the same as us and part of our everyday social relationships, but the propaganda makes him a spy–hero, and it turns his biography into a hagiography. Even in the Gorbachev era, the KGB propaganda continued to describe the spy as a combination of superior qualities. One month after the death of the most famous Soviet spy, the American Morris Cohen, Russian President Boris Yeltsin awards him the posthumous title Hero of the Russian Federation.[78] (Note how often the spy wants to write memoirs so that his work will not be forgotten. Richard Tomlinson, the British MI-6 officer who participated in the operation of transferring Mitrokhin's KGB archive to Britain, became famous after his imprisonment in 1997 when he published a book about his career, violating the British Official Secrets Act of 1989 for the protection of official information related to national security. Retired KGB agent George Blake published his memoirs in 1990. The French lieutenant colonel Le Roy Fenville, Head of the Department of the French Counter-Intelligence Service SDESE, published a book entitled *I Spied on My Friends* (1980), which caused a series of scandals.[79] George Tenet, CIA Director from 1995 to 2004 also published his memoirs in 2007, and so on.)

Poe's literary successor Robert Louis Stevenson shed some light on the issue of the secret services as well. Stevenson is the author of the *Strange Case of Dr. Jekyll and Mr. Hyde* (1886). He locates the problem with the culprit in the duality of the person's character–who would have thought that the murderer is an "animal?", Borges writes.[80] The criminal was discovered with shrewdness, using the testimonies of those who entered the room before the crime, and everybody recognized the strange, hoarse voice. The Spaniard believed that it was a German, the German that it was a Dutchman, the Dutchman that it was an Italian, etc., that the voice of the criminal was an "animal voice." In ideological stories, however, the dissident regularly gets the "voice of a monkey." He is one of us, but he speaks strangely, and when he says something that everybody understands he talks like a foreigner. KGB Directorate C, published in 1999, threw an unpleasant light on this fact–besides the vast diversity of the professional KGB spies abroad (among them was an ambassador in Costa Rica and a piano tuner for the governor of New York), one of the darkest surprises of the secret KGB Directorate lay in the fact that though charged largely with a foreign policy intelligence role, the main task of the KGB spy remained connected with work against the national enemy (although he is ours, he has the voice of a stranger), and the work of discovering and discrediting internal dissidents.[81] The battle against ideological subversion remains the main priority of all of the secret services in communism. This suggests that the KGB was basically invented for a war *with our own*; with those who dared to hold views different from "ours."

"Only Here is Poetry Respected. Poetry Kills People"

If communists and the small town hated the intimacy out of which poetry is created, if they didn't like the poets, then how does one explain my father's file full of poets–snitches? It is explained with the paradox that *the closest cooperation* was that between the secret services and the poets. Donald Rayfield writes that secret services and poets were linked by several similarities. Both desired fame, they admired the image of them as narcissistic missionaries, they had creative frustrations, they hated the world of provincialism and they couldn't discuss their work with normal mortals.[82] In the film, *The Recruit* (2003), Al Pacino plays a senior CIA instructor. On the first day of training he gives a speech to the recruits in which this "poetic" essence of the secret service is summarized: "Why are we here? Not for money. My salary is $75,000 a year, I cannot buy a decent sports car with it. Not for sex, there isn't much of that here. Fame? Our failures are public. Our successes aren't... So, not for money, sex or fame. Then why? I say we are here because we believe. We believe in good and bad, and we have chosen the good. We believe in right and wrong, and we have chosen the right. Our goal is justice. Our enemies ... are everywhere." When you work in the name of justice, who is bigger than you? That explains the orgiastic nature of the secret services. Nobody stands behind them, neither the Government, nor the party, nor the politics. Therefore, it is wrong to look for the profile of the spy only in the sadistic rubberneck (who, if he weren't paid, would have done it out of pure pleasure), what draws the spy is the implied, implicit possibility of immortality. The spy comes from nowhere. And he has the opportunity to become a poetic god.

Despite their close cooperation, however, the secret services didn't like the poets and the intellectuals. From Dzierżyński (Cheka) in Russia, to Stane Dolanc (KOS) and Ranković (UDBA) in Yugoslavia, all of the heads of the secret services despised the artists. The communists liked the illiterate man. But the cult of the illiterate man is not a communist invention. It is an inseparable element of the politics, as Stathis Gourgouris writes, in the whole of Western culture.[83] The illiterate man is "desired" because he talks from his experience, and he doesn't offer any interpretations of what he has been through. Rousseau glorifies the savage as good political "material." But if that is the case, why do we then say that drastic conditions for artistic creation existed in communism; isn't it that the capitalist ideology also likes the illiterate man? The answer lies in the paradoxical fact that communism took the creation process far more seriously than it did capitalism.

The Russian poet, Osip Mandelstam, declared "Only in Russia is poetry respected–it gets people killed. Is there anywhere else where poetry is so common a motive for murder?" Mandelstam died in 1938 in a transit camp near Vladivostok, because five years earlier in 1933 he wrote the *Stalin epigram*, a 16-line poem (popularly called "The 16-line death sentence"). Mandelstam's statement is correct. The attention socialism paid to culture is unimaginable for any democracy. Serbian historian Predrag Marković writes: "We cannot imagine the American Senate or the British Lower House dealing with issues of literature and art as the Central Committees of the Communist Parties dealt with them."[84] Capitalism has a different type of censorship, market censorship, and the system is organized in such a way that whatever you say or write, it will be lost in the sea of advertising and shock, about which Ursula Le Guin wrote in her essay, *The Stalin in the Soul* (1973): "I wonder if the reason why we have no Solzhenitsyn in this country, no Zamyatin, no Tolstoy, is that we do not believe in the possibility of art. The strange thing about the Russians is that they do believe in art, in the power of art to change the minds of men."[85] Communism believes in the potential power of the written word. Words are taken seriously, they have biblical power. "(Communists) are always interested in debating with intellectuals," says Žižek, "They are impressed by the word, it bothers them."[86]

It's astonishing how seriously the communists took art. Rayfield writes that only five years after the Soviet Revolution, in 1922, the Soviet Politburo became a *literary committee*. The members of the highest Soviet political body didn't allow anybody else to see their intelligence, they divided the various areas of reading among themselves, and they literally read everything. According to Rayfield, the most educated of the first communists, Trotsky, had piles of books to read. He was appointed the task of reading military and religious literature, and shared economics with Lenin. Zinoviev and Kamenev read journalism, whereas Rykov and Tomsky shared industry and agriculture. Stalin shared military literature with Trotsky, and Stalin had an additional responsibility for reading texts about ethnic issues.[87] "It has become necessary to move from preliminary censorship to punishing censorship," the GPY announced in October 1922.[88] The aim of observation is not only to identify dangerous material, but to spread paranoia as well. In 1922, Dzierżyński, the first man of the Cheka, agrees with Lenin on a list of collaborators in the newspapers, insofar as they must take over the leading editorial positions. Because they don't know how to master the intellectual spheres that they will monitor, Dzierżyński suggests a classification scheme according to group:

"We should divide the intellectuals by groups. For example:

1) Writers;

2) Journalists and political commentators;

3) Economists (here we have sub-groups: a) finance, b) energy, c) transport, d) trade, e) cooperatives, etc.);

4) Technology (more sub-groups): a) engineers, b) agronomists, c) doctors, d) general;

5) Professors and teachers.

Every intellectual must have a file… We must remember that our task is not only deportation, but also… active assistance to the party line with experts, i.e. causing disintegration in their ranks by favoring those who are ready to support the Soviet power without any reservations."[89]

The consequences of this action are remarkable. In the autumn of 1922, the cream of the Russian intelligence is brought to Ljubljanka (prison) by force, and most of the intellectuals are declared counter-revolutionaries. The Head of OGPU, Jagoda, orders their deportation to Germany, but the German Chancellor refuses them with the statement, "Germany is not Siberia." Jagoda boards them onto two big ships and deports them from Russia. According to Rayfield, those two ships are "the biggest gift from Russia to Europe and America."[90] "Trubetzkoy and Jakobson (structural linguistics and narratology), Berdyaev (existentialism), Melgunov and Kizevetter (historiography) are on the ships. Prague and Paris are enriched with entire theoretical schools, and the USSR is left without some of its greatest minds…" Rayfield continues that: "The deportations of 1922 were as catastrophic for civil society in the USSR as the executions of 1921."[91]

Yugoslavia didn't effect deportations of such (Soviet) magnitude because it didn't have open (and punishing), but instead hidden censorship. Does that mean that the Yugoslav and Macedonian artists were left alone? It does not. We often come across the thesis, as Predrag Marković writes, that: "In Yugoslavia, the number of authors and scientists who were exiled from the country was small; in Croatia they were mostly exiled for nationalism, and repression was probably the worst in Bosnia."[92] How then can we explain the fact that one out of 10 of all films produced in Yugoslavia were forbidden, either by the judiciary or by acts of self-management/censorship, and that a large number of writers and poets lived in pronounced disfavor, and out of half a million secret files kept on the Yugoslavs, (such) a large number were dedicated to intellectuals–dissidents?

There was hidden censorship in Yugoslavia, but the question is: Which is more frightening, the open or the hidden? In the DDR, where political censorship was the strongest, it was clear what was appropriate and what was not. On the other hand, if you were in Yugoslavia in the 1980s, you ran a magazine and you called "government officials" to consult on what you could publish, they would reply: "We are self-management, think for yourselves," Žižek explains in an interview.[93] When I publicly opened my father's file in 2005 and stated that the President of the Writers Association of Macedonia, Macedonian poet and member of the Macedonian Academy of Sciences and Arts, Gane Todorovski, did nothing to call on the Writers' Society to defend their fellow member, Todorovski told the journalist I talked to that he did everything in his power–he went to consult with the Party and was ordered not to interfere in the case. "We are self-management, think for yourselves," therefore it always came down to *think along the lines of the Party*. Where open censorship doesn't exist, where you "alone" determine the boundaries of your freedom, it all comes down to Party freedom. In life, artists are paralyzed and prevented from expressing resistance; and in art they escape into the avant-garde–they create abstract acts, in which it is unclear what is appropriate and what is not. If the artists protected themselves by "escaping into the avant-garde," the question remains as to how did it happen that some artists in Macedonia suffered? The answer most often given is that of the small town. The small-town mentality, in conjunction with communist ideology, produced a chaotic system that was used for revenge against those whom you couldn't stand. One such example is the fate of the Macedonian socialist poet, Kočo Racin. For a long time it was believed that he was killed as a victim of political calculation. The latest research, however, reveals that Strahil Gigov, a high-ranking communist official, ordered him murdered out of jealousy over a woman.

Another case that connects writers with high-ranking communist officials is the case of Metodija Andonov-Čento (first President of the Socialist Republic of Macedonia in the Yugoslav Federation) and the famous Macedonian writer Kole Čašule. Here, an excellent writer appears in the role of a judge of a pro-Macedonian communist official. Kole Čašule is the third judge (alongside Panta Marina and Lazar Mojsov) in the case against Čento, who was sentenced to an 11-year prison term. Kole Čašule later explains: "The trial was prepared in advance, not only the charges, but the sentence as well... Thus, we the judges, were ordered to convict Čento."[94] Here, we have a similar explanation as with my father: The executors apologize that they themselves were powerless, as everything was in the hands of the Party that "wanted that." In 2003, Kole Čašule was chosen as the third honorary member of the Macedonian Academy of Sciences and Arts, together with Josip Broz Tito and Edvard Kardelj (the founders of the first secret services in Yugoslavia). This list of honorary members of the Academy is more proof of the close relationship between the intellectuals and the police. Kiro Gligorov, the first President of the independent Republic of Macedonia admits in his memoirs, *Macedonia is All We Have* (2001), of "an unpleasant fact," writing: "We were all asked individually to write what we knew about different persons... I remember that I was writing too, what I knew, about the role of Čkatrov, Guzelov, Draganov."[95]

There are cases where the poets directly supported the police actions, and such is the case with the Macedonian poet Risto Lazarov (the editor of "Communist," the journal of the Communist Party of Macedonia in the 1980s), who on December 6, 1985 publishes texts after my father's imprisonment, in which he proclaims my father's sentence to be "deserved," together with a line of praise for Tito's regime: "Our brotherhood and unity, our unbreakable togetherness and unshakeable stride on Tito's road of construction of socialist self-management cannot be destroyed by any insane assaults..."[96] These texts were written five years after Tito's death and five years before the disintegration of the Yugoslav Federation. What is confusing here is not the retrograde thesis, strangely amusing even for the time, but the self-confident position the poet expressed in his assessment of the judges' sentences as deserved. As a result, there wasn't any critical reaction among the Macedonian writers–my father's colleagues–to Lazarov's pamphlet.

The reason for this absence of critical reaction is twofold: "indifference" (neutrality) always offers a comfortable position "on the stronger side," though the writers were also provincially obsessed with the "dignity" of their guild–how could they now *embarrass themselves* by reacting? In the book, *Policemen of the Spirit* (1979), by the influential and merciless Croatian critic Igor Mandić, is an article from 1976 entitled, "Writers and Bicycles", in which he mocks Macedonian poet Gane Todorovski's complaining (in an interview of the same year), that although he likes riding a bike he can't, but has to drive a car instead because:

It would be shameful when with *the beard, the weight and the years and the positions,* I would ride a bike. I would be crazy of course. Not for myself, but for the surroundings… *the kids would throw stones at me,* and I don't know… maybe *nobody would come to listen to me at the Faculty;* look at this one, they would say.[97] (my emphasis)

Mandić uses Todorovski as a paradigm for the (Yugoslav) small-town arrogance that comes from the "writer's dignity." The writer sees himself as the Messiah: "His existence and movement through the world is of crucial importance for our people," Mandić says, and he adds ironically: "For God's sake, who recognizes even our most famous writers in the street? …And if all of this weren't so funny, it would be tragic."[98] The writer under communism thought that he had to demonstrate *sobriety (a business-like attitude).* That of course limits choice, exhausts the energy, the spirit withers in some kind of quiet desperation and there is a sadness that cannot be humiliated, but the "unquestioned" spirit is at the same time proud–he provincially "gives up" the little things that are important to him, but at the same time, he gives in and over to dignity with all his strength, because in return, he is granted freedom from any critical responsibility.

As mentioned before, one of the last documents in my father's file before his arrest is the operative's note from July 3, 1985, in which the Macedonian poet Ante Popovski asks to be admitted into the UDBA services. After Ante noticed confusion and anxiety in my father, he (quoting from my father's police file): "told the source that he hadn't slept all night, and the next day, at 7 o'clock in the morning, went to see the source," and told the UDBA services about the anxiety he observed in my father during the drive (see more in the Chapter "Hard Wing"). Why did the Macedonian writer feel the need to talk to the police about his colleague's intimate distress? Why did the *poet*, as spokesperson of the intimate confessions of people, feel the need to automatically tell each intimacy to the police? The Macedonian poet, this time embodied in Ante Popovski, liked the position of freedom from any critical responsibility. If he relates what bothers Jovan Koteski, then Ante Popovski is free and absolved; it's not his business anymore. He will stand on the stronger side (of course, he will think about himself in terms of comfortable "neutrality") because he wants to remain dignified. Now, what intimate problems, what little things of his friend should serve as the subject of his thoughts and contemplations when he has his *years and positions*? Ante Popovski, too, would ride the bicycle of freedom, but he is a manager and a poet, and like Professor Gane Todorovski, has to drive a car so that *the children won't throw stones* at him *and think he is crazy*. That means that if a friend gets into his car and tells him about an intimate problem (the UDBA blackmail his friend lived with for decades), he will have to process that problem, he will have to activate the writers' membership, he will have to look to them for solidarity, though he himself cannot feel such solidarity; therefore, he has to work on that *seriously*, which really *exhausts the energy*, he doesn't sleep all night, and in the morning he has to talk to some police blockheads, but dignity costs, it has a price. He gives in to this business of informing with all his strength because he knows it is *only* that night and *only* that morning. Then, for months, he is free from any critical responsibility, he is free to ride in his ideological car. That comfort is another reason for the close cooperation between the poets and the secret police in communism. In the system where everyone is guilty proven otherwise, people who want to succeed must submit to the system of police informing in order to maintain their success.

The connection between poetry and the police was finally closed with the bloody disintegration of Yugoslavia, which was "worked" for the most part by the intellectuals and the poets. Žižek writes ironically: "If the standard definition of war is a continuation of politics with other means," than the fact that the leader of the Bosnian Serbs, Radovan Karadžić, is a poet, is more than a pure coincidence insofar as the ethnic cleansing in Bosnia was a "continuation of (that type) of *poetry* with other means."⁹⁹ Radovan Karadžić's arrest in July 2008, when it was revealed that 13 years after Srebrenica he was hiding behind the mask of a spiritual, avant-garde healer shows the merciless connection between the directing of a sweeping ethnic cleansing operation and his own "poetic" re-creation of (his) identity.¹⁰⁰ Unfortunately, Karadžić's case is not a mere rhetorical exercise. The Eighth Session of the Central Committee of the Serbian League of Communists on September 23-24, 1987, which is the turning point at which Yugoslavia enters the war (at that session Slobodan Milošević becomes the new ruler of Serbia and Yugoslavia), was enabled by the work of the artists, scientists and intelligence from the Serbian Academy of Sciences and Arts (SANU). Namely, two years prior, on May 25, 1985, SANU elects a body which will write the later well-known Memorandum–a critical evaluation of the situation in Yugoslavia at the time. Some 23 regular and associate SANU members (1/4 of the entire Academy) participate in the writing of the document, some 70 typed pages, which constituted the bloody disintegration of Yugoslavia.¹⁰¹

Communism and the Avant-Garde

When the Western analysts evaluate and summarize the art created in communism today, they are amazed by the presence of the abstract themes developed by the Soviet and Yugoslav avant-garde. In the process of writing this book, a lot of my friends reminded me that there was an avant-garde in Yugoslavia–wasn't that proof of (our) artistic freedom under communism? Those who ask this question do not possess a good understanding of the communist obsession with form. Not only was the avant-garde tolerated, it was advocated on the level of official doctrine. Before the cult of personality developed (in the Soviet Union in the 1920s, and in Tito's Yugoslavia following the Revolution), only the bohemian status was taken away from the avant-garde–and the avant-garde was immediately proclaimed an official doctrine. The regime didn't attack modern aesthetic experimentation, it supported it. In contrast, it forbade the naturalistic works that dealt with social problems. One of the rare works Tito attacked and formally prohibited was Dragoslav Mihailović's, *When the Pumpkins Blossomed* (although the

Serbian play was staged in 1968, the novel was published only after Tito's death in 1981)–a naturalistic portrayal of the tragic effect of the repression on the common people of suburban Belgrade.[102] Perhaps one of the answers to the problems of creative work in communism is to be found here: If you write about the village, about the common and fallen people, about poverty (as my father did), you are not very likable. On the other hand, if you create abstractions, you are more than welcome.

One such example lay in the faceless communist, non-figurative National Liberation Movement monuments scattered across the landscape of the former Yugoslavia, which fascinate(d) with their futuristic bravery; but that was the point, futurism was the preferred approach or genre. These concrete blocks don't remind us of anything or anybody, they are in iconoclastic *dispute* with the landscape, but that is good. One Western visitor left a comment on the Internet page dedicated to the National Liberation Movement monuments: "I wonder when a gigantic robot will throw itself into the picture to fight the monument."[103] This comment is very much to the point, communism liked science fiction; these concrete jets were there to challenge the Universe. On the other side, it was a problem to say that you or your neighbor was hungry. The "human" absence from these monuments was most desirable, as these monuments offered an escape from the themes of poverty and political misfortune. Behind the gigantic monuments is the message of the Emperor–deserter: It is difficult to be a leader. A similar expression of the "avant-garde" playfulness of the "post-nuclear landscape" is the Albanian bunkers, although they were built with a different purpose. A total of 750,000 bunkers were built across Albania on the principle of one bunker for every three Albanians. After cutting off all of the railway connections to the country, Enver Hoxha, like a Dali surrealist version of Albania, wanted to make sure that in the event of a war, no road would function and that people would be stuck–but they would have the theme parks of communist paranoia where they could hide. This solution is of the same "avant-garde" type–the fact that there are no roads is irrelevant; what's important is that there are surreal science fiction-like bunkers. (The bunkers were a favorite object and means of consolation to both sides in the Cold War: In East Germany, bunkers were built for a single person; one of the reasons for the depth of the Moscow underground system was to serve as protection in the event of nuclear war; and at the same time, bunkers were built in the back yards of America, with folding beds, which by day served as shelves laden with canned food and books.)

And the Bolsheviks–why did they like the avant-garde? Both communists and artists wanted to break with tradition. The *Manifesto of Russian Futurists* (1913) praises the epoch of "the whole brilliant style of modern times–our trousers, jackets, shoes, trolleys, cars, airplanes, railways, grandiose steamships."[104] When describing the Revolution, the Soviet artists didn't feel like humble "secretaries of society" like Balzac, they were not *only* documentarians of the Revolution. Instead, they claimed that they were *creating* the Revolution, they were the great directors of the New World. Mayakovsky spoke of making, "The streets… our brushes and the squares our palettes."[105] The Revolution was proclaimed a work of art. Malevich requested that his art group UNOVIS be granted the status of a party in art, his Vitebsk Art School would be the "Red Creative Committee," and branches would be opened across the entire country.[106]

Communism, too, began as a form of the avant-garde in politics. Prior to 1917, Lenin was an anarchist. He dreamed of self-management councils, a prototype of the Paris Commune; a political John Lennon, he had the idea that all private property would vanish and the country would be divided into "councils" (hence the name the Soviet Union); he dreamed that the factories, the Army and the Navy would be cooperatives for everybody. He didn't want to introduce state control or monopolies, he didn't like bureaucracy, he didn't think the police or army should exist at all. But here's the trick: As Buck-Morss suggests, the first *compromise* Lenin made with regard to his own anarchist platform was precisely the secret police![107] Lenin's suggestion to establish the first people's militia ("armed people") instead of the police and the army constituted his first renunciation of anarchism and the directing of his politics into the mainstream. And it is exactly this compromise that led him to the snitch-radicalization scheme directed at the people in general, and at artists in particular. Three years after the Revolution, Lenin puts an end to the craziness of the avant-garde artists and declares that everything that is created must be done so under political observation (when Korolev creates a cubist design for a monument to Marx in 1919, it is rejected as too avant-garde).[108] Nevertheless, even under Stalin and the harshest times of Soviet rule, it was possible to work with different avant-garde expressions. The avant-garde in communism almost always had a pluralist character. Marc Chagall worked during Stalin's rule, and though principally apolitical, he did focus on Jewish and folk themes. This strange hybrid wasn't bourgeois art for art's sake, but proletarian art for art's sake–even Malevich's squares didn't exist outside the Party context. Not only did the most avant-garde artists fight for state financing, but also the most figurative ones, as well as the social realists.

When the Bulgarian Marxist Todor Pavlov, glorified in Sofia and Moscow, developed the theory of reflection (in short, advocating socialist realism in literature)[109] in the book of the same name in 1947 in Yugoslavia, the reflectionists' debate was rejected as nebulous because in the 1920s Yugoslavia led extensive conversations about what art should be like in the well-known "Conflict in the Literary Left." The most important discussant, Croatia's best-known writer, Miroslav Krleža, contemplates Chernyshevsky's question, "What is more important: one sausage or one Shakespeare?" (to which Chernyshevsky answers–the sausage), as a question that always includes a political context. In 1927, Krleža wrote: "There isn't untendentious art. The Greeks advocate a Greek outlook on the world, the Gothic is church propaganda, Neanderthal art is a celebration of the cult of hunting and so on. But when in principle people attack art because of a tendency, that is an attack on the tendency, and not on the art."[110] And as early as in 1931, Krleža states that he is neither left nor right, he finds the leftist concept in art primitive because it reduces the script to a slogan, and he sees the right as silly and reactionary. During that same year of 1931, the Central Committee of the Soviet Railway Workers Union announces the following:

Poets, writers and playwrights! The Central Committee of the Railway Workers Union addresses you with the suggestion to use your talent and your capabilities for a fight for exemplary locomotives, for impeccable implementation of the socialist transport and conscientious accounting in the railway transport. Brand everything that hinders or endangers the transport with strong verses, sharp narrative or satiric comedy. Glorify everything that is best in the socialist competition in verses, plays or short stories.[111]

Three years later in 1934, Zhdanov declared that literature must become tendentious. In 1939, Krleža spoke against the madness spreading among the Yugoslav communists. He said that both the left and the right have dogmatic schemes, and didn't recognize nuance, distinction and contradiction. "Fascism is characteristic of the incapacity to move from mythology to reason." He wrote: "We will fight both, the left and the right, the left kitsch and the left embarrassment, but also the right catholic and national literature." Krleža's solution was simple: in art, talent, and in life, diligence. But in the decades between 1920-1950, there was no choice to think other than left. The left became aggressive and self-confident, and in 1940 a close associate of Tito, the Slovenian communist Edvard Kardelj said: "Who that is not with us, he is with the enemy." And as early as in 1940, the Montenegrin communist poet Radovan Zogović explained what the communist artist should look like:

If a talented man... tells us he doesn't have any inspiration on the topic of a magical creation of the new world, brotherly solidarity, the fighters for freedom, the invincibility of the progressive social forces, etc.–we are not going to be quiet and tell him, "What can be done, paint the yellow quinces or your wife's red coat." No. We will ask him: And why don't you find any inspiration in these topics... isn't inspiration a question of will, a question of consciousness raised to passion, a question of participation in the fight?[112]

And Zogović himself becomes an ideal poetic example of the new poetic technology, as is evidenced in this excerpt from one of his love poems: "When I work, when I don't see our room/You were between the walls and me/You stroll quietly across the room, as across a meadow/You whisper my thoughts, my stream."[113] These types of lyrics remain relevant even into the late 1970s. In the poem, *What Must Communism Be* (1977), by Croatian poet Goran Babić, which was dedicated "to the Old one" (Tito's nickname), there is a type of political masochism (which continues to be nurtured even into the 1970s and 1980s), which goes like this: "(Communism) must be first love/which left you once/ and went with somebody else/ and then you, all your life/love her, and him."[114]

We find another instance of masochist *excess enjoyment* in identification with the system in the Serbian painter Predrag Stojanović, who in the late 1980s copied the style and themes of the most rigorous socialist–realist practices of the most famous communist painters in Yugoslavia, Ismet Mujezinović, Gorge Andreević Kun and Božidar Jakec; and in 1988 he still painted the partisans as if they were active in the here and now, in his pictures the children read the newspaper "Communist," the landscapes are building sites and so on.[115] For Stojanović, as for Babić, the system remains utilitarian in its purest call, while his exhibitions under the name "The Revolution Continues" were exhibited at important social anniversaries in the Yugoslav People's Army halls for years.

But besides these periodic intrusions of the most banal utilitarianism in art, after Goli Otok (Yugoslav prison camp), Tito eases up on artistic freedom. Mica Popović is the first non-communist artist under Tito. When he exhibits his paintings in September 1950, the exhibition brochure speaks out against totalitarianism in art, and there were also texts about the absence of criticism in art in Yugoslavia. In 1963, the Serbian critic Sveta Lukić wrote about the "socialist aesthetics" and about the obsession with the avant-garde, and he said that communism supported the form in order to avoid the real problems. And that was exactly the problem with Yugoslav censorship. But abstraction was not a problem; on the contrary, as in the USSR, it was supported. One of the rare times Tito attacked the modernists was in the era of moving closer to the Soviet Union again, in 1962, when Khrushchev also attacked the modernists in the Soviet Union,[116] but that only lasted a very short time.

By the same token, however, there was support, at least in principle, for the avant-garde, of the some 900 films and 1,000 documentaries produced in Yugoslavia between 1945 and 1991, though every 10th film was forbidden. Of these, only four films saw a court ban (*Ciguli-miguli*, *City*, *Plastic Jesus* and *Oasis*), and approximately 70 films were forbidden via political or self-management acts. Frequently, the police did confiscate film rolls, and the censorship mechanism in Yugoslav film operated through both the Yugoslav Committee for Review of Films and through film councils. When a film was censored, nobody made a fuss about it, the film simply disappeared quietly and unnoticed. In the film *Plastic Jesus* (1971) by Serbian director Lazar Stojanović, the plot sees Tom from Zagreb trying to shoot a film in Belgrade; but he doesn't like the system, and he's constantly in conflict with the world around him. The film underscores the similarities between communism and Nazism, and in the background the events of 1968 can be felt. After the release of the film, Stojanović was convicted of producing enemy propaganda and sentenced to a one-year prison term, then to two years, and after an appeal to three years, which he serves in the Croatian Zabela prison. When on one occasion he tells an entirely childish joke about Tito, he is brought before the court again. His film *Plastic Jesus* (1971) was shown for the first time in 1991. Želimir Žilnik's and Dusan Makavejev's films were regularly on the censored list as well (see more in the chapter on "Intimacy"). In Macedonia, where there was little idea of provoking the system at all, let alone create something that could be potentially censored, the films that underwent ideological discussion were Ljubiša Georgievski's, *The Mountain of Wrath* (1968), Branko Gapo's, *Time Without War* (1969), Kiril Cenevski's, *Anguish* (1975), and Stole Popov's, *The Red Horse* (1980).

While it was unclear what could be written, one thing was certain–writing and publishing about Tito was a lucrative business. In Yugoslavia, 900 books about Tito were published in huge print runs, and the publishing company "Communist" published 30 volumes of the collected works of Tito. Tito was profitable, and the artists did a lot to extol his cult. In the first edition of *Articles on Josip Broz Tito Biography* (1953) by Dedijer, Tito's birth house in Kumrovec, which was pictured on the cover, is embossed with a water seal, but in the next edition it becomes "bigger." Tito's friend Stevo Krajacić orders the construction of another storey "because it is impossible that a person like Tito could have been born in such a small house."[117] In another book about Tito, Croatian novelist France Bevk writes: "What does Marshal Tito do from morning until night? ... (The lazy ones) think that he sleeps as much as he wants. They don't know that every morning, Tito is up very early. So early, that he could wake up all the sleepy ones..."[118] Tito enjoyed particularly good relationships with the writers. Serbian writer Dobrica Ćosic (later a supporter of the actions of the Bosnian Serb Army under the command of Ratko Mladić, and the top military general responsible for the Srebrenica massacre during the Bosnian wars of the 1990s) was his favorite, and he accompanied Tito on the monumental "Journey of the Peace Seagull" through eight African states, which lasted an entire 72 days–probably the most expensive foreign policy trip of any statesman in the 20th century.

Macedonia surpassed many with nebulous issues such as *Tito and the Musical Art* (Skopje, 1983) and *Tito and the Physical Art* (Skopje, 1986). While Tito's cult of personality starts to wane across Yugoslavia into the 1980s, a "Law on the Protection of the Person and Work of Comrade Tito" is passed; yet in Macedonia, it is then that the cult of Tito reaches its zenith (and it is the same decade that my father was imprisoned).

Doublespeak–on the Nature of Censorship in Communism

We know of extraordinary authors who could work under the regimes; how can this paradox be explained?

It is not explained by the simple fact that one is a genius (Tarkovsky) and therefore allowed to work,[119] and another isn't (Jakobson) and is deported from the Soviet Union. Both the Yugoslav writer Krleža and the film director Makavejev were avant-garde artists, and while Krleža was allowed to work, Makavejev wasn't– how can these seeming illogical disparities be explained? They can be explained through the mechanism of ideological "doublespeak," a term from George Orwell's novel *1984*. In order to explain the communist doublespeak, Žižek uses the example of the two Soviet composers, Prokofiev and Shostakovich, who explain well the (dualistic) nature of censorship in communism. Over the last 15 years of his life, Prokofiev was caught in the "Stalinist superego at its purest," Žižek writes, "Whatever he did was wrong."[120] When he was avant-garde, he was accused of anti-revolutionary formalism and bourgeois decadence, and when he tried to get closer to the regime and composed the cantos for the 20th anniversary of the October Revolution, based on the texts of Marx, Engels and Lenin, he was criticized for vulgarly profaning the Marxist classics by putting them in his music. Even when he was creating propaganda, or intimate music, the Soviet censors didn't like him. On the other hand, Shostakovich used a musical "doublespeak," his works talked about one thing, but something else was "read" into them. Shostakovich had one musical message to satisfy the Kremlin mentors, and another–his moral credo. His Fifth Symphony was greeted by the Soviet audience with an ovation that lasted for 30 minutes, but at the same time the audience felt the "sadness," the "hidden message" in his music. In other words, Shostakovich was a man "from the inside," somebody who properly understood the Soviet madness, and understood that if you wanted to create, you had to be with the regime, and you could only create if you expressed that madness. And this is done through doublespeak. Žižek correctly points out that it is impossible that the Soviet censors were so naïve so as not to see that extra element of criticism and irony in Shostakovich's music, though it seems as if they liked this mixture, staying with the system yet creating "your way." And he asks: "What if what they wanted from him was precisely the coexistence of two levels, propagandistic and intimate, while he was offering them either the first or the second?"[121]

And we remember the opening scene in Bulgakov's, *The Master and Margarita* (1928-1940), in which the editor of a literary magazine, Berlioz, is dissatisfied with the ordered anti-religious poem because the poet Bezdomny depicted Christ as too dark, while one should depict Jesus in a way that he will become irrelevant. Jesus should be a combination of regime negation and intimate dilemma, so that Jesus remains "avant-garde," and thus irrelevant. Prokofiev, like Bulgakov's Berlioz, took his assignment too seriously, and when he was writing appropriate regime music he did so with complete dedication. Consequently, although he wrote far more appropriate regime music than Shostakovich, it was Prokofiev and not Shostakovich who was subjected to censorship; he simply didn't have the dualistic ideological (avant-garde + regime) formula that Shostakovich captivated with. More important, however, is the following. "Can we really be so sure that the public bombastic music is meant ironically, while the intimate confessional mood is meant sincerely?", Žižek asks.[122]

We find a similar paradox in the "Conflict in the Literary Left"– the first and the most important debate on the status of art in communist Yugoslavia. In his essay, *The Dialectical Antibarbarus* (1939), famous Croatian writer Miroslav Krleža breaks with the prevailing communist politics and is thrown out of the Party in 1939. During World War II, he lives in isolation in Zagreb under the protection of the Independent State of Croatia, and though after the war, in 1946, he remorsefully writes an essay, *Stalin's Victory in Moscow* (in the journal "Borba"), this is not sufficient to incline him towards the communist leadership. Before becoming Tito's most intimate friend, Krleža is like Shostakovich. Look at Krleža's writing about the railway Brčko–Banovići (the famous communally-built railway by the Yugoslav youth) in 1946: "This is not the first railway in the world for sure, but it is the first railway built by the children and given to Tito, who is the first man in our politics, so he succeeds in tunneling into the darkest middle ages of our history. All of that has a deeper sense."[123] These lines by Krleža are an ode to the state, but because of the last sentence ("All of that has a deeper sense"), this ode can be easily read as irony, in the way that Shostakovich is and isn't a regime writer. But as with Shostakovich, in Krleža too you find it is difficult to decipher what is actually the ironic message. Is the irony in the last sentence directed towards the regime, or is the irony directed towards intimacy itself, towards his own ("stupid") criticism? To the contrary, post-war Krleža is similar to Prokofiev, already too distant from the plebs to employ Shostakovich's double formula. When Prokofiev comes back to the Soviet Union in 1936 at the peak of Stalin's purges, he drives an imported American car, wears dandy clothes from Paris, orders books and food from the West and ignores the madness and poverty around him.

Similarly, in Yugoslavia, when after the war Krleža becomes Tito's intimate friend, he gets a personal chauffeur for an entire 20 years, lives in an enormous villa on Tuškanac (the city's famous central park in the Croatian capital Zagreb). Politically, he becomes a mere shadow of the sharp, critical and ruthless fighter for literary freedom he once was between the wars (with the exception of the post-war incident of signing the Declaration of the Croatian Literary Language), but is creatively powerful; at the same time, he has the luxury of privately associating with everybody who crosses the line, with various dissidents (Franjo Tuđman among them), and certainly with Tito's knowledge. But the last, post-war Krleža is not like Prokofiev, as the Soviet composer was completely psychotically absent from society, and even the Soviet Government couldn't do much to "subdue" his madness. When he was forced to attend a meeting of the Composer's Union in 1947, where Zhdanov attacked him and other Soviet composers, he showed up drunk, commented loudly and rudely, and fell asleep on his chair in the middle of it ("miraculously, nothing happened, so accepted was his eccentricity"[124]). On the other hand, Krleža was not only an expression of the wisdom and dignity of the new Yugoslavia, he was also part of Tito's nomenclature. By the same token, however, that didn't guarantee that he would be ignored by the secret services–all writers, including those from the nomenclature, were the constant subject of police attention, and their words, from the footnotes to the margins, were considered weapons.

5

Lenin's Laughter

About the Status of Thought in Communism

How did it happen that the communists developed such a phobia of the word? In 1908, when Maxim Gorky was on Capri, he organized a philosophical debate together with a group of Bolshevik emigrants, and invited Lenin to be his guest. Although Lenin considered Gorky a bourgeois, he appreciated his talent and respected him as one of the rare Russian writers who could help the Revolution. Lenin immediately replied to Gorky, but clearly set the conditions of his visit: "Dear Alexei Maximovich, I should very much like to see you, but I refuse to engage in any philosophical discussion."[1] Lenin wasn't a naïve political strategist, he knew he would need support from all of the emigrants, yet excused himself from the debate in what Althusser called an act of "Lenin's laughter."[2] His excuse didn't follow, because Lenin was afraid of the connection between philosophy and politics, thinking that it would be devastating to the politics. Nor he was especially alarmed that he would be mocked as an unprepared philosopher–Lenin frequently sent letters to Gorky where he confessed, "I am badly prepared in this domain (philosophy–my comment). I know that my formulations and definitions are vague, unpolished."[3] But for Lenin, that type of philosophical "disadvantage" was of essential importance for the revolutionary, his most basic virtue. And thirdly, Lenin didn't excuse himself from the philosophical debate because he considered theory unimportant; on the contrary, Lenin was the creator of the doctrine of anti-spontaneism: "Without revolutionary theory, there can be no revolutionary movement"[4] he said, and that meant he wanted the masses to have a clearly distinct philosophy. But the philosophy he wanted was philosophical *innocence*, he wanted thinking to be only a *remnant* of politics.

Lenin doesn't directly forbid thinking; instead, he asks Gorky the most complex question about the nature of thinking. The ultimate philosophical question: And what type of thinking, Aleksey Maksimovich, is still possible today? What more can I, after Marx and Engels, deliver to you on Capri? (Lenin doesn't say this directly in the letter, but that is the meaning of his excuse). I don't forbid thinking–quite the opposite! Now I even encourage all the existing philosophers to think without stopping. But tell me, what will that thinking be like, after we have come to the threshold of the thinkable? Think that! Until then, I will laugh at your philosophical debates. That is the main content of Althusser's Lenin's laughter, laughing in the face of each thought. In 1908, Lenin poses the key question, which marks the communist thought of the 20th century: When thought has reached the threshold of the thinkable, *what will thought be like*? With this letter to Gorky, the era of Marxist intolerance towards philosophy gets it drastic start. There are no more philosophers that should be studied (with the honest exception of Marx and Engels), there are no more philosophies that are dear to me. The drama of the previously said places thought in the era of the unthinkable, in the sense in which Sartre declares Engels and Lenin to be "unthinkable."[5]

This position on thought lies at the root of the essential bias of communism towards the intellectuals and books, without exception–in all the forms of the so-called "Real Socialism." One of the most important sources for the theory of socialism is the monk Deschamps (considered Hegel's predecessor) from the 18th century. In his book, *The Real System or the Word of the Metaphysical and Moral Conundrum* (1769), he says that a condition for higher changes in the consciousness is to burn all books. Deschamps wasn't selfish, he thought that the last book that would have to be burned would certainly have to be his. In Emmerich's film *The Day After Tomorrow* (2004), such an extreme situation is described, the ultimate conditions under which *such magnitude* of the decay of thought is possible. A small group of people hides from the Ice Age, which threatens to destroy the planet, and one scene takes place at the City Library on 42nd Street in New York, where the survivors have to warm themselves with what they can find–the books. When a girl picks up a book by Nietzsche to throw into the fire, an elderly man tells her that one of the greatest philosophers in the world mustn't be burned. She replies that Nietzsche was in love with his sister. Are the radical surviving conditions closest to the communist ideal of tightening the canon to Marx and Engels? Is it that without critical mass and a well-toughened morality, the first thing that will disappear is thought itself?

Yugoslav Communist Party and Pure Philosophy

According to his *Memoirs*, when Tito sends his collaborator Tempo to Macedonia in the spring of 1942, Tempo receives "special authorizations" from the communist leadership for actions in Macedonia,[6] which consist of cleansing the party of intellectuals:

The most important is the organizational issue–that is the cadre devoted to the Party. There is almost no cadre who will implement the line. If there are clever intellectuals in the Party, small bourgeois elements, the line will remain dead. Our main task is to clear the Party of those elements, put the Party is in sound working hands, even though the workers don't know how to talk much.[7]

The party should be "cleared" of clever intellectuals and instead drag in people "who don't know how to talk much," a dead cadre is needed. The party comes to life when everybody is deadened. This "line" of clearing the intellectuals from the Party in Macedonia starts in 1942.

Six years later in Belgrade, we get a picture of the possible profile of the "welcome" party intellectual. Professor of Philosophy at the Belgrade Faculty of Philosophy Dušan Nedeljković, "who held almost all lectures himself" during the 5th Congress of the Yugoslav Communist Party in 1948, brought in a radio set so that his students could listen to the Congress live. He stood still and said: "Why would I teach, you don't need any books, this is pure philosophy."[8] Nedeljković is not naïve, he represents the first Yugoslavian "cleansed" profile of an intellectual, an offshoot of Lenin's philosophical laughter. Nedeljković understands the message of the communist revolution early on and correctly: In the new world, there is no place for philosophical debates or books, for thought in the old "bourgeois" sense; the thought becomes listening, as the Party's technological shortcut into the Academy.

And here is what the 5th Congress was about. In his talk, on July 26, 1948, Boris Kidrič (The Preobrazhensky of Yugoslavia) asked, and the entire hall cheered and answered together:

Do we have coal, and not only brown coal and black coal? Yes we do. We have more than we need. Do we have hard coal? Although not much, we do have it. Do we have oil? Yes, we do. We have it inland more than we need. Do we have iron ore? Yes we do. We have more than we need. Do we have copper, lead, zinc, nickel, chromium, manganese, antimony, mercury, mica, bismuth, gold, silver, selenium, aluminium? We do. Do we have phosphates? We do. Do we have the possibilities to produce sulphur? We do. Do we have the possibilities to produce nitrate and potassium? We do. Do we have cotton and wool and possibilities for their further development? We do.[9]

This is no ironic ideological gesture, as Nedeljković and Kidrič's unity frames the parameters under which the intellectual in Yugoslavia was formed.

In the fascinating Danish documentary, *Welcome to North Korea* (2001), there is one absurd and grotesque scene that takes place in the only library in the capital city of North Korea, Pyongyang (North Korea, together with Turkmenistan, is probably the last state in the world where the active history of "real-socialism" can still be studied in its most acute form, although those studies are nearly impossible because of the isolation of the countries). The only library in Pyongyang is called the "People's House of Education," and the two authors in the documentary, accompanied by three guards, enter the room where the books written by Kim Il sung are kept. Kim Il sung, the North Korean leader who died in 1994, is still glorified in the most grotesquely unironic way in this country of 20 million people. Still today, large posters of him, together with those of Marx and Engel, hang, entirely without irony, on the empty buildings of the Orwell-like empty capital.

In the scene, the documentary authors come to the room where the volumes of Kim Il sung's personal teachings are kept ("Juche Sasang" in Korean, the main thoughts of which constitute the official ideology of North Korea from 1972), and his teachings are collected into *3,078 volumes*! With this number, Kim Il sung became the most prolific writer in the history of civilization! Lenin's question to Gorky's circle: "What would we think when the thought is finished?", gets its concrete historical answer here. Kim Il sung's volumes are the most correct answer to Lenin's laughter. It is possible that the thought would continue once it reached the threshold of the thinkable, but that thought would take the form of Juche teaching. When we have reached the end of thought, thought can then produce an infinite number of volumes, and the more it produces, the more it will understand its own thinkable inexhaustibility. Juche ideology officially replaced Marxism-Leninism in 1972 (when North Korea split with Soviet policy) as a "creative application" of Marxism and Leninism–and this is correct. Juche ideology is *creative* in the sense that Kim Il sung held the answer that neither Gorky nor Lenin, nor even Marx himself, held.

Marx's Ambition

Shortly before he submitted *Capital* for printing (after he had worked on it for decades), Marx hurries Engels in 1867 to read the short story, *The Unknown Masterpiece* (1837), by Balzac. In the short story, the great painter Frenhofer spends 10 years painting and re-painting the portrait that will represent "a revolution in art," "the most perfect representation of reality." When Frenhofer, finally allows his colleagues Poussin and Porbus to see his masterpiece, to their horror they see a violent storm of accidental forms and colors scattered over one another, which are void of any harmony or sense. The painter wrongly understands their astonishment, and says: "Ah, you didn't expect such perfection," but when he hears Poussin's comment that "maybe Frenhofer really discovered the truth–he changed the portrait so many times that nothing was left of it," the great painter kills himself.

Francis Wheen writes that according to the testimonies of Marx's son-in-law Paul Lafargue, Balzac's short story, "made a great impression on him because it was in part a description of his own feelings."[10] Marx tailored his *Capital* for years in order to make it the perfect description of reality, but how can reality be perfectly described? Marx didn't want to publish *Capital*, as he studied math, he learned Russian in order to be able to follow the changes in the Russian landowning system, as well as collecting piles of books and statistics, all of which annoyed Engels, who offered that they served him only as a barricade, an obstacle to handing over his text for printing. Is there a way of presenting the perfect picture of reality? What type of madness are we talking about here? Balzac's short story is a perfect description of the love of the epoch towards abstract art (Malevich and his squares). Although he criticized beautiful writing as "intellectual babbling," "fictional fine-tuning," Marx nonetheless wrote with detailed precision–he wanted, says Prauer, to create a *literary* masterpiece.[11]

Marx also clearly thought of himself as a pure artist, and not a political theoretician or economist. "Now, regarding my work, I will tell you the plain truth about it," he writes to Engels in July 1865, "Whatever shortcomings they may have, the advantage of my writings is that they are an artistic whole."[12] Although *Capital* is most often categorized as a work of economy/economics, when the economists, political theoreticians and even the historians read it, they note that *Capital* is without form, incomprehensible, and frequently decry the clumsiness of the book. *Capital* was created as a radical collage of literary excerpts and thoughts, fragments of factory reports mixed with quotes from the Bible. In 1976, Professor Prauer wrote a book of 450 pages exclusively on Marx's literary references. Marx saw himself as *a poet* of dialectic materialism, while his ambitions were neither political nor economic, but literary. As a student of law, he published a collection of poetry, one play in verse and a novel, *Scorpio and Felix*, but when he saw his work next to the world classics, "all my creations crumbled into nothing,"[13] and he then had a nervous breakdown and his doctors advised him to take a long holiday. During this period he discovered Hegel, at that time a now-deceased professor of philosophy from Berlin. And it is true that Marx started studying political economy after many years of intensive analysis of literature and philosophy, after he had received a doctorate in philosophy, and after unsuccessful attempts in literature, as both a reader and a writer. Francis Wheen writes that in 1868, Marx copied a passage from Balzac's short story *The Village Priest* (1839) for Engels, and asked him whether Balzac's expression of reality corresponded to the doctrines of political economy.[14]

"According to Lacan, it was none other than Karl Marx who invented the notion of symptom," says Žižek, who asks: "How was it possible for Marx, in his analysis of the world of commodities, to produce a notion which applies also to the analysis of dreams, hysterical phenomena, and so on?"[15] Žižek answers that those two worlds share a fundamental homology, the same fetishistic fascination with the content hidden behind the form, with the secret of *the form itself*.[16] What lies behind the visible? Unmasking the place where value is formed–that had already been done before Marx in the field of political economy. The concept of surplus value had already been developed, and commodities also had a *secret*, namely that the secret of the value is the form itself. Pre-capitalist markets had an idea of equal exchange–I take to the market what I have produced, you bring yours, we make an exchange. Commodities don't have some universal character, and there is no absolute exploitation; at least in principle, the exchange is direct. But in capitalism, a new paradoxical type of commodity emerges–the work force, the worker, which/who is sold on commodities. With this new commodity, the commodity itself becomes its own negation. Then surplus value appears, and the owner assumes it. That is a symptom, a type of market hallucination, a kind of ghost world. All of this was known before Marx, but Marx wanted a world without this point of symptom, a perfect world of the dream; he wanted the universal without symptom, universal without exception.

Marx's Silence

The last and most famous thesis from Marx's *11 Theses on Feuerbach* (1845) is as follows: "Philosophers have hitherto only interpreted the world in various ways; the point is to change it."

With this thought, Marx announces the starry spectacle of his philosophy. It is interesting that after announcing an end of interpretation, Althusser says there was a philosophical silence from both Marx and Engels that lasted 30 years (the next work they would publish would be Engels's *Anti-Dühring* in 1877).[17] Althusser notes that when you proclaim an end of interpretation, you are left with nothing else but to shut up. Marx himself becomes paralyzed before his own dictate: "Enough interpretations, now we will make changes." If we make changes, then why any philosophizing? Lenin was right when he asked Gorky the impossible question. Do we have the capacity to continue thinking after this call? Marx himself didn't have a solution to this philosophical straying, nor did Engels or Lenin. They couldn't do anything but stand amazed before the last thesis on Feuerbach. Where to from here? If everything thus far had been interpretation, than the 11th thesis itself is nothing else than one more bourgeois thought. Is it to be considered a part of the "old" system of thought, or is it just some bourgeois discharge? The consequences of the theater called, Absence from Marxist Philosophy begins here.

For analytical purposes, everybody who threw him/herself at a systematic reading of Marxist literature felt this vertigo of a proliferation of words that in the end served nothing, that monstrous absence of sense incorporated in Marxist texts. (As the woman working the photocopying machine at the Macedonian National Library asked me, with amazement–why would I want to read books that no one had borrowed for decades?) The main problem of reading this literature can be overcome, at least on a philosophical level, if we approach that production of thought as a *symptom* of something. But of what? It is a symptom of frozen time. If one should be silent, one should also talk without interruption–these two are two sides of the same coin.

There is a brilliant insight into the jovial chatter made by the French psychoanalyst Jacques Lacan in his analysis of a patient from the cabinet of the Hungarian psychoanalyst Balint. One charming lady began coming to Balint's sessions. She was likeable, interesting and chatty, actually she was so garrulous that she belonged to the type who talk and talk, and in the end don't say anything. The problem (for which she unsuccessfully attended various therapies) consisted of a certain neurosis which could not surface, and it couldn't because she always talked about largely unimportant things. At one session, after an hour of tiring chatter, Balint suddenly gently touched the place that didn't want to be discovered. The charming lady received a recommendation for a new employment position, and the recommendation said that she was a "completely trustworthy person." The anxious moment lay in the fact that she didn't want to be seen as trustworthy. But nobody could rely on her word because the word obliges and she would have to start working and stop talking; and work has rules, laws, working hours, work demands and the respecting of agreements, which puts us in the position of slaves; and if she stopped talking, she would have to start working.

Lenin's laughter at Gorky is of the same type: "I refuse, Alexei Maximovich, to engage in any philosophical discussion," which at the same time means, "You, therefore can talk uninterruptedly." That is a pact that turns philosophy into chatter about the same thing:

Each *general* which is not connected to the individual and special, which doesn't turn into them, which doesn't objectify into them, which doesn't exist in them and through them (and, of course, vice versa, each individual and special) is unreal, empty, abstract, subjective and dead *general*.[18]

This is an excerpt from the interpretations of Hegel, by the Bulgarian communist leader and Doctor of Philosophy, Todor Pavlov. The communist generation produced horrible redundancy, a deadly repetition of the same mantras and tautologies as a style of living. On the other hand, tautology is the highest form of thinking, at least according to Hegel, as Kierkegaard cynically wrote: "This kind of tautology is especially useful for rostrums and pulpits, where one is expected to say something significant."[19] Lenin's laughter was not philosophically naïve. He announced that: (1) If there are no more philosophers, professional thinkers, and philosophy has done its work, then (2) Everybody can become a Marxist philosopher. In its shortened form, Slovenian communist Edvard Kardelj said the same thing in 1977: "Of course each communist or trade union official shouldn't be a scientist. But everybody must rely on Marxist theoretical thought."[20]

W.C. for Communists

There is a Yugoslavian joke about two cleaners taking an exam. The first one enters, "Tell me, what does the sign of the man's shoe on the door mean?" "W.C. for men." "And a woman's high heel?"

"W.C. for women." "And the five-pointed red star?" "W.C. for communists." She passes. She gets out and the other asks her what kind of questions she had. She replies: "Two general knowledge and one Marxism."

This joke illustrates Lenin's thesis about partisanship in philosophy.[21] If the whole of philosophy becomes partisan, then everybody can continue thinking. That doesn't mean that the cleaner will be raised to the level of an expert in Marxism, but precisely the opposite, as in the joke–now philosophy has been diminished and becomes amateurish, everybody can be occupied with it. Althusser says that Lenin believed philosophy doesn't even happen, philosophy has no real history,[22] and if it has no history, it is empty, so it can be filled by anybody. When Engels says in *The German Ideology* (1845) that philosophy should disappear, he says that philosophy is like a craftsman's laboratory–it is time to close that laboratory and now everybody, with a little bit of training, can open their own, the same one.

Thus, Marxism came to a thesis about the "universal man." At Marx's grave in 1883, Engels pays him respect with his posthumous speech: "But in every single field which Marx investigated–and he investigated very many fields, none of them superficially–in every field, even in that of mathematics, he made independent discoveries."[23] What made Marx such a brilliant mind that whatever he touched he made radical discoveries? More importantly, what guarantees that each of Marx's successors will be capable of the same endeavor? The guarantee is the materialistic characteristic of Marxism. In the same speech, Engels says: "Just as Darwin discovered the law of development of organic nature, so Marx discovered the law of development of human history."[24] Hence, Engels is the first to move Marx's thought from philosophy to science and that science gets its name–historical materialism. One of the consequences of such guaranteed scientific status is the fact that you can make no mistake!

If you receive recognition in communism, you know that the recognition is worth nothing, that it is fake, but you also know that there isn't anything above or beyond this, wrote Croatian historian Stanko Lasić in 1970.[25] The communist world is a world without self-reflection. Communism cancels God, and it establishes itself as the absolute. If you poke the balloon of the absolute, it will explode and everything will fall apart, therefore you mustn't question the balloon because it is the only thing that guarantees your existence. Before falling to disgrace, the most famous Yugoslavian dissident Milovan Ðilas taught the communists: "We should be happy if a person kills himself in the name of his world view, that's how the Revolution gets stronger." The man is released from alienation because the suicide also becomes an input into the system; even if you commit suicide, you are not free from the system. There is no exit.

When Althusser playfully concludes that there is "historical materialism," but there isn't "chemical materialism,"[26] that doesn't mean it will not be introduced. Communism becomes an era of the so-called proletarian sciences, as opposed to the bourgeois ones. In the Stalin era, two new theories were introduced: Japhetic theory in linguistics and Lysenkoism in biology. The powerful Stalin linguist, Nikolay Marr, developed the thesis that people from one class speak a more similar language, even if they are from two different countries, than people from different classes living in the same country. He called that theory the Japhetic theory of language. The Russian worker can communicate more easily with the French worker than the Russian worker can with the Russian bourgeoisie, because the Russian worker "somehow" developed a "version" of the Russian language that is much closer to the language of the French worker. Even Stalin had problems with this stupidity, and after Marr's death in 1950 he proclaimed his theory as an incorrect implementation of Marxism.

Stalin's director at the Genetics Center, Lysenko, who was glorified by the Soviet media as a genius, didn't even develop a theory with any factual substance—all he said was that there was a way out of the crisis in Soviet agriculture of the 1930s. The way out was the following: Because of their innate shrewdness and intelligence, the peasants themselves will achieve the best results in agriculture! That was the theory that elevated him to the top of Soviet science. He drove away the biologists and the agronomists, and his "science" was soon translated into a hysterical government request for agricultural self-coping with the crops. Mao Zedong implemented this science in China. He ordered Lysenkoism to become the leading approach in "solving" the problems in agriculture.

II

Phenomenology of Communist Intimacy

1

Paranoia

Sexual Hieroglyph

In communism, paranoia is the main "material" that human intimacy is made of, which applies to the "neutral citizens," to the nomenclature and to the victims as well. Let's proceed with the nomenclature. We usually believe that the top communist leadership in Yugoslavia lived an abundant life, while in truth the higher cadre never, even for a moment, forgot that they were the encoders of an order of a frightful semantic system saturated with signs; every associate said something, but the issue was how to read what they were saying. Everything around the party's top leadership was congested with hieroglyphs; the political destiny of each cadre member depended on the correct decoding of these hieroglyphs.

An illustration of this is "the Đurić case," an equally comic and tragic example of the communist empire of signs at the top of Tito's machinery which, as the ill-mouthed foreign reporters from the Congress in Zagreb jokingly commented, nearly turned the Sixth Congress of the Communist Party of Yugoslavia of November 1952 from the SIX(th) congress into a SEX congress. The event was also covered by "Time" magazine in their issue from November 17, 1952, in an article entitled "The Indiscrete Comrade."[1] Ljubodrag Đurić, a Secretary General and later minister, also a close associate of Tito and Ranković, and who also stayed for some time with Tito in the White House, accompanied him on lunches and dinners, to film screenings, pool games and hunting. There were no secrets between them. He lived alone with three children from his previous marriages, but Tito and Ranković suggested that "it is inappropriate for him to appear at receptions without an escort" and pressured him to remarry. When he found a woman that was his match, Ranković, at that time the Minister of Interior and first man of the military intelligence service OZNA, congratulated him on his choice of wife with the words: "The right woman for you, we checked her along all lines."[2] During one of the breaks at the congress, Đurić's fellow countryman from the Serbian town of Užice, Petar Stambolić, also a Congressional delegate, approached him and tauntingly remarked that Đurić's present wife was previously married to him. When they returned from the break, Đurić asked the president, Đuro Salaj, if he could have the floor for a moment to address "the communists' true problems." He approached the stand and visibly disturbed, said: "I cannot understand the act of certain functionaries, such as the one that happened to me–when comrade Stambolić, a member of the Central Committee of our party, stole my wife from me..."[3] (Here, Đurić, either confused or ashamed, changed the subject of his complaint and instead of saying that he himself was not aware that he had married Stambolić's former wife, said that his wife had been stolen by Stambolić.) The delegates jumped from their seats and began shouting: "You are lying!", while Tito ordered: "Remove this madman." Đurić was immediately taken away by the UDBA services in Zagreb and Đilas (later, the most famous Yugoslav communist dissident) approached the stand and tried to calm the delegates: "Comrades, I asked for the floor solely because I am familiar with his political background and therefore cannot consider his words to be a provocation, but merely an instance of insanity." There followed a break after which Tito took the floor, and in his turn gave an entirely different interpretation from Đilas'. "Comrades and lady comrades, I felt it necessary to offer my opinion regarding this unfortunate incident... I have indications and therefore I am deeply convinced that the enemy is behind this madman (approval and long applause) who wanted to compromise our Congress with some dirty excess and deal it a moral blow."[4]

This case provides, in miniature, insight into Lenin's doctrine of "anti-spontaneism."[5] In order to realize the revolution, the communists cannot be guided by spontaneous impulses (Lenin) because of the danger that they might stray from the path. Đurić's spontaneity equals political suicide–although cadre material fit for the Revolution, with an impeccable political portfolio, his moment of weakness, his "indiscrete" sign, becomes the subject of paranoid interpretation. Đilas's interpretation was naïve (Đurić was normally a faultless communist who was merely disturbed at this particular moment), and even that naivety was proof that even Đilas himself was not so successful in mastering the communist empire of signs, and it explains the real reason why he was later removed from Yugoslavia's historical records.

Unlike the above interpretation, Tito's interpretation reads that each sign is a conspiracy, Đurić does not speak of some alleged immorality of the Party, but rather what speaks through him is the "extended arm of enemy activity." The change in the interpretation from Đilas to Tito indicates how the communist "empire of signs" was built. The Party was a body that could not embrace those who were not like-minded. In his last speech before the Party, Trotsky said: "I know that to be right and at the same time against the party is impossible because history has not created other paths leading to the realization of justice."[6] There was no truth outside the party truth. The true communist did not hear what was spoken to him/her, as he/she saw *through* the speech. This turned communist speech into what Lacan called "empty speech." Whatever a person said was not really what he/she was actually saying. In Tito's jargon, the word was that which was transformed into a hieroglyph that required interpretation. In the strict hierarchy, Đurić was not supposed to say anything that was outside the established "empty talk" rules. If one was upset, he/she sent signals that required verification from the Party. In the communist hierarchy, no one thought and no one listened; furthermore, no one really spoke. Instead, all posted and read signs. One example of this is the naivety with which people repeatedly went to rebuild "democracy" in Yugoslavia at elections. There was no enforced voting in Yugoslavia such as, e.g. in Enver Hoxha's Albania (where, starting from early dawn, the party cadre would go around and gather the voters, while the Albanian radio announced: "It is 6:15 and already 48% of Albania has voted," and where Hoxha party candidates always won at least 97% of the vote),[7] but in Yugoslavia there was a type of "small town" coercion ("the neighbors should see me voting"). Žižek says that when people went to vote collectively for the *only* candidate, that meant that they did not perceive communism as being *real*, people were trained to read the exact opposite behind the phrase "rebuilding democracy." Don't rebuild democracy at any price! This created an apathetic distance–why should we even try when everything has already been resolved at the top? The worst option is for people to start taking the phrases of democracy seriously because that would mean that "they cared," and then they would really start acting in accordance with those phrases.[8] If they would take the call that the Communist Party should be rebuilt via a democratic process seriously, it would have meant the deterioration and destruction of the Party itself.

Another example is the case of the former commander of the Second Proletarian Brigade and railway manager, Ljubiša Veselinović, who committed suicide by shooting himself in front of the Monument of the Liberators of Belgrade in 1986 as a sign of protest against the "complete disintegration of Yugoslavia," and who stated in his letter to the President of the Union of the Communists of Yugoslavia:

My decision to end my life in this manner somehow grew commensurately with the stagnation of the new Yugoslavia–with its persistent transition from early socialism into late feudalism. I underline that I am not trying to do anything spectacular; my aim is rather to achieve some effect. Namely, if this protest of mine expressed through committing suicide (setting oneself on fire is more painful, more anachronic and has a religious quality to it) provokes people in the state and Party forums to think, then it won't all be in vain... And if, as it happened with many similar cries, it does not reach the consciousness of the main directors of today, then let this sacrifice of mine join the mass of the 1,700,000 buried in the foundations of the imagined, free, socialist and unified Yugoslavia.[9]

Veselinović's act was proof that the party phrases should always be accepted with a certain *distance*. (Žižek points out that the comedic humor in the novel, *The Good Soldier Schweik* (1923), by Jaroslav Hašek resides in the fact that Schweik understands and obeys orders in the most literal way, and while doing so simultaneously twists the orders to the point of absurdity.) The party used phrases that under no circumstances should be understood exactly as they were spoken, one always needed to read the message *behind* the phrase. With a bit of improvisation, it can even be said that one part of the dissidents in communism were those who truly understood the calls for freedom and democracy.[10] Communism was structured in such a way that every refusal to read the messages *literally*, outside the interpretation of paranoia, created victims. Communism was a place of ultimate replacement for those who listened by those who didn't listen (but not in the sense of disobedience, but in the sense of the biblical phrase, "And they have eyes wherewith they see not." If you see, then you are in the way of the ideology. Speech is not merely speech directed at someone else, but at myself as well. While I speak, I am not only speaking to the other person, but I am also hearing myself, Lacan wrote in his seminar, *The Psychoses 1955-56* (1997).[11] The sender is already the receiver of his/her own words. When the regime speaks, it speaks to other people, but since the others are not here to reply in words to the regime, but only to hear it, after a while the regime ceases to hear anything but itself.

The key question related to clinical paranoia is "Who is speaking?" This question becomes central to the regime as well. When Đurić is speaking, who is speaking *behind* him, *through* his speech? The world the communist enters becomes magical; everything is bursting with meaning, just like a paranoiac's world. The regime thinks that someone is constantly gossiping about it; that the people are spreading rumors among themselves, that someone is talking quietly, secretly, in ambush. The most important effort becomes an ability to "read between the lines." That means under no circumstances should you ever believe what someone is telling you, but to look for a hidden meaning. One of the big troubles that arose from this operation was that one could never be entirely sure what the other was actually trying to say. Everybody's speech was rife with hieroglyphs, but you didn't know in which direction to lead the subtle range of possibilities for its interpretation. Communism rendered people some type of encoders, therefore the entire learning process was that of learning how to read the signs. So people developed to perfection their social ability to understand not what the other was telling them, but what he/she "actually" wanted to tell them. The modi through which people functioned, from the lowest instances of neutral citizens up to the nomenclature, were simply large *factories* for the producing and reading of the signs of the communist empire. Paranoia is a communist disease, as communism considers everything. Everything becomes a sign. If a red car passes on the street it didn't just accidentally go by at this very moment, at this very location. Paranoia adds (new) meanings. The regime notices that there are things happening on the street. But what are those things? The totalitarian regime does not know and the people even less so. They all simply know that the meaning is going through a strange distortion. In his seminar *The Psychoses, 1955-56* (1997), Lacan says: "Very often, (a person) doesn't know, if you look closely, whether things are favorable or unfavorable towards him, but he looks for what is revealed by the way his counterparts act, or by some observed feature in the world..."[12] Like the paranoiac, the regime also says that when it experiences an illusion, there is some meaning behind it. But it does not know what that meaning actually is.

One famous case is the one in which Yugoslavian general Peko Dapčević asked General Jovo Popović, Head of the Surveillance Department within the State Security Service (the latter was also known as "Tito's doppelganger"): "Tell me Jovo, but truthfully, are you tapping my phone?" Popović answered: "No matter what I tell you, comrade Peko, you are going to get upset. If I tell you that we are tapping your phone you will be upset. But you will get even more upset if I tell you that we are not tapping your phone, you might think to yourself 'Am I worth so little that you won't even bother tapping my phone?'"[13]

Not only is the paranoid regime spied upon, observed, monitored, not only do the people talk, point, stare and wink at it, but a certain mercilessness spreads to the world of inanimate objects. Every microphone, every pin, the collar, the way the glasses are set on the table, all of this has meaning, and although the paranoiac is often incapable of saying what that meaning is, whether it is positively inclined and favorable or threatening, what is certain is that those words and those objects are not here without a reason! At the seminar *Psychoses, 1955-56* (1997), Lacan explains the manner in which a paranoiac mind works; the world gets meaning, as do the objects in his world, because his world "is never purely and simply inhuman since it's man-made."[14]

Such *humanization* of objects is present in the case of the so-called "Lenin's Testament." When Lenin was heavily stricken with a disease in December 1922 and his right arm and leg were paralysed, he was granted permission by his doctors to dictate to his stenographer for a few minutes each day, because he was disturbed by issues concerning the Soviet future and wanted to leave behind his characterizations of some of the members of the most immediate leadership of the CC.[15] Lenin requested his notes be made out in five copies and classified as "highly confidential," one of which was to be sent to his secretary and opened after his death. Lenin's notes became "an object winking" at the communists. When Stalin immediately succeeded Lenin as leader of the Party, the communists were still wondering: What about the notes? The communists, just like the Soviet emigrants, became involved in extensive secret analyses: What messages were Lenin's notes actually winking at them? Was the state obeying Lenin's will? Why did Lenin leave the notes in such a secretive manner, and under such strange circumstances? As could be seen in the notes, even Trotsky, whom Lenin favored over Stalin, had to distance himself from a misreading of Lenin. When the American Trotskyite, Max Eastman, published "Lenin's Testament" (as the Soviet emigrants referred to those notes) in 1925, Trotsky became very disturbed and immediately appeared with his own text in the newspaper "Bolshevik", severely criticizing the very existence of "Lenin's Testament":

No will should be allowed in our party. Vladimir Ilyich did not leave any "will." And the very character of the Party itself precluded the possibility of such a "will"… All talk about concealing or violating a "will" is a malicious invention… All gossip regarding the possibility of concealing or misusing the "will" is a malicious creation.[16]

The paranoiac himself "utters what he says he hears," says Lacan in his seminar on psychoses.[17] Trotsky is saying what he thinks he hears Stalin saying. Now, will I stay alive?–is what Trotsky ultimately asks Stalin in reference to the Lenin notes "that wink at Trotsky."

Tempo's Hardships (The Production of Generations)

Reading signs was the main driving force behind the "production" of communist sons, the driving force behind generational shifts. In Tempo's *Memoires* from 1985 (Tito's chief executioner in Macedonia), we find many examples of such "uneasy admiration" of the signs sent by Tito's party.

When Tempo appeared on television in October 1966 as the President of the Yugoslav Syndicate (the occasion being the bad economic situation), he was provoked at one point, and stated: "If the workers have it bad, let them go on strike then."[18] This outburst is the reason why "at around 7 o'clock" the very next morning his office was visited by the show's editor Ščekić, who was out of his mind, telling Tempo that he hadn't slept all night from worrying about the interview and that he had been taken to the hospital where he'd stayed overnight.[19] Now Tempo also became upset. As a functionary of a higher rank, he immediately turned to Tito:

"I hadn't visited Tito in a long while, so I asked for a meeting with him. I wanted to find out what he thought about my reaction. Of course, Tito immediately agreed to meet me. We discussed the current situation... 'What do you think, Old Man, of my outbursts on television?' Tito responded: 'I watched the first show. You were quite sharp, but what you said was true. A somewhat bitter truth, but the truth nonetheless. I didn't watch the second show. I was away.'"[20]

After being reassured somewhat, Tempo seems to calm down– at least he seems to. Because in *Memoires* he tells us that he couldn't find the peace he once knew. What about the second show that he missed? What if the *others* also requested to meet Tito and gave him different interpretations? "The problem is not in the fact that they are informing Tito, but *how* they are informing him,"[21] says Tempo. The time for the Brijuni meeting had come, and on the train that took the top party cadre to the Adriatic island of Brijuni, Tempo is approached by Žarković, who tells him: "I know with certainty that comrade Tito disagrees (with your views)." [22] Disgusted, Tempo goes to bed, but cannot sleep a wink:

I was surprised by the certainty with which Žarković told me that Tito disagreed with my texts. How could he possibly be better informed than me? ... Maybe Pajković told him that, and Pajković himself heard that directly from Tito at their last private meeting? What if Tito has changed his mind?[23]

And so it went, without end. The communist cadre member was someone who needed to be trained to be infinitely alert, ensuring that he/she remained informed of current actions and circumstances pertaining to the signs that were being sent. Colleague X requested a meeting with colleague Alpha, who then may have implied that colleague Y informed Alpha of the meeting of X with Z, etc. (Here, as Žižek says, we can freely add all kinds of behind-the-scenes meetings, court plots and shady conspiracies.) Alertness was key. If one was alert, then one knew where and when he/she could jump in with a personal intervention in the interpretation of the court dealings. Bared of substance, the paranoid game of party incidents and punishments now revolved around generational approval: Is this "son" (Tempo) guilty, is this "father" (Tito) going to punish him? Tempo addresses Tito as "Old Man;" Stalin's code name was "Grandfather," etc. This was no mere ideological drama, but an essential familial, Oedipal drama, set and located in the ideological world of paranoia. Paranoia is always most acute towards those who are closest to us. Tito's most loyal guard in the Revolution, his personal bodyguard for eight long years, Boško Čolić, who survived the war with an unlocked gun in his holster," was sacrificed when Tito's phobia/fear that someone wanted to kill him first kicked in (and later become more frequent). As an experienced agent of the Comintern, Tito had the professional habit of changing the people surrounding him, especially those closest to him, for fear that those who were closest to him were precisely the ones who were going to kill him. Čolić was Tito's guard for eight years, and was sacrificed in 1952 when he was asked to confess that on following orders from Moscow he planned the assassination of the Marshal together with Tito's private shoemaker and the former chief of Tito's cabinet. Due to a lack of evidence, they ended up accusing Čolić that in 1946, having Tito's permission to do so, he talked to the Russian actor Igor Bersenyev while he was making the film *In the Mountains of Yugoslavia*, and on that occasion discussed Yugoslavian war history with him. For this, he was convicted and sentenced to death by shooting; his punishment was later changed and he was sent to Goli Otok, and then to the St. Grgur camp. When he was finally released after 10 years of imprisonment, he had to sign a statement that he had never in his life seen the Marshal.[24] (Due to the paranoia that, as with the majority of communist leaders, Tito suffered from, his personal staff, which was charged with checking and securing all the food he ate and the premises he occupied, employed in its various configurations larger and smaller, somewhere between 1,000 and 1,500 members.)[25]

Which is why the following issue remains acute: What happens with the shift of generations, does there come a moment when the Son fills the empty space left by the Patriarch? Will he be rewarded for his indefinite trust? Or is the Son never going to succeed the Father, for the father is essentially immortal? In his novel, *The Successor* (2003), Ismail Kadare writes about the life of Mehmet Shehu, who was to be Enver Hoxha's successor in communist Albania. Shehu dies in 1981; however, his death remains an enigma, as the official announcement claimed suicide, though rumor has it that he was murdered. In his book, Kadare writes:

(The successor's life)... was a "dog's life." I was he who would come after. Preassigned to fill the Guide's shoes... that one day he would not be there anymore, whereas I would go on existing. Some days, the thought of it terrified me. I wondered how he could bear it himself. How could he tolerate my being there, how could he tolerate all the others who had accepted the pact? Why didn't he rise up and (start) shouting...[26] And further on: "I was Pasardhës. He who comes next. But nextness was not a question of distance...nor was it a chronological nextness, referring to the years I would reign after him... We were impossible fathers, and so we could only have impossible wives, sons, and daughters."[27]

The impossibility of a generational relationship is linked to the very sense of utopias that represent "reversed flow." In Gorky's novel, *The Mother* (1906), the son sells his dream to his mother. Utopias are possible only if the biological sequence is disturbed, as they are based on the act of rotating the places of generations. In Wolfgang Becker's film, *Goodbye Lenin* (2003), while the son is recreating East Germany as it was to his mother who is in a coma, he softens the harsh voice of the Party, he creates a world of communism that he himself would have been proud of.

However, another issue is of greater importance to us: What

happens if the shift of generations happens simultaneously with an ideological shift? Is the Oedipal question rotated in post-communism: Is the Son going to take over the license to kill from the Father, and whom shall he turn it against–against himself or against his communist parent? The Russian film *Twelve Angry Men* (2007) by Nikita Mihalkov is a perfect illustration of the ideological dynamics of the father and son in post-communism. The 12-member court jury is to take a verdict as to whether the Chechen student who is on trial is guilty for the murder of his Russian stepfather or not. The verdict is supposed to be unanimous, but due to the refurbishing of the court the jury is summoned into the gym hall of the nearby school (as a replica to Beslan), and in that closed atmosphere the jury begins a complex ideological debate on the father-son relationship in the post-communist ideological universe as the temporal, but also substantial, successor of communism. Following the disintegration of the Soviet Union, the question was now: Is this Son/Daughter (Chechnya) guilty of the murder of this Stepfather (Russia)? Or in the case of Yugoslavia, the permission from "outside" for emancipation of the last Yugoslav "child," Kosovo; the disputes between Serbia and Croatia in March 2008 over the heritage of the Olympic medals where Serbia responded to Croatia that since Croatia stepped out of the Yugoslav family, it automatically left behind all the medals in the possession of the "home," etc. In one moment from Mihalkov's film, while the votes whether the Chechen student is guilty for killing the Russian stepfather are divided, one of the jurors suddenly remembers his father, who was the party secretary on Ural. To this, another juror comments that his father was privileged and that that case cannot be of any help, but the communist son replies: "What kind of communist privileges are you talking about? We never saw our father. Three months after he retired he left this world." The privilege in question is a Bond type of privilege, "a license to kill;" the party secretary from the Ural trades family peace for the privilege to hold "a license to kill," but now, here stands the Son, who is demanding revenge because the father was involved with bloody politics instead of being the desired "family" dad for both his own children and his ideological children. The reminiscing of the "party secretary of the Ural" is an important moment in Mihalkov's film. "We never saw him, he passed away in three months, what privileges;" this response is the communist lament over generational stories, and it is indeed an accurate one, at least in the same sense as Đurić's political incident (which we already discussed at the beginning) becomes fatal, not only for his political career, but for his entire family as well: His sister was dismissed from work, his other sister was exiled, his brother was retired and the name of Đurić's older deceased bother was deleted from the list of the Teacher Training School in Uzhice.

Prison as a Central Life Experience

When we say that the communist universe is saturated with signs, is that not true for all of life's various aspects? Love relationships are full of signs, as are art works; is there a difference between the ideological signs and the love and artistic signs? In Sofia Coppola's movie *Lost in Translation* (2003), Charlotte and Bob arrive in Japan and cannot understand the Japanese signs. They intuitively come to the conclusion that there is some kind of excess in the signs that is lost, some kind of deprived thought that cannot fully be translated. Bob is an actor who goes to Japan to make a commercial. The first replica is when Bob lands in Tokyo and the man waiting for him says: "Welcome to Tokyo. My name is Kawasaki. Nice to meet you." To this Bob responds, "I've heard of you, thank you." That is comical, and at the same time it means that Bob gets lost in this totally ambiguous Japan. How should one translate the signs without getting lost in the process? The moral of Coppola's film is the opposite, insofar as during the time he is in Japan, Bob can actually finally exhale. The new country and the foreign culture compel him to surrender to the process of getting lost, as conventional signs here only have a *probable* value, and they cannot be understood despite the great effort, intelligence and good will that are put into their understanding. Bob's Japanese lesson is that the signs cannot always be understood. What remains an excess can become an insight–what occurs is the *unmasking of ideology as a system of phantasms*. Bob eventually realizes that being unable to read the signs actually frees him from any direct identification with the ideology. In Coppola's film, freedom is not presented as being a false conviction that living outside an ideology is possible; instead, it has the form of some ironic point *that life within ideology is always already a type of prison*. "I am preparing to break out from prison," Bob tells Charlotte. Bob speaks of life as an assumed prison, of life within any ideology as a prison. What about a communist prison? Has the meaning been lost in the translation of the communist prison experience?

In the German documentary about the secret police of the DDR, *No Lost Time* (2004), by Christopher and Marc Bauder and Dörte Franke, a four-member group of DDR dissidents is interviewed, two young men and two young women, who were incarcerated in 1979 and 1980 for distributing flyers with citations from the book, *Alternative*, by Rudolf Bahro, which was prohibited at that time in the DDR. When they were arrested, they were sentenced from two to five years in prison. What struck me as terribly sad in the movie was the unclear feeling of the vainness of their prisons. The film was made in 2004 in contemporary Germany, and these dissidents mentioned that life had improved much from what it was then in the DDR of that time, which is indeed true, both in a political and historical sense. But there is an obvious contradiction in the film between their verbal statements and their non-verbal, carnal sadness. Their statements are full of confidence, stability and assuredness; they say that their battle was worth it, that it made sense, that finally, according to the statement of one of the dissidents, they considered the time spent in prison as "No Lost Time," hence the title of the film. But their lostness in the translation between the two historical systems, the personal injustice that was done to them with that very translation, is what is seen independently from the ideology in which they believed at that time or in which they believe today. One of the dissidents, Günter Herrig, says in one of the scenes: "The prison is your central life experience, everything that you have ever been or will be amounts to the prison." And he was possibly more successful than all the other dissidents in wording the key message concerning the translation between the two ideologies:

We ended up being sentenced twice. On the one hand, we were not given any explanation of the possibility for an alternative. On the other hand, we were dealing with a force... We tried to find solutions; could things be made to be different? But we failed to find a solution because they arrested us before we found an answer.

This is something that could ideologically even be considered a "successful" outcome. Namely, there is a double paradox with the prison experience in totalitarian regimes, which is that the most excruciating life experience is an experience that elevates you as a subject of political "virtue." A friend of mine once told me that people who had survived ideological prisons, such as my father had experienced, have a philosophical depth, a wisdom that derives from the intensity they endured while in prison. Contrary to that, I think that the prison experience breaks people, however my friend is still right about one thing–if political prisoners, after all their ideological turmoil, still think that is was worth it, that it was not all in vain, that feeling which was, paradoxically enough, rendered from prison was a legitimization of the "political" virtue.

There is a well-known anecdote in which the main actor is the most famous Yugoslav dissident, Milovan Đilas, who in 1979 went to the State Security Service to take back his trophy weapon that the Service had taken away from his apartment "while acting in accordance with the security situation," and who jokingly said to them: "Arrest me more often, this will boost the sales of my books abroad."[28] That is indeed true. As Verdery says, the most important dissident tool was attracting the attention of Western countries,[29] and the dissidents accrued moral capital; they were without any formal political authority, while the idea of suffering, arrests, prosecution and torture gave them political authority. To be noticed by the West was what counted as moral capital in communism, such as that of Václav Havel and Jan Patočka in the Czech Republic, Doina Cornea in Romania, Adam Michnik in Poland, Gyorgy Konrad and Iván Szelényi in Hungary, and in some cases, as in the case of Václav Havel, the political prisoner becomes a political leader mainly owing to the moral capital acquired in the socialist era. To show that someone suffered in communism became an important moment, it strengthened one's moral authority.

The Serbian painter and sculptor, Ilija Šoškić, who in Rome in 1968 joined a group of Italian Maoists gathered around the newspaper "Metropoli" owned by Scalcone, Negri and Poperno, would write later on in his memoires that he did not regret anything connected to his diversionary and dissident activity in Italy, except for one thing:

"Sometimes I only regret that in my life I was not sentenced to prison. At least in that way I would have perceived myself as a somebody. As things are now, I don't know what to do... I don't believe anymore that politics can bring change. Perhaps I can maybe sit on a motorbike and drive away somewhere."[30]

"Perhaps I will maybe get on a motorbike and drive away somewhere." But where? We remember the fate of Hesse's *Siddhartha* (1922), which achieved planetary success in the 1960s. After being a sinner in the big city, Siddhartha goes to the guru to eventually leave both hedonism and asceticism behind, and to find his peace with a fishing pole in his hand, standing alongside a desolate river. One of the most censored directors in Tito's Yugoslavia, Želimir Želnik, who made the ironic documentary, *Tito, for the Second Time among the Serbs* in 1994, is an example of the exact opposite. When on one occasion I met Želnik in Budapest in 1999, he told me: "There are no ideological themes, all there is is biology (he had personally come to film a porn fair), and biology is freedom." Similar to Šoškić and Želnik, Hesse also argues that freedom is possible only if ideology is escaped. But, escape from ideology is an adolescent dream. Both the river and the fishermen, even Hesse's fish, although Hesse does not tell us this, are part of the exchange within strictly defined ideological frameworks. Šoškić's motorcycle can only run as part of the existing traffic culture. And the porn fair, as well as the porn workers and the porn audience, are part of a porn culture which has its established rules. Laws may be more or less totalitarian or liberal, but there is no space where ideology ceases to be relevant. Nature too is a system of "ideological" constructs, and nature imposes its own "ideological" demands on the fisherman. But that is why it is important what material the ideology is made of, whether it is more or less restrictive when it cannot disappear anyway. To go back to Coppola's *Lost in Translation*: Bob is also imprisoned in the capitalist universe, but Japan is not the same for Bob as DDR prison is for Günter Herrig from the documentary *No Lost Time*. "I am preparing to break out from prison"–for Bob this is not only a phrase, it is the minimal difference with which Bob ceases to be a prisoner compared to Herring's imprisonment. In each ideology, one can *feel* as if thrown into a large prison. That is when you get the philosophical insight that the world is a big prison. But if capitalism is

Bob's prison, for Herrig the prison is where the Lacanian blow to the Real takes place, not a prison as philosophy, but a prison that abolishes philosophizing, even when, similar to Šoškić, one decides to proclaim prison the ultimate point of one's personal ideological freedom. If in a Hegelian sense there is no way of explaining the future, but only a way of understanding the forms in which the past exists, then we are obliged to compare and grade the possibilities of freedom of the different ideologies and to tell them apart.

If reading signs is not only a communist discipline, if the artist and the lover also produce signs, and not only the politician, is there a difference between these types of signs? The reason why we like the signs that love and art send us is because love and art free us from the obligation to interpret signs, we can get lost in the signs as a precondition to start enjoying the reading, or the love. Just like Bob in Coppola's film, one is free precisely because one has been allowed to "lose oneself in the signs." Things are not the same when it comes to the communist signs. The communist signs deprive one from freedom and with that, from time. In the novel, *In Search of Lost Time* (1913-1927), Proust's narrator is incredibly tense because of the "requirement" to properly read the ideological signs (in Proust, these are the snobbish signs) sent to him by high society in order for him to find his place of luxury in the narrow nomenclature of a semantically saturated world. The project ends with the paralyzing confession of Proust's narrator that while decoding ideological signs of others, he irrevocably lost his own historical time. In the fiction universe constructed by Proust, you enjoy yourself, while the narrator is the one who is doing all the work. As a reader you get lost in the signs in order to gain insight into the meaning of freedom. Life is not such. The signs sent by communism required one to rise up to a level of social perfection in order to avoid making a mistake by misreading a sign. That left people without any space to learn anything else but that. The reading of signs, "judging from the viewpoint of actions, appears to be disappointing and cruel, and from the viewpoint of thinking, stupid,"[31] says Deleuze.

The historical and cultural devastation that communist paranoia leaves is brilliantly described in Robert Carver's book, *Accursed Mountains* (1991), which is about post-communist Albania. "Everyone I met (in Albania) showed a staggering ignorance… Conversations suddenly ground to a halt when someone would ask: 'What is a hippy?' or 'Who is Freud?'"[32] But not be naïve, travel journals are a post-colonial discourse. If you don't know who the Beatles are, the Beatles have no significant effect on the quality of your life. Quite the opposite, the saturation with information in the capitalist universe functions similarly to paranoia in communism. In that, these two systems are related, one stacks information (capitalism), the other one encodes it and conceals it (communism), while both do what they do in order to anesthetize all action to the point of paralysis. As we already know from Baudrillard, information does not produce sense, "information has nothing to do with signification," and "information is directly destructive of meaning and signification,"[33] "information dissolves meaning and dissolves the social, in a sort of nebulous state dedicated not to surplus of innovation, but, on the contrary, to total entropy."[34] Information (because of the medium) often has a purely instrumental meaning, implying that a blind spot neutralizes the subject and does not allow it to react. But these two, although related systems, still leave the following issue unanswered: If information is an important action factor, at what point is the *action most frozen*? Is it at the point of not having any information or at the point of having too much information? Totalitarian systems depended on the monopoly over information, when too much information started to leak through the iron curtain thanks to fax machines, phone and computers,[35] the system of closed information caused its own deterioration. If too much information leads to a "blind spot," it also carries auto-referential information; the awareness of the system according to the Escher principle can carry potentials for resistance in capitalism, which by no means implies that it indeed carries them. The heritage that we take with us from the communist systems should take into account this overwhelming fact–that we come from a system of cruelty and stupidity as the elementary substitute for thinking, dedication and empathy. Yet it is most certain, keeping in mind the experience of Guantanamo Bay, that we have entered a similar world of systematic cruelty and stupidity, of a new series of victims not a product of "the empire of signs," of "empty speech," but rather a product of the horrifying acceleration of the media, which the more they are "filled" with information, the more paradoxically, they empty the probability of any other action but the same kneeling before ideological blindness and cruelty. However, the scalability of the two systems is important, and that scalability shows the striking consequences that our "Eastern world" survived by getting stuck in the worst of the two ideological alternatives.

2

Intimacy

Stealing Intimacy

"Dogme 95," the school of Lars von Trier (see the films *Dogville* (2003) and *Manderlay* (2005)), brutally dispersed the illusion of the existence of such a thing as "my intimate space," or simply "my space." In the book, *Cultural Intimacy* (2005), Herzfeld writes that, "a few are innocent when it comes to intimacy."[1] Every human intrudes on the privacy of others and is him/herself threatened by them. The sign (No Trespassing!) cultivated by the bourgeoisie culture as a place that I fence away from the world (physically and symbolically) was brutally proclaimed a farce in the postmodern culture of the "market families" of reality television shows. In the book, *I-Spy* (2006), Mark Andrejević writes that today every major Internet company claims that it safeguards your privacy, the paradox being that the very same company gathers your private data as its own property by referring precisely to the right of human beings to their privacy.[2] And Andrejević adds:

A cousin of mine who works at one of the nation's largest database companies [in Australia, my comment] refused, on the grounds of privacy, to send me a copy of the information the company had about me. But when she sent a copy of the information about her– including only the public record information and not the additional proprietary information (gathered from the commercial sector and law enforcement), it was more than 20 pages long and included not only a list of all the places she'd lived, but of all her former roommates, and all of the cars she'd owned. This was just the lowest resolution "data image" available, and yet it contained much more information than most of us would have realized is routinely gathered and stored about us.³

This is how dramatic things are in the world today, as far as when and where intimacy is concerned. In his novel *Postsingular* (2007), Rudy Rucker, Hegel's great-grandson and one of the best SF writers of today, provides a visionary description of a world in which intimacy is literally *non-existent*. In Rucker's world, small nano-robots, at any and all times, freely enter and exit your premises while you are eating, peeing, or making love, and every inhabitant of the planet can log into the direct streaming from your room and follow you in your most banal daily life if they find you are interesting enough. However, the dramatic moment in Rucker's novel is that the canceling of privacy occurs *abruptly;* there are no serial acts, education or getting used to, there's no revolution, just the technological inescapability that people accept even without having any idea of resistance. How is this possible?

The word intimacy, from the Latin "intimus," signifies something "most inherent," "one's innermost nature." But although we consider intimacy to be something of a self-evident phenomenon, Henry Lefebvre warns us that to start with, intimacy is always "abstracted" from the public space, and only then is it gradually proclaimed as privacy. Intimacy per se does not exist, it is what people steal from the public space, "demarket" it from the world and subsequently proclaim it as theirs. In contrast, every ideology considers human intimacy as "its own property" (similar to Internet companies), while people only have the illusion that they "own" their intimacy.

When I visited the State Archive of the Republic of Macedonia in 2006, demanding non-restrictive access to my father's dossier, the officer directly in charge of the dossiers unexpectedly responded with a personal confession:

My uncle's police file is in the cabinet to my right, it has been within my reach for years, and have I attempted to open it? No. And why haven't I? Because it is *here* that a higher agency is involved. What is the benefit for me, or my uncle for that matter, from the act of opening?

Herzfeld described this type of unclear homogenization of the community concerning state intrusions in the intimacy of others with the notion of "cultural shame." In times of crises, people practice a kind of solidarity with the secret services, services that they would otherwise find appalling. With regard to the student demonstrations of the late 1990s in Macedonia, a leftist friend of mine told me that if the state hadn't secretly monitored the leader of the demonstrators, he would have personally felt endangered–meaning that in times of crisis even the greatest non-conformists tend to act as citizens unusually loyal to the secret services. And they are not alone. The bureaucrats themselves are caught up in the same closed circle, seeing that the state is not a monolithic agency, but rather something of a mobile complex of people and roles; it often happens that the bureaucrat at the window complains about the system with the same passion as the most dissatisfied client. People are ready to tirelessly protect even the most notorious operations of their ideologies as their own, personal ones, expecting in return that the institutions will offer them (civil) security for their loyalty.

What's up with communism? "I should immediately explain that I do not consider houses with rooms as compulsory, and I think that the notion of a 'room' shall mean only the former human's formerly inhabited space."[4] This is the writing of the Russian thinker Shchekin in his book, *How to live differently* (1925), which was based on Trotsky's ideas. After the October Revolution, communists instantly sketched out the new intimate space, and said: There are not going to be any rooms anymore. Rooms shall be physically destroyed. If one of the rooms survives, it shall survive solely for its museum value, as an artifact that was inhabited by a former human, who shall automatically become a past human. Why were communists so inclined against rooms? Shchekin offers an answer: "The solitude of the rooms is something that the collectivist human does not need... On the other hand, the solitude needed for several hours of love can be satisfied in the special gardens of pleasure, where a man and his female comrade can find the required comfort."[5] The garden of pleasure–the public pornographic space, becomes the recommended way of living, and sex becomes collective, not in the sense of a liberating orgy, but in the sense of a perverse insight into the intimacy of the other (this ideal was finally achieved through capitalism by using more sophisticated means).

The room is a den, it is unclear what dark moments may seize the communist in the solitude of the room; the room is a shelter for various forms of deviation. What is recommended are the gardens of pleasure, before the eyes of all.

Already in the first great book of socialist ideas, *Utopia* (1516), by Thomas More, we have descriptions of the rooms, doors, clothing, food and entertainment of the citizens of the ideal state. While reading More, one soon realizes that the houses and clothing are not just socialist décor, they are the most intrinsic feature of the ideal society. More describes in detail the *doors* that led to the ideal state: "The doors are two-winged, they open and close on the slightest touch and then, by closing themselves, they let everyone in."[6] This 16th century description perfectly fits the saloons of the Wild West–the socialist utopia of an ideal home paradoxically finds its ideal system of closure in the capitalist cowboy public space. There are no private rooms in More's writings, and although there are still houses, their doors are permeable. The door is a threshold, it opens and closes, it is a passage from the private into the public. For More, the door becomes the key to the ideal society. Transform the door into a passage into the world (abolish intimacy) and what you get is the ideal society. This is actually an idea from ancient times, as Plato wrote that private property and the home should be abolished, saying: "The principle of individuality is merely an abstract idea"[7] Marriage should also be abolished, children should, immediately after birth, be taken away from their mothers and put in kindergartens, etc. Communists read the utopian teachings and concepts; the *Communist Manifesto* said: "Destruction of the family!", while Engels wrote: "The upbringing of all children from the moment they can manage without their mothers' help must be the concern of the state and financed by the state."[8] The Soviet communist Ljadov elaborated: "Every conscientious father and mother will say: If I want to free my child from the private owner dwelling in each and every one of us, I must isolate him/her from me... The sooner the child is separated from its mother and turned over to the social kindergartens, the greater the guarantee that the child will be healthy."[9] Women go through the same process. Capitalism exploits sexual desire, while the radical communist response to this was to deprive women of their "marketability" and treat them in a discrete manner. "The family must be replaced by the Communist Party"[10]–this is the thesis of Preobrazhensky from the very beginnings of the Soviet Union. "I shall not greet the uninvited guests, I never asked them to come" goes a memory from Lukacs's childhood. Childhood is constantly under threat, in a crisis, as just about anything can bring harm to the little person, with Lukacs–the child, before becoming Lukacs–the ideologist, saying: I didn't invite you, you have imposed yourselves on me. But this was, however, before the euphoria of communal life caught up with him. In Kafka's "Process," Josef K. is arrested after the machinery enters his room. Josef K. sees his anonymous executors at the very threshold: "Who are you?" K. asked, immediately half-sitting up in bed. But the man ignored the question, as if his presence there simply had to be accepted."[11] Why is it normal for the regime to force itself through the door uninvited? The room is the space where you can still hope, the core of resistance. Even resistance *towards* the room is shaped *in* the room.

If no ideology favors intimacy, how then is communism different? The communist defines "good" as something that has been cast away by the bourgeois. Having a family house and a family car formed the essential core of the bourgeois dream. When the USA and the USSR organized a cultural exchange in Moscow in 1959, the Americans did not bring paintings or books with them; instead, they brought a highly prosaic model of a modern-equipped American kitchen, and Nixon and Khrushchev were photographed standing in front of it and talking about the comparative advantages of the family models–in what was called "The Kitchen Debate." The capitalist response to communal socialism was this: Here is this kitchen, so how would you feel in it? Capitalism does not deceive people, it tells them openly that the factory is an ugly place that makes routine of movement and humiliates people; but capitalism promises them that what they have been deprived of as manufacturers shall be returned to them as consumers, says Buck-Morss.[12] Domestic space becomes a place for such a correction; the home becomes the primary axiomatic value–a place for rest and intimacy. Communism tries to *correct* this correction. It diverts the emotions to the factory (public dining halls, kindergartens, joint dining rooms, hot meals at work, leisure clubs, worker's summer resorts, sport halls), the factory is to become a home. Mayakovsky wrote: "Let's put a stop to the production of useless paraphernalia. With all these dogs, mermaids, little devils and elephants, it invisibly approaches the petty bourgeois and is creepy. Clean your rooms!"[13] But when avant-garde living space concepts ("communals") were transformed into joint apartments, it was an idea born more out of a lack of space than of futuristic visions. In the Bosnian city of Zenica in 1969, Yugoslav communists discussed the matter of how the workers could be cultivated, as they had no time to go to the opera, meaning that the opera had to come to them, into the work halls. The paradox, however, lies elsewhere. Capitalism turned the *home into a factory,* into a sector of capitalist production, which was equipped as a service with sewing–and washing machines, refrigerators, vacuum cleaners, electric irons, as homes became small production halls, they were industrialized,[14] but more importantly, what it did was turn the home into a *pornographic space,* and instead of tearing down houses, capitalism told people–go home from work and rest, and we shall bring the cameras into your houses and we shall attack intimacy in the very place where it is created. And you will even desire this! Unlike the naïve communist attempts to physically destroy the home, capitalism succeeded by doing so ideologically. If someone does not put me under a magnifying glass, I shall personally place a camera and broadcast myself on the Internet 24/7. Someone is *bound* to see me.

Macedonian Goats and Soviet Potatoes

The chronology of Macedonian communism in the period from 1943–1991 by Macedonian historian Violeta Ačkoska in 2001 presents a sequence of events, incidents and processes related to Macedonian communism that *entertain* us with various, unusual phenomena. One in particular attracted my attention. If we exclude the events related to Josip Broz Tito, all other occasions for which Macedonians organized *en masse* were represented in the summits of exotic countries. For example, in December 1967 the People's Republic of Macedonia announced a "Week of Solidarity with the Vietnamese people." In December 1960 in Macedonia, an action called the "Month of the Algerian children" was organized as an aid to the children in the French–Algerian conflict. In February 1961, protest gatherings were organized in the cities of the People's Republic of Macedonia against the murder of the Congo national leader Patrice Lumumba, and a gathering of 70,000 citizens was organized in the city square known as Marshal Tito. In September 1966, the Swedish King Olaf V visited Macedonia and the Macedonian citizens organized a huge welcome, etc. The question is what did the Macedonians have in common with Algeria, Congo, Vietnam or Sweden, i.e. why hadn't they demonstrated such solidarity in large numbers for some great injustice in their close communist neighborhood (Bulgaria was blanketed in information darkness due to the split between Yugoslavia and the USSR in 1948), but what about the events in Serbia, Kosovo, Albania, Bosnia? We find an answer in the communist *concept of the home*, which found a strange "understanding" with the mentality of our small town. The small town is aware that it is banal and gives up the illusion that it has sensationalism. The small town actually likes that banality of the ever-unchanging stasis, which guarantees the eternalness of the small town. But, at the same time, the small town wants sensationalism, it recognizes the duality: "usual" (for us) and "unusual" for the (world), usual–unusual, closed–open, the small town nurtures this dualism and believes in it–it considers itself to be "an island amidst the sea of banality, but a fantastic island,"[15] as Konstantinović writes, while it believes that *real* life "retreated to the zones of unusualness" somewhere out there in the world, and the small town wants to *mingle* with it. Life is a phenomenon of exclusiveness that can only be reached when domestic banality is excluded, and for a moment it connects with the unusualness of the world, out there somewhere. The communist phenomenon of "a home outside the home" (of the communist "Internationale," of the "workers have no state," of the whole planet is our home and similar, in our country in the form of Tito's "nonaligned" movement) was an ideal match for this small-town ideal of the unusualness of the world "outside." Aside from the asceticism and avant-garde disgust of flowers and useless paraphernalia in petty bourgeois homes, the communist home still preserved one recognizable bourgeois phenomenon–the ficus. In *all* communist countries (including in the Soviet Union, its satellites and in Yugoslavia), the ficus was tolerated, not as a remainder of the bourgeois greenhouses, a "poor relative of the geranium," a common ornament on the flowerboxes of middle-class houses, as Svetlana Boym put it,[16] but because the ficus was experienced as some kind of imperialist impulse, communist "Internationale," the idea that the exotic world *too* is our home (how shall I turn this room into a home? By introducing a flower that has nothing to do with my *habitat*). This insistence on the "exotic" can be found in both communism and capitalism, with the difference being that capitalism had a clearly defined imperialist impulse, while the adapted ficus was seen as *colonial loot*. Communism, on the other hand, had no idea that this artifact was foreign, it felt like an international good. The lucky charm of the third world becomes a frequency captured with the communist Internationale, but also a small-town vibration for banishing the banality of what is ours, and a plug into the unusualness of the world.

How to destroy the rooms of intimacy? One of the approaches was the physical. In the 1920s, Soviet architect Vladimir Tatlin broke the pavement in the yard of the Leningrad Academy of Art and planted potatoes in the exposed soil.[17] Communism required a redefinition of the bourgeois relationship towards nature. In 1844, Marx wrote that since people are part of nature, when nature is destroyed, they destroy themselves as well and in order to abolish alienation, people need to make peace with nature.[18] But paradoxically, this call was not read as an ecological cry, on the contrary, it was primarily interpreted as a call for the destruction of nature itself. As Marcuse wrote: "Nature ceases to be true nature... the material is given a negative status."[19] Communism does not recognize a "positively" privileged matter, all that intrudes with the New Form is cleared. This is also behind the explanation of the strange goat slaughter of September 1947 in Macedonia ordered by the hard-line communist Lazar Koliševski, when the government of the People's Republic of Macedonia adopted a "Regulation for Prohibiting the Farming of Goats, i.e. restricting their number," which was popularly called Lazar's Law. In 1948, it was changed into the Law on Prohibiting the Farming of Goats on the Territory of the People's Republic of Macedonia. Lazar's Law brought the number of goats in Macedonia down from 516,831 in 1947 to 69,350 in 1952.[20]

What fetish status were the goats assigned at that moment in

Macedonia, and why was their slaughter necessary? A pragmatic explanation would be that the goats destroy the forest, they graze the breech, the oak, the acacia, the box bushes, they also eat shrubs, thorns, nettle, and although the farming of them is economical and they provide tasty meat, being omnivores, they are becoming a kind of closest natural competition for humans. But, as Žižek writes, communists didn't recognize the simple difference between nature and culture, culture too is part of nature (from a cosmological aspect); the communist premise was that the world should free itself of all the traces of the dirt of the former (bourgeois) corruption.[21] The goats were an accidental and stupid choice, but no less stupid than Tatlin's act of planting potatoes in front of the Leningrad Academy of Arts in 1920. The general logic behind the two operations was that if some something was there before, it should now be destroyed to make way for the new.

If goats were once here, let there be civilization now (the Macedonian case), and if there once was an Academy here, then let there now be potatoes (the Soviet case). Although these events concerned different transfers (a trade of culture for nature and vice versa), both operations amounted to a process of reducing the "truly" existing nature to a *raw material* that was sacrificed for the construction of the New World. Faith says that following the action of destruction, "*something will remain*, the sublime '*indivisible* remainder,' the paragon of the New," as Žižek writes.[22] This "irrational cruelty served as a kind of ontological proof... that we are dealing... not just with empty plans–the Party is ruthlessly brutal, so it must mean business..."[23]

But that business was not easily achievable. It is difficult to uproot the room and one possible way to do this would be to displace it, so often and persistently that it finally becomes a mobile room. If the room is constantly on the go, one cannot fall into the temptation of settling into bourgeois cosiness. The consumerist West sensualized objects, fed homeostasis and rendered people passive. In Paris, the Soviet communist Rodchenko saw the "endless bidets" and "indecent postcards" and had the urge to puke from the Brie and Roquefort cheeses.[24] Communists, just like a bunch of Freudians, were aware of the blind spot of pleasure, and in the end it was Marx who coined the term "symptom" and not Freud, as Žižek points out.[25] Marx noticed the object's bite on the bourgeois and that already at the point of cosiness, a nauseous feeling and alienation appear, in the sense and spirit of Goethe's words: "There is nothing more difficult to bear than a series of beautiful days!"[26] If the agreeable, benign objects do not diminish the alienation, but rather increase it, then the solution would be the radical separation of objects from people. In the Soviet Union, Vladimir Tatlin published an article, "The Problem of the Relationship between Man and Object: Let Us Declare War on Chests and Sideboards."[27] So the solution was to create *mobile* objects. Susan Buck-Morss writes that when Walter Benjamin visited Moscow in 1926-1927, he noticed the astonishing dimensions of experimentation with room objects: "Indeed, what distinguishes the Bolshevik, the Russian Communist, from his Western comrade, is this unconditional readiness for mobilization."[28] The beds were constructed in such a way that they could immediately be turned into a table or armchair, kitchen appliances could be put in small packages, chairs could be folded away when not in use, and so forth. Mobility, speed and an absence of stagnation become the imperative, and frequent moves are supported. Mayakovsky wrote: "If you so desire, just put on wings and wheels and take off, the house and all the objects in it."[29] And not only the houses–let the people fly off too. Susan Buck-Morss shares a comical detail that between 1929 and 1931, Tatlin created a "new object" in Moscow that was unknown to capitalism. It was actually a flying machine that worked like an air bicycle, and he named it Letatlin after himself, hoping it would become widely used and would help people regain their innate flying capacity since "we have been robbed of our feeling of flight by the mechanical flight of the aeroplane."[30]

The paradox, however, is that the "flying" rooms of communism found their final realization precisely in the capitalist expansion of tourism! Communism constantly spoke of some kind of mobility: "to walk that difficult path," "to walk the true path"–those euphemistic determinants were to be connected to the bourgeois desire for mobility, the accumulation of capital and climbing the social ladder. And although both ideologies were similar in this respect, the difference was otherwise–the world of real-socialism remained in essential immobility. The Soviet Union and Albania are probably the only countries in the world (today, also North Korea) in which, in the era of the harshest communism, literally only two pedestrians would be seen walking along the streets. In the documentary, *Welcome to North Korea* (2001), by Peter Tetteroo and Raymond Feddema, fantastic visualization is made of the still acute immobility of North Korean communism. In one of the scenes, the traffic police officer continuously regulates traffic at the largest intersection in the capital of Pyongyang, where not even a single car passes during the day. In the enormous hotel, the authors of the documentary are the only guests, and aside from them, there are 20 other people sleeping in the hotel–the hotel staff. There are no elderly people in the streets, and everyone that is above a certain age is forcefully moved from the city because they do not fit the designed image. The empty city is constantly getting ready for visitors who never actually come to visit. When people wonder about the force underlying the communist project for maximum mobility that ended in a total paralysis of life, they overlook the fact that *to want and not to want* are the same thing–not to want (objects) is the same as to want not to want them (the objects). The capitalist overestimates the objects and calls that love. The communist underestimates the objects, but also calls that love. This is only one of the explanations as to why the two ideologies essentially shared the same attitude towards intimacy and its displacement, though with the difference that communism wanted to displace intimacy in order to nail the possible points of resistance of people in their homes, while capitalism decided to leave people in the comfort of their passive homes, but also entered them with the most sophisticated ideology for the (voluntary) dissolution of intimacy.

Thomas More understood utopia early on as a uniformity of the population. In the 16th century, More wrote with sympathy about the world of uniformity and grayness: "Throughout the island they wear the same sort of clothes, without any other distinction except what is necessary to distinguish the two sexes and the married and unmarried." And: "When they appear in public, they put on an upper garment…; and these are all of one color, and that is the natural color of the wool."[31]

More imagined uniforms as if he were the director of an ancient theater. In the ancient theatre, the actors wore exaggerated masks–

the men, black, the women, white, and the elder, wrinkled. The masks were enormous, the actors stood on platform shoes and the clothing was *expressive*. But this solution came from the technical conditions of the amphitheaters where the acoustics were perfect, but the viewers in the furthest rows had no video beam, therefore they needed exaggerated clothing, i.e. a uniform, to help them see and distinguish the actors on stage. Contrary to this, communism proclaims technical conditions as essential. The uniform becomes something literal, the mask becomes the face and human individuality is exchanged with the role. The entire world becomes a theater with strictly defined and accentuated roles in order to make society totally transparent (see the chapter entitled "UDBA Code Names"). In the first year following the October Revolution, Tatlin designed a workers' uniform (a coat and a suit) in five variations.[32] Communists impose the uniform by force.

What about capitalism? Is there a difference between the communist and the capitalist uniform? The cult British punk documentary *UK/DK* (1983) by Christopher Collins describes the life of street punks in London. In the 1980s, they say the only thing they want from the world is the right to variety in clothing. They would work at whatever, as long as they could go to work in their own clothes. For example, they would work as cashiers in supermarkets, but with Iroquois hairdos, if it wouldn't disturb the customers. The punks demanded clothing be seen and tolerated as an expression of their internal emotions, and they demanded people stop pretending that they did not care, and to stop pretending it is all the same to them. At the same time, the corporations were designing a more successful dress strategy for the world. They appeared to be giving individuals the right to choose their own clothes, but this applied only to clothes worn in one's leisure time. No one stands in the way of the chief of the supermarket who, after wearing the work uniform from 7 a.m. to 3 p.m., spends his afternoon as a punk under the bridge, and that permission is regarded today as a great democratic achievement. But precisely with that "permission for freedom," corporations were only buying time for a more serious yet hidden process, in which they managed to make uniform casual clothing itself. If you work as a salesperson at a Gap store, you can choose your uniform from the five offered shirts with the Gap logo.

In that way you will not feel as if you have put on a uniform, but that you are even (in a way) a Gap model. Also, you aren't wearing anything that you wouldn't otherwise wear in your leisure time. The perversion is that the customer in the boutique is offered the same choice of shirts with the Gap logo. If you shop at the Gap, you are also somehow selling for Gap. There is no outside and inside. You wear the uniform on both sides of the shop door, during working hours and also in your free time. The freedom to choose a uniform amounts to the freedom of choosing between S, M or L. Even this choice is not a free one. This means that capitalism finally managed to make uniforms for the world, and that it did so in a very "communist" manner. It was done sophisticatedly, without external force (like Tatlin's uniforms), but by entering peoples' "intimate" choices and convincing them that they, by their own free will, chose the exact same uniforms the corporations wanted to sell them.

Bourgeois Marriage ("Comrades Are Marrying Whores")

"Bourgeois marriage is a public community in which women are shared. The communists shall be condemned only because they want to officialize the open, shared possession of women, instead of the mendacious, hidden one."[33] This is what Marx and Engels wrote in the explanation of the call from *The Communist Manifesto* (1848), "Destroy the Family!" What they sought is the freedom of love, and not the prison of marriage. But the problem is that the French Revolution itself (the official beginning of capitalism) recognized marriage as a "ridiculous institution." This is actually said by one of the characters in Beaumarchais's play, *The Marriage of Figaro* (1784), which was published and performed just five years prior to the bourgeois revolution in 1789 (which Napoleon says is the "first great announcement of the changes to come in the status of society"). Today, Figaro, the work's protagonist, is somewhat of a bourgeois folklore tale. He is the description of the bourgeois intimacy that bothers Marx, which is why it is important to take a closer look at the drama. In it, the piano teacher Bazile says: "Among all the most serious things in the world, marriage is the most ridiculous." He uses this sentence to convince Figaro's future wife, the maid Suzanne, to sleep with their employer, the Count Almaviva. Bazile is actually saying that there is a certain marital paradox. Marriage as an institution with serious obligations which, at the same time, is an amusing facade because the most serious of all obligations–marital faithfulness–is one of the most commonly violated ones. People are aware that adultery is forbidden, but that does not stop them from being unfaithful to their partners. And in order to "spare" her from the marital paradox of faithfulness, Bazile proposes that Suzanne should accept the code of an obligatory lover. "If you become the Count's mistress, what was prohibited yesterday (adultery), will tomorrow be prescribed as a duty," he claims.

The paradox is that Marx and Engels act similarly to Bazile. They see the world of bourgeois marriages, and naïvely believe that the problem with adultery shall be overcome if the need for adultery is overcome. And they say that now family is abolished, there are no restrictions as regards adultery, as anyone can love anyone else as they please. The naïvety they propose is similar to Bazile's indecent proposal. When Bazile suggests to Suzanne that she should accept the code of "obligatory lover" he, even before Marx and Engels, predicts that if adultery becomes an obligatory "duty," being monogamous will be interpreted as resisting the law. The symbolic order that maintains social harmony is specifically based on the double nature of the laws. There is one publicly articulated law (for example, faithfulness), but behind it, as a shadow, there is always the illegitimate adultery. This is visible in all aspects of life. For example, a person spits on the street when no one is looking, runs a red traffic light, etc., in other words, a person would violate the law here and there, not as an act of resistance to the community, but paradoxically, in the name of the *desire for imaginary identification* with the "communal spirit." This is because the order is ambivalent, and it sends out contradictory signals. Those signals force people to regularly connect pleasure with violation. Notice how no one believes that a family man is sexually satisfied; he must find a lover to convince the community that he has finally started enjoying himself. Other examples are the paradoxes around liberal and conservative upbringing. In the film, *American Pie* (1999), by Paul Weitz, the father is trying very hard to introduce his son to the secrets of sex, but paradoxically the father's obscene behavior only instills a feeling of shame in the son and a desire to retreat. The father would actually help the son if he would most conservatively forbid him to date girls, to which the son would respond with resistance. Or recall the screenplay disaster of *Emmanuelle 2* (1975), from the erotic series about Emmanuelle by Giacobetti, that followed after the married couple agreed to live in an open marriage. Another example is the behavior of the adulterers themselves. When they are caught in flagrant adultery, they deny it with all their might because they intuitively know that an admission of adultery is a more dramatic blow to the relationship than the act of adultery itself. "If he/she is ready to admit, that means that he/she really does not love me." If there is no prohibition and everything is allowed, then paradoxically, nothing is allowed, as many philosophers have pointed out. This is also one of the reasons why erotic alternatives such as Komaja (a Croatian-based spiritual community which cultivates communally approved polygamy) are unsuccessful. When adultery becomes an "agreement," it automatically becomes an impossible "patriarchal" task to have (more) partners. In other words, Marx overlooks the fact that in the ideological world a *dual law* is always in play–the visible one (the allowed) and the hidden one (the obscene). Where does this *split* in the law come from, why is the law split in two and why is one thing propagated and another "obeyed?" Why do people intuitively break the law, and why do they feel the need to be "criminal" with regard to laws? That is because the law is not all encompassing, laws are insufficient and can never cover all areas of legal permissions and offenses. The Russian formalist, Bakhtin, wrote extensively about the essence of carnivals, and the joy they incite is *not* to turn the world upside down, but that the world needs to empty itself, a periodical *public acting out,* liberating from the rigid signalization of the public law. Since ancient times, carnival celebrations saw men dressed up as women and princes transformed into slaves; for that one night, all of them got a chance to free themselves from the meaningless roles imposed by and around sex and class. There is a story about Queen Elisabeth of Hungary, a gorgeous princess who, however, loved to publically humiliate herself. Carnival behavior was an opportunity to relieve the tension of the "imposed" social categories and order, to "suspend the law." And paradoxically, what holds the community together is not the publically declared law, but this violation of it. We violated the law, we are alive; now, we shall calmly obey the laws until the next time. When Marx and Engels proclaim the obscene law (free love) a public law in *The Communist Manifesto*, when they legalize the very violation (adultery), they paradoxically open the dark side of *illegality*, of offense. The ideal realization of *The Communist Manifesto* is an annihilation of all laws, the disintegration of the entire social fabric into widespread criminality of all against all.

The capitalists had Freud, while the communists despised him as a doctor for the bourgeois. Hence, the communists recognized "their own, socialist psychoanalysis" in the work of Freud's successor at the Viennese clinic, Wilhelm Reich, who joined the communist party, proclaimed that neuroses were more of a pest and more persistent in poor people, and decided to open sex counseling services for the workers. Generally speaking, Reich claimed that both the bourgeois and the workers share the same problem–they don't fuck enough and when they do, they do it badly.[34] In 1933, Reich left the Soviet Union disappointed and fled to the US. There, in the era of McCarthyism, he was arrested as a German spy and was sentenced to two years in prison, where he died of a heart attack. When the Serbian film director, Dušan Makavejev, visited Erich Fromm in Switzerland, he asked him about his opinion of Reich. Fromm told him: "Reich is exceptionally talented and praised, but because women were crazy about him, people's insane jealousy destroyed him. On the other hand, he acted so superiorly and provokingly, as if he was the only one on the planet who can actually fuck."[35] Makavejev made a documentary film about Reich in Yugoslavia, the prohibited *Mystery of the Organism* (1971) or *W(ilhelm) R(eich)*, i.e. *W(orld) R(evolution)*. Makavejev considered himself to be the continuer of the Russian avant-garde in Yugoslavia. He claimed that communist asceticism was destroying the Revolution, and that the Revolution was impossible without sex. He worked for two-and-a-half years on the film, which included Reich's friends, relatives, followers and patients. The story evolves around the revolutionary who holds sexual speeches, while her roommate actually lives them out. She is innocent up until the moment she meets Vladimir Ilyich, a Soviet ice skating champion. In Yugoslavia, the film was prohibited by the Public Prosecutor's Office in Serbia even though it had the proper censorship card, while at the screening in Novi Sad in 1971, the local community requested that the author be arrested and hung and the film destroyed. In the West, the film was received as "one of the rare promising films coming from the socialist countries."

Although communism claimed that it stood opposed to the greatest bourgeois ideals–sentimental love–in practice, things were not quite that simple. Innocence was only considered unimportant in principle, and the fact that someone had multiple partners was only tolerated in principle. When Alexandra Kollontai used the metaphor, "Sex was just like drinking a glass of water,"[36] the reality was that misunderstandings regarding free love were the reason for political failures and exiles. The case with Tito's high functionary, Đurić, only confirms that claim. When Đurić met his future wife, who was also a party member, she captured his heart with the thesis: "We were good enough for you in the war, but now the female comrades are old maids so the comrades are marrying whores, ballerinas and bourgeois women."[37] Aleksandar Ranković, the head of the Yugoslav Secret Service, checked her along all the party lines and approved her as candidate for a wife, but Đurić himself was quite surprised when he found out that his chosen bride had been the mistress of 34 of the delegates at the 6th Congress of the Communist Party of Yugoslavia, after which the sex scandal (previously described in the chapter "Paranoia") was revealed. Communism had a nice idea. It wanted to reveal the true relationship between people–if people are polygamous, then they should stop pretending and just be themselves. "The (marriage) registration procedure is a surviving remainder from bourgeois relationships, and it is going to disappear" (stenographic record from the session of the Pan Russian Central Executive Committee, Larin's speech). "The Court, according to the general rule, shall be guided by the principle of the well-known truth: To whom the truth known by the majority shall apply, the court shall pronounce as the father (laughter)" (the same session, from the speech of the Minister of Justice, Kursky).[38]

Communism wanted to rid itself of the hypocrisy surrounding sex, but the issue remained–how to regulate polygamy once people fall in love or once they become jealous. Returning to the "nostalgic" times when people lived "purely" was not at all as easy to achieve as it sounded in theory. Capitalism played another hand–it used the strategy of "intentionally false indexicals." Adultery is not allowed–this means that all can practice it, as long as they don't get caught. Intimacy is performed and not affirmed. Or when you read the nametag of the McDonald's employee "Alexander," you know that there is nothing personal on this nametag, even in the case when the employee's name is indeed Alexander. The card will not bring Alexander closer to you–the card remains a convention, a package of politeness mimicking a real relationship. Its role is to "evoke" nostalgia for the non-corrupted relationships, "when people knew each other," "when there was a well-known truth" (Kursky's speech at the Congress), while the gesture in capitalism remains a non-intimate gesture, it only acts out the "investment called emotional labor," as Herzfelf explains.[39] There is a well-known joke about Lenin, who tells his wife that he is at his mistress's house and tells his mistress that he is with his wife, while he is actually in the attic, studying, studying, studying. Žižek reads this joke as the middle path, a balance in ideology, a deviation both from the impossible Marxist idea of free love and the bourgeois ownership over "his" wife. But the paradox is that there is no "middle path" in the joke, as Žižek would have it. It is a joke about the strength of the "homo(sexual)" dogma–what Lenin wants when he "studies, studies and just studies" is just Marx. Engels is a much "gentler" example. He was the author of the communist Family Bible, he never married. He lived together with two girls, sisters and he stated that without women, life would make no sense. As the holder of the nomenclature, he allowed himself the possibility to choose, but did not extend this to others.

A woman's bra is not perverse, politics is perverse. When sex became a proletarian race for the breaking of records ("The fetus is the socialist property of the whole of society," said Ceaușescu),[40] the number of creative solutions for "senseless" (non-reproductive) sex outside grew: benches, parks, woods, abandoned buildings, trains, cars and summer camps. People made love everywhere and public pornographic spaces (conveniently called by Shchekin, "gardens of pleasure") indeed become a reality, not because of the ideology, but because of the common flats, the so-called "komunalki." At the 11th Congress of the Communist Party in Romania of November 1976, the plan for the urban development of Romania was confirmed, and according to this plan, habitat centers were to be built using less land (land was needed for agriculture). In 1966, this resulted in the average flat (of non-nomenclature) of 40 square meters with four or more tenants, where it was impossible to have sex.[41] If anyone can enter the communist room, and just because one can, that is why one will–then the room shall move into the open and the "garden" shall be turned into a room. Another way to destroy the room was to fill it to the extent that it becomes a "komunalka," with five families in the shared kitchen, so that in the end everyone will want to escape it in order for sex not to become impossible in an Oedipal sense. The same moment that sex moves outside, the whole machinery also moves outside–police units overflow the gardens in order to catch those having "non-reproductive sex," and that is when another solution appears in the form of cinema halls. In many communist countries, the repertoire started at 10:00 in the morning with advertising/news. However, these places were not visited for staring at the ideological screen. In Ceaușescu's Romania, the price for a day cinema ticket (an option with which you could watch all of the films showing that day, on average five, mainly re-runs) was about 60 cents. The repertoire consisted of old Russian films, Soviet propaganda or Western westerns. Bad seats, bad acoustics, cold in the winter and warm in the summer, mice, these were the spaces of instant intimacy for students, the newly-hitched and the adulterers, for all those who wanted to have sex. In 1966, Romania comes up with a five-year reproduction plan, which planned for the population to grow to 30 million by 2000–which meant that on average every woman should give birth to four children. That same year, abortion was prohibited under Romanian law, contraception was made illegal and the title Heroic Mother was introduced for mothers who gave birth to five or six children. Once even the most optimistic prognoses were exceeded, and having meaningful sex had become a national competition, the criteria for being granted this prestigious title became even more rigorous. Children born in that year were called "decree children," but when they in turn wanted to have sex, there were no rooms that provided at least the minimum intimacy for having sex. For 20 years (from 1966 to 1986), the Romanian population grew by 20 million, which was very much in line with the prognoses of the five-year plan.

What is interesting is that among the first things that the new right-wing governments did after the fall of communist unions was to unleash the rebellion against the 35-year legality of abortion in communism. It was said that "17 million young Poles in embryo" and "5 million Hungarians in embryo"[42] were killed, and in Abasár in Hungary, an "Embryo Memorial" was mounted for the embryos aborted in communism. With this "review," women who aborted in communism became allies to the communists, and anti-feminism automatically became capitalist. But not even the initial feminization of society in communism was that rosy in practice. Although abortion was legal, contraception was not easily accessible. The principle equality at work amounted to the fact that women were primarily secretaries in the parties, while the key functions, the bureaucracy, heavy industry and the army were almost exclusively in the hands of the men. Even when women did receive political functions, they were always graded lower. The only real equal representations of men and women were apparent in the field of education, culture and health.

3

Waiting Room

Zero Time

Communism created a specific kind of waiting room paradox, just as in Beckett:
Why aren't you coming?
I am coming.
It is said that it is not easy to make a good representation of communism because nothing ever happens there. But this "nothing" is a lie. Naturally, people live their lives. Žižek writes:
Heiner Miller compared the socialist mentality to the waiting for a train announcement. The first announcement is that the train will arrive at 18.15, but it never arrives at 18.15. The next announcement is that the train will arrive at 20.10, and so on, while all still keep on waiting in the waiting room, although they very well know that the train will not be arriving. And yet, it suddenly proves to be good to hear the call over and over again.[1]
Each promise has an inherent distance, which is implied even without being publicly announced. "I shall love you forever," means that I could leave you tomorrow. "I will be there at 3 o'clock," means that I might be late. "We are waiting for communism" was the greatest historical promise of our generation, but that does not mean that people were alert. People intuitively knew that the promise was also used in order to *stall*, for the purpose of bringing the event closer. And people instinctively adapted to the joke with the arrested historical time, and performed the joke of socialism. They did this naturally. Unaware, they came to the philosophical

insight that life is a big theater. Waiting for communism did not make life difficult for the "neutral citizens." On the contrary, only then did life finally become "unbearably light" (Kundera). Light, because nothing frenetic ever happened in communism. People started to look around, into the inert materiality and all of a sudden they saw *life itself*, whatever that may mean; the acceleration common to the consumerism-oriented West was missing, and people took comfort in passivity and in contemplation, says Žižek. [2] They didn't go crazy, sitting on Pullman armchairs that took tokens to drive through the full shelves of capitalist supermarkets, crazed with the dilemma: Should I buy Coca-Cola or Pepsi? There was no consumer choice, but nor was there any sense in the quality of life depending on that choice.

But life was also unbearable, because time was well frozen. There is a joke from the time of communist Romania. The question was: "What do we celebrate on May 8, 1821?" And the answer is: "100 years *to* the founding of the Communist Party of Romania."[3] Socialism announced the end of all bourgeois phenomena, including the time phenomenon. Time, as it was tracked by the capitalists, was deleted and time was restarted. That is why time before the Revolution is just time *to* the Revolution. Mircea Eliade called this socialist tracking of time the most glorious of all modern political eschatologies.[4] In order to create the New Man, communism introduced new time points by changing calendars, regulating curfews, working hours and the like; all religious holidays were banned and replaced by profane ones: May 1st, Women's Day, etc. In 1978, Jug Grizelj published a text in the Serbian newspaper "Nin," in which he suggested using religious holidays to establish the communist ones. He saw the Day of the Republic, November 29th (the birth of Socialist Federative Republic of Yugoslavia), as being a kind of communist Christmas, so he said: "Why don't we come up for that occasion with at least some of the nice, mysterious and attractive games that are part of Christian Christmas?" He pronounced May 1st ,"the true resurrection of our working man/woman liberated from exploitation,"[5] as the communist Easter, and so on. The Croatian writer Igor Mandić created a mocking scheme of the communist versus religious holidays of the new Federation:

The Day of the Republic–Christmas
May 1ˢᵗ–Easter
Veterans Day–All saints
May 8ᵗʰ–St. Virgin Mary
May 25ᵗʰ–Halloween

This integration of Christian cosmology into communism, however shocking and comical it may be, was based on the belief that time was restarted; we are starting anew. But people, however, know that there is no *ideal* zero at the beginning, and that after all there *was something* there previously. We shall treat that *something* as "used time," time that existed only for the purpose of creating this "zero" time. When Lenin says in the 1917 revolution: "History will never forgive us if we miss this opportunity,"[6] this means that the communist cannot wait endlessly for realistic conditions to come around *in* time for the revolution. No time is ideal for a decision, there are no ideal preconditions for revolution, one creates one's preconditions by him/herself and only afterwards interprets them as created, in the sense that conditions are always already minimally present. If time cannot be stopped objectively, all one can do is to *declare* the end of the old time. This was the communist operation for restarting time, for starting to measure time as *zero* time, a radical intersection in the time continuum, with the aim of having time start with *me*.

In his *The Aesthetics of Disappearance* (1991), Paul Virilio asked the question: "Why were totalitarian regimes negatively inclined towards Einstein's time theory?", and answered: "Because for them, time was not assigned, it was locally created."[7] But the problem with Virilio's explanation is that it covers all ideologies. Anthropologists warn that *all* time is locally created. "Time per se" does not exist. That is why the same operations of *restarting* were also reversely activated after the disintegration of communism. When the Kremlin designated November 4ᵗʰ as the Day of the Victory of Russia over Poland in 1612 holiday in 2004, it was in lieu of November 7ᵗʰ, the day when the Bolsheviks came to power in 1917. From 2005, this day has traditionally been celebrated in Russia as a "gift" for the neo-Nazi groups; in 2007, 5,000 Russian nationalists demonstrated in Moscow against people with darker skin color, primarily from the Caucasus region and from Central Asia. Establishing new holidays always means modeling time anew. Using ideological mechanisms, new time is organized as appropriate and inappropriate: First it was the capitalists, today it is those with different skin color, but there are always those who are included and those who are excluded and who suffer because of the social definition of time. If time per se does not exist, if time is always locally created, then how was "zero time" created and what did that creation mean for the communist empire?

There are Three Tenses and all Three of Them are Future Ones

The "zero time" of communism was established through the announcement, "Communism is coming." That call was messianic, borrowed from the Christian register: "Thy will be done." It is not accidental that communism saw its greatest enemy in religion. The communist leader was the Messiah. Therefore, despite the obviousness that communism was not coming, people still wanted to hear, repeatedly, the announcement that "Communism is coming." That announcement sent people a message that they were not living, but that they were in some kind of pre-dress rehearsal, in some type of *pre-life*. That gave them great relief. They could now calm down. There was no way they could go wrong.

In Skopje in March 2007, while I was carefully searching through the pile of socialist literature no one had opened in decades at the National and University Library, "Sv. Kliment Ohridski," I saw a notice on the toilets: "Please, before leaving, leave the toilet in the condition that you found it in before using it." More than Marcuse and Althusser, this notice captures the key determiner of communist mentality stemming from zero time that, as we have witnessed, is not dying away at all that quickly. The proper communist citizen is not the already dead one, but the one who has not yet been born. If the time is zero, then no one exists in "real" time yet. He/she acts as if they are not alive, and the message that he/she gets is "don't infect the project with your presence," be invisible! But paradoxically, this opened up endless possibilities for the citizen. It freed him from guilt. People stopped worrying. Whatever it was that they dirtied with their presence, it was still nothing compared to the unstained upcoming future in communism. That is why they were relaxed and left toilets in a totally unbearable condition. When time is frozen, it is impossible to make any mistake in it. That brought about infinite advantages. There is nothing to worry about over this "transitional" toilet.

The favorite saying of generations of Yugoslavs–"It's better to live a 100 years as a millionaire than seven days in poverty"–spoken by Grunf in the Italian comedy, *Alan Ford*, shows what kind of unpredictable games with time plans socialist zero time opened up. Time that belongs to the people becomes somewhat "compressed." *Alan Ford* was never as popular, even in its country of origin, Italy, as it was in Yugoslavia in the 1980s, because the intelligent reader identified it as the cynical response to the empty rhetoric, like Tito's most famous call: "Live as if there will be 100 years of future peace, but prepare like there will be a war tomorrow." These paroles simulated serious dissension with the world when there was actually no conflict within them. If there is war tomorrow, there will surely be peace today. They were not spoken in the present tense, and the call, "Live as if there will be 100 years of peace," also concerned the future, the same future that the possible war concerned as well. Time becomes a moving image of eternity that has not yet come. Both war and peace are part of the future. The start is postponed, indefinitely. And while the socialist leader talks about the future that shall arrive at any moment, communism's "neutral citizens" talk of the apocalypse all the time, of the time that has passed.[8] In a certain sense, these two tense types are the same "absent" zero time. Verbs in socialist texts were sacrificed for nouns. Wherever possible, the verb, as the carrier of the tense, was replaced with an undefined timelessness. The communist style, formally called *la langue be bois*, indicated the final entry into zero time in the text, the legitimatization of the empty phrase that covers the absence of thought and concrete information. This provoked an unusual, controlled trance, some sect (Marxist) "variant" of Plotin's ancient offering: "There are three tenses, and all three are present tenses." Communist zero time made it possible to make a peculiar theological connection of the three tenses, but not in the present, as in Plotin's case, but in the future. Hence, the most accurate communist definition of time would be this: There are three tenses, and all three are future ones.

Capitalist time is also "dictated," "created" time. Early capitalism imposed a certain rhythm on the body so that it could exploit it. It turned agricultural cycles into a linear sequence of the same value units. In capitalism, time is linear, and that holds not only for work, but for pleasure as well. The film, *About a Boy* (2002), by Chris and Paul Weitz, tells the story of the comfortable life of Will Freeman as a single, rich Londoner, who does not have to work because he has inherited money and just idles the days away. But, idling the day away is something that should be endured. Will also organizes his leisure time in a "capitalist" fashion, in order not to feel either effort or boredom. His day is divided in "time units"–one such unit is 30 minutes, if there are more minutes, the idea that time goes by slowly will wear him out. According to Will's system, showering is one unit, surfing erotic sites–two units, lunch–three units, hairdresser–four units and so on. "It is incredible how the day is filled and to be totally honest, I often ask myself whether I would have any time for work, ever," says Will. Will is the product of the capitalist belief that man is the master of his own time, his favorite maxim is, "I am an island, I am fucking Ibiza," as a counter-replica to the maxim, "No man is an island," by the 16th century renaissance poet John Donne. Renaissance ideology had it that people are not isolated, but instead interconnected and interdependent. Capitalism begins when time is proclaimed an "island," virtual, where no one really meets anyone. Or in Will's words: "Now is the time to be an island. This is an island era." Capitalism has faith in the notion of a person's control over his/her time, in his/her independence from other people. But the paradox of the life described in the film by the Weitz brothers is that Will is also employed, employed in the most difficult workplace in the world–he *has to* enjoy himself in an organized, capitalist fashion, and leisure in capitalism is restructured in precise time units.

In order to draw out greater profits from him, capitalism organized the body as a military–political machine. That is why it accelerates time greatly; man becomes a cerebral automat in cycles of charges and discharges. Electroshock treatment was discovered by the Italian psychiatrist Ugo Cerletti in 1938, at a time when fascism was roaring, and it became the standard method used by the secret police, especially in Latin America.[9] But the abuse of the body, using a principle of cycles and its acceleration to a point of madness, for the then exhausted body, to become the ideal object for interrogation and monitoring, was commonplace for capitalism. The fascination with planes and automobiles, and with a city beat, was part of the capitalist understanding of time, and has been ever since the beginning. "Beware of the car"–says Mercier in his piece, *Tableau de Paris*, from the 18th century–"Here comes the black cloaked doctor in his carriage, the dance instructor in his cabriolet, the fencing teacher in his one-seat car and the duke with a six-horse carriage galloping through the open field... The threatening wheels of the rich go faster than ever on the stones covered with the blood of their unfortunate victims." Don't think that Mercier was exaggerating: In France, the mail wagon, which was introduced in the 17th century, killed more people annually than the later introduced railway,"[10] Branka Arsić writes: "A modern city is born in blood..., the blood of the casualties that have encountered speed."[11]

In capitalism, stopping equals death. The connecting of the moment of departure with the one of arrival in late capitalism finally led to a certain contraction of space-time in concentration points as virtual, "non-existent" points. E-mail, which began in the 1990s as a series of "pleasure buttons," the loving, seductive and playful "touches" of friends and potential lovers, has wound up today transformed into mobile offices, and virtual communication has become duller than the dullest office meetings in the real world. But the meeting itself of lovers in real time achieved a speed similar to military–technical movement; acceleration has a final aim, the "disappearance of the partner or partners in time and space,"[12] as Virilio writes, in the virtuality of the capitalist "world without a world."

In socialism, another type of time annihilation prevailed. Although leaders claimed that socialism was a dynamic system, they acted as if time were on their side–when they promised something, they were not constrained by the date. Time was static, but with arrhythmic quakes, periods of acceleration (five-year plans) and slowings down (waiting in queues). Gorbachev's Perestroika admitted, for the first time ever, that the temporality of socialism is unsustainable, that the linearity of capitalism tramples it underfoot. Gorbachev wrote that the delay should be made up for, development accelerated, sluggishness should be cast aside, but that was now impossible, and Verdery correctly says that the fall of socialism came about in part due to the mess that resulted out of its clash with capitalist acceleration.[13]

For capitalism, timing is everything; it includes timely accommodation towards the margins, a softening of the subversive angles. A friend of mine from London was telling me that when *Monty Python* started working in Britain as an alternative, experimental discourse, it was immediately bought by the BBC, which started airing it for all to see. As a result, *Monty Python* instantly became mainstream. Capitalism not only tolerates, but actually *exploits* the alternative forms of humor, politics, ideology and sexuality, which is not a sign that capitalism has an unlimited patience for and tolerance of the subversive, but rather the opposite–it just has a good notion of timing. What can be said about capitalism is that the maxim "seize the day" from Peter Weir's film *Dead Poets Society* (1989) actually applies. But don't the communists share the same idea? In a letter to Kugelmann from 1867, Marx wrote: "The first success does not depend on conscientious critique, but, to put it bluntly, on making a big deal out of things, on sounding the drum, that will even make the enemy talk…, but above all–time should not be wasted!",[14] which is similar to Lenin's thesis that "History cannot wait any further." The two leading philosophers of the revolution say that waiting was not the solution; however, communism is a slippery route, a "new project," and it is unclear how to speed things up. If you wait for too long, nothing radical happens, it you act immediately, you might jeopardize your project. What to do? The solution starts with Lenin. Lenin was the first communist leader who started to experiment with *unpredictable* action. No one was able to predict the speed of the next cycle–would the next phase be a shock-work one or a relaxing one? People find this baffling, as they don't know what to think. Capitalism is a long run in the same direction, with increasing speed, whereas socialism is a *zigzagging* movement in an unknown direction. That is why socialist time is arrhythmic, at one moment it is dynamic, at another it is slowed down. "The arrhythmia of these ritual temporalities echoed that of socialist production patterns, with their unpredictable alternations of slackness and "storming" to fill production quotas," says Verdery.[15]

This zigzag phenomenon of socialist *accelerated* and *slowed* movement is best illustrated with two phenomena: Stakhanovism and ritual waiting. Stakhanovism is the second name for socialist competitions. Stalin launched the competitions in the 1930s, within his politics of "wide socialist appearance," which were named after the young miner Alexey Stakhanov from Donbas who, in August 1935, collected 102 tons of coal with a regular mining pick and managed to break the set daily norm by 15 times. In the Soviet Union, the fame of Stakhanov and his feat took on dimensions of fame enjoyed perhaps only by Western film stars. One of the fan letters that he received, read: "We are pleased to know that our society can turn an ordinary miner into a celebrity." The Yugoslav version of Stakhanov was Alia Sirotanović, the miner from the Bosnian mine Breza, who in 1949 managed to break Stakhanov's record by 40 tons. Top communist leaders Svetozar Vukmanović Tempo and Đuro Salaj sent Sirotanović on a month-long luxury vacation in the Croatian coastal city of Opatija, and by special order from Tito, his home village immediately became connected to the electricity grid.[16] Vihid Mutapić, a bricklayer and employee of the wire coil packing factory in Sarajevo "Žica," wanted to get into the Guinness Book of Records, and worked continuously from November 2-6, 1984, and in 96 hours managed to pack 2,175 wire coils, securing his entry into the Guinness Book, though within this socialist country his achievement was promoted as a communist awareness of shock endeavors. Shock work was the main form of work organization in communism, in which the worker either performed shock work or no work at all. The American factory owner and automobile innovator, Henry Ford, warned: "A great business is too big to be human,"[17] but Lenin was impressed by the possibilities of shock work. Admiration and a passion for work were most dramatic at the beginning of the (communist) era, when there was a general work craze. In 1930, the Russian novel, *Foundation Pit*, by Andrey Platonov was published, in which the supervisor tells the workers: "But you must stop working, you have already been working for more than six hours (on a Saturday), and the law is the law," to which the workers respond: "The law is only for the tired."[18]

In theory, this was somewhat differently formulated by Marcuse, one of the most famous American Marxists, and author of the thesis of work as a game. While capitalism is a type of endless metonymic hunger for pleasure-inducing objects, communism is a type of "suspended pleasure"–repressed genital sexuality, in which Marcuse wanted to connect Freud and Marx, and the whole body becomes a pleasure instrument; while working, the body enjoys the repressed sexuality. As Epstein writes, in that shock work atmosphere of "seduction erotics" of Soviet labor, "The truly hardworking person feels like a traitor."[19] Communists were the first to make people work out of idealism, rebuilding the country from the ruins of war. But when everything turned into "endless work," they no longer wanted to work; they started thinking of ways of getting their hands on money without having to work, as Carver writes in connection with Albanian communism.[20] That is most feasible in the gray economies of communism. A well-known example in Albania is the one of the factory for the production of fake Marlboro cigarettes in the Albanian city of Pogradec, which was managed by the secret services, Sigurimi. It was equipped with high-quality machines and used original boxes and wraps, only the tobacco was local. Via the Macedonian city of Ohrid, those cigarettes were then sold to the Yugoslav secret services in exchange for dollars, while Yugoslavia, which was the only country that practiced actual trade with the West, was a good source of goods in the Eastern Block, which is why it sold the cigarettes further on in Russia, the Ukraine and Central Asia in exchange for convertible currency, or sometimes trade in kind. And when traded in kind, the cigarettes themselves were treated as currency.[21]

Alongside the acceleration of time, socialism also continued to equally frenetically dictate endless delays. "Every year on August 23, Romania's national 'independence' day, thousands of people were massed as early as 6:00 a.m. for parades that actually began around 10:00 or 11:00," Verdery writes.[22] These immobilized bodies waited and waited without any logical explanation. The explanation that they needed to be organized in order to prevent any possible disorders is incorrect—when forced to wait for no reason, people tend to get nervous and aggressive. In 1987, when the Romanian authorities realized that those hundreds of thousands of bodies who were waiting idly for the local leader to appear could create disorder for no apparent reason, the masses were gathered later and later each time and the security at stadiums improved, until the whole practice of waiting was abandoned altogether. In anthropology, Verdery says, this type of waiting is called "ritual waiting,"[23] which is the time that the élite takes away from others to fame itself. In brief, ritual waiting does not mean that the one who you are waiting for is tied up with other work; instead, it accentuates the difference–the "ordinary" man is forced to give away his time to the "cadre." Also in Yugoslavia, when Tito or some other important visitor passed by, lectures were interrupted as was work, people were immobilized to wait in the streets and to wave every three seconds while Tito's car passed; those three seconds were preceded with hours of immobilized waiting for the leader.

Plan Fetish and the Immobilized Body

Communism is a plan fetish era. There is a joke, where the Russians and the Bulgarians are planning the next production cycle. The Russians: "You will make clay pots; we shall trade them with the Germans for machinery, trade the machinery for innovations from the Japanese, the innovations for Argentinean wheat, and the wheat for technology." "And what do we get?", ask the Bulgarians. "You get the clay for the pots."

The *promise* is the fundamental social contract in communism, as everything begins with central planning. A plan is made for what and how much should be produced, and an estimate of the required raw material is then prepared. Plans are doubled, but the raw materials don't arrive on time and in the required quantities. Therefore, the directors start negotiating about the plan, but they also ask for more raw material because they really do need it. The remainder is kept for the next production cycle or traded with another enterprise. The main problem of the enterprise is not the market, but how to get hold of the raw material. Capitalists compete to sell the product and communists to negotiate a deal with the supplier. That is why in capitalism it is the salesperson who is polite, while in communism it is the buyer. Products are not made to be competitive on the market, they are piled up at headquarters or sold off at lower prices, and practically given away. What is important is the realization of the plan. Aside from the excess raw material, directors create excess workers as well because they never know how many workers they really need for the realization of the five-year plans. That is how the state effect was achieved–no one shall be unemployed. And Verdery explains that compared to capitalism, workers are in a better position, but they also create a cult of non-work and they work as little as possible for their pay.[24]

Evidence of the absolute absurdity of planning is given by Mihailo Švabić, who was responsible for the first big work action, the Bosnian Brčko–Banovići railroad, which was built in 1946, and was the famous communal-built railway in Yugoslavia. Immediately after the liberation (WWII), Švabić was made Head of Youth and Work Actions within the secretariat of the Central Committee of the Union of Communist Youth of Yugoslavia. Before the war, he read some news that the Russians in Siberia managed to construct a grandiose channel project with 200,000 people in just 14 days. Not wanting to be remembered for less significant things– "a fixed bridge here, a repaired school there"–he decided to make something big from scratch. "At that time, the Belgrade–Zagreb railroad was not yet constructed, and the few roads and railroads that existed had been destroyed… It was indeed pointless to build a new railway when we hadn't fixed the old ones yet… (but) since the main priority was 'land reconstruction,' we decided to make a new railroad," Švabić would later say.[25] Many were against it, but Tito liked the megalomaniac project; he saw "the youth initiative as something more than just a material effect." And why was that precise route chosen? Švabić got the idea from the then Assistant Mining Minister Tadija Popović, who claimed that the route allowed for an optimal exploitation of the mine, and that was the only reason for choosing to build a road precisely there.

Capitalism invents needs; advertisements are there to convince you that you need something that you were not even aware that you were missing. Communism only promises the satisfaction of basic needs. Capitalism *invents* desire in the form of new products and then advertises them. Communism maintains the desire through constant deprivation, the psychology of queues, etc.[26] Verdery says: "What was rational in socialism differed from capitalist rationality. Both are stupid in their own way, but differently so."[27]

These days, at the Natural Science Museum in London, if you

want to see the dinosaur exhibit on a Saturday, you are notified that you have a 15-minute waiting time from your spot in the queue before you reach the starting point. The queues are extremely long in front of all of the museums in Paris; for the sake of maintaining the principle of entry on the bus, people in today's post-communist Kiev spontaneously get in queues when the bus comes along according to the sequence to which people had come to wait. Buses literally come every few seconds, but the number of people in these cities is enormous. Capitalism has become a victim of its own insistence on speed, and the traffic of people rushing in capitalism is frightening. In capitalism, queues are not created for the purpose of waiting for someone; on the contrary, they are created for the purpose of rushing, reaching the next point as soon as possible, and rushing from that point to the next and never stopping, in a manner Virilio calls "deadly comfort,"[28] a kind of replacement of the human being with a rushing machine.

Waiting in communism unfolded in accordance with a different principle. The communist cadre wanted to plan the phases of rest and speed, of laziness and shock work, which is why it ordered the meaningless waiting and racing, not allowing the body to independently determine those rhythms. The communist cadre "takes care," it wants both progress and breaks; these dictates are not led in accordance with the internal order of the body, they are led by the chaos of the system itself. The Serbian communist Vladimir Ribnikar was the first in Yugoslavia to describe the queues in front of the shops in the Soviet Union in 1927. "Without patient waiting nothing can be achieved, not in a store, nor in an office, nor in the theater, nor in a tram."[29] These impressions were published in the Serbian daily "Politika" only once, and they were republished only after the separation with the Soviets. Verdery writes that in 1960, Soviet citizens spent 30 billion hours waiting in queues for food, or the equivalent of a year's work for 15 million people.[30] In the communist states, the state and local authorities had the right to control the people's enormous quantity of time. Workers were primarily hanging around the factories and offices doing nothing. The most famous worker's motto in Yugoslavia was "Idle the day away, for pay." The time the worker could spend on home production was being stolen. If the worker had time to plant something in his/her "own yard," the state would decide the quantity that one was allowed to produce "for oneself," and then it would have the same taken away via a "compulsory buyout" at a ridiculous price. People couldn't choose when to take a bath and when to cook because there were frequent electricity restrictions. There was a popular joke in Romania. Question: "What did we have before candles?" Answer: "Electricity."[31] Contraception was not allowed, so people were forced to adjust their sexual activity in accordance with the natural cycles. Party meetings were scattered irregularly throughout the week, so one never knew when one was supposed to be available. When a bus would come, it was so jammed that it was impossible to read or work on it, which also meant deprivation of time. Socialism amounted time to two basic operations: securing food and going to work and home. There were special shops for the party élite and the secret police, the bureaucracy managed by leaving work two hours earlier, but the workers (those who were treated by socialism as the leading class, in the name of which the entire ideological project was implemented), were, paradoxically, the only ones who couldn't manage, it was their time that was most thoroughly stolen. Time was also stolen at various offices and inquiry desks. Verdery mentions a 1988 case from the city newspaper, Flacara Iașului, from Bucharest, in which in the section entitled, Questions and Answers, a reader asks: "For some time now, there has not been a return bus ticket to Iași (a city in Romania) available, why is this so?" And the editorial board replied: "As the bus company director informs us, new dispositions from the Ministry of Transport stipulate that tickets should not be sold in advance, which is why the ticket office is closed."[32] The authorities didn't bother to explain why they controlled people's time, they simply created a situation in which the man did not know whether he would be able to travel that day, nor would he be able to plan anything; he will have to get up early, but still he does not know whether the ticket office will open that day.

Why does socialism create such time arrhythmia? One of the responses is: to keep people subordinated. The arrhythmia of time invoked social instability. Verdery says: "(O)ne effect of temporal regularity is to create the background expectancies upon which our sense of the 'normal' is erected; a possible consequence of socialism's arrhythmia would have been to keep people permanently off balance, to undermine the sense of 'normal' order and to institute uncertainty as the rule."[33] A person is forced into immobility, one's time is stolen and he/she cannot do anything about it. The stealth of time created *immobilized bodies*, as all initiative has been taken away from the immobilized body. The immobilized body cannot plan anything and cannot take any initiative. Aside from the most flexible and spontaneous things, all other things (traveling to another city, the university exam, when one is allowed to drive his/her car, when the bus is going to come, when food will arrive in the shops, etc.) cannot be planned, therefore the body waits in tune with *the incidental*. This immobilization provides at least a partial answer to the question: How is it possible that communism has not experienced any substantial resistance, even though so many people where against it? One of the reasons for the dramatic success of the pyramidal savings bank scheme in post-communism is also explained with immobilized bodies. Verdery offers a brilliant insight into the pyramidal savings bank "Caritas" in Romania, which operated such that people waited to pick up the voucher and then waited at another window to once again deposit the money; they operated by activating the psychology of queues from communist times.[34] Finally, in some analyses of the queue phenomenon in communism, it is emphasized that, paradoxically, waiting helped not only the accumulation of state power, but the accumulation of products as well. People could not do their shopping with a certain dynamic, which means that the state had a reserve of products and in this laid its power.

4

Prosthesis

Berlin, Two Prosthetic Scenes

Berlin, 1961–On November 20th 2007, on the day of the celebration of the 18th anniversary of the fall of the Berlin wall, the TV channel "Discovery" commemorated Berlin Wall Day with a photograph that was chosen for an advertisement. The photo, which was taken in the early 1960s, depicted an anonymous man standing on one side of the river in divided Berlin, holding his hat on a stick so that he can be seen by the other man standing on the other side of the city. This photograph shows that only by putting the hat on a stick, only by "amputating" the head, can this "headless" person be tall enough to be seen from the other side of the Wall. He no longer has a head that is placed on a live body, it is now placed on a wooden *throat*; he becomes a type of political Pinocchio, a prosthetic city dweller. And more importantly, this "amputated" man's head, once symbolically detached, can now begin a political life of its own. This photo shows what becomes of the head of the so-called politically neutral citizen. It is a head that no longer feels any pain and feels no ecstasy. The neutral citizen is the one who mounts his/her head on a stick–as an act of resourcefulness (let them build walls, I shall erect myself *prosthetically* in order to see those close to me, in the end it *is* some type of resistance), but at the same time it is also an act of acquiescence–of the head under political anesthesia.

Berlin, 1929–Berlin, 30 years earlier: In 1929, Freud returns to Germany to have his prosthesis replaced, the one that was inserted due to throat cancer. "The huge prosthesis, a sort of magnified denture or obturator, designed to shut off the mouth from the nasal cavity, was a horror; it was labeled 'the monster,'" writes David Wills.[1] Freud enjoyed the advantages of the prosthesis, and when he returned to Berlin to change the prosthesis, this was only shortly after he had finished his most famous study, *Civilization and Its Discontents* (1930), in which Freud wrote about the relationship between humans and culture, on "the civilization (and) the consciousness of guilt," as he explains in a letter to Lou Salomé. With this orthopedic extension in his mouth, with this *wooden throat,* Freud tries to answer the question–can we enjoy culture, its ideological solutions, and yet avoid something getting stuck down our throat?

In *Civilization and Its Discontents* (1930), Freud explains what the next grandiose man is going to be like: "Man has, as it were, become a kind of *prosthetic God.* When he puts on all his auxiliary organs, he is truly magnificent… (my italics)."[2] This is the Freudian anticipation of the forthcoming world. Freud, who personally enjoyed the advantages of his prosthesis, said that the prosthesis would become the only condition for enduring the intensified ideological sadism in the world. The grandiosity of the human will be achieved by bringing the organic closer to the prosthetic. The human with the "prosthetic throat" on the photograph of the separated Berlin 30 years later confirms Freud's diagnosis–culture becomes so impossible, so uncomfortable, that a person can bear to stand it only with a prosthesis between the symbolically separated and the biologically attached head. Freud actually says that the mechanical culture of the 20th century that marked the beginnings of communism, of New Deal capitalism and fascism, has been organized with the help of the *prosthesis of aggression*: Berlin walls, cars, machines, camps…, but at the same time, it can only be tolerated if prosthetic additions are implanted. The prosthetic additions are a way in which a person eases aggression in culture, the person bears his/her political fate less painfully, and least in the sense in which Freud quotes Rűckert: "What we cannot reach flying, we must reach limping."[3]

Prostheses are important for the communist universe. Communism was designed as the final solution against the metaphysical restlessness of man, against the question–is everything around me an illusion? This question was raised by Marx in *Capital* and everywhere, where in describing the material universe (consumer goods) he says that they "appear as ghosts," as "an illusion," he says that the material world is "a mirage." The bourgeois economy hides the true relationships of people behind masks; these relationships hide the pathology, while the truth is that all there is is just the scandalous nature of exploitation. The comment that "reality is a mirage" is not essentially Marxist; it is among the most elementary experiences of people viewing the world. People say that "life is but a dream," "reality is a fantasy," the world is an illusion, etc. But, when people say this, they are not only intimidated on a poetic, folklore level, they are also intimidated on an *ideological* level. In the most successful science-fiction film of the 20th century, *The Matrix* (1999), by the Wachowski brothers, which was made exactly a decade after the fall of communism, the world is a huge computer simulation, a Matrix, a sophisticated virtual reality of exploitation, and people are only prostheses attached to the large Matrix body. While in reality people eat oysters in restaurants, travel by car, in *real reality* people are just a mirage, an illusion, feeding prostheses of the Evil Genius; what really exists is only the unnamed dark force that commands us and does not allow us to wake up into real Reality. How can I know that I am me and not merely some prosthesis of the Evil Intelligence? This issue is one of the oldest philosophical dilemmas of mankind, and was posed with renewed certainty by Descartes in the 16th century. In his most famous, disturbing work, Descartes says that, considering that when we dream, what we see seems true and real; isn't that sufficient proof that what we see when we are awake is in fact some kind of dream, an image without reality? And Descartes says that one may doubt the existence of the entire world and all the things in it, I can doubt even myself, but while I doubt–I think. And being that I think–I exist. That was the basis of Descartes' teaching and the Enlightenment adopts his argument. Descartes convinced us that we are fine, we are not mistaken when we say that we exist, and that the meta-question itself, "do I exist," is evidence of it since it is not asked unless someone truly exists. Descartes provided the magical solution to our metaphysical quake. But the end of the 20th century, after the experiences with communism, revived these questions with a new intensity. The Josef Rusnak film, *13th Floor*, came out the same year that *The Matrix* was made. The tagline for the film was Descartes's sentence "I think, therefore I am," but in the movie, although they do pose meta-questions, people are merely a simulation, they are Marx's apparition.

Not by coincidence, these films were created a decade after the fall of communism. That was the death of hope, that communism would cure the world of the scandalous nature of exploitation, from turning people into prostheses. Communism was a movement *against* the prosthesization of the human. Marx described the worker as the prosthesis of the machine and believed that in capitalism people are replaced by automats, creatures that feed the system, life simulations and prostheses of the Evil Genius of exploitation. Another science fiction film, *Blade Runner* (1982) by Ridley Scott, which was crucial for the revival of Descartes's thought in pop-culture in the late 20th century, described a world in the near future inhabited by replicants (Nexus sixes) who are artificially created people, who don't have a mother and father and who have no childhood, but who have an artificially integrated memory of a non-existent childhood, and most importantly, are not even aware that they are not human. Because of their superior intelligence, they also have doubt and since they have doubt, this is a playing with Descartes' idea of proving that man is not an illusion. In Ridley Scott's film, *everyone* is in doubt–both the people and the "people," how could one tell them apart? The main character, Deckard, a kind of Americanized version of the French philosopher (Descartes), works as a hunter of replicants and in one of the films' key scenes faces the replicant played by Daryl Hannah, and we hear her ironic comment: "I think, therefore I am." But she is, despite all the evidence and for which the words "here is evidence that I exist" apply, the integrated memory, the artificial childhood, the automat, the prosthesis pretending to be human. As we see, the relationship between the *prosthesis* and the *human* is crucial in the defining of each ideology. A successful ideology is one that knows how to offer a sophisticated yet simple solution for the "true" human nature. Marx said that the world is a mirage, that the worker is a prosthesis, so let's free him! The sooner the world realizes that freedom is our destiny, the better for the world. All others shall remain among the charred fields of history. Freud offered the opposite: The sooner all agree that the prosthesis is our destiny (both in a physical and metaphysical sense), the sooner humankind will become a grandiose one, and all others shall remain among the charred fields of history. Who was right?

Communism began as an era of obsession with machines. Machines disturbed Marx, as he realized that people were becoming prosthetic extensions of the machines. But the Soviets were also thrilled by the mechanical revolution. Stalin did not hide that he was attracted by the mechanization of the US, by Western industrial developments and practices and by the hardworking American people, as well as by the general spiritual and physical health of Americans, writes Ivo Banac.[4] The first national hero of Soviet industrialization was none other than Henry Ford, the founder of the automobile industry, the wealthiest American industrialist of his time and the man who first introduced the conveyor belt into the manufacturing process in his factories. Freud in theory, and Ford in capitalist practice, provided the determinants for the mechanical galaxy that started to rule the 20th century, in which prostheses play a key role. Wherever machines are present, there are also prostheses for arms, legs and heads that have been cut by the machines. In his autobiography, *My Life and Work* (1923), Ford wrote that in order to produce the Model T, 7,882 different operations were required, but only for 12% of those tasks, i.e. for 949 operations, are "strong, able-bodied, and practically physically perfect men" required. "The remaining 3,595 jobs were disclosed as requiring no physical exertion…, and we found that 670 could be filled by legless men, 2,637 by one-legged men, two by armless men, 715 by one-armed men, and 10 by blind men."[5] Ford was the first great exploiter of the 20th century, in the most rigid sense of the word, of which Marx could only dream in the 19th century. And the paradox is that social change in the USSR came about precisely with the help of the man who had no scruples. By 1926, Stalin had ordered 24,000 tractors from Ford, "a figure equal to about 85% of total Soviet production,"[6] and the greatest share of the Soviet Five-Year Plan consisted of buying services from Henry Ford. Ford's autobiography, *My Life*, appeared in eight Soviet translations, four alone in 1924, and became widely read literature for party members, economists and technical students.

The tangents between the three dominant ideologies of the 20th century, capitalism, communism and fascism, are linked with the fact that Hitler, just like Stalin, was also fascinated by Ford. Hitler respected the anti-Semitic views of Ford, was personally fascinated by cars and had a huge poster of Ford, the only American mentioned in *Mein Kampf*, on the wall of his workroom. Volkswagen, as the car of the German people, was modeled after Ford's Model T, and Ford was the first great capitalist who worked with both the US and the USSR, and who also played an important role in the mechanization of Nazi Germany. Ford is the ideological creator of the first *workplace snitches*. Ford founded the controversial "Social Sector", which employed 50 snoops, whose business was to follow the lives of the employees so that they would be productive. Ford's invasion of the private lives of employees was criticized all around America, and only in his memoirs from 1933 did Ford confess that "paternalism has no place in industry," in the sense that "welfare work that consists in prying into employees' private concerns is out of date."[7] However, the paradox lies elsewhere. While in the West, factory production was already the image of horror that the workers lived daily, in the early Soviet Union, on the contrary, the new machine culture was the source of general delight. The Soviet Union was a semi-agricultural country, and in it "the cult of the machine preceded the machines themselves,"[8] writes Susan Buck-Morss. The Soviets neither had the machines nor the workforce to operate them, as the country was fighting to restore pre-war industrial capacities; however, the ecstasy with which the idea of the machines was accepted is *shockingly contrary* to Marx's warning that machines prosthetisize humans. In his film *Stalker* (1979), Tarkovsky depicts post-industrial garbage, piles of industrial waste, and in this respect the Soviets beat the West in anticipating the price of industrialization, even before the appearance of the machines–the piles of machine waste are the place where the "capitalist urge is on vacation," writes Žižek. And the irony is that communism developed a greater sensitivity towards the point when capitalism would come to want to rest, precisely owing to the fact that the communists came from the place of rest itself, from that place prior to the emergence of mechanized work.

Stalin–Automat (The King is a Thing!)

When the Yugoslav leader Maslarić took students to the harvest in the DDR, he saw Stalin at the May Day parade from afar, on the official stage, and described him just as he had experienced him: "We couldn't see Stalin and the rest of the leadership very well; looking at them from the side, they seemed well fed and indifferent. But the movement of their hands and the salutations to the laborers seemed somewhat *mechanical*. As if made by *automats* (my italics)."[9] Stalin adopted the reason of the Automaton, as he himself became a conglomerate of the technological; not only is his revolution externally supported by socialist prostheses (ships, machines, spectacles), but this is what the aesthetic (beautiful, clean, philosophy), the social (political) and the personal performance should become–the Leader himself should become the Automaton. Indifferent, just like an automat, Stalin's mechanical salutations and arm movements were as if made by an automat. Freud's prosthetic diagnosis from *Civilization and its Discontents* is an important anticipating of the future Leader. The leader is the one who becomes the prosthesis himself, his generosity is not achieved by replacing *some* part of the body with a prosthesis, but by replacing the entire body with a giant prosthesis. Stalin is no longer glorious with several prostheses *here and there*, Stalin himself *becomes* a prosthesis. In Shakespeare's *Hamlet*, there is a sentence that brilliantly explains the dictator's place: "The King is a Thing"–says Hamlet when Rosencrantz asks him, "My lord, you must tell us where the body (of the king) is." Hamlet responds: "The body is with the king, but the king is not with the body. The King is a thing." The starting point for every government is this radical emptiness, this "leader without a body;" all meaning must be evacuated from the leader, in order for the Leader to be able to position him/herself at the point of absolute power. When, in the same scene, Hamlet sees Rosencrantz for the first time, this is how he describes his face: "Ay, sir, that soaks up the king's countenance, his rewards, his authorities," meaning that the people are the form, the substance that this emptied body, this thing, this prosthesis for the human, sucks in.

In 1954, Sarajevo hosted the conference, "Human characters in Marx, Engels and Lenin," and a scandal broke out when the Serbian philosopher, Ljubomir Tadić, said that Marx and Lenin were undoubtedly greater minds than Engels, but he personally preferred Engels because Engels "(o)nce stated that life without French women would make no sense."[10] This scandal was to be expected. One should note that the Yugoslav generations in their historical time never found out anything significant about the lives of their leaders, but an explosion of discussions followed after the fall of communism when books on Tito's intimate life appeared, which told of his wives and calculations on the number of his known and unknown lovers, as well as the fascination incited by the documentary film, *Tito–A Post-Mortem Autobiography* (2003), by Sergej Kostina, with a long opening scene in which the Marshal is shaving. The message is not that Tito is "human," and that it is human that his beard actually grows; instead, this Marshal can even shave and put on cologne, but these "daily" operations do not turn the leader into "human material," as his origins shall remain mysterious and blinding. Even today, every few years in the countries that emerged from the disintegration of Yugoslavia, the phantasmagorical question is revived: Who actually was Tito? (Was he an Austrian aristocrat who later assumed the identity of a Croatian peasant, etc.?) Seeking a metaphysical exit from the political jungle, seeking salvation and sense, the communist universe introduces the figure of the Tyrant as the most desired form of ruler, at the same time investing in the infantile idea of his/her "divine" origin. This is strange, though if we take a look at the regular massive, unreserved support with which the people from communist countries *exclusively* greeted their tyrants, and the moderation with which they greeted their democrats, then it becomes clear that there is a certain innate human need to desire a tyrant as one's political leader and to invest in him the desire for a personal and collective closure of the drama called life.

In Hamlet, Shakespeare also offers excellent insight into the question–where does the opposition come from? Hamlet rises against the new king only after the ghost of his dead father asks of him to start restoring the old, moral order. This is a Shakespearian response to the question of where the opposition, the discord, comes from. It comes as a call from the dead, from the point of the ancestors. As Lacan interprets him, Hamlet's ideal father occupies a dubious place: The father can give out orders, but he can no longer accept any because he is no longer among the living, and therefore he can only be a distant conductor of Hamlet's rhetorical drama ("to be or not to be"), and simultaneously a phantom of opposition. The cases in which Khrushchev succeeds Stalin and Gorbachev succeeds Khrushchev (via Brezhnev, Andropov and Chernenko) (see the chapter on "Kremlinology as a Symptom" in the first part herein) demonstrate the fact that both of them could talk against the system, and that they were even personally damaged by the system (Khrushchev's son, Leonid, was a victim of Stalin; the families of Gorbachev and his wife were arrested as kulaks and sent to gulags),[11] but they talked of the systematic injustices only after they were both no longer leaders. Logic says that in communism, not even the leader himself can position himself as the opposition of his predecessor.

Marx's *Capital* (1867) was written under the direct influence of Aristotle's concept of Automaton, with Marx representing the first great confrontation of the workers and the machines. In London he saw how the big factories gobbled people up, how the machines became people and the people became machines, and he saw the human as the *prosthesis of the machine*, so in order to describe the phenomenon he used Aristotle's concept of the Automaton. An Automaton is a lifeless being who blindly repeats its routines: it wakes up, brushes its teeth, goes to work, arranges tomatoes or peppers, files receipts, has lunch, arranges tomatoes or peppers, files receipts, returns, has dinner, watches TV, brushes its teeth again and sleeps. The Automaton does not perform any real act, it has no opportunity to transgress meaning, no possibility to see itself "behind" the routine in which it repeats the actions. Marx saw these operations as being closely related to that of the worker. One of the most prominent socialist thinkers, Fourier, saw that the same operations were performed by the peasant, whom he describes with obvious repulsion: "(The peasant is) a live *automat*... judging by his/her utter primitiveness, he/she is far more similar to the animals than to people."[12]

Both Marx and the socialist nurtured a deep hatred of the Automaton, but Marx is among the first philosophers in the world to see that labor was the cause behind the appearance of the Automaton. Philosophers before Marx were obsessed with the mind and to talking about work, and making money was considered a shameful act. But industrialization was so shocking that Marx couldn't resist. Hugh Griffith writes that Marx was perhaps the first philosopher who ever took the notion of work seriously,[13] which is paradoxical seeing as Marx himself had hardly done a day's work in his entire life. During all his years living in London's Soho, Marx never managed to keep any work engagement for any lengty period of time; he was always on the verge of bankruptcy, and of the six children he had together with his wife Jenny, three died due to the poor living conditions in Soho. When he moved to London in 1849, he found peace in reading in the British Museum, where he read from 9 o'clock in the morning to 7 o'clock in the evening. He lived in a two-room apartment in Soho, under terrible conditions, with the entire family with numerous children sleeping in one of the rooms, and the other room used as a workroom, playroom and kitchen. When he didn't go to the museum to read, Marx would often sit idly for days. But he did the opposite as well, as Marx could work for days and nights without stopping, he had no fixed time for work and rest, and he would often stay up all night and then sleep in his suit on the sofa until dinner.[14]

In a letter to Kugelmann, Marx wrote: "I have become used to night work–I study by day and write by night. That, and all daily concerns, private and public… (make me) neglect a regular diet and exercise, and that is enough to create turmoil in the body."[15] The only work that Marx managed to keep over all these years was to send two weekly columns to the "New York Tribune" for two dollars per text. Marx was constantly in debt, largely owing to his unbalanced character, which would not let him give up easily on spending money that he didn't have. Marx was hopeless when it came to being economical; although he didn't have a dime to cover his debts, he still paid for piano lessons for his daughters, never gave up holidays and continued his bourgeois lifestyle. He also made fun of his situation: "I don't suppose anyone has ever written about 'money' when he was so short of the stuff."[16] But there was always Engels, who helped Marx financially until the end of his life. For more than 30 years, Engels covered all of Marx's financial debts. Engels managed the family business, elegantly and precisely, just as he led his private life. He was a businessman, with time for books, letters and journalism, and throughout his life maintained a high style, with horses and expensive wines. Marx, on the contrary, lived amidst chaos most of his life, in poverty and unemployment. When they first met in Paris, Marx and Engels made a deal to write a pamphlet of 40 pages together, with each writing 20 pages. Engels finished his part in several days, while after several months Marx, for his part, had produced around 300 pages.

Marx could never stop himself from getting carried away in extensive episodes and couldn't maintain his stream of thought; as Francis Wheen writes: "(He) was the kind of writer who could never resist a distraction."[17] The same was true for *Capital*: For years, he wasn't even close to finishing the book, and after announcing a deal with the publishers, he let 20 years go by before he finally handed it in. Engels immediately knew that he was not going to be the dominant partner in the relationship, which he accepted without envy, offering Marx both intellectual and financial support. They had no secrets or taboos between them, and as Francis Wheen writes, "Their correspondence was a pungent stew of history and gossip, arcane economics and schoolboy jokes."[18] Marx was also loyal to Engels. When Kugelmann told Marx something unpleasant about Engels in a letter, Marx said: "You don't know my relationship with Engels well. He is my most intimate friend. I don't have any secrets before him. If it wasn't for him, I would have been forced to find some kind of 'work.'"[19] Even with the only work that Marx actually managed to keep over the decades, as a columnist for the *New York Tribune*, Engels still helped him. When Marx would struggle with his deadlines for the column, Engels would write it and sign it with Marx's name. Once, when things indeed became unfavorable, Marx applied for the position of clerk at the London railways, but was turned down for his illegible handwriting.[20] Engels was the only one who could understand his handwriting, but after Marx's death in 1883, when Engels was left with a heap of Marx's notes (Engels prepared the second and third volumes of *Capital* for publishing), he trained Karl Korsch and Kautsky to read Marx's almost illegible handwriting (Kautsky's task was to prepare the fourth volume, which came out under the title, *Theories of Surplus-Value*). Engels was frustrated from the aggravation of trying to decode Marx, and he told the German socialist Bebel of the impossible task he was confronted with: "Alongside parts that have been completely finished are others that are merely sketched out, the whole being a draft with the exception of perhaps two chapters. Quotations from sources in no kind of order, piles of them jumbled together... (and) there is the handwriting, which certainly cannot be deciphered by anyone except me, and then only with difficulty."[21]

Marx's entire work is an astonishing 50 volumes. Although he was capable of condensing complex ideas into reasonably understandable sentences, he wrote extensively and took notes on all that he would read, yet wrote slowly and painfully, with many breaks and holes. He had endless inspiration, and yet in his lifetime he saw only the first volume, out of a total of six, of *Capital* (1867) published. The next two volumes were published, handwritten by Engels, after his death. Soon after he began writing *Capital*, Marx realized that he already had more than 3,000 pages (such manic writing was typical for him); at the same time, he realized that most of what he had written was not suitable for publishing, as it had to be revised, and this is what he did for 20 long years.[22] Today, it is generally thought that *Capital* was written in a way that turns people off or away from reading it, and those who think so are indeed correct. But the basis of Marx's teaching is simple and can easily be summed up. Work is the most important form of self-realization. A person works not only to buy things that make him/her into the person they desire to be, but while a person works, he/she is already becoming the person he/she wants to be. The problem appears when the capitalist so desperately exploits people that work becomes a condition for alienation. In the work process, you are no longer a human being, but merely an automaton, a prosthesis of Capital. After the Industrial Revolution, people became "impoverished prostheses" of the machines, and did not enjoy ownership over the machines and over the process, which was actually owned by someone else. Marx did not consider this paradox to be inherent in work per se, but rather in capitalism. Therefore, he offered the prognosis that capitalism was going to fall apart. This proved an incorrect diagnosis, however, as capitalism has never been more stable than it is today. In the documentary film, *Žižek!* (2005), the Slovenian philosopher says: "Thirty, 40 years ago, communism, capitalism and fascism were still debated; on the other hand, people are obsessed with the end of the world caused by viruses and Armageddons, which means that we find it easier to imagine the end of the world than the change in capitalism." But although Marx's definition of the end of capitalism proved to be incorrect, what remains true is his detailed analysis of the capital that today transforms in all possible ways (lower pay, the transfer of large corporations to Third World countries due to cheaper available labor, etc.), and this is the reason that Marx remains a disturbing, relevant reference without which the 21st century cannot be viewed.

Marx enjoyed Gothic metaphors. In *The Communist Manifesto* (1848), the first sentence contains a Gothic, demonic metaphor: "A *spectre* is haunting Europe–the *spectre* of Communism" (my italics).[23] The first sentence of *Capital* (1867) also contains a haunting description: "The wealth of those societies in which capitalist mode of production prevails, *presents* itself as 'an immense accumulation of commodities,' its unit being a single commodity (my italics)."[24] Entering *Capital* is like entering a "world of shadows and ghosts," says Francis Wheen.[25] Wherever Marks describes the objective world, he speaks of it as a "phantom" world, "immaterial," a "mere illusion," a "false representation." Although an advocate of materialism, it is interesting that Marx explains the real universe with irrational epithets, as everywhere he talks about objects, he says that they "appear as." He does so in order to say that the world is paradoxical, that what is a mirage, is essence, and essence a mirage. In the fourth volume of *Capital*, Marx offers this example that the water consists of two highly explosive gases, and concludes: "Scientific truth is always paradox."[26] This dilemma (illusion or essence) is most evident with objects that we buy and sell. Their inherent value is one; when traded, it is completely different. Bread costs 50 cents, and a plate of rare oysters covered in fine olive oil costs 50 dollars. Rubber boots are 5 dollars and their purpose is to protect one from external outside influences, but Louis Vuitton boots are 2,000 dollars and their purpose is not to protect one from external influences; they have a signaling role. What role is this? If the trade is made exclusively according to the versatility of both commodities, bread should cost *100 times* more than the rare oysters, just as the rubber boots are far more *valuable* than the Louis Vuitton boots.

What happens, asked Marx, when a certain type of commodity

is transferred to the market, what mysterious logic, what perverse value is added to it there? What occurs there is something along the lines of *phantom operations*. Bread is not cheaper because it is less useful, but because in order to produce the oysters, a *third value* is added. And that is the labor of the worker that is integrated in(to) them (the oysters are hard to find, they are difficult to pick, etc.). The work integrated into them is the *surplus* value that is profited on by the capitalist. This is the basis of Marx's teaching. Marx's critics today find certain points that Marx had foreseen in his analysis. Why would anyone pay thousands of dollars for a napkin that Salvador Dali used? According to the labor invested in them, they would cost several dollars, but their value is built on fetishism, not a fetishism of the commodities (of which Marx speaks in the chapter of *Capital* of the same title), but on cultural fetishism–the status that is given to the object, irrespective of the labor integrated into it. But his criticism does contain the genius intuition that there is a strange phenomenon that *sticks* to objects, something *phantom*, and something along the lines of *shadows*. Marx speaks of metaphysics and of theology when he speaks of objects, and this is a brilliant insight into the nature of our civilization. Objects become ghosts, they take on a life of their own and disturb the life of the living, and the dead come alive. At the same time, people who are alive become dead prisoners of the trade that only brings profits to the capitalist.

In Marx's opinion, machines don't bring about any improvement, they are irrevocably *malignant*–the mechanical monster fills both the factories and the people, and turns them into machines. But, in his historical time, Marx couldn't even imagine the level of monstrous alienation caused by mechanization as we know it today. The brilliant film, *The Machinist* (2004), by Brad Anderson, describes Trevor Reznik (played by Christian Bale), a mechanic in a factory whose work alienates him from people, food and sleep (one of the workers says to him, "If you were a bit thinner, you wouldn't exist"), and as a result of his terrible insomnia, he accidentally cuts off another worker's hand at his workstation. Reznik becomes something closest to a machine (he disappears physically, functionally cuts off arms–just like a machine–and leaves arms that need prostheses), but on a psychic level his insomnia results in paranoia.

The main issue in the film is this: How can a machine develop paranoia? The Machinist becomes a paranoid, *human machine.* The film describes the symbiosis of the ill person and the machine–the world of hallucinogenic paranoia. A dialogue between Reznik and Ivan, the machinist's hallucination, follows:

> Ivan: "You look like as if you've seen a ghost."
> Reznik: "Strange that you would say that. The colleagues from work think that you don't exist."
> Ivan: "Aha, so this is the reason why I can't get a raise."

And true enough, one of the consequences of turning people into machines and machines into people, which in Marx's opinion is irreversible, is that the richer the capitalist becomes, the poorer the worker becomes, and then what follows is a moment where he (the worker) no longer has anything, not even himself. This prognosis that Marx offered is, as we know, not entirely true if we take into consideration today's worker, who owns cars and has microwave ovens (impoverishment, to the extent that Marx announced, never really happened), but Marx often explained that for him the proletariat is the lowest class segment, what is known as a subclass today: the unemployed, the sick, the elderly, the outcasts and the homeless.[27] Finally, Marx did announce that in capitalism, an absolute decrease in wages would never happen, only a relative one. If the capitalist turnover increases by 20%, a 20% increase in the worker's salary will not necessarily follow, and this is how things still are today. In 1970, as Wheen writes, the theory of so-called "leisure time" appeared on account of automatization; now no one will have to work as much, people will idle their days away and become lethargic. But this did not happen because statistics tell us that workers today work more than they worked, e.g. in the 1980s.[28]

"Freedom or Death?" (Master or Servant?)

Marx didn't want to have anything to do with the workers. He didn't want to take an active role in political groups or actions, and when he agreed, out of pure curiosity, to be the leader of the "International Association of Working People" in 1864, he wrote to Engels, complaining that it was "a terrible waste of time." Žižek offers the anecdote that when Marx was told that the workers were planning a revolution, he answered: "Tell them to wait a while, I'm writing *Capital* at the moment." Geoff Eley writes that: "Marx first encountered workers in the educational meetings of German migrant artisans in Paris in early 1844."[29] Three years later, Engels formed an international association of workers that they called the Communist League. The note that was later prepared at the League congress in London, several weeks before the French Revolution, became the *Manifesto of the Communist Party* (1848). Although the Revolution was active and popular, no one in Europe had the guts to launch a revolution of global proportions. However, Marx rarely spoke of the *contents* of the Revolution; he concentrated on the description of the situation, philosophically, just as Kierkegaard and Hegel, and as Aristotle before them. If he desired a change in the circumstances of material life, he imagined the changes as a joint transformation of society through a change in the working class. But Marx was most certainly accepted in Russia, and with that by one-third of the planet. If there is a weakness in Marx's work that he failed to notice, then it is the fact that the same logic of transforming commodities into fetishes becomes valid for his *Capital* as well. Placed on the market of commodities, *Capital* quickly became such a fetish good, and such single-century adoration, that it swallowed millions of living people. There is probably no 20th century book whose ideas changed the lives of millions of living people so significantly, turning them into dead meat because of the critical ideals of *Capital*. Marx created a book that precisely fit his definition of the mysticism of objects; his *Capital* became precisely such an autonomous figure, which started living a life of its own and started bothering the living. To rephrase Marx, the person who writes a text, even if it is just for him/herself, is actually making a product. But the moment he/she sends it to be printed, it becomes a commodity. It seems as if Marx had no *self-reflection* that the work he himself was making would fall under the heading of commodities that created surplus value. The fate of *Capital* is more relevant proof of its accuracy than all the analyses contained therein. The Mexican critic, Ludovico Silva, writes of capitalism as a metaphor for transferring life from subjects to objects, from people to objects, with this ontological schism finally turning against the book of the critique itself and offering it as an example of all the tragedy that the book described, but did not anticipate of/from itself.

Money has a similar fetishist schism. "Our children, when they grow up, shall recognize money only as something from their memories, and or grandchildren shall know of them only according to the images in history schoolbooks"–this was written in 1920 by Jury Larin, the man who led the Ministry of Finance of the VSNH.[30] Based on the analysis of materiality of money by Alfred Sohn-Rethel, Žižek writes that there is a "fetish disavowal" in money–"I know very well that it is only money, but still...," "I know that money is a material object, but still... [it is as if it were made of a special substance over which time has no power]."[31] Money is a sublime object, made of a physical body, but there is another body in it "a body within the body," an immaterial substance, some "pre-phallic" anal object.[32] Money becomes a "real abstraction," it is real, with a metal weight and form, but at the same item its value is abstract. Money is subject to the same fetishist inversion–the material characteristics ("useful value," the form, etc.) stand opposite the "real abstraction," the fascinating force. One of the reasons for the success of the pyramidal saving banks in post-communism, nicely explained by Verdery, is the obsession with the fetishist immateriality of money. The pyramidal savings in Albania, in the Czech Republic, Slovakia, Bulgaria, "Caritas" in Romania, "MMM" in Russia, "TAT" in Macedonia, etc.–the pyramidal savings banks that appeared after the fall of communism have become Marx's fetishism, as people have learned that objects are actually faceless, no one is behind money in a particularly personal sense, they turn around independently of the will of political subjects as a natural force that no one is responsible for, the money is not *my* money, it becomes something like an abstraction that happens somewhere away from me. In other words, the pyramidal schemes have created an environment ready to accept capitalism and its different moral, i.e. its lack of morality,[33] in the sense that for the capitalist the market is *amoral*, money is an abstract economic factor, but it is not moral. It makes people start thinking whether money is directly linked to work, is there any money without work, is greed natural, what does wealth mean, is money dirty and what is money? People understand that money also multiplies without any visible work–this is not imaginable in socialism, except in the form of the lottery as one of the rare gambling fields that socialism allowed–that money can be traded, while socialism regarded trade as a type of immoral behavior and the traders as "thieves."

Marx's *Capital* (1867) was not much read in the West. When Marx finally sent the manuscript after working for many years on it, Engels was worried–he considered that the book was difficult to read, he required of Marx to shorten the chapters, to give them sub-headings, to make it look like a textbook, and not to be unappealing to the readers: "The fourth chapter is almost 200 pages long, and only has four sub-sections,"[34] complained Engels. When *Capital* came out, Engels tried to increase the interest for reading it, so he anonymously wrote negative critiques about the book in German magazines and newspapers. He also forced their common friend, Kugelmann, to do the same, and although Kugelmann published several attacks of *Capital* in Hannover, he himself never understood Marx's idea, so he didn't know how to attack it accordingly. A 1,000 copies of *Capital* was published in its initial run, and took four years to sell. Marx's daughter, Jenny, identified the problem correctly when she said: "If workers had an inkling of the sacrifices that were necessary for this work, which was written only for them and for their sakes, to be completed, they would perhaps show a little more interest."[35] That is true in the sense that the book that was written for the workers was not understandable to them, while those that could understand it–the elite, were not happy with it. The French edition (only one small part) only appeared after 1875, and also after at least five translators in the course of five years gave up the work because they were exhausted from the material, while the British showed almost no interest in the book.

The book suddenly had an uncommonly warm acceptance in a strange place–in Russia. The Russian translation was published as early as 1872, and managed to pass the czar's censors because there were very few references to Russia; furthermore, it could not be applied there. The Russians didn't have a developed industrial life, i.e. they were still in feudalism. The censors removed Marx's photo from the cover to prevent the developing of a cult for the person, and they thought that it would not be read much, even less understood, but after a year all 3,000 copies were sold. "Isn't it an irony of fate"–Marx would write to Engels, "that the Russians, whom I have fought for 25 years, always want to be my patrons? They run after the most extreme ideas the West has to offer, out of pure gluttony."[36] After the book was not accepted in the developed world, the world that it addressed to, it was accepted in Russia. The translator of *Capital* in Russian, Nicolay Danielson, was the leader of the "Narodnik" movement, which believed that Russia could move directly from feudalism to socialism, and entirely circumvent capitalism. Opposite to this, the more orthodox Marxist, Plehanov, stuck to the opinion that industrialization was a condition for socialism, that the peasants must be made into proletariat, and only after they survive the exploitation, would they will be able to build socialism. A fraction of the "Narodnik" movement, "The People's Will," assassinated Czar Alexsandar II, and later tried to assassinate Alexsandar III. One of the activists who was hung after the assassination failed and the assassins were arrested was no one else but Vladimir Ilyich Uljanov, later known as Lenin's brother.

Because it remained unclear as to whether Russia could go directly from feudalism into socialism or wait for capitalism, Plehanov's friend, Vera Zasulich, wrote Marx a letter in 1881 and asked for his opinion. In the letter, Zasulich says: "You are not unaware that your *Kapital* is enjoying great popularity in Russia. But, what you probably do not know is the role which your *Kapital* plays in our discussion of the agrarian question." She also asked if he could please settle his "ideas on the possible future of our rural commune and the theory of the historical inevitability for all countries of the world to pass through all phases of capitalist production?"[37] Marx agonized over his response for several weeks, and even prepared five versions of it. In the end, he only sent a small comment that his theory of necessity of the historical phase of capitalism "is *expressly* limited to the *countries of Western Europe.*" And he vaguely added that his analysis of capital in Western Europe "does not adduce reasons either for or against the viability of the rural commune."[38] In the first version of the answer, however, Marx was more determined. "To save the Russian commune, a Russian revolution is needed… If revolution comes at the opportune moment, if it concentrates all its forces so as to allow the rural commune full scope, the latter will soon develop as an element of regeneration in Russian society and an element of superiority over the countries enslaved by the capitalist system."³⁹ Marx had never before imagined the change from capitalism into socialism as an act of *terrorism*, he always perceived it as a collective action of the working class. In 1881, after he spent several years convincing the socialists that the terrorism was simply foolishness, he was already sick, tired and old, and had waited so long for the proletarian revolution, which never happened ("it is a bad thing to be old at this moment," he said), that he decided to "give" a green light to the revolution. All of the architects of the October Revolution used Marx as a reference, and most certainly, the Soviets had no conditions for a communist revolution of the kind that Marx supported. However, there is a correspondence between Rosa Luxemburg and Edward Bernstein, in which Luxemburg says that there is *no such thing* as a *premature* revolution. The essence of history, Žižek writes, is that the *mistake* is an integral part of history. When in Sophocles' *Oedipus the King*, Oedipus runs from the father and the mother to prevent the gods' prophecy that he will sleep with his mother and kill his father from happening, he does everything that is within his power to avoid this fate. But, the paradox is that Oedipus is led with a steady hand *precisely* towards the realization of the prophecy. He runs away from the parents who adopted him and comes to the city where his mother and father live, and where he then kills his father and marries his mother. In Žižek's words: "Without the prophecy, the little Oedipus would live happily with his parents and there would be no 'Oedipus complex.'"⁴⁰ According to Žižek, the same goes for the revolution. Should a prophet like Marx appear to say that there will be a revolution, there will be one even on a principle of error, but there will also be one as a realization of the prophecy. Whether it shall appear in the wrong place, in the undeveloped East, instead of the developed West, that is irrelevant to history. The mistake here, Žižek says, arrives *before* the truth, because "this 'truth' itself becomes true only through… the error."⁴¹ The mistake appears here in the form of a *subjective stake*. When Bernstein tells Rosa Luxemburg that the revolutionaries should wait and be patient for the objective conditions to appear, she answers that we shall not live to see that real moment, we should create the moment, and that there is a history that occurs because I am leading it in that direction. If Luxemburg's position is already a creation of history, the more important question then appears: What does actually happen *after* the revolution?

In *The Communist Manifesto*, Marx says that with the end of exploitation, the state shall also die, but what this would actually be like remained unclear; Marx never gave a description of the situation *following* the victory, which left the Russians in a quite unpleasant situation. Speaking from the aspect of philosophy, if the Revolution starts with an act against the bourgeois, then it begins with an act of unlawfulness, as well as with an act of crime. But after that, a series of making that act legal must follow, and the revolution shall continue as a legitimate act. The issue still remains as to whether the first Crime results in other ones, and whether it shall stabilize in the repeating of crimes as a historical necessity? Shall the system, initially sparked from murders, integrate them? When the Revolution happens for the same time, it is an Act, an Event. Does this act then lose its symbolic meaning, and how is Marx's "permanent revolution" to be carried out on a daily basis? Hegel developed a concept of *unhappy conscience*, in which he approached the problem of the crime and said that the first murder would result in a guilty conscience. When murders follow, they follow not because of the need to *repeat* the revolution, they follow as a payment for the symbolic debt incurred with the first murder. That is why, only afterwards, were the dimensions of the act made with the Revolution realized. Only afterwards is Bernstein's question activated again, let's wait, let's postpone. Postponement now has the form of paying back a debt of the hasty revolution. And paradoxically enough, that form of returning the debt may occur only by repetition of the debt, though another set of murders.

The most severe researchers of human freedom and labor before Marx were Kierkegaard, Hegel and Freud, all of whom concentrated on what automated repetition means? How does one become an "automaton?" Just like Marx did later on, Kierkegaard placed the Automaton in the field of labor: "What does this life mean, anyway? If we divide people into two classes, we can say that the first group works to live, while the other does not need to do that. But, working for one's living can't be the meaning of life... To say that the meaning of life is to die seems again to be a contradiction," Kierkegaard wrote.[42] Kierkegaard was not partial. He said that both the servants and the masters are Automatons. The servants work to survive, while the Masters destroy the conditions for their work (they are not the ones working, the servants work for them), which means that the self-realization that work gives you is impossible for the masters to find. Where do they find their self-realization? In destroying the working conditions for the servant! Neither can the servant be without the master, or the other way around. They are both caught in a circle, and both are alienated from themselves. With his *unhappy conscience*, Marx's teacher, Hegel, developed a theory for the two categories: the master (in Hegel–the lord) and the servant (with Hegel–the bondsman). The servant works for the master, who takes the results from his labor. The servant must give up his/her signature on the product, as the signature belongs to the master, as Judith Butler explains.[43] Moreover, the servant is not only exploited economically, but also cognitively. All human senses, all movements of the worker are paralyzed, in some delirium of the automaton, of the doll (the term comes from historical materialism). Thus far, it is clear why the servant is in alienation. Here comes a twist–it is true that the servant is forced to give up the signature on the product, but he/she stubbornly clings to the work because while he/she is working, he/she is not yet completely subordinated. The servant has the choice to create lasting products, objects that shall outlive him/her. There is a different type of philosophical senselessness on the master's side. The master starts off as self-realized, as he/she does not need to work, he/she does not have to produce anything and he/she can just spend. Everything seems to be all right. But while he/she spends, he/she deforms the objects that the worker creates. The sadism that he/she directed at the worker now turns against him/her, as the master now starts to take an alienated look at him/herself.[44] He/she does not work, and does not have anywhere to get self-realization from. Now the master falls into endless contradiction. With Hegel, both the master and the servant are in a fundamental metaphysical drama.

Freud threw a slightly different light on alienation. For Freud, the automated repetition of a meaningless operation is a dictation that comes from the outside, as a work dictate and a need for self-preservation. Repetition, of course, is not moved by the principle of comfort (but by mere survival), but by one more *additional factor*. When a person endlessly repeats an operation, the person does that in order to master the trauma that would arise if he/she *saw* the work in its essence. When the workaholic works continuously, he/she repeats the action in order *not* to realize that the work is senseless. Repetition saves you from the meeting with the truth, which is an "unsuccessful encounter" with the senselessness of work. Therefore, Freud has no negative attitude towards the human's prosthetic nature. (Take a look at the children Lacan advises in his seminar, *The Four Fundamental Concepts of Psychoanalysis* (1998), in which he analyzes Freud's notion of repetition–children want you to tell a story in the same way as yesterday.[45]) The story must be repeated, word for word, yesterday the *same* as the day before, brought to the level of ritual, with a clear request that the details should remain unchanged, as they were previously carefully memorized by the child. If you skip the contents of Red Riding Hood's basket, the child shall tell you to go back, to list all the articles from yesterday's storytelling. If the child shows an appetite for something new, the idea that the world is changeable returns, and that there are *other* things in it that it needs, even if it does not need them, in the interest of the new, as some consumer impulse opens. That impulse is monstrous; to avoid seeing the new piling up, man turns to automatization. The automaton is a buffering of the "surplus sense," a need to forever stabilize in the same. As we see, Freud for the first time ties the psychic dynamism between the master and the servant to the dramatic question, "Freedom or Death?" The servant says: There is no freedom without life, and he/she chooses life. The master says the same, but chooses death. In this way, the master gives up his/her being–as a result, he/she becomes alienated. If you choose freedom (as the servant), you lose both, if you choose life (as the master) you lose freedom. This *deadly factor*, as Lacan describes it, is proof that there is no choice for self-realization, either for the servant or the master. When Lenin applied Marx, he decided to ignore these insights from Kierkegaard to Freud. Lenin said, let's create work conditions in which work shall become a positive value for all. For Hegel, work was a negative activity; when the worker worked on an object, he/she negated the form that he/she worked on, *he/she de-formed it*. Lenin wanted to affirm the work process, when the worker finished the product, he/she should get back to the "un-deformed" product, which in Hegelian terms would mean that Lenin wanted to see the worker in a process of *doing nothing*. For both Hegel and Freud, labor was a philosophical problem, not an empirical one, and there was no way for work to be a positive, affirmative value. To affirm a certain project meant that nothing should be done to it, the object should not be touched. But this is not how it was imagined in the communist universe.

Lenin was also obsessed with the machines, just as Stalin was, but Lenin's obsession with machines did not come directly from Ford, but from the Dadaists–it is there that he first saw the prosthetic nature of the people after the First World War. The war invalids were a frequent topic of the Dadaists. Before returning to Russia to organize the Revolution in 1917, Lenin lived in Switzerland, only a few meters from the Cabaret Voltaire in Zŭrich, the most important gathering place of the Dadaists, a place where they wrote their manifestos and had their most famous performances. In the book, *Lenin in Zŭrich* (1975), Solzhenitsyn follows the personal development of Lenin, trying to find the roots of the Soviet Empire, and the majority of thoughts that Solzhenitsyn tries to assign to his narrator Lenin are comprised of combinations of aristocratic and bourgeois manners and concepts–the masses made him sick, the avant-garde thought of the Dadaists as being close to him. However, it is important to stress that the avant-garde was not the one to blame for Lenin's later achievements, Dadaists did not support the totalitarian tendencies, and Dada's counterparts in the Soviet Union were regularly sent to the Gulag.

The Dadaists developed a concept of a "laughter Revolution," and said: "Revolution *without* a goal can still be a revolution *with* effect."[46] This was important for Lenin's undertaking in 1917–you can laugh at the revolution, you don't have to take it seriously, but even if it is funny, the revolution will never be in vain. Every revolution always means an exit from the closed circle of automatic acts, exit from the Automaton. Between the two world wars, the Martinetti's futurists and the Tristan Tzara's Dadaists were obsessed with technology, and they presented the body as a prosthesis of the machine. Lenin looked at the Dadaist images–post-war world of victims with prostheses, and the Dadaist's tried to coin the term "anti-human humanism;" they first discussed the price that humans have to pay for technological modernization. Just like Marx, the Dadaists were obsessed with Aristotle's Automaton, and they too had an attitude of disgust towards machines. The machine is a continuation of the human, the machine is a prosthesis which is neither a part of me (since it is mechanical), neither an object (because it is a part of me, it replaces my arm, leg and mouth). At the same time, Dadaists considered the prosthesis to be an ideal mechanism for a final and complete assimilation of the human.

In his famous *Dada Manifesto* (1918), Tristan Tzara, the leader of the Dadaists said: "Dada is working with all its might towards the universal installation of the idiot." Lenin was aware of the price of industrial production, but just like the Dadaists, he was thrilled by the duality of the concepts, as he knew that the price of material production was turning people into automats and automats into people (Lenin claimed to have read *Capital* when he was 18, in the old kitchen of his grandfather's flat[47]), but Lenin didn't have any strength to perform a total prosthetization of the Soviet culture. Stalin, on the other hand, had that strength. Lenin wanted to introduce industrial production into the Soviet Union, but only to take over the form of work without importing exploitation, but as Buck-Morss writes, he missed seeing that "the capitalist form *is* its content."[48] It does not exist, just like Hegel said, work without exploitation. Stalin had no such anarchistic fantasies, he was a "realist!" In 1929, five years after Lenin had died, Stalin placed an order with Henry Ford to build an automobile industry in the Soviet Union, and Henry Ford sent his best engineers to set up the factory, "The Automobile Institute," in Nizhi Novgorod (Gorky at that time). That same year, Stalin completely abolished private property, introduced total collectivization of the villages, turning the country into kolkhozes (Soviet collective farms) and sovkhoses (state-owned economies).[49] The communities were constantly losing money, but Stalin's regime lied and published optimistic numbers, and it was only in 1956 on the 20th Congress of the Central Committee of Soviet Union, three years after Stalin's death, that it was admitted that only in 1953 did production reach the same level as in 1928.[50] The results of obligatory buyout were quite disastrous.

How the Small Town Dreams of Communism?
(From the Six Macedonian Tractors to Apollo 9)

Yugoslavia desired communism, but as in the Soviet Union, there were major conditions missing: machines that would exploit workers so they would feel as if they were prostheses of the machines, a work class that was to be exploited by the masters in order to create a revolution and Marxist literature that would explain what communism was. The first two factors were missing in Russia as well, the difference being that, while in Russia *Capital* was widely read, people from Yugoslavia didn't have the faintest idea of what Marxism was. In the exceptional study on the history of the Left in Europe, *Forging Democracy* (2002), Geoff Eley writes: "The countries of weakest diffusion (of the *Communist Manifesto*–my comment) were those of the Iberian Peninsula, where anarchism dominated, and the Balkans and parts of Eastern Europe, where there was no labor movement yet and little literacy."[51] Eley writes that until 1918, *The Communist Manifesto* appeared in more than 20 languages, including in Japanese and Chinese, and it was published in Russian in over 70 editions, but in the Balkans and parts of Eastern Europe, Marx was primarily read by the movement's intellectuals, but the actual diffusion of Marxism among the cadres was limited, as people had acquired only garbled versions of his writings and they knew only a few basic ideas, e.g. like the broadness of the readers of Marx in Russia.[52] The rest was the same.

Both Yugoslav and Soviet communism did not have the required infrastructure for a revolution against the owners of the machines for the simple reason that there were no machines. According to historians, at the outset of the Second World War in Yugoslavia there were approximately 2,300 tractors, 1,200 ploughs, 10,000 tying machines and 12,000 mowers.[53] This was the entire basis for production, as one-third of the peasants literally worked by hand, meaning that they didn't even have the most primitive working tools. In Macedonia, things were even worse. Before the start of the Second World War, there were a total of *six tractors* in Macedonia, six sowing machines and 20 threshing machines.[54] Those six tractors were supposed to bring the country into an era of brilliant socialist industrialization. Since there were no machines, the question was how to get money to buy them? In the Soviet Union it was

Preobrazhensky who offered a solution–the money should come from the villages because it was only there that there was some "realistic" and not virtual money, an idea that he called the, "Theory of initial socialist accumulation."[55] That meant that exploitation was being transferred onto the peasants. From favoring the bourgeois over the worker in capitalism, advancement was made to the favoring of the worker over the peasant, and communism ended up like a system with two privileged classes (workers and the bureaucracy), which was embodied in the maxim: "Now we have only one bourgeois (the Communist Party), and all others are exploited."

The Preobrazhensky of Yugoslavia was Boris Kidrič, who stated that: "There is a lot of money in the villages."[56] That is because in Yugoslavia in 1939 76.6% of the entire population worked in agriculture.[57] How to obtain this money? The answer lay in the obligatory buyout that was done in accordance with Preobrazhensky's model. The Federal People's Republic of Yugoslavia entered into the collectivization phase from 1949-1953, in which village communities were built based on the Soviet kolkhozes. There was a nominal difference between Yugoslavia and the Soviet Union, but in practice it all amounted to nothing. Stalin completely revoked private property in 1929, while Yugoslavia basically allowed private property with the "Law on Agrarian Reform and Collectivization" of 1945, but due to the obligatory buyout, all that the peasants produced the state actually stole from them. Furthermore, in the Soviet case there was at least no hypocrisy, as it was clear that all went to the state, which was the thief in the eyes of the peasants. In Yugoslavia, aside from the fact that there was a theft, there was this fake concept that all that was stolen was actually yours (the parole: "The land belongs to the one working it").

Aside from not having any machines before communism, Macedonia had only one clear legacy–the Ottoman form of feudalism. Ottoman feudalism had a peculiar relationship *towards technology and machines*. As reported to the French traveler Victor Bérard, a late 19th century Turkish governor provided a fascinating solution of how to resolve the technological drama of dealing with the issue of progress. He said: "If we followed Europe in all its caprices, our life would pass in building roads, then in transforming them into railroads, and transforming those in turn into electrical vehicles.

Better to wait and not decide, until we will have learned of progress' final word."[58] A certain *duality* lies in the essence of the Ottoman Empire. The Ottoman Empire was not organized according to a capitalist principle, nor to classical European feudalism. The peasants "owned" the land, the urban class held the reigns, and the link between the two was the taxes that were used to pay the army. This is how the sultan protected himself from the possibility of some small sultan endangering him, which also offered the peasants some kind of protection. The state was the nominal owner of the land, something like a central landowning agency, but it was the owner only in name, as the Ottoman state was the absent and faceless owner. On the contrary, the peasant was the "real" owner, which is what Marx wrote about. The central government interfered in the affairs of local communities as little as possible; when a peasant could not afford to pay his taxes, the taxes were paid by the local community that the peasant belonged to. The army and the peasants were really in a constant antagonism, which brings to mind the same as that in capitalism. When European colonial interference (due to international interests) began, this antagonism was irrevocably destroyed. European capitalism introduced a reform in the taxes that lead to local riots, as the peasants started to sell their labor in accordance with the market norms, which resulted in tears in the communal bonds. That is how the pre-capitalist form of production begins.[59]

When communism began, there were barely any traces of a pre-capitalist market economy in Yugoslavia, and what was there was insignificant. In Yugoslavia, and especially in Macedonia, there was no industry. According to the census from December 1945, there were 140 factories in Macedonia, 163 enterprises, 8,873 work posts and 3,391 employees, the lowest number in all in Yugoslavia, which in turn had the lowest compared to all of Europe (for comparison purposes, Slovenia had 1,094 factories, 222 enterprises and 87,113 work posts). Only 4% of the total industrial enterprises and 3% of the work posts were stationed in Macedonia.[60] Yugoslavia started off with terrible losses during the war with the Allies, reporting a material loss in the amount of 9,100,000,000 US dollars (17% of the total loss to the Allies).[61] Because of the semi-feudalism and lack of infrastructure, when Yugoslavia adopted the first Five-Year Plan in

April 1947, and with it the planned increase of industrial production by five times compared to 1939 and agricultural production by one-and-a-half times,[62] it was completely nebulous in regard to the realistic conditions in the field. Aside from factories, there was no working class in Yugoslavia as well–in 1939, 76.6% of the entire population of Yugoslavia, and above 80% of the population of Macedonia, worked in agriculture.[63] While Marx talked of exploitation of the workers in the West, in Yugoslavia the class that knew how to operate machines (that were yet to be bought) was just emerging in order to be exploited. That ideally closed circle of absurdity showed that communism in Macedonia started off as an ideology *without any connection* to the conditions in capitalism that Marx wrote about. Macedonia was actually ideally undeveloped if one considers that communism succeeded only in the most undeveloped countries.

But the great communist dream to conquer the universe also caught on in semi-feudal Yugoslavia. The small town enjoyed the exoticism (see the chapter with the same title); therefore, the first impulses for top technology were linked to space fantasies. When the Americans launched the space mission "Apollo 9" in 1969 at the peak of the Cold War, the Serbian singer–songwriter Obren Pjevović wrote the song "Apollo 9," which was performed by Masinka Lukić, the most notorious example of the cyber dreams of Yugoslav communism:

> In a wooden bed I sleep and whine
> and my Mile in Apollo 9
> on Venus, where our lads climb
> and girls gathering food for a nice time
> planets and prunes–dried
> while a child on Earth cried
> bread and salads it will need
> a hungry child, well indeed![64]

This sarcastic intervention from 1969, the same year that Konstantinović published his brilliant study on Yugoslav provincialism, contains the correct paradoxes between which the small town and the communist ideology oscillated. During the launching of "Apollo 9," the most (only) famous commentator on the American and Soviet space programs in Yugoslavia, Milivoj Jugin, commented: "The noise the motors of this shuttle makes sounds like what millions of Beatles records played at the same time would sound like,"[65] which is an ideal sublimation of the entire ideological–propaganda mess in which Yugoslavia ended up 10 decades after abandoning feudalism, jumping into capitalism and launching communism. If, from the Ottoman heritage, the resulting small towns listened to the Beatles, then the six tractors could magically be launched into communist space. For years, Pjevović's song was the subject of ridicule by the Yugoslav alternative youth; however, it was the most sublimated description of the Yugoslav communist superego, much better that the deconstructive attempts the Yugoslav rock scene made in the two decades that followed (the 1970s and 1980s).

Henri Ford died in 1947, and Yugoslavia missed the opportunity to invite the great industrial giant to raise the Yugoslav mechanical communism into the space of the five-year plan. But the obsession with Ford did not circumvent Yugoslavia, which was proven by the parodic lyrics from the song "My Ford" by the Bosnian band "Nervous Postman" from the 1980s: "My Ford, although old/Is still worth gold/It is not just talk/With Ford/I was never a police mock." Between these opposites, Yugoslavia reached fame by redesigning capitalist brands: *Stoyadin* was the name for the Fiat-based automobile from the late 1970s, *Cocta* was the Yugoslav response to *Coca-Cola*, etc. From beauty pageants, avant-garde animated film schools, relatively good cartoons and design, blues and jazz festivals–these phenomena were part of the reason for today's nostalgic remembrance of Yugoslavia as the variant closest to the West and furthest from Soviet Union. Yugoslavia launched its own special *communist expression* through its partisan movies–Tito himself once made a cameo appearance in the movie, *This People Shall Live* (1947), which was however before his cult grew stronger; later, the problem was who was going to embody him, so in a movie called, *Sutjeska* (1973), he was played by Richard Burton. Yugoslavia profited largely from its adopted pop culture, which was exported to the East, especially in the countries of the Soviet bloc (78% of all translations of Western books in Yugoslavia were sold to the East[66]), and when the famous

East German skater, Katerina Vitt, visited Zagreb at the height of her fame, the only thing she asked for was Ljupka Dimitrovska's (Yugoslav pop singer) signature–that's how significant her status was in the DDR.[67]

5

Body

Chosen Body, Mortal Body

The famous Soviet apparatchik, Vyechislav Molotov, advised his associates that: "A disciplined man can never catch a cold."[1] Those who caught a cold were state enemies, and if you had an ache or pain, communism advised you that you could conquer every bodily nerve. The communist-to-be was the one who was held back by the insight that he/she could not give up, as his/her body was chosen for a special purpose. This fit well with Lenin's general philosophy that the true communist can fool the body, and that the body of the communist is comprised of "a special texture," it is a "special type of non-pathological excess above and against physical incarnation," as Žižek writes.[2]

When Stalin met Lenin for the first time, in Finland in 1905, he was immediately disappointed by his appearance: "The most ordinary-looking man, below average height ... (was) in no way distinguishable from ordinary mortals."[3] But when Lenin died, Stalin literally began the eulogy with the words: "We, the communists, are not like other people. We are made of a special stuff."[4] For Stalin, there were ordinary bodies (the "ordinary" human is only historical "material"),[5] but there was also the special body of the cadre–it is the body that is "historically necessary" and because it is aware of this necessity, the body cannot experience a deviation; the spirit in that body does not know any deviations, it can stand all kinds of stress and stormy weather; however, it should not be subjected to death.

When, shortly before his death, the Hungarian communist János Kádár turned to the Congress of the Communist Party of Hungary in 1989, he recognized his bodily weakness as Marxist weakness: "The doctor told me that my illness is a result of the constant reflecting over my responsibility. Because in a biblical sense, I am a scapegoat." [6] Using Kádár's vocabulary, the first sentence means that he suffers from the enormous stresses in the Party, while using Stalin's vocabulary, the second part means that he must be the "scapegoat" since his illness is evidence that he is not historical material, but merely ordinary *flesh* that does not recognize historical necessity. The illness is the key evidence that Kádár is not cadre–the deviation of the body is a *signal* of the deviation of the spirit in that body. These are the roots of the communist pathological fear of death.

When on one occasion, the Albanian communist leader Enver Hoxha visited his birth city of Gjirokastër, among the masses of people he met a distant relative of his, an old lady, whom he addressed with the words "You shall live long," to which she responded: "No, you and I are old, we shall soon die." Hoxha went pale, his body went numb, and Ramiz Alia responded: "No, great comrade Hoxha, you shall live to be a 100 because that is in your genetic code, but you will receive a 20-year bonus from socialism," after which a huge, relieving applause from the gathered masses followed.[7] The absurdity of the *socialist bonus years* for the leader is explained by the faith in the subliminal body of the cadre; the cadre is not integrated in his body as a material fragility; to the contrary, it is some upgrade *beyond* history, he is the absolute historical Subject which, due to the grandiosity of the historical project, receives bonus years.

The standard salute of Hoxha subordinates–"Take years from our lives Great Leader, and add them to your life"–already existed in the Ottoman salute to the sultan of Turkey, the Padishah, "May Allah take years from me and give them to him."[8] But while the formulistic salute to the sultan objectified the sympathy towards the leader, of course people *knew* the sultan was mortal and it is precisely due to his mortality, to the awareness that leaders pass away, that people were expressing good will to him. Communism, on the other hand, promulgated a free-of-interest conviction in the realistic "exception," the leader shall *break from* the circle of mortality, therefore the act of "giving bonus years" is not a gesture of personal sympathy towards the leader, but a confirmation of the aforementioned personal, objective truth: The leader *is* the one who overcomes death, otherwise, he would not be a leader, but a traitor.

When Lenin was suffering a severe illness in December 1922, his right arm and leg paralyzed, the doctor allowed him to dictate to his stenographer for five minutes a day in order for him to express his latest concerns about the Soviet future. Lenin ordered that the notes be made out in five copies, with one copy designated as "strictly confidential," which was to be given to his secretary and opened only after Lenin's death. Following her own interpretation, the stenographer Krupska, "refused to write the words 'the death of Lenin.'"[9] There was no gesture of personal sympathy in Krupska's censure, but only the belief that through an exception from the cycle of birth and death could the leader be asserted as the leader; death is denied thanks to the fetishist confirmation of the historical necessity of the Leader. The manner in which this fetishist schism works is best illustrated in the documentary, *Welcome to North Korea* (2001), which reveals the absurd belief of the North Korean people that Kim Il-sung still lives behind the walls of his grandiose palace in some transposed eternity ("carried away by birds," "protected by flowers," etc.). This schizophrenia of the public symbolic Law confirms that the communist social scene is directed in this way, and that death is denied from a place there. Or, we witness the necrophilic apotheosis in the form of the diagnosis of Stalin's death published in the newspaper "Pravda" in 1953, which demonstrates how medicine must bow before the Symbolic laws of the communist universe—death is not a matter of medical verification, *death is a question of style* so to speak, only the one who cannot conquer death in the field of literature dies.

This is the road by which the doctor becomes the enemy in communism. The doctor was some kind of objective instance, an alternative for the immortal universe, and it is probably the only profession that served as an effective threat to the immortal symbolic authority of communism. "The truth is dead, and if there is one at all, it is known only by those who died, if they died,"[10] Branka Arsić writes with customary poignant irony. The most cynical comment on the communist attitude towards death is offered by Erofeyev in his book, *The Good Stalin*: "In the Soviet Union, it was considered that death does not exist. Death is willfulness. Marxist philosophy passed by death holding its nose. The deceased were treated badly, just like deserters. The undertaker's job fell to the lowest status level. For many years after the Revolution, close to the cemetery one could still smell the unburied corpses."[11]

This general communist relationship with death completely matched the manner in which the small-town mentality works. Konstantinović writes that, "The style (of the small town) does not recognize the dead."[12] The small-town spirit is present everywhere, and it is also *forever*. Konstantinović writes that the curiosity for historicalness often present in the small town most often signifies the opposite: When it peaks into the past, the small town does so to see whether any secret is left from the past that shall be absorbed in the eternal small town. "The peasant goes everywhere in order to satisfy his/her needs, in his neighborhood, but also in time: He/she loves the past as his/her own confirmation, but also dislikes it for the very same reason."[13] For the small town, it is not the man who dies, but some abstract X instead. "The closer we are to concreteness, ... the closer we are to death."[14] That is why the small town does not recognize death, just as the communist universe does not.

Doctor (About Tito's Leg)

Tito's leg–the more it shrank, the more Yugoslavia's political life extended. This leg is an ideal occasion to enquire into the relationship between medicine and the Yugoslav communist movement. What happened when the Marshal's body disintegrated, if his body was a symbolic stake for the entire community? In the final phases of Tito's dying, there were transfers of life: The Marshal's shrunken body expanded (the previously condensed) ideological world. For Yugoslavia, this meant a spinning disassembling of the system, with great forceful speed and violence–the same kind with which it was assembled. When in 2007, the autopsy findings from Tito's death were discovered in the notorious box number 36 in the archives in Ljubljana, they ended all speculation of the Yugoslav "doctor conspiracy" that had spread among the people for decades.

According to these so-called theories, Tito died due to "a doctor's cardinal error," that "the doctors killed Tito," etc., similar to Stalin's thesis that the doctors killed the leaders, and not Death. A reading of the autopsy findings today shows that the Marshal had: "Blood vessel sclerosis, particularly accentuated in the leg arteries... heavy thrombosis (which in the first period) was bridged with a bypass of the blood vessels, and later an amputation above the knee was performed. In the later course of treatment, some damage to the organs occurred. The heart gradually weakened, the oxygen levels fell (causing damage to the brain), the weak kidneys collected poison in the body and the liver was not functioning, which in turn brought on hepatitis; a lung infection was diagnosed, then a bladder infection and finally the heart stopped and death occurred."[15]

Tito "couldn't get over the leg amputation," his nephew, Joška Broz, remembers: "Once Badurina said to him, 'Old friend, Roosevelt lived 20 years without a leg.'" Tito got angry and said "I came into this world with two feet, I want to leave it that way." He categorically declared "I am not giving up my leg."[16] Just like Stalin, Tito was a paranoiac. His food in the hospital in Ljubljana was brought in every day by his personal butler, Jožef Oseli, in a black Mercedes at the back entrance of the Clinical Center in Ljubljana. Tito's doctors' consilium also ate from the food that was prepared in the kitchen of the Brdo Palace in Kranj. Just as Stalin made his bodyguards try the dishes, the Yugoslav Marshal was also terrified of sabotage. But Tito was far less paranoid than Stalin, and far more narcissistic. Until the moment he died, he was obsessed with his looks, as he stood up straight, insisted on walking quickly and tanned himself to mask his age spots. Tito's entire later life was one big battle to look younger and to achieve the possibility of eternal life. He wore gloves to hide his age spots, he colored his hair every 15 days and he had a perm done with huge quantities of hairspray, with the hairdresser visiting the hospital every day.

Tito's personal doctor, Matunović, offers: "Tito did not fear death, he didn't even think of it at all. Tito simply *didn't believe* that he was going to die. Until the end of his life, he did not accept the fact that he was a *biological being*. He considered himself *immortal*"[17] (my italics). Much like Enver Hoxha, Stalin and Lenin, Tito also entertained some "hazy idea" that death circumvents the leader.

The communist leader is the Absolute historical Subject. He stands above death, not as a threat, but as an investment in the historical movement–all die, but the absolute leader is spared from such senselessness.

Bolshevik hatred of medicine is well documented, and the relationship between the Bolshevik movement and doctors was quite tense. The style (literature) could even shut its eyes before death, but not the doctors, and that is why the doctor was the most efficient threat to the communist fascination/obsession with eternal life. The paradox lies in the roots of the so-called "doctor conspiracy" dating back to 1953, when Stalin ordered the most famous doctors of the Kremlin to be taken before the court, led by his personal doctor. They were accused as being part of the Jewish conspiracy to poison the Soviet political and military leaders. The newspaper "Pravda" called doctors terrorists and saboteurs, and they (the doctors) had to confess that they deliberately "covered up" Zhdanov's heart attack, that they shortened Schebyakov's life, etc. In the first wave of this process, 37 doctors were arrested. Later, the number grew to hundreds and the outcomes of the trials were either swift execution or the gulags. These doctor conspiracies were looked for (and found) in all of the Soviet republics–for example, 36 doctors were arrested in the Ukraine. Stalin's obsession with doctors began long before 1953. In 1934, Stalin asked his doctor, Shnayderovich: "Doctor, just tell me the truth: Do you occasionally feel a desire to poison me?"[18] In 1937, Stalin turned to the Kremlin doctor Valedinsky during a dinner party, and apropos of nothing, told him: "There are enemies of the people among the doctors." In 1952, already sick and paranoid, Stalin claimed that all of the doctors must be replaced with new ones, and the next year he lost his nerves entirely in the demonic battle with his paranoia and ordered the arrest of all the Kremlin doctors, together with their torture, until they admitted that they were part of the international conspiracy to kill the Soviet leaders.

According to medical data, Stalin was in constant pain, and as the pain increased, so did his paranoia from doctors. Stalin requested his medication be ordered under false names, his bodyguards tried the pills before he did, and near the end of this life he completely lost any trust in doctors and sought health consultations only from veterinarians.[19] The fascination with this phenomenal transfer from *Stalin the automaton* into *Stalin the animal* can only be explained with the ancient paradigm of the monstrous hero, who in his solitude (cannot be in a community he does not trust) oscillates between assuming the form of God (the Automaton) and a wild beast (the animal).

The Bolsheviks used sickness as an argument against all kinds of "deviations" of the mind. In Lenin's letter to Gorky from the autumn of 1913, Lenin, deeply disturbed by Gorky's attitude towards the so-called "construction of God," writes to Gorky that his theses are the result of bad nerves: "Take care of yourself more seriously, really, so that you will be able to travel in winter *without catching cold* (in winter, it is dangerous)." And: "Concerning the 'construction of God' perhaps you didn't write that seriously? Good heavens, take care of yourself a little bit better."[20] Those whom he couldn't kill or deport, like Gorky, who was precious to him, he sent to a sanatorium. Rayfield reminds us that when Gorky refused to be quiet or pack, Lenin insisted: "Tut, tut, this is really shameful and irrational. In Europe, you will have treatment in a proper sanatorium and work three times as much. Really… Go away, get cured. Don't be stubborn, I beg you."[21]

New Body and Sanitary Sweepings

The mindless bonus years for a leader (Ramiz Alia's reply to Enver Hoxha, "You shall get 20 years bonus from socialism") was "compensated" for with the lack of life for the ordinary person, with the treatment of so-called ordinary death. Stalin defined this double balance well when he said: "A person can be broken, run over, ruthlessly swindled, but that is done with the goal to create the new man"–and that deadly calculation was taken to the limits of the animalistic in Stalin's fury in his sweep in the Ukraine and Russia during the "Great Hunger" of 1923 when 11 million people were killed. That kind (and scale) of mindless death of the ordinary person rests on the faith that following the wreaking of destruction, as Žižek writes, "Eventually something will remain, the sublime 'indivisible reminder,' the paragon of the New.'"[22] In a different variation, the same is said by Preobrazhensky, one of the most influential ideologists of the early Soviet Union, when he writes: "From a socialist point of view, it is completely senseless for each individual member of society to see his/her body as implicit personal property."[23]

The doctrine of the new body did not include any a priori positive content, as the frame was not filled with positive provisions; on the contrary, the New Man was treated only as a Frame, a Still that was yet to be given substance. The revolutionary mess with which the order was destroyed establishes the void which, in the first period, was nothing but a frame, similar to the *Black Square on a White Ground* (1915) by Kazimir Malevich. Žižek puts it this way: "The essence of the cadre is to provide a *cadre* (square, frame) for the essence itself."[24] The problem with the obsession with the *form* lies entirely in the fetishistic fascination that there is some hidden content behind the form, while if there is no content there is also no form for that content either.

"The party strengthens through sweepings." This is the thesis that Lenin adopts from the German socialists.[25] Following the October Revolution, there is one truth for Lenin: The world is fecal, the fecal product called people is the burden of the world, and it shall have to disappear into oblivion, into nullity. Zinoviev says: "If from 100 million people we have managed to lure 90 million for our goals, that is success." This means that 10 million are considered to be justified killings, but unfortunately the calculation of "sanitary rubbish," especially in Stalin's era, already drastically surpassed Zinoviev's original calculations. Inside of two months–September and October 1917–Lenin killed approximately 10,000 people, and in 1918 Lenin and Trotsky opened the first camps. Lenin's executioner and later Stalin's as well, the monstrous Dzerzhinsky proclaimed: "We need no justice, we are now at war;" Lenin said the same, but with a milder tone: "It is better to arrest 100 innocent than to leave one counter-revolutionary alive."[26]

It is interesting that all of the compromising parts of Lenin's texts were also later carefully cleansed, the sanitizing of Soviet communism includes not only the people, but approaches history in an Orwellian fashion as well. The action to clean human garbage takes on drastic proportions when Lenin turns against the peasants. In one of his texts, Lenin calls the peasants "medieval trash," and in May 1918 he introduced the term "kulak" for a rich peasant, together with the thesis, "Death to all kulaks." It was not clear how to execute the kulaks in the most efficient way because they were the most numerous demographic of the Soviet Empire. Lenin first recommended hanging kulaks in groups of 100 in front of the people gathered in (Moscow's) Red Square for all to see, with everything in accordance with the medieval public guillotine executions. But then he needed some fecal swamp that would just gobble them up, a *Black Square on a White Ground*, a solution for a toilet that swallows the fecal excess of people from the Soviet Union, the excess "medieval trash," in order for the Empire to be able to launch itself out of feudalism directly into Apollo 9 communism.

There was no other alternative to Lenin's sanitation project than Stalin's. On November 7, 1929, Stalin issued a decree for collectivization with which a new classification of the kulaks was made, with extermination dictated according to three categories: shooting for the first, distant gulag for the second and nearby gulag for the third category. In 1932, Stalin surrounded the villages with political police so that the peasants could not leave the kolkhozes, thus giving way to the greatest communist genocide of the 20th century. Khrushchev personally signed a list for the execution of over 41,000 kulaks, and in 1932 and 1933 over 11 million people died from hunger, mainly in the Ukraine and Russia. As early as 1927, and particularly from 1937, Stalin's sweeps did not circumvent even the last line of permitted sanitary cleaning–the Party itself. The era of spectacular public processes began, as every day on Stalin's desk there were lists with over 40,000 Party members to be liquidated, even though the total number of party sweeps is represented by "only" 8 to 9% of the total number of victims. Sweeping people away was not a cheap task. In 1937, the famous act with which Stalin directed that people had to be cleared in each and every region of the Soviet Union was adopted. The lists contained three columns: in the first was the name of the region, in the second the number of people to be shot, while the third was the number of people to be exiled to Siberia. The lists for liquidation were executed immediately. During the execution process, new lists were begun and Stalin signed all of them, while the ones behind these executions were Stalin's monsters, Jezhov and Berija. Seventy-five million roubles were used for this operation, and after the sweeping of counter-revolutionaries, priests, sailors and kulaks was over it was the nationalists' turn. In 1940, 27,000 Polish functionaries were terminated. During the war, the mortality rate among the exiled rose to more than 60% for children under the age of four and the elderly, who suffered the most of the exiles. The sanitizing continued with the cleansing of the next area, the prisons. In 1938, orders were given for the execution of the workers in the gulags–the only reason being to provide space for new prisoners. Up until 1953, the mortality rate in the Gulags ranged from 0.3 to 24%, meaning that in some years one-fourth of all those imprisoned died–a total of over 15 million prisoners. In the war years–1940 to 1945–the mortality rate rose to 60%, thereby exceeding the rate of the Nazi death camps that were also projects for cleaning society of the bodies of the filthy population. The Nazi and communist totalitarian cleansing of bodies were two branches of the same tree. While Nürnberg happened to Nazism, nothing happened to communism. The Germans take their children to the former camps to show them what Nazism meant–but that is not what former Soviet citizens do.[27]

Bronze Body

"Dead bodies, of both flesh and bronze, were essential to symbolizing (and thus helping to produce) the end of socialism," says Verdery.[28] When Lenin's statue in Yerevan (Armenia) was removed from its throne, put on a truck and driven around the central square, the onlookers threw sticks and coins, just as is done for a funeral. In Mongolia, one of Stalin's monuments, which was taken down a bit later, in 1990, was sprinkled with milk on the occasion because the Mongolians believe milk prevents an evil spirit from haunting them or returning–like an act of burying communism itself. Dead bodies were excavated and revalued, e.g. Imre Nagy, the leader of the Hungarian revolution from 1956, was reburied as an *anti*communist.[29]

Why did death in communism manifest itself through the *politics of corpses* by excavating them, reburying them, kidnapping them, attacking cemeteries, fetishizing the dead bodies, etc.? What kind of investment did the corpses represent? It seems that *necromania* emerged as a consequence of the lack of a sacrificial attitude towards communism and the lack of acts and processes for reconciliation with the past, and because the state didn't know what to do with its communist heritage, people began practicing the ritual needs of the community on their own initiative through "renewed" funerals, vendettas or reconciliations, which was manifested on the bronze bodies. In 1989, Lenin's statue in Volchov, near Saint Petersburg, was scheduled to be torn down, but one very persistent citizen guarded the monument every day. Initially, the citizens had no sympathy for the guerrilla soldier, but they didn't feel any antipathy either, so they joined forces and came up with a third solution: The statue stayed, and underneath it they hung the text, "Give me money." Life was ritually returned to the bronze Lenin, but as that of a beggar; he continued to fulfill the request of the community, as his bronze body was to be the downgraded symbol that would represent what he did to other bodies. Unlike him, the bronze body from the grave of Todor Zhivkov, who ruled Bulgaria for 35 years, was kidnapped from the central cemetery in Sofia in November 2007.[30]

The dead bodies of the communist leaders still incite "excitement" because, as Louise Burgoise says: "If the past is not destroyed, you are not living your life." The leader should die *for you* for you to continue living. In a certain sense, the dead Lenin from Volchov is indeed deadened where he was symbolically superior, in his social belief, which was the ideal that Lenin lived for. What is worse than a symbolic death with a begging sign? On the contrary, the kidnapped Zhivkov is alive, he is still a body that exercises effects, as people are not indifferent. There are Lenins making money abroad. In Dallas, Texas there stands a statue of Lenin in front of a McDonald's restaurant, on which it says "American Victory." This Lenin earning money in America is not here to commemorate the past. The children from Dallas probably know little or nothing about the communist leader, but employed as a doorman at McDonald's, Lenin still materializes affection. This Lenin is not begging, he is historicizing an instinct for food at a place where the communist and capitalist ideologies connect in the frightful question: "How to feed these people?" Only under threat, that's how. There are personal Lenins as well. A citizen from

Zimbabwe contacted the main sculptor of the Soviet era in Belarus, ordered a 1.2-meter-tall statue of Lenin from him, and installed it in his garden in Harare. This Lenin was never used to stand in squares, he only owns the sentiment that his owner had never even enjoyed–that is a sentiment of a past lost, not my own.

In May 2007, the tomb of the Hungarian leader János Kádár was vandalized and the bones and skull stolen from it, as well as the urn of his wife Maria Tamaska. In the Hungarian media, this was interpreted as "perverse fetishism," and "occult political economy."[31] At the crime scene, it read: "Killers and traitors don't belong in the Holy Land 1956-2006." And the message is this: It is still too early for him to be buried; communism might return, let's wait and see. There are also people statues. The largest bronze Stalin, standing 15.5 meters tall and 22 meters wide, stood in Prague from 1955 to 1962. The man who modeled for the sculptor never managed to get rid of the nickname "Stalin," and died three years after the statue was erected.[32] This is a case where the body becomes a statue, and for the people it created the effect of a living Stalin–the live mannequin becomes the dead Leader's hostage.

Naturally, there exists a converse scenario as well–when the leader was afraid of statues and therefore employed *live statues* during his/her lifetime. This was the case of Enver Hoxha in Albania who, although he enjoyed a powerful cult never allowed, as a paranoiac afraid of sabotage, statues in his image, nor did he allow his image to be put on banknotes. In order to prevent possible assassinations, Hoxha ordered a "sosi," a double to be hired. Peter Shapalo was a dentist from North Albania, whose resemblance to the leader was discovered by the Albanian secret services, Sigurimi. He was brought to Tirana, where he underwent several plastic surgery procedures, and was taught to walk and talk like Hoxha. In order to make the secret secure, the surgeons and trainers were killed in a bus heading for the Adriatic Sea, while his wife and two daughters were killed immediately after his arrival in Tirana. Hoxha's double often appeared in public, he opened halls, visited factories, held speeches and was recorded as the Great Leader. When he was not needed, he was kept in a villa in Tirana, without any clothes of his own nor any documents. He had to read everything that Hoxha read, and he developed a taste for French literature and Marxist dialectics. He was not allowed to watch television nor read newspapers, and he never actually saw the real Enver Hoxha. His food was weighed so he wouldn't weigh any more or less than Hoxha. When Enver Hoxha died, the Services apologized to him. He left Tirana, but wherever he went, people were scared to look at him, as he was marked as the wandering spirit of the dead Hoxha. When the communist regime collapsed alongside many others in 1991, he tried to get a visa for the West and climbed onto the wall of the Embassy of West Germany, but was attacked by others who were waiting. In a state of depression, he cut his face with a knife, took out one of his eyes and died shortly afterwards.[33] Josip Broz Tito had two doubles, who were mentioned for the first time in 1963 when the Marshal went to meet John Kennedy in America.[34] To date, there is no information on the first one, as all the data on him was kept as a war secret. The second was General Jovo Popović, a legend of the Yugoslav army and the police, and one of the people who introduced Arkan (one of the most notorious paramilitary leaders during the ex-Yugoslav war of the 1990s) to the secret services. He was educated at the NKVD "Felix Dzerzhinsky" academy in Moscow, and was a wealthy member of Tito's nomenclature, with a luxurious villa in Dedinje. Popović played Tito on several occasions, once during the demonstrations in Pristina of 1968 and once during Tito's official visit to New York in 1971.[35] While before the entrance of the Waldorf Astoria Hotel, where Ustashi and Chetniks were demonstrating, Popović would enter the hotel in his general's uniform and Tito would take the stairs to leave his suite.

"Of all the prostheses that mark the history of the body, the double is doubtless the oldest,"[36] says Baudrillard in his celebrated work, *Simulacra and Simulation*. Communism knew how to use this prosthesis because it guaranteed that death could be overcome and that the Leader would remain alive forever.

Josip Broz Tito's monuments endured very different fates throughout the time of the former Yugoslavia. Vojislav Šešelj[37] sold Tito's monuments at public auction; some Tito monuments still exist in the former Yugoslavia and some initiatives for fashioning new Tito monuments appear from time to time (in October 2006, such an initiative was given by the then President of the Republic of Macedonia, Branko Crvenkovski); some of Tito's bronze bodies ended up "used" in the "Simna" company (which trades in secondary raw materials, e.g. Tito's famous monument in Užice, the work of Fran Kršinić), while a part of Tito monuments experienced an "ideological encounter," when in 2004 Tito's monument at his birth place in Kumrovec was damaged in an explosion.[38] Tito's bronze body from the Museum of the First Proletarian Brigade in Rudo, the work of Antun Augustinović in 1994, was sold as scrap iron in the whirlwind of the Bosnian War when the employees of the Museum calculated that for the 400 kg Tito, they could get the equivalent of six-month's salary. This is how the sadistic ideological cycle ended, from Tito's cult on which the Yugoslav federation rested, to Tito's bronze body, which literally served to make weapons in the bloody disintegration of the federation. A decade later, in 2006 at a square in Mostar, one of the main sites of urban slaughter in Bosnia, a monument of Bruce Lee was erected with the explanation that he was "a good boy and a fighter for justice,"[39] the final ironic response to the dramatic disintegration of Yugoslavia and its bronze ideals.

And finally we have the destiny of the "bronze" Stalin from the city of Khashuri (Georgia). When he was removed from the main square, the local citizens did not destroy him, but instead buried him. In 2008, they dug him out and returned him to his original place, and several thousand people visited the ceremony for the rebirth of the dead Stalin.[40] In ideologies, the categories of alive and not alive are only *spatial determiners*, they indicate above–or under the ground. Ideology in itself is neither alive nor dead. It can resurrect. In February 2008 in Cyprus, a member state of the European Union, the hard real communism option won the elections, which only goes to show that communism is not just in the past, but that it can be renewed and resurrected as a potential future.

6

Why is it Good to be Good?

The Left, the Psychoanalysis and the Ultimate Good

What ethics never managed to avoid is the following, very concrete problem: When speaking of the good, the ethic immediately starts to convince us that the good and pleasure are identical, that it is good to be good because the good brings pleasure.

Psychoanalysis, however, convinces us of the opposite. Maybe it is good to be good, but that has nothing to do with pleasure. To the contrary, if you are good, it is always on account of your pleasure. The good and pleasure are two terms that contradict each other entirely, says Lacan in his seminar, *The Ethics of Psychoanalysis*.[1] What is good does not offer pleasure, and that which offers pleasure is not good. Sex without any restrictions is not good, eating fresh vegetables does not offer pleasure (except the enjoyment you derive surrendering to the vague commands of the Super Ego that you are doing "something good for yourself"). It is believed that psychoanalysis is involved with things of a lesser caliber (family, personality), while politics is involved with social communities. Quite the opposite, says Guatari in his lecture, *Everyone Wants to be a Fascist* (1973), things are quite the other way around: Everything that really exists is the *politics* of the individual desire, a desire that manifests itself on a large political scale; while desire is the object of psychoanalysis and can only be understood through it.[2] Those who believe that the political must be conducted according to political methods alone are mistaken. On the contrary, a discipline must go *out* of its restrictive field in order to provide results *within* the discipline itself, which is what Laclau says: Plato's philosophy comes from Greek math; Galileo's mathematization of nature is behind 17th century rationalism. Laclau says: "(W)e are still living in the century of Freud, and I would go as far as to say that most of what is fruitful and innovative in contemporary philosophy is, to a large extent, an attempt to come to terms with Freud's discovery of the unconscious."[3]

If politics amounts to the postulate–don't do evil, then the politics so understood is closely connected to ethics, and ethics, on the other hand, with the name of Immanuel Kant. Kant's most famous maxim was, "Don't do to others what you don't want others to do to you." This sentence, says Badiou in his book, *Metapolitics* (2005), underscores the difference between the principle according to which you operate and the principle according to which you judge.[4] Between the act and the judgment there is a certain irreconcilability of ethics and politics. Ethics has associations of some ideal substance, almost religious or metaphysical, and it never overlaps with the political. Politics is not only action, it is also thought. Who is political thought directed at, who is the recipient? The logical response is all of us, what we call the public, mass, people. "Politics is a public exercise of judgments," says Badiou.[5] "This is my opinion"–this is, in brief, politics, and in a democracy we think we find in that right something that is comprehensible, but it is a valuable right that took many centuries to gain, and is constitutionally guaranteed today. This means that our conversations in front of the local store and on the park bench, the comments we read in the newspapers, all of that is politics, says Badiou, and it is often *of the same quality*–good and bad, just like the debates in Parliament. Indeed, that valuable right does not mean a thing for the truth of things, even truth gets lost in the multitude of individual judgments (known as Ockham's razor),[6] which turns politics into commentary, says Badiou. And what is more, in parliamentary democracies, people go out to vote, but that has nothing to do with the truth. The one who votes does not perform an act of truth, even if he/she expresses *his/her* truth. If you allow people to vote, we would still vote that we live in a geocentric universe, says Badiou.[7] That means that politics is not a process of truth. Politics is a public judgment of things, a so-called doctrine of consensus, and truth has very little to do with it (as in the question: Didn't free elections bring Hitler to power?").

We are used to thinking that the capacity to think is connected to the ability to tell good and evil apart–that the critical mass of people is enough. That people are guided according to "common sense." That "common sense" naturally leans towards goodness. That people shall know to choose good. But (most) often this is not true, and the other way around as well. Several years ago, a friend claimed that too much "thinking" leads to Nazism. He took his examples from Serbia and Germany: The first, as the most progressive republic in Yugoslavia, ended up preparing the field for the genocide of another people; and the second, as the most advanced European civilization prior to the First World War, invented Nazism. Consequently, my friend believed that too much thinking is dangerous because it leads to the point where no distinction between good and evil is made. In any case, one thing is clear. People do not choose good *by default*. There is no instance *on that side* of our being that guarantees that we shall choose good. People can be inclined towards evil, and be easily seduced by it as well. That is why the concept radical evil" exists, it says that evil is more powerful than good.

Plato's question, "Why is it always better to be just than unjust?", has received various answers throughout history. Rorty classifies the answers into two large groups.[8] The first group is made up of those who support one in each of the following pairs: Good–Evil, Moral–Hedonism, Freedom–Slavery, primarily the first of each. The second group of thinkers says that these oppositions are not so simple and advocate a combination of the two. (There is a third Hegelian path, and according to Žižek it is not to support the Good, not to support a balanced synthesis of the Good and the Evil, but to support the Evil because at the moment one clearly chooses Evil, at the same moment, one rejects that option as impossible and other alternatives open up–the only way to come to the truth is to start with the "wrong choice."[9] Personally, this version seems like an extremely irresponsible meddling with the meaning of ethics.) If we ask people whether war is good, they shall all, in chorus, answer in the negative. However, politics remains closely related to wars. It seems as if there is a breach between the public judgment against war and the paradoxical quality with which it regularly turns into collective military behavior. This is similar to Kant's paradoxes–

your judgment about something is one thing, and your action is another. People say that *war is evil*, but on the other hand, people and the public are *constantly fighting in wars*. Where is the origin of the problem? What happens in that interim interval between the desire to be good and the manifestation of that goodness? Why isn't the desire to be good enough? What more is needed?

There is a strange scene, key to understanding the extreme conditions of goodness, in Cervantes's *Don Quixote* (1605). The Knight of Goodness meets a group of silk merchants and he stands before them in military fashion, requiring that they should admit that no girl is more beautiful than his Dulcinea; otherwise he will consider them to be the enemy and shall have to fight with them. The merchants stand completely stunned by this totally absurd request, and in the first moment rationally answer that they would, without reservation, admit to the superior beauty of the girl if Don Quixote offered them some proof, a portrait, or anything else for that matter. Don Quixote answers: "If I were to show her to you, what virtue would there be in confessing such a manifest truth? The important thing is for you to believe, confess, affirm, swear and defend without ever having seen her…"[10] In a nutshell, this controversial scene contains the most radical position that one should start from when pondering the good. At first glance, Don Quixote poses the unrefined question of trust, and trust is not received for obvious reasons–it is silly, even dangerous, to testify in regards to something of which you know nothing, and as such is commonly reflected in the legal world of today. But Don Quixote's experiment is more complex than the request for trust without grounds. Don Quixote *appears before* people with a grandiose project–to test the capacity of the world for ultimate goodness, whether the world carries goodness, and therefore, he basically experiments with a religious issue–I ask of you to believe me without seeing (just like the church asks of one to believe in God without even seeing him). The question is posed with childish naivety and childish cruelty, but notice that the concept of ultimate good is impossible without that combination of infantilism and cruelty, because from the philosophical aspect–a religious belief that God exists without offering any proof of his existence–is infantile. Don Quixote is like Prometheus, but unlike Prometheus he has very little or no political experience–that is why it is a paradigm closest to Jesus; another similar example in literature can be found in Dostoevsky in the shape of *The Idiot* (1869), Prince Myshkin. Dostoevsky, like the philosophers, says that the radical good can only be thought of in terms of idiotism. Does this mean that the concept of good can unconditionally be placed only in the realm of childish phantasms and idiotism?

The thinkers of the first group ("it is good to be good") are the ones who believe that the sky *is not closed*, either because they are religious or because they believe that there is life on other planets. In the first version, the sky has no limits because God exists; his heaven should be deserved. In the second version, there is life on other planets; instead of conflicts around the limited resources on our planet, let's strengthen humanity, let's turn people into an equal, global star force aiming to become an ethical formation that shall investigate space and humanize the cosmos. This is the scientific explanation of why it is good to be good. Closest to the second view is Lenin when he said to H.G. Wells: "If we manage to establish contact with other planets, all our philosophical, social and moral ideas shall have to be revised, our potentials shall become unlimited and violence shall not be the necessary means for progress."[11] This viewpoint implies that there is *one* time, but there are different *spaces*. Other variants of this argumentation are present in various New Age ideologies according to which there is *one* space (for example, this planet), but there are various time streams in it (parallel to this universe). In all cases, it seems as if the idea of good regularly includes belief in a *higher level* (God, another world, parallel time), and that higher level lends goodness to philosophical sense.

There is also another, more common "folk" approach to goodness. When people say that it is good to be good, they believe in altruism, in the inherence of goodness, although philosophically speaking rightfulness is "a transparent attempt to make altruism look more reasonable than it is,"[12] as Rorty says. People have always formed unfair communities, and when they try to create a good community they are led either by the need for *private* self-realization or *self-creation*, i.e. from irrationality or the need for aesthetics ("it is nice for the world to be good"). Finally, for the utilitarian, Good is defined as of or having *instrumental value*: To say that something is good means that it is useful, that it serves a purpose. It is good to be good because good is useful. Lastly, there is also trust that the good in a political sense is manifested through neutrality, but even neutrality is a defeatist choice. In "small dimensions," neutrality is the most common choice of citizens, and they think that things don't at any rate depend on them, therefore it is not up to them to react (see chapter on "Neutral Citizens"). Things seem worse on the larger political scene. When in January 2008, George Bush, while visiting the Israeli memorial center dedicated to the holocaust, asked Condoleezza Rice: "Why didn't we bombard this?" (referring to the railway tracks leading to Auschwitz where between 1.1 and 1.5 million Jews were killed), the question is not a naïve one at all. For years, experts on Jewish issues have used the problematic nature of political "neutrality" as a theme: If the US (that up until Pearl Harbor led a so-called Politics of Neutrality) had intervened (earlier), the entire holocaust could have been avoided, at least the proportions of it. Therefore, neutrality always means that you are actually choosing the convenient position, to silently be on "the side of the stronger," at least until you are not personally involved.

How to Recognize Evil?

When people believe that it is good to be good, they believe in the inherence of goodness, in some implanted chip of goodness, in the Freudian "ocean feeling" that all share; if that chip is missing in some people, then it is considered a deviation, and we believe that that missing chip is easy to recognize. A simple insight into what ultimate evil looks like is given in the dark film, *8 mm* (1999), in which the character played by Nicholas Cage finds the brutal murderer and sadist John Higgins and takes his mask off. Behind the mask he suddenly sees an everyday, normal, neighborly face. The sadist, with the nickname Machine, tells him: "What did you expect, a monster?" And he adds something along these lines: "I had a normal childhood, I was not abused by mummy and daddy; you have to accept that I am what I am." And this is true in the spirit of Hanna Arendt's work, evil is banal, evil does not come in the shape of the elegant Mephistoteles from Goethe's *Faust* (1805).

We witnessed a similar case when Radovan Karađić first appeared in The Hague in July 2008. Was this nice looking old man really capable of genocide? Evil is not dramatic, it is banal. Another version of these themes are the films of Lars von Trier's, *Dogville* (2003) and *Manderlay* (2005), in which although people initially start off with relatively good intentions, things somehow get twisted in the very beginning, and our regular, everyday people from the neighborhood turn out to be made of the most brutal essence, which they pursue with sadistic dedication. So, how do we recognize evil? In her book, *The Shortest Shadow* (2003), Alenka Zupančič analyzes the genius black comedy, *To Be or Not to Be* (1942), by Ernst Lubich. At the beginning of the film, there is a scene in which a group of actors are rehearsing a play about Hitler, and the director is criticizing the lead actor because he simply fails to resemble Hitler. He comments on his make-up, on his appearance and the general complaint that what he sees before him is just an ordinary man. One of the actors didactically reminds the director that Hitler is an ordinary man, after which the director suddenly sees a photo with Hitler and triumphantly declares: "This is it! This is what Hitler looks like," and the actor playing Hitler, answers: "But sir, that is a picture of *me*!" Zupančič analyzes this scene in relation to the Deleuzean concept of "minimal difference,"[13] the difference with which I think I can *tell* the villain *apart* from the non-villain, good from evil–but that difference is just an illusion. Stripped of the mystique that is around us, Evil paradoxically appears on the face of each one of us. The director is trying to represent Evil, but as in *8 mm*, all he manages to show is the banal, even ridiculous, object. When I want to catch Evil and seize its meaning, I see the face of the ordinary person appear before me and it obscures my apprehension of the great Evil. Even Deleuze lacks the capacity to bring us to the source of evil; on the contrary, evil itself appears as essentially unrepresentable, you can't separate it and point a finger at it and exclaim–There, that's it, that's evil! A similar "minimal difference" is noted in one of the myths about the KGB–that they built exact replicas of the typical American suburbs somewhere on the Ukrainian plains so that the agents could "train" for everyday American life.[14] This was a communist attempt to apprehend a representation of evil–rotten American capitalism, evil personified, that which cannot be apprehended, that dark villainous "moment." The KGB village, even if an ideal replica of the American suburb, remains a mere attempt, similar to Lubich's notion of the enemy as always a notion of ordinariness.

This only serves to show that the concepts of Good and Evil are actually totally void of any attributes whatsoever. Jeremy Bentham had a theory that paved the way for Kant's "transcendental idea." Bentham says that Good and Evil are *immaterial*, that they have no substance; in other words, the root of ethics it not in materiality. Bentham also comes to the idea that ethics is a form, an empty bureaucratic machinery, like the empty Stazi offices (see chapter entitled "Communist Crimes and Political Anesthesia"), and since it is a form, it is also *fiction*. Bentham continues the idea of Thomas Hobbes's social contract and says that all social contracts among people function on the principle of fiction. Not only did the sovereign not sign a social contract (Hobbes's premise), but neither did the citizens sign such a contract (Bentham's addition). The Law treats us as if we have all signed a social contract, while in reality no one of us has made such a contact[15]–yet the valid legal premise insists that "ignorance is not an excuse." Paradoxically, the most dramatic describer of the world with a closed sky is at the same time one of the most important political theorists. Thomas Hobbes, the author of the idea of social contract, gave a grim vision of the world in the so-called "natural state," for a world without a state and authority. If there is no authority, there are also no limitations to tame the human sadistic urges. Unlike the peaceful image of ourselves that we nurture of our transparent I, of the cogito–the truth is usually the opposite, that the cogito is a pure kernel, a core of sadism, excessiveness, immoderation, as well as a sadistic joy from enjoying without restrictions. In a world without a state and authority, there is no good and no evil in the classical ethical sense; the natural man is guided by natural urges: the fear of death, the need for security and the desire for authority; it was Hobbes who first clearly said that the natural state is not paradise; to the contrary, it is a war of every man against every man;[16] life in its natural state is "solitary, poor, nasty, brutish and short."[17] For Hobbes, there is only one will, to survive, and that will is in regular conflict with the will of others who also want to survive. Therefore, the creation of some contract that shall put an end to the natural state and shall mean safety for the population is unavoidable. With that contract, the people give up a significant part of their rights and surrender them into the hands of the ruling sovereign, whereas on the other hand, he does not sign any contract, he rules only based on the power of attorney that is given to him.

In an episode of *Star Trek*, the student, Wesley Crusher, asks the first officer, William Riker, how to make an important decision because he is afraid that the decision he makes might be the wrong one: "And what if someone dies because of my decision?" William answers: "If you are not sure, think of what Pickard would do if he was in your place." "But Pickard is the captain," answers Wesley, "I never question his decisions." To that William responds: "Ask yourself this question: Why do you never question his decisions, and you will be able to make a decision." This is an excellent dialogue on the technology of authority. The position of the commander is in a way in a position in which trust must be invested for the "contract" to have meaning. For the sovereign to be able to ensure security and peace, his authority must be absolute, and no one should restrict it, and that makes him a dictator. Only under the rule of the dictator, the idea of righteousness emerges (righteous is what the ruler decides it to be), and only under his authority it is possible for people to start with a network of subcontracts, with which they shall improvingly regulate the relationships between them. An important issue comes up, one that Kołakowski formulates in this manner: Anarchists and Marxists thought that if the state was abolished, people would live in peace and solidarity. In contrast, Hobbes considers that that shall mean a war of all against all. Who is closer to the truth?[18] Who guarantees more freedom–the Marxists (and anarchists) or Hobbes?

Marxists believed that if the classic role of the director was abandoned, the world would be a better place. The practical expression of this in communism was the so-called worker's self-management, whose Yugoslav author was the Slovenian teacher Edvard Kardelj. Worker's self-management meant that instead of a traditional director who tells everyone what to do, the employees themselves make decisions how and where work will be done, how the work is going to be distributed and how much is going to be produced (in accordance with the general five-year plans). The idea of worker management is present in all utopian texts as early as from ancient times, but as an economic movement, it finds its defined form in the 19th century. Anarchists supported self-management, although self-management only survived in practice for a short period (in the Paris commune, in the Spanish civil war, in the well-covered "layoffs" over a period of several months (and then re-employment) of the managers of the LIP watch factory in France in 1973 and in the "recovered factories" movement in Argentina). And of course in Tito's Yugoslavia, where worker's self-management lasted for several decades and as such, directly influenced the intimate coordinates of the people, discovering not only human nature, but also the madness of surviving in an "experimental" life without hierarchy. In the film, *Red Room* (1999), by Yamanouchi, a philosophical light is shed on the problem of an absent hierarchy. When interpreted, not having a strict hierarchy means that hierarchy belongs to the one who first manages to grab it. The ultimate permission that is hidden in the self-governance law is the allowance of a general war, of all against all, just as in Hobbes' "natural state." In Yamanouchi's film, four players are faced with an extreme game–they are closed in a small, red room with cards, and the one who draws the King shall have the opportunity to tell the other two players what to do. If they don't execute the order appropriately, they are disqualified, while the one who remains in the game after all the impossible sadist games goes home with a 10 million yen award. The simple game opens up an opportunity for millions of perversions and torture. At the beginning, the players use psychological tactics, but as the game becomes more desperate, they become more and more evil, and show that there is no depth to which human evil cannot sink.

In the strictly legal sense of the word, self-management contracts meant a form of suspended laws, as they committed no one to anything,[19] which is why ultimate self-management was perceived as a mafia transaction; the best realization of self-management in our region was the corruption scandal of "Agrokomerc." Using the established self-management practice of financial deals without security, this food giant from Bosnia and Herzegovina from the late 1980s "produced," through director Fikret Abdić, millions of dollars according to the currency exchange rates of the day.[20] The "Agrokomerc" case is interesting in its revealing of the powerful side of self-management. As is well known, in the military break-up of Yugoslavia Fikret Abdić was the first to extract the mini-state of the Republic of Western Bosnia–the question being: What mechanism was behind Abdić's power? As something more than just simple mafia dealings, worker's self-management opens an *auto-referential shaft*. The people's people, although generally left to their own devices in the process of making decisions related to their work, do not even for a moment forget that the abstract dictate "all belongs to all" was masterminded by "someone from the top," from the nomenclature.

Does that mean that people shall "liberate" the inner freedom that is guaranteed to them under the self-management law, and submitting to it, they shall be free on dictate, or shall they constantly be aware that there is an abstract hierarchical point "from above" that allowed this? If the Super-Ego instance liberates people from external coercion, do they obey the order to be free or instead choose to subvert the order for freedom to, through that act, *regain precisely the freedom that was ordered of them*? An example of this is the legendary scene from, *The Life of Brian* (1979), by Monty Python, in which Brian tells the masses, "You are individuals!", to which the masses reply in chorus, "We are all individuals," while only a single voice from the masses replies, "I am not." In other words, isn't the dictate, "No one has the right to impose on you how you will organize yourselves!" an *even more perverse dictate* than the order for non-freedom? Is perhaps the abstract order, "there is no boss," "you are free," the new point of non-freedom? Now I have no other boss, except for the boss who told me that I don't have a boss! Through a twisted message the film, *House of Nine* (2005), by Steven Monroe, speaks of the solution that can potentially become the only possible solution for a world of absent hierarchy. The nine "candidates" are kidnapped from the street and dragged into a closed house from which there is no escape. Only one of them is allowed to leave the house with a $5,000,000 reward, but *only* if he/she is the only survivor, which means that he/she must kill the others. The game has been created by "someone from above" who never even appears in the movie. This movie stands out from the many others with similar themes (*Cube, Battle Royale, Saw, House on Haunted Hill*), even from the *Red Room*, owing to the final minutes of the film, in which instead of the expected catharsis comes a final message related to life in Hobbes' "natural state." The final minutes show us the last survivor leaving the house though a door that is, at the same time, also the entrance into another house in which there are 20 other people, each holding $5,000,000. This film shows that the ultimate solution behind the "permission for freedom" is the fight of all against all, in which each exit door is an entrance door to another bloody cycle more monstrous and more sadistic than the previous, something similar to the "natural state" Hobbes writes about. In an interview, Žižek says that, "Worker's self-management socialism created the conditions for war in Yugoslavia."[21] This is true in the sense in which Fikret Abdić, the last (best) surviving protagonist in the House of Yugoslav self-management from the "Agrokomerc" food factory, entered into the "Bosnia of the 1990s," the best mastermind of Kardeljian self-management, which resulted in a game with even more "permissions for freedom" with an even greater stake; this time it was the "permission" to draw up *"territorial" self-management*, with the break-up of Yugoslavia and the war in Bosnia.

In Death

If the sky is closed, then the people, in the most elementary sense, can be treated as prisoners of the earth. If there is no greater "life meaning" than just surviving in the prison called Earth, then that means that people are sentenced to cooperate. What type of cooperation is the best, and at the same time the only possible one, for life in prison to be more tolerable for all? In the theory of games, there is a problem called the "prisoner's dilemma." The classical form in which the "prisoner's dilemma" is presented in the theory of games is the following. Two suspects are arrested by the police, though the police do not have enough evidence to convict the prisoners, and they then separate the prisoners. Each one of the two prisoners is offered a deal. If one of them testifies against the other and the other is quiet, the first one will get out of prison free, and the other one will get a 10-year prison sentence. If the two are quiet, they shall each get six months in prison. If they both testify against each other, they each get a five-year prison sentence. Each one of the prisoners must decide for himself whether he/she will testify against the other or remain silent. Each of them is sure that the other one won't know if he/she has been betrayed until the end of the investigation.[22] How should both prisoners react? They have the choice of either cooperating with each other or surrendering the other. Paradoxically, the only rational decision in which there is fair play is for the two players to *play on betrayal,* although if they cooperate they will receive the greatest award, but that would also mean that they would have to unconditionally trust that other one will also play fair; they will have to trust the principle based on which Don Quixote required the trust of the silk merchants. However, I am mentioning this theory for a completely different reason. The analysis of the "prisoner's dilemma" shows that if the game is repeated indefinitely, then *cooperation* can be expected, although the threat of betrayal from the other will always linger.

In the film, *A Beautiful Mind* (2001), by Ron Howard, there is a scene in which the mathematician John Nash discovers the "Nash equilibrium"–he enters a café with three friends, and there are five girls there; he connects the "actors in the game" and realizes that the ideal equilibrium will be achieved when each of the four friends tries to *most selfishly* realize his own interests; those interests will constantly be in conflict with the selfish interests of the other members of the group, meaning that each of them will "profit" best if they don't court the most beautiful girl. In popular interpretation, this means that the cooperation between people is best, not when people try to be altruistic towards the others, but when they most selfishly try to realize their own interests; those interests will regularly be obstructed by the selfish interests of the others and in that interaction, with equilibrium, people learn what type of cooperation is the only possible one for all. That means that the best cooperation is achieved not when there is no "social contract" (because anarchy is an open permission, i.e. the one who will be the first to use force to come to the "desired good"), but when the contract implies the optimal cooperation of all personal interests with all other personal interests. The theory of the "prisoner's dilemma" showed that following the numerous trials and errors on the Gaussian Curve, the most cooperations will take place at the beginning and at the end of the game. That means that "self-government" will be most successful with the setting up of the project and its eventual closure, which in a social sense cannot occur because, unlike the "prisoner's dilemma," which is a mathematical strategy, an abstract situation, life doesn't have such an abstract ending and instead is an endless interaction of a multitude of social factors. This theory provides an unclear awareness that the long enough attempts at human cooperation can only improve. People somehow *teach themselves* that it pays to be good, to cooperate. Although it is believed that the conduct of people is irrational, states, however, do have very loyal and good people; people are also mainly aware that they play some game of smaller and greater gains and losses with the world, which means that when they play, although people are led by selfish interests, those interests are regularly corrected by the selfish interests of the others and the ultimate result is that people *indeed do* play *rationally*, while only the results of their actions are irrational.

In a different way, the same result was reached by Hegel, whose most famous dictum was: "What is rational is real, and what is real is rational."[23] Hegel was incorrectly interpreted in the 20th century, as his theory was not a miserable recommendation that current state regimes should be accepted as reasonable (it is real, therefore it is wise). On the contrary, he recommended the questioning of the realistic nature of the state regime (to see whether that regime is maybe only "mimicking" reality, while leading humanity to the verge of destruction), but how can we know what the case is with every state regime? For Hegel, that is evidently based on the principle of known negations. Each phase in the development of history is here in order to be annulled. From Hegel, we don't profit much from referring to the universal moral good; we don't have a clear picture of what the ideal world should look like. Every reference to the moral is a battle already lost, as the moral cannot do anything before the progress of history. But, if the real is intelligent, "It would be a pitiful result when it would be the last word of Hegel's philosophy," says Kołakowski.[24] In any case, there is a certain totalitarian trap that lies in Hegel's theses, and he was rightfully convicted for philosophical hallucination; his influence was demonstrated in the terrible consequences to the political world of the 20th century. Hegel cannot help us explain why on a large historical scene, both Nazism and communism are good. One thing is clear, the issue of goodness, presented as a political issue, is generally the most difficult philosophical issue ever. There are disciplines outside philosophy, and related to religion, that solve these issues with unusual lightness. But for the cynics, they are just not enough. Naturally, to this sequence, from Hobbes to Hegel, 10 more philosophers can be added before, between and after them. With greater or less subtleties, they shall say the same–that it is not easy to answer the question: Why is it good to be good?

When it comes to myself, I admit that I feel somewhat "barbaric" when it comes to ethics. I don't see any sufficiently "natural" reason to be good–aesthetics, self-realization, altruism, empathy, even usefulness or utility–all responses amount, in the end to these things, and just like emotions and to a degree, actions, these explanations are close to philosophical kitsch. Philosophy simply cannot provide a (satisfactory) response to the question–Why is it good to be good?–except with heavy mental loopings, meaning that good does not come to it naturally. To claim that good is reachable by conspiring radical evil is also meaningless. In that way, it turns out that the only thing one can know, without moralizing, is why it is not good to be good. One step astray from this safe, cynical field and everything already amounts to boring moralization or to consoling religion. If the root of evil is of a biological nature and no social change can overcome it, what follows is that the question "Why is it good to be good?" is neither proper, nor improper and the solution for it, the disappearance of social living, would mean a lack of any physical contact between people, a kind of asceticism, which is actually known in all intermediary forms of religion, as well as sci-fi visions. Neither variant was familiar to me.

After several years of struggling with this dilemma, I finally decided to give up the entire thing. I don't know why it is good to be good (philosophically), and I know less in terms of how that is organized (politically).

Concerning this story, at least it had some formal "closure." It was July 2008 when the Macedonian poet Risto Lazarov called me. He had written pamphlets against my father in 1985 while my father was in prison and now, 23 years later, he had just received the Macedonian poetry award. "A newspaper called me to give a statement. The statement is not that important, I wanted to meet you, to tell you I am sorry," he said. When I closed the telephone, I thought–injustice is public, the rage around them is loud, but just like sorrow, reconciliations are quiet and away from the eyes of the world. The same thought came to me even before I started this on this entire endeavor–that it makes sense to settle things with systems, but that it is always morally difficult, although historically necessary, to assess the individual stakes in that past. However, I thought the same as at the beginning of this book: That there are acts of humiliation and acts of crime, but that there are also acts of reconciliation. Where does *I'm sorry* fail to be enough? I don't know. All stories are personal. Nonetheless, "sorry" is what is needed on the large historical scene.[25] Lazarov's role in my father's case was certainly irrelevant, it can even be said that aside for his petty editor's comments, his role was insignificant. As such, it was neither a reason, nor could it be a consequence of this theme. But then, it was not only he that called; it was also that he called after the Macedonian journal "Fokus" had called him to ask for his statement; they had found Lazarov's texts on the Internet where I put them after I found them in June 2008 in my father's personal archives. So, virtually an entire circle was closed, although not a very important one. On a human level, however, I was pleased. It even happened that some idea of justice stayed with me for several days.

But for all that time something else was also clear to me. As my Macedonian publisher Kolja put it when he saw the manuscript: "You whine too much. Many people in this country feel that injustice has been done to them with regard to many things; if you want yours to melt into that Macedonian mentality of shedding crocodile tears over graves, let it be so." At the same time, he also wrote: "But in a country in which history lasts between two white and black bumblebees,[26] or tops 0-21 years, your work is important." And it remained at that. I remembered Erofeyev: "The love of fathers and children has no common denominator of thankfulness, but is rather full of endless offenses and misunderstandings which bring about the bitterness of belated compassion… The parents are the shield between us and death. As great artists, they don't have a right to age; our unavoidable rebellion against them is biologically appropriate and equally morally revolting. Parents are our most intimate possession. But when family intimacy grows to the scale of an international scandal, as it happened to us, even unwillingly, thoughts, memories and analyses come up."[27]

The victim philosophy popular at the end of the 20th century was not unknown to me. Had I nestled myself into this family story in that long line? Couldn't I have been brave and said that bygones are bygones, and simply go on? Was I living with the trauma because the trauma became such a great part of me, or is it precisely the opposite, because it never managed to really nestle in me, because it remained a "distant" theme; while others were rotting in prisons, I was the child with the good grades, "the normal one;" is this book not the same?

Lastly, where was my generation standing? What happened to my *intergeneration*, with us who were the children of that system and the parents from this? What was the graveness of our doings–in which the requirement for confronting the past was systematically necessary, proper in the sense of civilization and historically important–and where did we pass the limit of not afflicting pain? My brother went into the army two days before they arrested my father; the same morning when my father went to prison, I started in high school. In a few days, we were allocated to three different institutions, which were actually quite similar. When he completed his army service, my brother chose a life turned towards the future. A psychologist who I spoke with several years later at one of the sittings confronted me with my first, private "prison dilemma" when he asked me: "Your father got out of prison in 1987, your brother in 1986, when did you get out?" They are so funny I thought to myself, I will get out when everybody else does–in death. I don't know whether the years that followed brought me more wisdom than this childish instant nihilism. If nothing else, at least this response in a way answered the ethical issues, least of all in the sense that all are *good enough* in death, right?

Skopje, Budapest, Berlin, Kiev, Rawa,
2006–2008

Children to Compare

It was a Saturday when I decided to write this book, and eight years have passed since then. I arrived at my mother's with my (newborn) son, and my mother was sad. "They are talking about the Struga Poetry Evenings, your father is not mentioned anywhere." I probably got cross with her and fell asleep with worry. The district of my childhood remained mournful, that never changed. I was sitting all worked up, as if everything depended on me, as I knew what my mom was talking about. All had some kind of life in the world with themselves, some past to happily look back to. Only at my mother's front door did the past and the world not ring the doorbell, not even we, ourselves, we rang it as if *extradited* from this world.

My brother has a letter which I donated to the State Archive. He wrote it when he served in the Yugoslav People's Army in Mostar, Bosnia for my father, who was serving his prison term in Skopje, Macedonia. In it, our childhood is explained with one sentence, all that my brother didn't like and despised in my father, in addition to everything he realized when my father went to prison.

Today, my brother studies atoms, he became an atomic physicist and does not live in Macedonia. One morning (he had come on leave, he was 18, I was 14) while my father was in prison, my brother said that the time had come for us to part, and that he would no longer recommend books for me to read or movies to watch. He said that he was starting on his path and that I would have to choose my own. I agreed, though I had no choice. Today, my brother is researching atoms at the institute in Berlin and in Belgrade. Physics and metaphysics for him are something that is closely related, as he is interested in the future, and not in the past. I somehow stayed with the family issues. The prison catapulted us into two different directions; we each unconsciously chose to continue one of the two themes of my father.

In a letter to my father, my brother explained everything that I never managed to, although I intensively lived with it all. If my father hadn't gone to prison, I would have probably dedicated my life to something else. I couldn't even write a proper letter to my father in prison at that time. I wrote how many good marks I had, how much I missed him and how we spent the New Year holiday. That is what my letters were like. Later, I remembered Freud: "What we cannot reach flying, we must reach limping." And that is how this book came about.

And this is my brother's letter. All that I always wanted but never managed to tell my father were in these several lines:

Dear Dad,

Quite some time has passed since we last saw each other, so I decided to write this letter. I would have done it earlier, but I waited for my leave, to try to find you and to talk about this whole situation. Indeed, I came to Skopje (in the period from March 21-March 25), but my attempt to get in touch with you failed. However, nothing else remains, but to try to explain with words what my opinion is of this entire newly occurred situation.

Five-six months ago when I first found out, I was perfectly convinced of your innocence. Very well aware of your ideas and views (that I largely accepted), I knew that all you had done was done with a deep panhuman and humane intent. I was sure that you were not involved in any terrorist actions because I knew that you never approved of terrorism, neither as a means or a goal. Every human being that knows you at least a little bit will confirm that in life you have been led by one sole purpose—to help others, to give even your last piece of bread if needed. Everyone who has ever been near you must admit that your endless fight against injustice not only does not put you in prison, but places you higher than all thrones. I don't know. Maybe someone thinks differently, but I know that everyone who thinks this way can only envy you. Many people, great by spirit and by deed, have been to prison. Prove to all sycophants, mediocrities and evil tongues that you can be great even there. Here is a chance to confirm who were and who still are your true friends.

Coming to Skopje, not only was I not scared, but on the contrary, I was proud to be your son. I was not the least bit concerned about people's opinions, but I soon discovered that many of them gave me complete support and that they were convinced that your views were correct. If there was among them a pitiful or malicious look, from them I only receive more strength and stamina.

Now, I must confess that maybe you and I have had our moments in the past when we have not agreed on various things. But that was only so because I was not capable of understanding that a father does not always have to be interested in driving cars, buying furniture for the home, or, not to have to mention all, any other thing that average dads do. Only now do I understand that it is not most important who earns how much or whether someone has missed a film or a game on TV. A thousand times more important is the spiritual development of the human that you nurture and thousands of others abuse. Only now do I see that you are not a below average–but rather an above average father.

What more can I say? You and I are now in the same position. I know how you feel, but I believe that you will endure. I am deeply convinced that people will realize the mistake and that, soon, surely much sooner than you expect, everything will pass. I understand your being there not as a punishment, but as a test that life puts before a person. Endure because not everyone gets an opportunity like that. Many live their life in a hermetical, semi-transparent atmosphere of their home that does not allow them to see further than their nose. They will never find their true purpose or the meaning of life. Only people like you have a true purpose; creators and ideologists, those who strive towards the universal, neglecting their own interests. These careerists, these feeders of their own ego are not worthy even of contempt. Maybe one day they too will realize that humanity has had enough separation and division, both physically and spiritually. Maybe they will understand that by raising themselves, they will contribute to the panhuman good. Some are already aware of that. Some already feel that they are represented by something that is above them, as Tagore said.

I know that you are like that and that I share your ideas. If one is put in prison for those ideas, then my place is there too. Finally, the whole of life is just a game, an illusion and nothingness compared to the eternity that awaits!
Love, Vasil

Bibliography

Adler, Nanci. *The Gulag Survivor, Beyond the Soviet System*. New Brunswick, New Jersey: Transaction Publisher, 2004.
Althusser, Louis. *Filozofija in spontana filozofija znanstvenikov*. Ljubljana: ŠKUC/Filozofska fakulteta (zbirka Studia humanitatis), 1985.
Althusser, Louis. *Lenin and Philosophy and Other Essays*. New York: Monthly Review Press, 2001.
Andrejević, Mark. *I-Spy, The Limits of Interactivity*. Lawrence: The University Press of Kansas, 2007.
Andrew, Christopher and Mitrokhin, Vasili. *The Sword and the Shield, The Mitrokhin Archive and the Secret History of the KGB*. New York: Basic Books, 1999.
Arendt, Hanna. *Eichmann in Jerusalem. A Report on the Banality of Evil*, New York: Penguin Books Ltd., 1992.
Arsić, Branka/ Bajić, Srđan. *Rečnik/Dictionary*. Beograd: Dental, 1995.
Eš, Timoti Garton. *Istorija sadašnjice*, (English translation: Ash, Timothy Garton. *History of the Present*), Beograd: Samizdat, 2002.
Ачкоска, Виолета. *Задолжителниот откуп во Македонија 1945-1953*. (English translation: Ačkoska, Violeta. *The Obligatory Purchase in Macedonia 1945-1948*) Скопје: ИНИ, 1995.
Ачкоска, Виолета. *Македонија во југословенската федерација 29.11.1943-8.9.1991*. (English translation: Ačkoska, Violeta. *Macedonia in the Yugoslav Federation 11.29.1943-09.08.1991*) Скопје: ИНИ, 2001.
Ачкоска, Виолета. *Братството и единството 1944-1974 помеѓу хармонија и дисхармонија*. (English translation: Ačkoska, Violeta. *Brotherhood and Unity 1944-1974. Between Harmony and Disharmony*) Скопје: ИНИ, 2003.
Badiou, Alain. *Manifesto for Philosophy*. Translated, edited and with an introduction by Norman Madarasz. Albany: SUNY Press, 1999.

Badiou, Alain. *Metapolitics*, London and New York: Verso, 2005.
Banac, Ivo. *Sa Staljinom protiv Tita*. (English translation: Banac, Ivo. *With Stalin Against Tito*). Zagreb: Globus, 1990.
Baudrillard, Jean. *Simulacra and Simulation,* Michigan: The University of Michigan Press, 1994.
Buck-Morss, Susan. *Dreamworld and Catastrophe. The Passing of Mass Utopia in East and West,* Massachusetts: The MIT Press, 2002.
Butler, Judith. *The Psychic Life of Power. Theories in Subjection.* Stanford: Stanford University Press, 1997.
Butler, Judith. *Antigone's Claim. Kinship Between Life and Death.* New York, Chichester, West Sussex: Columbia University Press, 2000.
Borhes, H.L. *Usmeni Borhes*. (English translation: Borges, Jorge, Luis. *Borges's Lectures*), Beograd: Reč i misao, 1990.
Boškovič, Dragan. *Islednik, svedok, priča,* (English translation: Boškovič, Dragan. *Prosecutor, Witness, Narration*), Beograd: Plato, 2004.
Boym, Svetlana. *The Future of Nostalgia.* New York: The Basic Books, 2001.
Carver, Robert. *The Accursed Mountains*. London: Flamingo, 1999.
Cervantes Saavedra, Miguel de. *Don Quixote*. Translated, with Notes by James H. Montgomery. Introduced by David Quint, Indianapolis: Hackett Publishing Company Inc., 2009.
Châtelet, François, Duhamel, Olivier et Pisier, Evelyne. *Dictionnaire des œuvres politiques*, Paris: Presses Universitaires de France, 1989.
Churchill, Winston S. *The Second World War. Triumph and Tragedy*, New York: Houghton Mifflin Company, 1995.
Courtois, Stephane, Werth Nicolas, Panné Jean-Louis, Paczkowski, Bartošek Karel, Margolin Jean-Louis. *The Black Book of Communism. Crimes, Terror, Repression.* Massachusetts: Harvard University Press, 1999.
Даниловић, Рајко. *Употреба непријатеља. Политичка суђења 1945-1991 у Југославији,* (English translation: Danilović, Rajko. *The Use of an Enemy. The Political Trials in Yugoslavia 1945-1991*), Ваљево: Ваљевац, 1993.
Dedijer, Vladimir. *Tito Speaks. His Self Portrait and Struggle with Stalin.* London: Weidenfeld and Nicolson, 1953.
Deleuze, Gilles. *Proust and Signs*. London: The Athlone Press, 2000.
Deleuze, Gilles. Guattari, Fèlix *Kafka: Toward a Theory of Minor Literature.* Minnesota: The University of Minnesota Press, 2003.
D'Encausse, Hélène Carrère. *Le Malheur Russe. Essai sir meurtre politique,* Paris: Librairie Arthème Fayard, 1988.
Derrida, Jacques. *The Politics of Friendship*. New York, London: Verso, 2005.
Драгутиновић, Војислав. *"Странпутице у развоју једне литературе",* The *Nepoznati Krležijanci ili Prilozi raspravama o sukobu na književnoj*

levici, (English translation: Dragutinovich, Vojislav. *The Astrays in the Development of a National Literature. The Unknown Krlezhians or the Additional Debates in the Conflict on the Literary Left*.) (Београд, 1938), 1986.
Dubil, Helmut. *Niko nije oslobođen istorije*, (English translation: Dubil, Helmut. *Nobody is History-Free*), Beograd: Samizdat B92, 2002.
Eley, Geoff. *Forging Democracy. The History of the Left in Europe1850-2000*, Oxford, New York: The Oxford University Press, 2002.
Engels, Fridrih. *Uloga sile u istoriji*. (English translation: Engels, Friedrich. *The Role of Force in History*), Beograd: Kultura, 1961.
Engels, Fridrih. *Konspekt "Kapitala"*. (English translation: Engels, Friedrich. *A Synopsys of Capital*), Beograd: Kultura, 1961.
Engels, Fridrih. *Za radničku partiju*, (English translation: Engels, Friedrich. *For the Working Class*), Beograd: Kultura, 1962.
Engels, Friedrich. "Karl Marx's Funeral," in: *Marx Engels Archive. Der Sozialdemokrat*, March 22, 1883 See: http://marxists.anu.edu.au/archive/marx/works/1883/death/dersoz1.htm (accessed November 5, 2006).
Evropski diskurs rata (zbornik) (English translation: *The European Discourse of War*, collection), Beograd: Beogradski krug, 1995.
Ford, Henry. *My Life and Work*. Charleston: BiblioBazaar, LLC, 2008.
Foucault, Michael. *Discipline and Punish: The Birth of the Prison*. New York: Random House, 1975.
Foucault, Michael. *Abnormal: Lectures at the College de France, 1974-1975*. New York: Picador, 2004.
Fowkes, Ben. *The Rise and Fall of Communism in Eastern Europe*. London: MacMillan Press LTD., 1995.
Friedman, Tomas L. *The World is Flat*. London, New York: Penguin Books, 2006.
Freud, Sigmund. *Beyond the Pleasure Principle*. Translated and edited by James Strachey. Introduction and notes by Gregory Zilboorg. New York: W.W. Norton & Company, 1961.
Freud, Sigmund. *Civilization and its Discontents*. Newly translated from the German and edited by James Strachey. New York: W.W. Norton & Company, 1962.
Guatari, Felix: "Everybody Wants to be a Fascist", lecture delivered in Milan for Colloquium "Psychoanalysis and Politics," December 1973, in: *Chaosophy*, Semiotext(e), 1995, 227.
Goldman, Lisjen. *Marksizam i humanističke nauke*. (English translation: Goldmann, Lucien. *Marxism and Humanistic Disciplines*), Beograd: Nolit, 1986.
Gorbachev, Mikhail. *Perestroika*. London: Collins, 1987.

Gourgouris, Stathis. *Dream Nation, Enlightenment, Colonization, and the Institution of Modern Greece*, Stanford: The Stanford University Press, 1996.

Грамши, Антонио. *Одбрани текстови*, (English translation: Gramsci, Antonio. *Selected Works*.) Скопје: Македонска книга, Култура, Наша книга, Комунист, Мисла, 1978.

Harald, Hauswald/Lutz, Rathenow. *Ost-Berlin Life Before the Wall Fell*. Berlin: LVD, GmbH, 2005.

Hegel, Georg Vilhelm Fridrih. *Istorija filozofije II*. (English translation: Hegel, Georg Wilhelm Friedrich. *History of Philosophy II*), Beograd: Kultura, 1964.

Hegel, George H.W. *Philosophy of Right*, S W. Dyde, translator, New York: Cosimo, Inc., 2008.

Herzfeld, Michael. *Cultural Intimacy*. New York and London: Routledge, 2005.

Hobbes, Thomas. *Leviathan*, with an introduction by Jennifer J. Popiel, New York: Barnes and Noble Publishing, Inc., 2004.

Džejmson, Frederik. *Marksizam i forma*. (English translation: Jameson, Frederic, *Marxism and Form*), Beograd: Nolit, 1974.

Jerofejev, Viktor. *Muškarci*. (English translation: Erofeyev, Viktor. *Men*), Beograd: Plato, 2002.

Jerofejev, Viktor. *Dobar Staljin*. (English translation: Erofeyev, Viktor. *The Good Stalin*) Beograd: Geopoetika, 2005.

Jones, Dafydd. *Dada Culture. Critical Texts on the Avant-Garde*, New York: Editions Rodopi B.V. Amsterdam, 2006.

Kadare, Ismail. *The Successor*. Edinburgh, New York: Canongate, 2006.

Kafka, Franz, *The Trial*. A new translation by Mike Mitchell, Oxford: Oxford University Press, 2009.

Карајанов, Петар. *Тито за Македонија, Македонија за Тито*, (English translation: Karajanov, Petar. *Tito for Macedonia, Macedonia for Tito*), Скопје: Здружение на граѓани кои го почитуваат ликот и делото на Јосип Броз Тито, 2005.

Kardelj, Edvard: *Pravci razvoja političkog sistema socijalističkog samoupravljanja*. (English translation: Kardelj, Edvard. *Directions of Development of the Political System of Socialist Self-Management*), Beograd: Izdavački centar Komunist, 1977.

Kardelj, Edvard. *Subjektivne snage u samoupravnom socijalističkom društvu*, (English translation: Kardelj, Edvard. *Subjective Forces in Self-Managing Socialist Society*), Sarajevo: Svetlost, 1982.

Kierkegaard, Søren. *Either/Or, A Fragment of Life*. London: Penguin Books Ltd., 1992.

Kołakowski, Leszek. *Šta nas to pitaju veliki filozofi?* kniga druga i treća, Pančevo: Mali Nemo, 2006 and 2007. (English ed. Kołakowski, Leszek. *The Two Eyes of Spinoza and Other Essays on Philosophers*, Chicago: St. Augustine's Press, 2004).
Колишевски, Лазар. *Аспекти на македонското прашање.* (English translation: Kolishevski Lazar. *The Aspects of Macedonian Question)*, Скопје: Наша книга, 1979.
Константиновић, Радомир. *Филозофија на паланката.* (English translation: Konstantinović, Radomir. *Philosophy of Provincialism*), Скопје: Лист, 2000.
Korš, Karl. *Karl Marks*, (English translation: Korsch, Karl. *Karl Marx*), Beograd: Nolit, 1984.
Котески, Јован. *Поезија.* (English translation: Koteski, Jovan. *Poetry*), Скопје: Три, 2000.
Lacan, Jacques. *The Four Fundamental Concepts of Psychoanalysis.* Book XI. Edited by Jacques-Alain Miller, New York, London: W.W. Norton & Company, 1998.
Lacan, Jacques. *Television. A Challenge to the Psychoanalytic Establishment.* New York and London: W.W. Norton & Company, 1990.
Lacan, Jacques. *The Ego in Freud's Theory and in the Technique of Psychoanalysis 1954-1955.* Book II. New York, London: W.W. Norton & Company 1991.
Lacan, Jacques. *The Psychoses 1955-56.* Book III. New York and London: W.W. Norton & Company, 1997.
Lacan, Jacques. *The Ethics of Psychoanalysis 1959-60.* Book VII. New York and London: W.W. Norton & Company, 1997.
Lacan, Jacques. *Écrits: A Selection.* London and New York: Routledge, 2003.
Laclau, Erneso "Identity and Hegemony," in: Butler, Judith; Laclau, Ernesto and Žižek, Slavoj. *Contingency, Hegemony, Universality, Contemporary Dialogues on the Left,* London, New York: Verso, 2000.
Lasić, Stanko. *Sukob na književnoj ljevici 1928-1952.* (English translation: (Lasić, Stanko. *The Conflict in the Literary Left 1928-1952*), Zagreb: Liber, 1970.
Ле Бон, Гистав. *Психологија на толпата.* (English translation: Le Bon, Gustave. *The Crowd: A Study of the Popular Mind*), Скопје: Култура, 1997.
Le Guin, Ursula. "The Stalin in the Soul," in: *The Language of the Night: Essays on Fantasy and Science Fiction,* edited and with introduction by Susan Wood, New York: Perigee, 1980.
Лексикон на ЈУ митологијата. (English translation: *Lexicon of Yugoslav Mythology*), Скопје: Темплум, 2006.

Лењин, В.И. *Последња писма и чланци*. (English translation: Lenin, V.I. *Last Letters and Articles*), Београд: Слово, 1973.
Lopušina, Marko. *Ubij bližnjeg svog: Jugoslovenska tajna policija 1945-1997*. (English translation: Lopushina, Marko. *Kill Your Neighbor: Yugoslav Secret Police 1945-1997)*, Beograd: Narodna knjiga, 1997.
Lopušina, Marko. *KOS, Tajne vojne službe bezbednosti*. (English translation: Lopushina, Marko. *KOS, Secrets of the Military Security Service)*, Beograd: Evro, 2004.
Mandić, Igor. *Mitologija svakidašnjeg života*, (English translation: Mandić, Igor. *Mythology of Everyday Life*), Zagreb: O. Keršovani, 1976.
Mandić, Igor. *Policajci duha*. (English translation: Mandić, Igor. *Policemen Spirit*), Zagreb: Globus, 1979.
Marić, Milomir. *Deca komunizma*. (English translation: Marić, Milomir. *The Children of Communism*), Beograd: Mladost, 1988.
Marković, Predrag J. *Trajnost i promena*. (English translation: Marković, Predrag J. *Continuity and Change*), Beograd: Službeni glasnik, 2007.
Маркс, Карл. *Писма Кугелману (1862-1874)*. (English translation: Marx, Karl. *Letters to Kuglemann [1862-1874]*). Београд: Култура, 1951.
Marx, Karl. *Nadnica, cena i profit*. (English translation: Marx, Karl. *Wages, Price and Profit*), Beograd: Kultura, 1960.
Marx, Karl. *Najamni rad i kapital*. (English translation: Marx, Karl. *Wage-Labor and Capital*), Beograd: Kultura, 1960.
Marx, Karl. *Kapital*. (English translation: Marx, Karl. *Capital*), Zagreb: Školska knjiga, 1975.
Marx, Karl (with Friedrich Engels). *Communist Manifesto/ Wages, Price and Profit/Capital (selections)/Socialism: Utopian and Scientific*. London: CRW Publishing Limited, 2004.
Марксистичка философија на XX век. Избор и редакција Предраг Враницки (English translation: *Marxist Philosophy of the 20th Century*), Скопје: Наша книга, 1985.
Miłosz, Czesław, *The Captive Mind*. New York: Vintage International, 1990.
Milošević, Nikola. *Polemike*. (English translation: Milošević, Nikola, *Polemics*), Beograd: Beletra, 1990.
Nikolić, Miodrag. *Informbiro*. Knjiga 1 и 2. (English translation: Nikolić, Miodrag. *Cominform*. Books 1 and 2), Zagreb: CIP, 1989.
N\osztalgia–Ways of Revisiting the Socialist Past. Editor Isabella Willinger. Budapest and Berlin: Anthropolis, and Rejs e.V., 2007.
Orwell, George. *1984*. New York: Penguin, 1971.
Panovič, Zoran. *Dozvolite da se odjavimo*. (English translation: Panovič, Zoran *Allow Us to Unsubscribe*), Beograd: Statussteam i Službeni glasnik, 2007.
Pearson, Owen. *Albania as Dictatorship and Democracy*. London and New York: I.B. Tauris and Co Ltd., 2006.

Pfaller, Robert. "Negation and its Reliabilities: An Empty Subject for Ideology," *The Symptom*. No. 4. (2003), http://www.lacan.com/pfaller.htm (accessed April 12, 2008).

Plekhanov, George V. *Fundamental Problems of Marxism*. New York: International Publishers, 1992.

Plehanov, Georgi. *O materijalističkom shvatanju istorije*. (English translation: Plehanov, Georgi. *The Materialist Conception of History*), Beograd: Kultura, 1961.

Plehanov, Georgi. *Anarhizam i socijalizam*. (English translation: Plehanov, Georgi. *Anarchism & Socialism*) Beograd: Kultura, 1961.

Prauer, S.S. *Karl Marks i svetska knjizevnost*. (English translation: Prauer, S.S. *Karl Marx and the World Literature*), Beograd: Nolit, 1983.

Rayfield, Donald. *Stalin and His Hangmen*. London, New York: Penguin Books, 2005.

Rebić, Đuro. *Špiuni na tekućoj vrpci*. (English translation: Rebić, Đuro. *Spies on Assembly Lines*), Zagreb: CIP, 1990.

Ricoeur, Paul. *History and Truth*. Evanston: Northwest University Press, 1965.

Ристески, Стојан. *Судени за Македонија (1945-1985)*. (English translation: Risteski, Stojan. *Convicted for Macedonia*), Охрид: Македониа прима, 1995.

Rorty, Richard. *Consequences of Pragmatism*. Minneapolis: University of Minneapolis Press, 1982.

Rorty, Richard. *Contingency, Irony and Solidarity*. Cambridge: Cambridge University Press, 1989.

Шафаревич, Игор. *Социјализам као појава светске историје*. (English translation: Shafarevich, Igor. *The Socialist Phenomenon*, Цетиње: Издавачка установа Метрополије Црногорско- приморске, 1997. (First ed. И.Р.Шафаревич. Социализм как Явление мировной истории. Paris: YMCA Press, 1977).

Sharaf, Myron. *Fury on Earth. A Biography of Wilhelm Reich*, New York: St. Martin's Press, 1994.

Schmitt, Carl. *Political Theology. Four Chapters on the Concept of Sovereignty*. Translated by George Schwab. Cambridge, London: The MIT Press, 1985.

Schopenhauer, Arthur, *The World as Will and Representation*, translated from the German by E.F.J.Payne, New York: Dover Publications, Inc., 1969.

Slapšak, Svetlana. *Ratni Kandid*. (English translation: Slapšak, Svetlana *War Candide*), Beograd: Radio B 92, 1997.

Solzhenitsyn, I. Aleksandr. *Lenin in Zűrich*, Wilcox & Follett Book Co., 1976.

Tempo, Svetozar Vukmanović. *Memoari: kampanja ili polemika*. (English translation: Tempo, Svetozar Vukmanović *Memoirs: Campaign or Polemics*), Beograd, Zagreb: Narodna knjiga, Naprijed, 1985.
Tempo, Svetozar Vukmanović. *Memoari: 1966-1969. Neslaganja*. (English translation: Tempo, Svetozar Vukmanović. *Memoirs: 1966-1969. Disagreements*), Beograd, Zagreb: Narodna knjiga, Naprijed, 1985.
Tito- Partija Zbornik radova sa naučnog skupa "Tito-Partija" održanog od 2. do 5. decembra 1987. godine u Kumrovcu, (English translation: *Tito-Party. A Collection of Articles from the Conference "Tito-Party," December 2-5 1987 in Kumrovec*), Beograd: IRO Narodna knjiga, 1988.
Trotsky, Leon. *Terrorism and Communism. A Reply to Karl Kautsky*. (Slavoj Žižek Presents Trotsky). London and New York: Verso, 2007.
US President, Public Papers of the President of the President of the United States, Harry S. Truman (Washington, D.G.GPO, 1964, p. 232). From the text by Robert M. Blum: *Appendix A: Surprised by Tito: Anatomy of an Intelligence Failure*, August, 2006, 686. See at: http://www.necenzurirano.com (accessed February 5, 2007).
Verdery, Kathrine. *What Was Socialism, and What Comes Next?* Princeton: Princeton University Press, 1996.
Verdery, Katherine. *The Political Lives of Dead Bodies*. New York: Columbia University Press, 1999.
Вирилио, Пол. *Естетика на исчезнувањето*. Скопје: Магор, 2006. (English edition: Virilio, Paul. *The Aesthetics of Disappearance*, MIT Press, 1991.
Vlaisavljević, Ugo. *Lepoglava i univerzitet*, (English translation: Vlaisavljević, Ugo. *Lepoglava and University*), Sarajevo: Centar za interdisciplinarne postdiplomske studije Univerziteta, 2003.
Volkov, Vladimir, K. *Staljin je hteo drugačiju Evropu*. (English translation: Volkov, Vladimir, K. *Stalin Wanted Different Europe*), Beograd: Narodna knjiga, Alfa, 2007.
Valerštajn, Imanuel. *Posle liberalizma*. Beograd: Službeni glasnik, 2005. (First ed. Wallerstein, Immanuel. *After Liberalism*. New York: The New York Press, 1995).
Wallerstein, Immanuel. *Utopistics*. New York: The New York Press, 1998.
Wills, David. *Prosthesis*. Stanford: Stanford University Press, 1995.
Wheen, Francis. *Marx's Das Kapital. A Biography*. London: Atlantic Books, 2006.
Woodard, Colin: "Objects of Disaffection in Eastern Europe", *The Chronicle of Higher Education*, Budapest, June 15, 2007.
What's Left of Theory? New Work on the Politics of Literary Theory. Editors: Butler, Judith/Guillory, John and Thomas, Kendall. New York, London: Routledge, 2000.

Zajednica sečanja. Tranziciona pravda u istoriskoj perspektivi. Editors: Obrad Savić and Ana Miljković. Beograd: Beogradski krug, 2006. (English translation: *Community of Memory. History of Transitional Justice*).

Zamyatin, Yevgeny. *We.* Translation by Mirra Ginsburg. New York: EOS, Harper Collins Publishers, 1999.

Zupančič, Alenka. *The Shortest Shadow. Nietzsche's Philosophy of the Two.* Cambridge Massachusetts and London: The MIT Press, 2003.

Žižek, Slavoj. *Druga smrt Josipa Broza–Tita,* Ljubljana: DZS, 1989. (English translation: Žižek, Slavoj. *The Second Death of Josip Broz–Tito*).

Žižek, Slavoj. *Tarrying with the Negative.* Durham: Duke University Press, 1993.

Žižek, Slavoj. *Metastaze uživanja,* Beograd: Biblioteka XX vek, 1996. (English edition: Žižek, Slavoj. *The Metastases of Enjoyment. Six Essays on Woman and Causality,* New York, London: Verso, 1994).

Žižek, Slavoj. *The Sublime Object of Ideology,* Verso, London, New York, 1999.

Žižek, Slavoj. *Manje ljubavi–više mržnje!* (English translation: Žižek, Slavoj. *Less Love–More Hate!*), Beograd: Beogradski krug, 2001.

Žižek, Slavoj. *Repeating Lenin,* 2001 http://www.lacan.com/replenin (accessed: May 17, 2005).

Žižek, Slavoj. *The Spectator's Malevolent Neutrality.* Lecture presented at the Theaterformen Festival, Brunswick, Germany, June 8, 2004.

Žižek, Slavoj. *The Universal Exception.* London and New York: Continuum, 2006.

Žižek, Slavoj. *The Parallax View,* Cambridge, London: MIT Press, 2006.

Žižek, Slavoj. *Leninism Today: Zionism and the Jewish Question,* 2007 http://www.lacan.com/zizbarabajal.html (accessed February 5, 2008).

Žižek, Slavoj. *In Defense of Lost Causes,* London, New York: Verso, 2008.

VIII Sednica CK SK Srbije. Nulta tacka "narodnog pokreta". (English translation: *VIII Session of the Central Committee of the Serbian League of Communists. Zero Point of "People's Movement"*). Beograd: Službeni glasnik, 2007.

Notes

I. INTIMIST

1. On the Emptions that Remained on a Bus

1. UDBA–Yugoslav State Security Administration.
2. Judith Butler, *Antigone's Claim: Kinship Between Life and Death* (New York: Columbia University Press, 2000), 24.
3. Dedinje (Belgrade), Pantovčak (Zagreb) and Vodno (Skopje) were the famous communist nomenclature districts in Serbia, Croatia and Macedonia.
4. Viktor Jerofejev, *Dobar Staljin* (English translation: Erofeyev, Viktor. *The Good Stalin*) (Beograd: Geopoetika, 2005), 50.

2. Intimist

1. Јован Котески, Поезија (Скопје: Три, 2000), 23. (English translation: Koteski, Jovan. *Poetry*, (Skopje: Tri, 2000), 23.
2. The Macedonian historians (Violeta Ačkoska and others) estimate that Jovan Koteski's file originally consisted of more than 6,000 pages. At present, approximately 3,000 pages from his file are still available at the State Archives of the Republic of Macedonia.
3. Laibach (Slovenian avant-garde music group) and NSK (Neue Slowenische Kunst, controversial Slovenian political art group)–both from the mid-1980s. They adopted the symbols and mannerism of the state enemies to provoke the Yugoslavian state apparatus, and exaggerated everything to the point of parody. For more see: Slavoj Žižek's analysis of the NSK phenomenon in "The Universal Exception," New York: Continuum, 2006, pp. 63-67.
4. DBK–short for State Security Administration of Yugoslavia, also known as UDBA.

5. "When the poet Jovan Koteski was imprisoned, his friends/intellectuals kept silent. The famous Macedonian Writers' Society was mute. Nobody called… because everybody was afraid for themselves, nobody for him, and certainly at least two or three of them who played cards with some important politicians from the Central Committee or, who were politicians themselves, could do something for their colleague. What they didn't do was done by a non-Macedonian intellectual, Predrag Matvejević, who at that time was the Secretary of the International PEN Center," writes Eftim Kletnikov, "Intellectuals", *Dnevnik*, July 8, 1998.
6. Ефтим Клетников, "Интелектуалци". (English translation: Eftim Kletnikov, "Intellectuals"), *Dnevnik*, (Skopje, July 8, 1998).
7. The poem "Lambada" from my father's collection *Shivers* (1991) testifies about Šumski's role as a police extortionist.

> Jovan Koteski
> Lambada
>
> *To Vasil Atanasovski-Šumski*
>
> Believe me, I'll come to your funeral,
> It will be my pleasure
> I'll light you a Lambada candle
> and I'll remember you ran horned between the bare walls.
>
> I'll come to your funeral
> to see
> where the stamen of evil was scattered,
> and I'll light you a Lambada candle
> for cruelty to burn with praise.

8. SDB–State Security Service in today's Macedonia.
9. Acronym for "Republic Secretariat of the Interior" within the State Security Service.
10. UBK–State Security Service in today's Macedonia.
11. How did the system watch the potential power of the thought? We can find the answer again in my father's file. It reveals a group of poets and intellectuals who have a different role from his "friends"– snitches in the highest literary circles. They show antipathy or at least dissatisfaction at my father's imprisonment, but that attitude puts the police on them as well. In an operative note from February 4, 1986 while my father was in prison, there was a report with the title:

"Glorifying the work of the recently accused poet Jovan Koteski." It is stated there that on November 8, 1986 in the house of the linguistics professor, Dimitar Pandev, "for the occasion of the religious holiday Mitrovden," "around 20 guests... from the cultural spheres in Ohrid, mainly young people" gathered. The snitch is among them and he conveys the entire event. The house was "lit with candles in order to look poetic'" (the irony is in the report), and when the guests gathered, Dimitar Pandev tells them (quoting from the operative note of ISDB-Struga): "This night is dedicated to the greatest poet, the rebellious Macedonian Jovan Koteski", and afterwards (quoting): "Pandev read a poem by Koteski from one collection of poems. After him, Slave Banar read, and then several other persons. While the poems were read, the present people quietly sang the Macedonian folk song 'I was born with suffering.'" The snitch reports that: "We find these people of interest to us because of the Macedonian nationalism, and because at the same time they gather around the editor-in-chief of the literary magazine 'Spizalit,' Pasko Kuzman (followed by crossed out lines)." In the operative note, the snitch added the personal details of Dimitar Pandev and Slave Banar (dates of birth, addresses, professions), and the inspector stated the following operative measures: "These persons deserve our more pronounced interest. It would be good to... (illegible, and then crossed out with a black felt-tip pen)." This type of inspector measures for observation stand beside the names of many poets, who according to the operative notes in the file, expressed dissatisfaction with my father's imprisonment, including among others, Metodija Fotev, Tome and Tamara Arsovski, Branko Cvetkovski, Liljana Dirjan, Eftim Kletnikov, Todor Calovski and others who cannot be recognized because of the black felt-tip pens, and their dissatisfaction probably contributed to opening police files for them as well (if they weren't opened already).
12. Blaže Minevski, *Focus* No. 554, February 10, 2006, 21-25.

3. Communist Crimes and Political Anesthesia

1. Игор Шафаревич, *Социјализам као појава светске историје* (English translation: Igor Shafarevich, *The Socialist Phenomenon*) (Цетиње: Издавачка установа Метрополије Црногорско–приморске, 1991), 11.
2. Katherine Verdery, *What was Socialism and What Comes Next?* (New York: Columbia University Press, 1999), 11-12.
3. Quoted in: Carl Schmitt, *Political Theology. Four Chapters on the Concept of Sovereignty* (Cambridge, London: The MIT Press, 1985), 15.

4. Slavoj Žižek, *The Universal Exception* (London, New York: Continuum, 2006), 121, note 20.
5. Игор Шафаревич, *Социјализам као појава светске историје* (English translation: Igor Shafarevich, *The Socialist Phenomenon*), 297.
6. Predrag J. Marković, *Trajnost i promena* (English translation: Predrag J. Marković, *Continuity and Change*) (Beograd: Službeni glasnik, 2007), 48.
7. Quoted in: Susan Buck-Morss, *Dreamworld and Catastrophe. The Passing of Mass Utopia in East and West* (Massachusetts: The MIT Press, 2002), 49.
8. Quoted in: Susan Buck-Morss, *Dreamworld and Catastrophe. The Passing of Mass Utopia in East and West*, 44.
9. Igor Mandić, *Policajci duha* (English translation: Igor Mandić, *Policemen Spirit*) (Zagreb: Globus, 1979), 82.
10. Игор Шафаревич, *Социјализам као појава светске историје* (English translation: Igor Shafarevich, *The Socialist Phenomenon*), 21.
11. Nanci Adler, *The Gulag Survivor, Beyond the Soviet System* (New Brunswick, New Jersey: Transaction Publisher, 2004), 15-18.
12. Ibid, 18.
13. From the French documentary *La Faute à Lénine (par Ukraine Europe)*. (2001). TV channel France 5, February 1, 2004, 16:00. Magazine "Les repères de l'Histoire": "La faute à Lénine" de Daniel Leconte, Débat avec Jean-Jacques Marie et Alexandre Gratchev.
14. Donald Rayfield, *Stalin and His Hangmen* (London, New York: Penguin Books, 2005), xxiii.
15. Ibid, xx.
16. Hanna Arendt, *Eichmann in Jerusalem. A Report on the Banality of Evil* (New York: Penquin Books Ltd., 1992), 11.
17. Ibid, 12.
18. Michael Bond, "I Walk in Ghosts and Shadows", *New Scientist*, February 23, 2008, 44-45.
19. Jacques Lacan, *The Four Fundamental Concepts of Psychoanalysis*. Book XI. (New York, London: W.W. Norton & Company, 1998), 134.
20. Slavoj, Žižek, *The Universal Exception*, 45.
21. Slavoj Žižek, *Sunday at two*, Interview for Croatian TV, Zagreb, February 3, 2007.
22. In the late 1960s, the historians in Czechoslovakia discovered shocking details, which were published in the Report of the Investigation Committee of 1968. They described the first victims from the nomenclature who exchanged correspondence with Stalin for the liquidation of the local leaders.
23. Ben Fowkes, *The Rise and Fall of Communism in Eastern Europe* (London: MacMillan Press LTD, 1995), 47.

24. Ibid, 208, footnote no. 57.
25. Jacques Lacan, *Television. A Challenge to the Psychoanalytic Establishment* (New York and London: W.W. Norton & Company, 1990), 51-52.
26. Donald Rayfield, *Stalin and His Hangmen*, xx.
27. Ibid, xx-xxi.
28. Quoted in: Nanci Adler, *The Gulag Survivor, Beyond the Soviet System*, 7.
29. Ibid, 42.
30. Ibid, p. 89, footnote 98.
31. Vasili Mitrokhin was a senior archivist for the KGB, and co-author with Christopher Andrew of, *The Sword and the Shield, The Mitrokhin Archive and the Secret History of the KGB* (New York: Basic Books, 1999).
32. Christopher Andrew and Vasili Mitrokhin, *The Sword and the Shield, The Mitrokhin Archive and the Secret History of the KGB* (New York: Basic Books, 1999), 3.
33. Ibid, p. 90, footnote 111.
34. See the book: Ivo Banac, *Sa Staljinom protiv Tita* (English translation: Ivo Banac, *With Stalin Against Tito*) (Zagreb: Globus, 1990).
35. Katherine Verdery, *What was Socialism and What Comes Next?*, 37.
36. Slavoj Žižek, *The Universal Exception*, 44.
37. Ibid, 42-60.
38. Susan, Buck-Morss, *Dreamworld and Catastrophe. The Passing of Mass Utopia in East and West*, 209.
39. Jacques Lacan, *The Ego in Freud's Theory and in the Technique of Psychoanalysis 1954-1955* (New York, London: W.W. Norton & Company, 1991), 42.
40. Quoted from: Susan, Buck-Morss, *Dreamworld and Catastrophe. The Passing of Mass Utopia in East and West*, 114.
41. Ibid, 114.
42. Ibid, 114.
43. Ibid, 114.
44. See the book: Stanko Lasić, *Sukob na književnoj ljevici 1928-1952* (English translation: Lasić, Stanko. *The Conflict in the Literary Left 1928-1952*) (Zagreb: Liber, 1970).
45. Miroslav Krleža was a famous Croatian writer and later a close friend of Marshal Tito.
46. Jacques Lacan, *The Ego in Freud's Theory and in the Technique of Psychoanalysis 1954-1955*, 51.
47. *N\osztalgia. Ways of Revisiting the Socialist Past*. Editor Isabella Willinger. (Budapest, Berlin, Anthropolis and Rejs e.V., 2007), 6.
48. See: Robert Pfaller, "Negation and its Reliabilities: An Empty Subject for Ideology", *The Symptom*. No. 4. (2003). http://www.lacan.com/pfaller.htm (accessed April 12, 2008)

49. Artyom Kosmarski and Tanya Zamirovskaya: "Protest, Nostalgia, and National Consciousness," in: N\osztalgia. *Ways of Revisiting the Socialist Past*, 25.
50. Søren Kierkegaard, *Either/Or, A Fragment of Life* (London: Penguin Books Ltd., 1992), 44.
51. Søren Kierkegaard, *Either/Or, A Fragment of Life*, 51.
52. Viktor Jerofejev, *Muškarci* (English translation: Erofeyev, Viktor. *Men*) (Beograd: Plato, 2002), 18-21.
53. Nanci Adler, *The Gulag Survivor, Beyond the Soviet System*, 15-16.
54. Interview with Jozef Oseli, *Nova TV* Croatian Television, March 30, 2008.
55. Marko Lopušina, *KOS, Tajne vojne službe bezbednosti* (English translation: Lopushina, Marko. *KOS, Secrets of the Military Security Service*) (Beograd: Evro, 2004), 84.
56. Boris Oresić, "Tito's Underground Airport," *Globus*, Zagreb, (23 March 2007): 115.
57. US President, Public Papers of the President of the President of the United States, Harry S. Truman (Washington, D.G. GPO, 1964, p. 232). From the text Robert M. Blum: *Appendix A: Surprised by Tito: Anatomy of an Intelligence Failure*, August 2006, 686. See at: http://www.necenzurirano.com (accessed February 2007)
58. Ibid, 694.
59. All the foreign sources quoted in this book are unanimous regarding this information. They are stated here from the book: Ivo Banac, *Sa Staljinom protiv Tita* (Banac, Ivo. *With Stalin Against Tito*), 21.
60. In the declassified CIA documents, the American agent Cabot states that, "The partisans, although inspired and led by communism, are a very heterogeneous group. The effective resistance to the Soviet domination is more likely to come from the partisan lines than from the opposition," and that nationalism, more than the ideology, will be the core which will holds the Yugoslav actions together and it will be a basis for political pursuits, but it is interesting that when his document got to the State Department, the under-secretary crossed out the document and wrote "rubbish" over it.
61. Ivo Banac, *Sa Staljinom protiv Tita* (English translation: Banac, Ivo. *With Stalin Against Tito*), 21.
62. Ibid, 27.
63. Ben Fowkes, *The Rise and Fall of Communism in Eastern Europe*, 52.
64. Ivo Banac, *Sa Staljinom protiv Tita* (Banac, Ivo. *With Stalin Against Tito*), 31.
65. Ben Fowkes, *The Rise and Fall of Communism in Eastern Europe*, 48.
66. Ivo Banac, *Sa Staljinom protiv Tita* (Banac, Ivo. *With Stalin Against Tito*), 33.

67. See: Marko Lopušina, *KOS, Tajne vojne službe bezbednosti* (English translation: Lopushina, Marko. *KOS, Secrets of the Military Security Service)*, 57.
68. Ibid, 61.
69. Ibid, 64.
70. Ivo Banac, *Sa Staljinom protiv Tita* (Banac, Ivo. *With Stalin Against Tito*), 36.
71. Ben Fowkes, *The Rise and Fall of Communism in Eastern Europe*, 48.
72. Ibid, 49.
73. Ivo Banac, *Sa Staljinom protiv Tita* (Banac, Ivo. *With Stalin Against Tito*), 34.
74. Ben Fowkes, *The Rise and Fall of Communism in Eastern Europe*, 47.
75. Ibid, 49.
76. Ibid, 50.
77. Ivo Banac, *Sa Staljinom protiv Tita* (Banac, Ivo. *With Stalin Against Tito*), 35.
78. At the famous Moscow Conference of October 1944, Stalin and Churchill made a decision for the division of spheres and influences. In the percentage agreement, the Soviets agreed that their influence would be restricted to Hungary, Romania and Bulgaria, and it would remain 50-50 in Yugoslavia, although Molotov tried to increase the Soviet interests to 60%. In his memoirs, Churchill describes the devision like this: "The moment was apt for business, so I said: 'Let us settle about our affairs in the Balkans. Your armies are in Roumania and Bulgaria. We have interests, missions and agents there. Don't let us get at cross-purposes in small ways. So far as Britain and Russia are concerned, how would it do for you to have ninety per cent predominance in Roumania, for us to have ninety per cent of the say in Greece, and go fifty-fifty about Yugoslavia?' While this was being translated, I wrote out on a half-sheet of paper:
Roumania: Russia 90%, The others 10%.
Greece: Great Britain (in accord with U.S.A.) 90%, Russia 10%.
Yugoslavia 50%-50%.
Hungary 50%-50%.
Bulgaria: Russia 75%, The others 25%.
I pushed this across to Stalin, who had by then heard the translation. There was a slight pause. Then he took his blue pencil and made a large tick upon it, and passed it back to us. It was all settled in no more time than it takes to set down… After, there was a long silence. The pencilled paper lay in the centre of the table. At length I said, 'Might it not be thought rather cynical if it seemed we had disposed of these issues, so fateful to millions of people, in such an offhand manner?

Let us burn the paper.' 'No, you keep it,' said Stalin." From: Winston S. Churchill, *The Second World War. Triumph and Tragedy* (New York: Houghton Mifflin Company, 1995), 198.
79. Ivo Banac, *Sa Staljinom protiv Tita* (Banac, Ivo. *With Stalin Against Tito*), 30.
80. US President, Public Papers of the President of the President of the United States, Harry S. Truman (Washington, D.G. GPO, 1964, p. 232. From the text: Robert M. Blum: Appendix A: Surprised by Tito: Anatomy of an Intelligence Failure, August, 2006, p. 1, or 83. See: http://www.necenzurirano.com.
81. Ben Fowkes, *The Rise and Fall of Communism in Eastern Europe*, 2.
82. Cominform (Communist Information Bureau) was an idea of uniting all the communist parties which formed governments (mainly in Europe). The members–founders were Yugoslavia, Bulgaria, Romania, Hungary, Poland, the Soviet Union, France, Czechoslovakia and Italy, and what's interesting is that Germany and Albania were not included, as well as China and Greece. It was founded in September 1947 in Poland, and the chairman was Zhdanov. He talks about two groups after the war, imperialistic and democratic, and he especially praises the Yugoslav communist line, where as a reward, the headquarters of the Cominform was moved (to Belgrade).
83. Ben Fowkes, *The Rise and Fall of Communism in Eastern Europe*, 72-73.
84. Marko Lopušina, *KOS, Tajne vojne službe bezbednosti* (English translation: Lopushina, Marko. *KOS, Secrets of the Military Security Service)*, 78.
85. Ben Fowkes, *The Rise and Fall of Communism in Eastern Europe*, 69-70.
86. Opinion by Ante Rastegorec, one of the UDB operatives on Goli Otok, quoted from Dedijer, see in: Ivo Banac, *Sa Staljinom protiv Tita* (Banac, Ivo. *With Stalin Against Tito*), 238.
87. Ugo Vlaisavljević, *Lepoglava i univerzitet* (English translation: Vlaisavljević, Ugo. *Lepoglava and University*) (Sarajevo: Centar za interdisciplinarne postdiplomske studije Univerziteta, 2003), 75.
88. Ivo Banac, *Sa Staljinom protiv Tita* (Banac, Ivo. *With Stalin Against Tito*), 234-236.
89. Svetozar Vukmanović Tempo was one of the high Yugoslav communist leaders.
90. Svetozar Vukmanović Tempo, *Memoari: kampanja ili polemika* (English translation: Svetozar Vukmanović Tempo, *Memoirs: Campaign or Polemics*) (Beograd, Zagreb: Narodna knjiga, Naprijed, 1985), vii.

4. Poetry Between the Small-Town Mentality and Secret Services

1. Radomir Konstantinović, *Filozofija palanke* (English translation: Konstantinović, Radomir. *Philosophy of Provincialism*) (Beograd: Nolit, 1981), 17.
2. Slavoj Žižek, *The Universal Exception*, 156.
3. Radomir Konstantinović, *Filozofija palanke* (Konstantinović, Radomir. *Philosophy of Provincialism*), 18.
4. Andrei Şerbulescu is quoted of 1991. See in: Katherine Verdery, *What was Socialism and What Comes Next?*, 49.
5. See the analysis in: Susan Buck-Morss, *Dreamworld and Catastrophe. The Passing of Mass Utopia in East and West*, 141-147.
6. Susan Buck-Morss, *Dreamworld and Catastrophe. The Passing of Mass Utopia in East and West*, 144.
7. Slavoj Žižek, *Leninism Today: Zionism and the Jewish Question*, 2007. http://www.lacan.com/zizbarabajal.html (accessed February 5, 2008).
8. Susan Buck-Morss, *Dreamworld and Catastrophe, The Passing of Mass Utopia in East and West*, 66.
9. Игор Шафаревич, *Социјализам као појава светске историје* (English translation: Shafarevich, Igor. *The Socialist Phenomenon*), 15.
10. Susan Buck-Morss, *Dreamworld and Catastrophe. The Passing of Mass Utopia in East and West*, 147.
11. Игор Шафаревич, *Социјализам као појава светске историје* (Shafarevich, Igor. *The Socialist Phenomenon*), 279.
12. Quoted in: Francis Wheen, *Marx's Das Kapital. A Biography* (London: Atlantic Books, 2006), 77.
13. Игор Шафаревич, *Социјализам као појава светске историје* (Shafarevich, Igor. *The Socialist Phenomenon*), 305.
14. Quoted from the book: Игор Шафаревич, *Социјализам као појава светске историје* (Shafarevich, Igor. *The Socialist Phenomenon*), 304.
15. Ibid, 304.
16. Slavoj Žižek, *The Universal Exception*, 50.
17. Петар Карајанов, *Тито за Македонија, Македонија за Тито* (English translation: Petar Karajanov, *Tito for Macedonia, Macedonia for Tito*) (Скопје: Здружение на граѓани кои го почитуваат ликот и делото на Јосип Броз Тито, 2005), 413.
18. Ibid, 412.
19. Ibid, 401-402.
20. Edvard Kardelj, *Pravci razvoja političkog sistema socijalističkog samouprav- ljanja* (English translation: Edvard Kardelj, *Directions of Development of the Political System of Socialist Self-Management*) (Beograd: Izdavački centar Komunist, 1977). 179.

21. Ibid, 180.
22. Петар Карајанов, *Тито за Македонија, Македонија за Тито* (English translation: Karajanov, Petar. *Tito for Macedonia, Macedonia for Tito*), 400.
23. Imanuel Valerštajn, *Posle liberalizma* (English translation: 1st ed. Immanuel Wallerstein. *After Liberalism*. New York: The New York Press, 1995) (Beograd: Službeni glasnik, 2005), 189.
24. Radomir Konstantinović, *Filozofija palanke* (Konstantinović, Radomir. *Philosophy of Provincialism*), 24.
25. Donald Rayfield, *Stalin and His Hangmen*, 119.
26. Ibid, 119.
27. Ibid, 64-67.
28. Radomir Konstantinović, *Filozofija palanke* (English translation: Radomir Konstantinović, *Philosophy of Provincialism*), 19.
29. Robert Carver, *The Accursed Mountains* (London: Flamingo, 1999), 42.
30. Slavoj Žižek, *Manje ljubavi–više mržnje!* (Slavoj Žižek, *Less love–more hate!*) (Belgrade: Beogradski krug, 2001), 124.
31. Žarko Trajanoski, "Have you heard the joke about?", 2006, from the blog *Zombification*. See: http://jasnesumjas.blogspot.com/2006/04/blog-post_114636585489062303.html (accessed April 30, 2006).
32. Карл Маркс, *Писма Кугелману (1862-1874)* (English translation: Karl Marx, *Letters to Kuglemann [1862-1874]*) (Београд: Култура, 1951), 41.
33. Donald Rayfield, *Stalin and His Hangmen*, 66.
34. Đuro Rebić, Špiuni na tekućoj vrpci. (English translation: Đuro Rebić, *Spies on Assembly Lines*), Zagreb: CIP, 1990, 5.
35. Radomir Konstantinović, *Filozofija palanke* (English translation: Radomir Konstantinović, *Philosophy of Provincialism*), 12.
36. Donald Rayfield, *Stalin and His Hangmen*, 70.
37. Ibid, 64.
38. Ibid, 79.
39. Ibid, 81.
40. Игор Шафаревич, *Социјализам као појава светске историје*. (Igor Shafarevich, *The Socialist Phenomenon*), 296.
41. Slavoj Žižek, *Repeating Lenin*, http://www.lacan.com/replenin (accessed November 17, 2006).
42. Donald Rayfield, *Stalin and His Hangmen*, 46.
43. Ibid, 20-21.
44. Ibid, 19.
45. Игор Шафаревич, *Социјализам као појава светске историје*. (English translation: Igor Shafarevich, *The Socialist Phenomenon*), 306.
46. Ibid, 305.
47. Ibid, 305.

48. Ibid, 305.
49. Karl Korš, *Karl Marks* (English translation: Karl Korsch, *Karl Marx*) (Beograd: Nolit, 1984), 233.
50. Slavoj Žižek, "Trotsky's Terrorism and Communism, or, Despair and Utopia in the Turbulent Year of 1920," *Slavoj Žižek Presents Trotsky. Terrorism and Communism. A Reply to Karl Kautsky* (London and New York: Verso, 2007), x.
51. Ibid, xi-xii.
52. Jacques Lacan, *The Ethics of Psychoanalysis 1959-60* (New York, London: W.W. Norton & Company 1997), 33.
53. Ibid, 53.
54. Ibid, 54.
55. Svetozar Vukmanović Tempo, *Memoari: 1966-1969. Neslaganja*. (English translation: Svetozar Vukmanović Tempo, *Memoirs: 1966-1969. Disagreements*) (Beograd, Zagreb: Narodna knjiga, Naprijed, 1985), 19.
56. Ibid, 19.
57. See: Marko Lopušina, *Ubij bližnjeg svog: Jugoslovenska tajna policija 1945-1997*. (English translation: Marko Lopushina, *Kill Your Neighbor: Yugoslav Secret Police 1945-1997)*, Beograd: Narodna knjiga, 1997. The book is available on the Internet: http://www.serbianunity.net/culture/library/Ubij_Bliznjeg_Svoga/index.html (accessed August 2, 2006).
58. Andrei Şerbulescu is quoted in 1991. See in: Katherine Verdery, *What was Socialism and What Comes Next?*, 24.
59. Ibid, 50.
60. Marko Lopušina, *KOS, Tajne vojne službe bezbednosti*. (English translation: Marko Lopushina, *KOS, Secrets of the Military Security Service)*, 164.
61. Ibid, 179.
62. Marko Lopušina, *Ubij bližnjeg svog: Jugoslovenska tajna policija 1945-1997*. (English translation: Marko Lopushina, *Kill Your Neighbor: Yugoslav Secret Police 1945-1997)*. On: http://www.serbianunity.net/culture/library/Ubij_Bliznjeg_Svoga/index.html (accessed August 2, 2006).
63. Marko Lopušina, *KOS, Tajne vojne službe bezbednosti*. (English translation: Marko Lopushina, *KOS, Secrets of the Military Security Service)*, 76.
64. Andrew Curry, "Piecing Together the Dark Legacy of East Germany's Secret Police," *Wired Magazine*, issue 16.2. (January 18, 2008).
65. Đuro Rebić, Špiuni na tekućoj vrpci. (English translation: Đuro Rebić, *Spies on Assembly Lines)*, 13.
66. Donald Rayfield, *Stalin and His Hangmen*, xxiii.
67. Christopher Andrew and Vasili Mitrokhin, *The Sword and the Shield, The Mitrokhin Archive and the Secret History of the KGB*, 1.

68. Ibid, 8.
69. Marko Lopušina, *KOS, Tajne vojne službe bezbednosti*. (English translation: Marko Lopushina, *KOS, Secrets of the Military Security Service*), 160.
70. Ibid, 36.
71. Marko Lopušina, *Ubij bližnjeg svog: Jugoslovenska tajna policija 1945-1997*. (English translation: Marko Lopushina, *Kill Your Neighbor: Yugoslav Secret Police 1945-1997*). http://www.serbianunity.net/culture/library/Ubij_Bliznjeg_Svoga/index.html (accessed August 2, 2006).
72. Quoted from the book: Ugo Vlaisavljević, *Lepoglava i univerzitet*, (English translation: Ugo Vlaisavljević, *Lepoglava and University*), 29.
73. Ibid, 43.
74. Ibid, 56.
75. Borhes, H.L. *Usmeni Borhes*. (English translation: Jorge, Luis Borges, *Borges's Lecure*) (Beograd: Reč i misao, 1990), 57.
76. Ibid, 54.
77. Ibid, 53.
78. From: Christopher Andrew and Vasili Mitrokhin, *The Sword and the Shield, The Mitrokhin Archive and the Secret History of the KGB*, 9.
79. Đuro Rebić, *Špiuni na tekućoj vrpci*. (English translation: Đuro Rebić, *Spies on Assembly Lines*), 48.
80. Borhes, H.L. *Usmeni Borhes*. (English translation: Jorge, Luis Borges, *Borges's Lectures*) 55.
81. Christopher Andrew and Vasili Mitrokhin, *The Sword and the Shield, The Mitrokhin Archive and the Secret History of the KGB*, 9.
82. Donald Rayfield, *Stalin and His Hangmen*, 76.
83. Stathis Gourgouris, *Dream Nation. Enlightenment, Colonization, and the Institution of Modern Greece* (Stanford: The Stanford University Press, 1996), 315.
84. Predrag J. Marković, *Trajnost i promena* (Predrag J. Marković, *Continuity and Change*), 42.
85. Ursula Le Guin, "The Stalin in the Soul," *The Language of the Night: Essays on Fantasy and Science Fiction*, edited and with introduction by Susan Wood (New York: Perigee, 1980), 215.
86. Geert Lovink and Slavoj Žižek, "Reflections of Media and Politics and Cinema," *Inter Communications*. No. 14 (1995). June 20, 1995. See: http://www.ntticc.or.jp/pub/ic_mag/ic014/zizek/zizek_e.html (accessed May 28, 2008).
87. Donald Rayfield, *Stalin and His Hangmen*, 118-9.
88. Ibid, 118.
89. Ibid, 116.
90. Ibid, 117.

91. Ibid, 117.
92. Predrag J. Marković, *Trajnost i promena*. (English translation: Predrag J. Marković, *Continuity and Change*), 48.
93. Slavoj Žižek, *Sunday at Two*, interview for Croatian Television HTV, Zagreb, February 3, 2007.
94. Македони„ум", March 4, 2007. See: http://makedonium.blog.com.mk/node/72117 (accessed May 5, 2007).
95. Kiro Gligorov, Excerpts from "Macedonia is All We Have" (2001), in: *Forum* (15 February, 2008, Skopje), 19.
96. Risto Lazarov, "With Bombs Against Freedom," *Komunist*, December 6, 1985.
97. Igor Mandić, *Policajci duha*. (Igor Mandić, *Policemen Spirit*), 57.
98. Ibid, 57.
99. Žižek, Slavoj. *The Universal Exception*, 165.
100. And isn't it that the world fame of philosophers Slavoj Žižek (Slovenia) and Julija Kristeva (Bulgaria), perversely even that of a politician Radovan Karadadzić (Bosnia), also a psychoanalyst, confirm that the Balkans are a fertile soil for a theoretical psychoanalysis? While the confession was established in the Catholic West, the Eastern countries invested a trust in the neighboring networks, which provided an infrastructure for confessions. Thus, the East has a history of substantially developed networks of observing and informing, fear of the interior "enemy" within me, which all wonderfully sums up to a metaphor for the psychoanalytic work on the unconscious. It can even be said that, besides fratricide, psychoanalysis might be the other most common denominator of the post-communist identity in the Balkans.
101. *VIII Sednica CK SK Srbije. Nulta tačka "narodnog pokreta"*. (English translation: *VIII Session of the Central Committee of the Serbian League of Communists. Zero Point of "People's Movement"*) (Belgrade: Službeni glasnik, 2007), 121-122.
102. Predrag J. Marković, *Trajnost i promena*. (English translation: Predrag J. Marković, *Continuity and Change*), 48.
103. "Communist Monuments of Yugoslavia," in: *Boing Boing*. 28.12.2007. See at: http://www.boingboing.net/2007/12/28/communist-monuments.html (accessed May 20, 2008).
104. Susan Buck-Morss, *Dreamworld and Catastrophe. The Passing of Mass Utopia in East and West,* 48.
105. Ibid, 55.
106. Ibid, 54.
107 Ibid, 24.
108. Ibid, 50.

109. Todor Pavlov's idea, also known as "Reification Theory," was promoted for the first time by the Hungarian Marxist György Lukács in his book *History and Class Consciousness* (1923).
110. Stanko Lasić, *Sukob na književnoj ljevici 1928-1952*. (Stanko Lasić, *TheConflict in the Literary Left 1928-1952*), 15.
111. Ibid, 31.
112. Ibid, 146.
113. Ibid, 192.
114. Igor Mandić, *Policajci duha*. (English translation: Igor Mandić, *Policemen Spirit*), 221.
115. Milomir Marić, *Deca komunizma*. (English translation: Milomir Marić, *The Children of Communism*) (Beograd: Mladost, 1988), 408.
116. Predrag J. Marković, *Trajnost i promena*. (English translation: Predrag J. Marković, *Continuity and Change*), 44.
117. Milomir Marić, *Deca komunizma*. (English translation: Milomir Marić, *The Children of Communism*), 235.
118. Tihomir Ponoš: "It was Lucrative to Publish Tito," *Booksa*, May 25, 2007. See http://www.booksa.hr/specials/14 (accessed: October 28, 2007).
119. Tarkovsky's film, "Andrei Rublev," is, e.g. completed in the winter of 1966, but it is shown for the first time in Moscow in 1969.
120. Slavoj Žižek, *In Defense of Lost Causes* (London, New York: Verso, 2008), 238.
121. Ibid, 244.
122. Ibid, 244.
123. Tihomir Ponoš: "It was Lucrative to Publish Tito," *Booksa*, of May 25, 2007. See: http://www.booksa.hr/specials/14 (accessed: October 28, 2007).
124. Slavoj Žižek, *In Defense of Lost Causes*, 245.

5. Lenin's Laughter

1. Louis Althusser, *Lenin and Philosophy and Other Essays*. (New York: Monthly Review Press, 2001), 11-13.
2. Ibid, 13.
3. Ibid, 17.
4. Ibid, 31.
5. Ibid, 14.
6. Виолета Ачкоска, *Братството и единството 1944-1974 помеѓу хармонија и дисхармонија*. (English translation: Violeta Ačkoska, *Brotherhood and Unity 1944-1974. Between Harmony and Disharmony*)

(Скопје: ИНИ, 2003), 33.
7. Ibid, 34.
8. Milomir Marić, *Deca komunizma*. (English translation: Milomir Marić, *The Children of Communism*), 8.
9. Ibid, 15.
10. Francis Wheen, *Marx's Das Kapital. A Biography*, 2.
11. Prauer. S.S. *Karl Marks i svetska književnost* (English translation: Prauer, S.S. *Karl Marx and World Literature*), (Beograd: Nolit, 1983), 314.
12. Qouted in: Francis Wheen, *Marx's Das Kapital. A Biography*, 5.
13. Ibid, 9.
14. Ibid, 5.
15. Slavoj Žižek, *The Sublime Object of Ideology* (London, New York: Verso, 1999), 11.
16. Ibid, 11.
17. Louis Althusser, *Lenin and Philosophy and Other Essays*, 20.
18. Stanko Lasić, *Sukob na književnoj ljevici 1928-1952*. (English translation: Stanko Lasić, *The Conflict in the Literary Left 1928-1952*), 203.
19. Søren Kierkegaard, *Either/Or, A Fragment of Life*, 54.
20. Edvard Kardelj, *Pravci razvoja političkog sistema socijalističkog samoupravljanja*. (English translation: Edvard Kardelj, *Directions of Development of the Political System of Socialist Self-Management*), 173.
21. Louis Althusser, *Lenin and Philosophy and Other Essays*, 39.
22. Ibid, 33.
23. Engels Friedrich, "Karl Marx's Funeral," *Marx Engels Archive. Der Sozialdemokrat*, March 22, 1883, See: http://marxists.anu.edu.au/archive/marx/works/1883/death/dersoz1.htm (accessed November 5, 2006).
24. Ibid.
25. Stanko Lasić, *Sukob na književnoj ljevici 1928-1952*. (Stanko Lasić, *The Conflict in the Literary Left 1928-1952*), 42.
26. Louis Althusser, *Lenin and Philosophy and Other Essays*, 23.

II. PHENOMENOLOGY OF COMMUNIST INTIMACY

1. Paranoia

1. "The Indiscreet Comrade," *Time Magazine*, Monday, November 17, 1952.
2. Milomir Marić, *Deca komunizma*. (English translation: Milomir Marić, *The Children of Communism*), 309.
3. Ibid, 307.
4. Ibid, 308.

5. Louis Althusser, *Lenin and Philosophy and Other Essays*, 31.
6. Игор Шафаревич, *Социјализам као појава светске историје*. (English translation: Igor Shafarevich, *The Socialist Phenomenon*), 296.
7. Robert Carver, *The Accursed Mountains*, 71.
8. Slavoj Žižek, *Druga smrt Josipa Broza-Tita* (Ljubljana: DZS, 1989), 34. (English translation: Slavoj Žižek, *The Second Death of Josip Broz-Tito* (Ljubljana: DZS, 1989), 34.
9. Milomir Marić, *Deca komunizma*. (English translation: Milomir Marić, *The Children of Communism*), 9-10.
10. Žižek says: Socialism fell apart not because it failed to reach Western standards, but its own normative standards, that is why socialism had the greatest dissidents–Slavoj Žižek, in *Sunday at Two*, interview on Croatian Television, HTV, Zagreb, February 3, 2007.
11. Jacques Lacan, *The Psychoses 1955-56* (New York, London: W.W. Norton & Company 1997), 21.
12. Jacques Lacan, *The Psychoses 1955-56*, 21.
13. Lopušina, Marko. *KOS, Tajne vojne službe bezbednosti*. (English translation: Lopushina, Marko. *KOS, Secrets of the Military Security Service)*, 155.
14. Jacques Lacan, *The Psychoses 1955-56*, 21.
15. Лењин, В.И. *Последња писма и чланци*. (English translation: Lenin, V.I. *Last Letters and Articles*) (Београд: Слово, 1973), 173-174.
16. Lenin's "Will" http://www.plp.org/books/Stalin/node13.html (accessed November 20, 2007).
17. Jacques Lacan, *The Psychoses 1955-56*, 23.
18. Svetozar Vukmanović Tempo, *Memoari: 1966-1969. Neslaganja*. (English translation: Svetozar Vukmanović Tempo, *Memoirs: 1966-1969. Disagreements*), 38-39.
19. Ibid, 38-39.
20. Ibid, 51.
21. Ibid, 106.
22. Ibid, 107.
23. Ibid, 107.
24. Marko Lopušina, *KOS, Tajne vojne službe bezbednosti*. (English translation: Marko Lopušina, *KOS, Secrets of the Military Security Service)*, 82-3.
25. Ibid, 84.
26. Ismail Kadare, *The Successor* (Edinburgh, New York: Canongate, 2006), 199-200.
27. Ibid, 206.
28. Marko Lopušina, *Ubij bližnjeg svog: Jugoslovenska tajna policija 1945-1997*. (English translation: Marko Lopushina, *Kill Your Neighbor:*

Yugoslav Secret Police 1945-1997).
29. Katherine Verdery, *What Was Socialism and What Comes Next?*, 8.
30. Milomir Marić, *Deca komunizma*. (English translation: Milomir Marić, *The Children of Communism*), 407.
31. Gilles Deleuze, *Proust and Signs* (London: The Athlone Press, 2000), 6.
32. Robert Carver, *The Accursed Mountains*, 25.
33. Jean Baudrillard, *Simulacra and Simulation* (Michigan: The University of Michigan Press, 1994), 79.
34. Ibid, 81.
35. Tomas L. Friedman, *The World is Flat* (London, New York: Penguin Books, 2006), 55.

2. Intimacy

1. Michael Herzfeld, *Cultural Intimacy* (New York and London: Routledge, 2005), 1.
2. Mark Andrejević, *I-Spy, The Limits of Interactivity* (Lawrence: The University Press of Kansas, 2007), 9.
3. Ibid, 9.
4. Игор Шафаревич, *Социјализам као појава светске историје*. (English translation: Igor Shafarevich, *The Socialist Phenomenon*), 275.
5. Ibid, 275.
6. Ibid, 274.
7. Quoted here from the book: Georg Vilhelm Fridrih Hegel, *Istorija filozofije II*. (English translation: Georg Wilhelm Friedrich Hegel, *History of Philosophy II*) (Beograd: Kultura, 1964), 239.
8. Игор Шафаревич, *Социјализам као појава светске историје*. (English translation: Igor Shafarevich, *The Socialist Phenomenon*), 25.
9. Ibid, 332.
10. Katherine Verdery, *What Was Socialism and What Comes Next?*, 64.
11. Franz Kafka, *The Trial*. A new translation by Mike Mitchell (Oxford: Oxford University Press, 2009), 5.
12. Susan Buck-Morss, *Dreamworld and Catastrophe. The Passing of Mass Utopia in East and West*, 203.
13. Ibid, 192.
14. Ibid, 202.
15. Radomir Konstantinović, *Filozofija palanke* (English translation: Radomir Konstantinović, *Philosophy of Provincialism*), 82-85.
16. Susan Buck-Morss, *Dreamworld and Catastrophe. The Passing of Mass Utopia in East and West*, 190.
17. Ibid, 122.
18. Ibid, 128.

19. *Марксистичка философија на XX век*. Избор и редакција Предраг Враницки (English translation: *Marxist Philisophy of the 20th Century*) (Скопје: Наша книга, 1985), 279.
20. Виолета Ачкоска, *Македонија во југословенската федерација 29.11.1943-8.9.1991 (хронологија)* (English translation: Violeta Ačkoska, *Macedonia in the Yugoslav Federation 29.11.1943-8.9.1991*) (Скопје: ИНИ, 2001), 56.
21. Slavoj Žižek, *The Universal Exception*, 268.
22. Ibid, 268.
23. Ibid, 268.
24. Susan Buck-Morss, *Dreamworld and Catastrophe. The Passing of Mass Utopia in East and West*, 120.
25. See: Slavoj Žižek, *The Universal Exception*, 81.
26. Sigmund Freud, *Civilization and its discontents*. Newly translated from the German and edited by James Strachey (New York: W.W. Norton & Company, 1962), 23.
27. Susan Buck-Morss, *Dreamworld and Catastrophe. The Passing of Mass Utopia in East and West*, 121.
28. Ibid, 121.
29. Ibid, 122.
30. Ibid, 123.
31. Игор Шафаревич, *Социјализам као појава светске историје*. (English translation: Igor Shafarevich, *The Socialist Phenomenon*), 126.
32. Susan Buck-Morss, *Dreamworld and Catastrophe. The Passing of Mass Utopia in East and West*, 55.
33. Игор Шафаревич, *Социјализам као појава светске историје*. (English translation: Igor Shafarevich, *The Socialist Phenomenon*), 25.
34. Milomir Marić, *Deca komunizma* (English translation: Milomir Marić, *The Children of Communism*), 377.
35. Ibid, 377.
36. Susan Buck-Morss, *Dreamworld and Catastrophe. The Passing of Mass Utopia in East and West*, 326.
37. Milomir Marić, *Deca komunizma* (English translation: Milomir Marić, *The Children of Communism*), 309.
38. Игор Шафаревич, *Социјализам као појава светске историје* (English translation: Igor Shafarevich, *The Socialist Phenomenon*), 333.
39. Michael Herzfeld, *Cultural Intimacy*, 7.
40. Katherine Verdery, *What Was Socialism and What Comes Next?*, 65.
41. Florin Poenaru. "Cinema-Sex-Scope, a Case of Nostalgic Discourse in Romania," *N\osztalgia–Ways of Revisiting the Socialist Past*. Editor: Isabella Willinger. (Budapest and Berlin: Anthropolis, and Rejs e.V., 2007), 77.

42. Katherine Verdery, *What Was Socialism and What Comes Next?*, 79.

3. Waiting Room

1. Slavoj Žižek, *The Universal Exception*, 47.
2. Ibid, 47.
3. Katherine Verdery, *What Was Socialism and What Comes Next?*, 57.
4. Ibid, 189.
5. Igor Mandić, *Policajci duha*. (English translation: Igor Mandić, *Policemen Spirit*), 83.
6. Slavoj Žižek, *The Universal Exception*, 106.
7. Пол Вирилио, *Естетика на исчезнувањето* (English edition: Paul Virilio, *The Aesthetics of Disappearance*, MIT Press, 1991) (Скопје: Магор, 2006), 124.
8. Katherine Verdery, *What Was Socialism and What Comes Next?*, 57.
9. Пол Вирилио, *Естетика на исчезнувањето* (English edition: Paul Virilio, *The Aesthetics of Disappearance*), 51.
10. Branka Arsić/ Srđan Bajić, *Rečnik/Dictionary* (Beograd: Dental, 1995), 29.
11. Ibid, 29.
12. Пол Вирилио, *Естетика на исчезнувањето* (English edition: Paul Virilio, *The Aesthetics of Disappearance*), 92.
13. Katherine Verdery, *What Was Socialism and What Comes Next?*, 36.
14. Карл Маркс, *Писма Кугелману (1862-1874)* (English translation: Karl Marx, *Letters to Kuglemann [1862-1874]*). (Београд: Култура, 1951), 40.
15. Katherine Verdery, *What Was Socialism and What Comes Next?*, 54.
16. Milomir Marić, *Deca komunizma* (English translation: Milomir Marić, *The Children of Communism*), 8.
17. Susan Buck-Morss, *Dreamworld and Catastrophe. The Passing of Mass Utopia in East and West,*117.
18. Ibid, 181.
19. Ibid, 181.
20. Robert Carver, *The Accursed Mountains*, 127.
21. Ibid, 131.
22. Katherine Verdery, *What Was Socialism and What Comes Next?*, 49.
23. Ibid, 49.
24. Ibid, 23.
25. Milomir Marić, *Deca komunizma* (English translation: Milomir Marić, *The Children of Communism*), 203.
26. "The term utopia has two meanings–imagining the ideal society that we know will never happen, and the capitalist utopia of new and newer, more perverse desires that we are not only allowed, but also

encouraged to realize", says Žižek in the documentary, Žižek! (2004), by Astra Taylor.
27. Katherine Verdery, *What Was Socialism and What Comes Next?*, 26.
28. Пол Вирилио, *Естетика на исчезнувањето* (English edition: Paul Virilio, *The Aesthetics of Disappearance*), 111.
29. Milomir Marić, *Deca komunizma* (English translation: Milomir Marić, *The Children of Communism*), 20.
30. Barry Schwartz: *Queuing and Waiting. Study in the Social Organization of Access and Delay* (Chicago: University of Chicago Press, 1975). Quoted in Kathrine Verdery, *What Was Socialism, and What Comes Next?* (Princeton: Princeton University Press, 1996), 241, note no. 12.
31. Kathrine Verdery, *What Was Socialism, and What Comes Next?*, 242.
32. Ibid, 48.
33. Ibid, 54.
34. See Verdery's analysis of the Caritas phenomenon in Romania in the chapter: "Faith, Hope, and Caritas in the Land of the Pyramids, Romania, 1990-1994." Kathrine Verdery, *What Was Socialism, and What Comes Next?* (Princeton: Princeton University Press, 1996), 168-207.

4. Prosthesis

1. David Wills, *Prosthesis* (Stanford: Stanford University Press, 1995), 92.
2. Sigmund Freud, *Civilization and its discontents*. Newly translated from the German and edited by James Strachey (New York: W.W. Norton & Company, 1962), 88-89.
3. Sigmund Freud, *Beyond the Pleasure Principle*. Translated and edited by James Strachey. Introduction and notes by Gregory Zilboorg (New York: W.W. Norton & Company, 1962), 58.
4. Ivo Banac, *Sa Staljinom protiv Tita* (Ivo Banac, *With Stalin Against Tito*), 37.
5. Henry Ford, *My Life and Work* (Charleston: BiblioBazaar, LLC, 2008), 101.
6. Susan Buck-Morss, *Dreamworld and Catastrophe. The Passing of Mass Utopia in East and West*, 110.
7. Henry Ford, *My Life and Work*, 120.
8. Susan Buck-Morss, *Dreamworld and Catastrophe. The Passing of Mass Utopia in East and West*, 105.
9. Milomir Marić, *Deca komunizma* (English translation: Milomir Marić, *The Children of Communism*), 20.
10. Ibid, 7-8.
11. Nanci Adler, *The Gulag Survivor, Beyond the Soviet System*, 48.
12. Игор Шафаревич, *Социјализам као појава светске историје* (Igor Shafarevich, *The Socialist Phenomenon*), 305.

13. Hugh Griffith, "Introduction," in: Marx, Karl (with Friedrich Engels): *Communist Manifesto/Wages, Price and Profit/Capital (selections)/Socialism: Utopian and Scientific* (London: CRW Publishing Limited, 2004), 13.
14. See: Francis Wheen, *Marx's Das Kapital. A Biography*, 24-25.
15. Карл Маркс, *Писма Кугелману (1862-1874)*. (Marx, Karl. *Letters to Kuglemann [1862-1874]*), 19.
16. Quoted in: Francis Wheen, *Marx's Das Kapital. A Biography*, 29.
17. Ibid, 18.
18. Ibid, 16-17.
19. Карл Маркс, *Писма Кугелману (1862-1874)*. (Karl Marx, *Letters to Kuglemann [1862-1874]*), 9.
20. Marx writes to Kugelmann: "I even decided to be a 'practitioner' as well, so I was supposed to start working in a Railroad Bureau at the beginning of next year. I don't know whether it was for the best or not, but I didn't get the job because of my bad handwriting." See: Карл Маркс, *Писма Кугелману (1862-1874)*. (Karl Marx, *Letters to Kuglemann [1862-1874]*), 6.
21. Francis Wheen, *Marx's Das Kapital. A Biography*, 38.
22. Prauer. S.S. *Karl Marks i svetska književnost* (English translation: Prauer, S.S. *Karl Marx and World Literature)*, 312.
23. Karl Marx (with Friedrich Engels), "Communist Manifesto" in: *Communist Manifesto/Wages, Price and Profit/Capital (selections)/Socialism: Utopian and Scientific* (London: CRW Publishing Limited, 2004), 19.
24. Karl Marx, *Kapital* (Zagreb: Školska knjga, 1975), 11.
25. Francis Wheen, *Marx's Das Kapital. A Biography*, 39.
26. Ibid, 80.
27. Ibid, 57.
28. Ibid, 59.
29. Geoff Eley, *Forging democracy. The History of the Left in Europe 1850-2000* (Oxford, New York: The Oxford University Press, 2002), 36.
30. In the article entitled, "Transformation of Life," in: *Pravda*, October, 17, 1920. Quoted from: Игор Шафаревич, *Социјализам као појава светске историје* (English translation: Igor Shafarevich, *The Socialist Phenomenon*), 325.
31. Slavoj Žižek, *The Sublime Object of Ideology*, 18.
32. Ibid, 18.
33. See Verdery's analysis of the pyramidal saving banks in post-communism in the chapter: "Faith, Hope, and Caritas in the Land of the Pyramids, Romania, 1990-1994," in: Kathrine Verdery, *What Was Socialism, and What Comes Next?* (Princeton: Princeton University Press, 1996), 168-207.

34. Francis Wheen, *Marx's Das Kapital. A Biography*, 83.
35. Ibid, 85.
36. Ibid, 86.
37. Ibid, 95-96.
38. Ibid, 96.
39. Ibid, 96-97.
40. Žižek, Slavoj. *The Sublime Object of Ideology*, 58.
41. Ibid, 59.
42. Søren Kierkegaard, *Either/Or, A Fragment of Life,* 49.
43. Judith Butler, *The Psychic Life of Power* (Stanford: Stanford University Press), 40.
44. Ibid, 45.
45. See Lacan's analysis of Freudian fort-da narration. Jacques Lacan, *The Four Fundamental Concepts of Psychoanalysis*, 60-64.
46. Dafydd Jones, *Dada Culture. Critical Texts on the Avant-Garde* (New York: Editions Rodopi B.V. Amsterdam, 2006), 20.
47. Francis Wheen, *Marx's Das Kapital. A Biography*, 97.
48. Susan Buck-Morss, *Dreamworld and Catastrophe. The Passing of Mass Utopia in East and West*, 104.
49. Виолета Ачкоска, *Задолжителниот откуп во Македонија 1945-1953* (English translation: Violeta Ačkoska, *The Obligatory Purchase in Macedonia 1945-1948*) (Скопје: ИНИ, 1995), 13.
50. Ibid, 14.
51. Geoff Eley, *Forging democracy. The History of the Left in Europe 1850-2000*, 43.
52. Ibid, 43-44.
53. Виолета Ачкоска, *Задолжителниот откуп во Македонија 1945-1953* (English translation: Violeta Ačkoska, *The Obligatory Purchase in Macedonia 1945-1948*), 18.
54. Ibid, 21.
55. Ibid, 15.
56. Ibid, 33.
57. Ibid, 19.
58. Quoted in: Stathis Gourgouris, *Dream Nation, Enlightenment, Colonization, and the Institution of Modern Greece*, 162.
59. Ibid, 61-62.
60. Виолета Ачкоска, Задолжителниот откуп во Македонија 1945-1953 (English translation: Violeta Ačkoska, *The Obligatory Purchase in Macedonia 1945-1948*), 22.
61. Ibid, 20.
62. Ibid, 16, footnote 20.
63. Ibid, 23.

64. The rest of the song goes like this: "Tell me Mile, cosmic brother of mine/is there salad on the Moon to dine/either salad, or prosciutto– aged/or is nudity all that's staged. A forward child I am too/and want to go to the planets with you/On Earth, the devil is near/since all from work stay clear. On Earth they spy/from some saucers that fly/from Apollo are they greater/or some other people that will come here later. Much a do/all 20th century through/we can't change, no/there's nowhere to go."
65. *Лексикон на ЈУ митологијата.* (English translation: *Lexicon of Yugoslav Mythology*) (Скопје: Темплум, 2006), 148.
66. Predrag J. Marković, *Trajnost i promena.* (English translation: Predrag J. Marković, *Continuity and Change*), 44.
67. *Лексикон на ЈУ митологијата* (English translation: *Lexicon of Yugoslav Mythology*), 101.

5. Body

1. Viktor Jerofejev, *Dobar Staljin* (English translation: Viktor Erofeyev, *The Good Stalin*) (Beograd: Geopoetika, 2005), 48.
2. Slavoj Žižek, *The Universal Exception*, 364.
3. Susan Buck-Morss, *Dreamworld and Catastrophe. The Passing of Mass Utopia in East and West*, 71.
4. Slavoj Žižek, *The Parallax View*, 151.
5. Slavoj Žižek, *The Universal Exception,* 364.
6. *N\osztalgia–Ways of Revisiting the Socialist Past*, 7.
7. Robert Carver, *The Accursed Mountains*, 58.
8. Ibid, 49.
9. Лењин, В.И. *Последња писма и чланци.* (English translation: Lenin, V.I. *Last Letters and Articles*), 173-174.
10. Branka Arsić/ Srđan Bajić, *Rečnik/Dictionary* (Beograd: Dental, 1995), 88.
11. Viktor Jerofejev, *Dobar Staljin* (English translation: Viktor Erofeyev, *The Good Stalin*), 30.
12. Radomir Konstantinović, *Filozofija palanke* (Radomir Konstantinović, *Philosophy of Provincialism*), 8.
13. Ibid, 9.
14. Ibid, 13.
15. Alen Galović, "Izveštaj o smrti predsjednika Jugoslavije," in: *Globus*, Zagreb, no. 843, 2007 (English translation: Alen Galović, "The Report on the Death of the President of Yugoslavia, Globus, Zagreb, No. 843, 2007) http://www.globus.com.hr/Clanak.aspx?BrojID=197&ClanakID=5432 (accessed October 9, 2008).

16. Ibid.
17. Ibid.
18. Donald Rayfield, *Stalin and His Hangmen*, 47.
19. Hachinski, V. (1999 Mar). "Stalin's last years: Delusions or dementia?", in: *Eur J Neurol 6* (2): 129-32, (accessed March 1, 2007).
20. Slavoj Žižek, *In Defense of Lost Causes*, 228.
21. Donald Rayfield, *Stalin and His Hangmen*, 117-118.
22. Slavoj Žižek, *The Universal Exception*, 268.
23. Игор Шафаревич, *Социјализам као појава светске историје*. (Alen Galović, "Izveštaj o smrti predsjednika Jugoslavije", Igor Shafarevich, *The Socialist Phenomenon*), 332-33.
24. Slavoj Žižek, *In Defense of Lost Causes*, 230.
25. From the documentary film, *La Faute à Lénine (par Ukraine Europe)*. (2001). TV channel France 5, February 1, 2004, 16:00. Magazine "Les repères de l'Histoire": "La faute à Lénine" de Daniel Leconte, Débat avec Jean-Jacques Marie et Alexandre Gratchev.
26. Ibid.
27. Ibid.
28. Katherine Verdery, *What Was Socialism and What Comes Next?*, 232.
29. Ibid, 232.
30. "Monument of Bulgaria's Communist Dictator Snatched from Tomb," in: *Novinite*, Sofia 11.21.2007, http://www.novinite.com/view_news.php?id=87733 (accessed June 30, 2008).
31. The first year refers to the Soviet tanks that destroyed the Hungarian revolution in 1956, which was lead by Kadar. The second anti-government protest was in Budapest in 2006, when Premier Ferencz Gyurcsány admitted to lying in order to come to power, and it is interesting that he was privately obsessed with communists and expecially with Lenin.
32. 'World's Biggest Stalin Monument Would Have Turned 50 on May Day' on: *Radio Praha*, 05.03.2005. http://www.radio.cz/en/article/66095 (accessed June 30, 2008).
33. Robert Carver, *The Accursed Mountains*, 96-97.
34. Marko Lopušina, *KOS, Tajne vojne službe bezbednosti*. (English translation: Marko Lopushina, *KOS, Secrets of the Military Security Service*), 85.
35. Ibid, 153-154.
36. Jean Baudrillard, *Simulacra and Simulation* (Michigan: The University of Michigan Press, 1994), 95.
37. Vojislav Šešelj, the founder and the leader of the Serbian Radical Party, currently on trial for war crimes in the former Yugoslavia in The Hague.
38. "U Kumrovcu srušen i oštećen spomenik Josipu Brozu Titu," in: *Na-*

cional from: 04.27.2004 http://www.nacional.hr/articles/view/9114/ (accessed May 30, 2008).
39. Bojana Pejić, "Kultura sećanja i politika zaborava," *Vreme,* from: August 9, 2007. http://www.vreme.com/cms/view.php?id=508258 (accessed May 30, 2008).
40. On the occasion of resurrection of the dead socialist body of Stalin in 2000, the leader of the communist party of Georgia, Panteleimon Georgendze, held a speech: "Ordinary people are more and more convinced that they were fooled with the so-called democracy in Russia and in Georgia. The Soviet Union shall become a great force when people come together again around the ideas of Josef Stalin." See: «Stalin Monument Restored in Georgian Town," in: *People's Daily* from: 05.08.2000. See: http://english.peopledaily.com.cn/english/200005/08/eng20000508_40314.html.

6. Why Is It Good to Be Good?

1. Jacques Lacan, *The Ethics of Psychoanalysis 1959-60*, 34.
2. Felix Guatari, "Everybody Wants to be a Fascist," lecture delivered in Milan for Colloquium "Psychoanalysis and Politics," December 1973, *Chaosophy*, Semiotext(e), 1995, 227.
3. Erneso Laclau, "Identity and Hegemony," in: Butler, Judith; Laclau, Ernesto and Žižek, Slavoj. *Contingency, Hegemony, Universality, Contemporary Dialogues on the Left* (London, New York: Verso, 2000), 72.
4. Alain Badiou, *Metapolitics* (London and New York: Verso, 2005), 10-15.
5. Ibid, 13.
6. Ockham's Razor consists of the following thesis: "Entities must not be multiplied beyond necessity," meaning that the thought should not be populated with an excess of constructs, with more philosophical principles than necessary.
7. Alain Badiou, *Metapolitics*, 15.
8. Richard Rorty, *Contingency, Irony and Solidarity*. (Cambridge: Cambridge University Press, 1989), xiii-xiv.
9. See: Slavoj Žižek, *The Parallax View*, 33-47.
10. Miguel de Saavedra Cervantes. *Don Quixote.* Translated, with Notes by James H. Montgomery. Introduced by David Quint (Indianapolis: Hackett Publishing Company Inc., 2009), 35-36.
11. Игор Шафаревич, *Социјализам као појава светске историје*. (Igor Shafarevich, *The Socialist Phenomenon*), 60-61.
12. Richard Rorty, *Contingency, Irony and Solidarity*, xiii.
13. Alenka Zupančič, *The Shortest Shadow. Nietzsche's Philosophy of the Two*. MIT Press, 2003, 175.

14. Slavoj Žižek, *Tarrying with the Negative* (Durham: Duke University Press, 1993), 84.
15. See: Slavoj Žižek, "On Radical Evil and Related Matters," *Tarrying with the Negative*, 86.
16. Thomas Hobbes, *Leviathan*, With an introduction by Jennifer J. Popiel (New York: Barnes and Noble Publishing, Inc., 2004), 146.
17. Ibid, xi.
18. Leszek Kołakowski, Šta nas to pitaju veliki filozofi? kniga druga i treća, Pančevo: Mali Nemo, 2006 and 2007. (English ed. *Leszek Kołakowski, The Two Eyes of Spinoza and Other Essays on Philosophers*, Chicago: St. Augustine's Press, 2004), 68.
19. Slavoj Žižek, *Druga smrt Josipa Broza-Tita*, 26-27.
20. This "fictive money" created an inflation of 250% in Yugoslavia at that time, and although that money is not the only reason for the galloping inflation in the later years of the existence of Yugoslavia, just like "Agrokomerc" was not the greatest and most important Yugoslav company, they confirm that self-government did not include any financial liability, i.e. that self-government is, to say the least, a permission for illegal financial doings performed by "the strongest ones."
21. Slavoj Žižek, *Sunday at Two*, interview on the Croatian Television HTV, Zagreb, February 3, 2007.
22. In the theory of games, this is the graphic presentation of the Prisoner's Dilemma:

	Prisoner B is quiet	**Prisoner B commits treachery**
Prisoner A is quiet	They get six months each	Prisoner A: 10 years Prisoner B: free
Prisoner A commits treachery	Prisoner A: free Prisoner B: 10 years	They get five years each.

23. George H.W. Hegel, *Philosophy of Right*, Translator S.W. Dyde (New York: Cosimo, Inc., 2008), xix.
24. Leszek Kołakowski, Šta nas to pitaju veliki filozofi? (English ed. Leszek Kołakowski, *The Two Eyes of Spinoza and Other Essays on Philosophers*), III volume, 16.
25. Who apologized? Clinton apologized for the slavery and racism, Australia to the Aborigines, the Netherlands to the ex-colonies, the Norwegians for the collaboration with the Nazis and the Pope for all the

crimes of the Roman-Catholic church throughout history. See: *Zajednica sećanja. Tranziciona pravda u istoriskoj perspektivi.* (English translation: *Community of Memory. History of Transitional Justice.*) Editors: Obrad Savić and Ana Miljković. (Beograd: Beogradski krug, 2006), 15.
26. Reference is made to a Macedonian TV show in which the popularity of a certain event or issue is voted for with black and white bumblebees.
27. Viktor Jerofejev, *Dobar Staljin*. (English translation: Viktor Jerofejev, *The Good Stalin*), 10.

www.ingramcontent.com/pod-product-compliance
Lightning Source LLC
Chambersburg PA
CBHW020737160426

43192CB00006B/227